# PLATO
## AND THE
# TYRANT

BOOKS BY JAMES ROMM

*Demetrius: Sacker of Cities*

*The Sacred Band:*
*Three Hundred Theban Lovers Fighting to Save Greek Freedom*

*Dying Every Day: Seneca at the Court of Nero*

*Ghost on the Throne:*
*The Death of Alexander the Great and the Bloody Fight for His Empire*

*Herodotus*

*The Edges of the Earth in Ancient Thought:*
*Geography, Exploration, and Fiction*

EDITED BY JAMES ROMM

*How to Have a Life:*
*An Ancient Guide to Using Our Time Wisely*

*How to Give:*
*An Ancient Guide to Giving and Receiving*

*How to Keep Your Cool:*
*An Ancient Guide to Anger Management*

*How to Die: An Ancient Guide to the End of Life*

*The Age of Caesar: Five Roman Lives*

*The Greek Plays:*
*Sixteen Plays by Aeschylus, Sophocles, and Euripides*

*Herodotus Histories*

*The Landmark Arrian: The Campaigns of Alexander*

*Plutarch: Lives That Made Greek History*

*Alexander the Great:*
*Selections from Arrian, Diodorus, Plutarch, and Quintus Curtius*

*Herodotus: On the War for Greek Freedom*

# PLATO
## AND THE
# TYRANT

*The Fall of*
GREECE'S GREATEST DYNASTY
*and the Making of a*
PHILOSOPHIC MASTERPIECE

## JAMES ROMM

**W. W. NORTON & COMPANY**
*Independent Publishers Since 1923*

For information about permission to reproduce selections from this book, write to
Permissions, W. W. Norton & Company, Inc., 500 Fifth Avenue, New York, NY 10110

For information about special discounts for bulk purchases, please contact
W. W. Norton Special Sales at specialsales@wwnorton.com or 800-233-4830

Manufacturing by Lake Book Manufacturing
Book design by Chris Welch
Production manager: Julia Druskin

ISBN 978-1-324-09318-3

W. W. Norton & Company, Inc.
500 Fifth Avenue, New York, NY 10110
www.wwnorton.com

W. W. Norton & Company Ltd.
15 Carlisle Street, London W1D 3BS

1 2 3 4 5 6 7 8 9 0

*For my dad, Alan Romm (1932–2022),*
*who never got to read it*

# CONTENTS

# ACT III.  THE THIRD VISIT

# ACT IV.  REVOLUTION

# ACT V.  RESTORATION

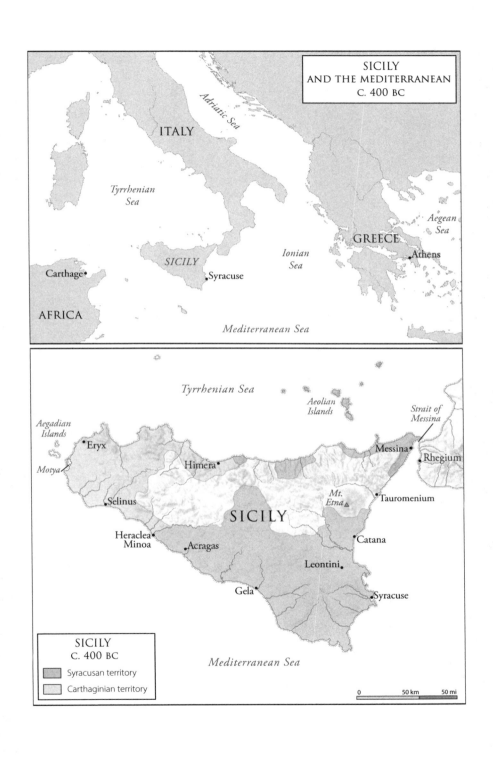

**SICILY AND THE MEDITERRANEAN C. 400 BC**

ITALY

Adriatic Sea

Tyrrhenian Sea

Aegean Sea

GREECE

SICILY

Ionian Sea

Athens

Carthage

Syracuse

AFRICA

Mediterranean Sea

Tyrrhenian Sea

Aeolian Islands

Strait of Messina

Aegadian Islands

Eryx

Motya

Himera

Messina

Rhegium

Selinus

Mt. Etna

Tauromenium

SICILY

Heraclea Minoa

Acragas

Catana

Leontini

Gela

Syracuse

**SICILY C. 400 BC**

Syracusan territory

Carthaginian territory

0    50 km    50 mi

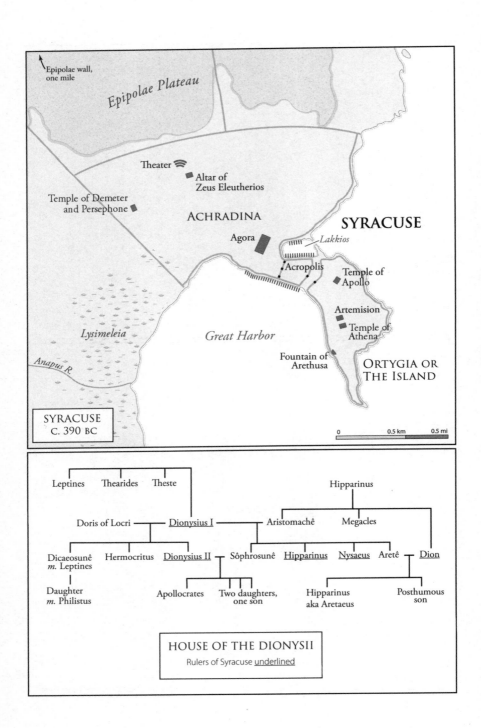

Epipolae wall, one mile

*Epipolae Plateau*

Theater
Altar of Zeus Eleutherios

Temple of Demeter and Persephone

ACHRADINA

**SYRACUSE**

Agora

*Lakkios*

Acropolis

Temple of Apollo

Artemision

Temple of Athena

*Great Harbor*

*Lysimeleia*

*Anapus R.*

Fountain of Arethusa

ORTYGIA OR THE ISLAND

SYRACUSE
C. 390 BC

0    0.5 km    0.5 mi

---

Leptines    Thearides    Theste

Hipparinus

Doris of Locri —— Dionysius I —— Aristomachê    Megacles

Dicaeosunê
*m.* Leptines

Hermocritus    Dionysius II —— Sôphrosunê    Hipparinus    Nysaeus    Aretê —— Dion

Daughter
*m.* Philistus

Apollocrates    Two daughters, one son    Hipparinus aka Aretaeus    Posthumous son

**HOUSE OF THE DIONYSII**
Rulers of Syracuse <u>underlined</u>

ITALY AND THE ADRIATIC
IN THE TIME OF DIONYSIUS I
405 BC–367 BC

········· Approximate location of wall
▫ Garrison towns

*Po*
Adria

ITALY

Ancona

*Adriatic Sea*

*Pharos*

*Issa*

ETRURIA

APENNINE MOUNTAINS

Caere

ILLYRIA

Lissus

Capua
Cumae
Neapolis

CAMPANIA

IAPYGIA

Brundisium

Tarentum

Elea

EPIRUS

Thurii

*Tyrrhenian
Sea*

LUCANIA

*Corcyra*

Croton

Hipponion▫

Lipara

*Ionian
Sea*

Tyndaris▫

Caulonia▫
Locri
Rhegium▫

*Mt. Etna*
Adranum▫ ▲ *Strait of
Messina*

SICILY

Syracuse

*Mediterranean Sea*

0          150 km          150 mi

*Plato's birthday celebrated by the Florentine Academy of the late fifteenth century. Canvas by Luigi Mussini (1813-1888).*

# INTRODUCTION

The first dictionary I ever used, a 1947 *American College Dictionary* that belonged to my father, bore on its austere black cover a cryptic inscription in Greek: ΛΑΜΠΑΔΙΑ ΕΧΟΝΤΕΣ ΔΙΑΔΩΣΟΥΣΙΝ ΑΛΛΗΛΟΙΣ. As a child I was perplexed by the strange, embossed characters; two decades later, after learning Greek, I understood them. "Those holding torches will pass them to one another"—the words come from Plato's *Republic*. They're spoken in the opening scene by Socrates, Plato's former teacher, who was executed in Plato's youth but then brought to life by Plato and others as the leading speaker in their "Socratic" dialogues. In their original context, the words describe a new kind of horse race taking place on the night that *Republic* is set; riders, Socrates says, will pass torches to their teammates as they gallop, creating an astonishing spectacle.

The dictionary's publisher had seen a metaphor in those words. Knowledge must be passed on from one hand to another. The flame must not go out or all is lost.

Plato's *Republic* has been passed on for nearly two and a half millennia, and its flame still burns bright. It stands at the center of the Western cultural canon; a 2016 survey of college syllabuses found *Republic* to be the most widely required text at top American schools.[1] Its historical influence has been immense. The project that lies at its heart—the

construction of an ideal state—has inspired a long series of efforts to rede-
sign political life, from Thomas More's sixteenth-century *Utopia* to B. F.
Skinner's *Walden Two*. Its dream—or, as some would say, its delusion—of
a ruler who unites perfect wisdom with absolute power has echoed down
through the ages and has given rise to a famous term, one that Plato himself didn't actually use: philosopher-king.

When I first studied *Republic* I found myself swept up in its transcendent visions: the perfect, eternal entities, known as the Forms, that it
urges us to reach out to with our minds; the ultimate Form, the Form of
the Good, shining with brilliance like that of the sun, compared to which
our earthly existence is as benighted as life in a cave; the soul's journey
after death through a cosmos filled with wonders, where the planets in
their orbits produce harmonious music. Plato's belief that these visions
are not only real, but bring sublime joy, seemed to me to have a kind of
religious conviction. I fell under "the spell of Plato," unaware as yet of a
book by that very title, the work of twentieth-century philosopher Karl
Popper—a book that decried *Republic* as one of the most deceptive and
dangerous texts ever written.

I was hardly the first to feel the power of this spell. In Renaissance
and Enlightenment Europe, the adjective "divine" was routinely affixed
to Plato's name in the standard Latin edition of his works, *Opera Omnia
Divini Platonis*. A new Platonic Academy formed in fifteenth-century
Florence; its members sang hymns to a bust of Plato as though revering a
saint. In 1814 Thomas Jefferson (who was himself no fan of Plato's *Republic*) wrote to John Adams that "Plato is canonized; and it is now deemed
as impious to question his merits as those of an apostle of Jesus."[2] As late
as 1929 a Columbia philosophy professor, F. J. E. Woodbridge, entitled his
study of Plato *The Son of Apollo*.

When I started teaching at Bard College, where *Republic* was required
reading for every entering class, the spell of Plato began to lift. My students focused not on the work's quest for the Good but on its political
doctrines, where goodness was harder to find. The "ideal" city-state
imagined by Plato looked more nightmarish than utopian to my students; it features all-powerful rulers backed by fanatical soldiers, censorship of art and literature, and state control of private life at a level that

rivals modern-day North Korea. My attempt to defend *Republic*—perhaps Plato was provoking us by allowing his spokesman, Socrates, to propose things he didn't support—didn't convince my classes, and I wasn't sure I believed that argument myself.

Again and again, I tried to steer class discussion, and my own thoughts, back toward the brilliant sun in the parable of the cave. Surely if Plato believed in that light, his politics must have been on the side of the angels? Then I began reading Plato's letters, and my doubts concerning *Republic* became more insistent.

I learned from the letters that Plato had tried to put his ideas into practice, not by way of a philosopher-king but via a notorious autocrat— Dionysius the Younger, ruler of the Greek city of Syracuse. These epistles told a tale of a political experiment gone horribly wrong, and of Plato's efforts to put things right and to cover up his mistakes. Plato's dealings with Dionysius, as revealed in the letters, had none of the purity of *Republic*. In Syracuse Plato had made moral compromises, committed errors of judgment, and gotten into jams he nearly couldn't get out of. He'd behaved like a real, and flawed, human being, not like the marmoreal figure I'd imagined up to that point.

I had never really encountered the letters before. They had not been put on the reading lists I'd been given or discussed in studies I'd read, beyond a dismissive sentence or two. They'd been treated by my classicist colleagues as inadmissible evidence because doubts have been raised as to whether Plato was actually their author or whether someone else was impersonating his voice. But as I began to research the authorship question, I came to believe that those doubts, in the case of at least five letters, were badly misplaced. I grew convinced that these letters are not only genuine but contain a story that needs to be more widely known.

Plato made three trips to Syracuse, the leading Greek state in Sicily, over the course of his life, and after his final departure continued to be involved in its politics. His engagement with Syracuse spanned nearly half of his life and the entire period when he was writing *Republic* (as well as most of his other dialogues). In Syracuse he developed two crucial relationships, one with Dionysius, an unstable sovereign who professed an interest in philosophy, and one with Dion, the ruler's brother-in-law, a

devoted student of Plato's teachings. A conflict between these two kinsmen, partly born of their rivalry over Plato, radically changed the lives of
all three, brought thousands of other lives to an end, and nearly caused
the destruction of Syracuse.

I wrote this book to explore the questions that first troubled me when
the spell of Plato was broken, and that troubled me even more when I
came to the letters. Did Plato, while extolling the Good as the source of
transcendent joy, end up collaborating with evil? Had he sought benevolent ends by using unsavory means? How far had he bent the noble ideals
of *Republic*—its unwavering commitment to justice—when he entered a
world where injustice prevailed? Was it thinkable—the most troubling
question of all—that he'd written *Republic* in part to explain his missteps
in Syracuse, or to obscure them?

Such questions seem all the more pressing in the current political
moment, when democracies again confront, as they did in Plato's era,
the allure of authoritarianism. Like many today, Plato thought that traditional governance systems were failing and only a radical transformation could stop the decline. In *Republic* he offered a route to redemption:
a new form of autocracy, philosopher-kingship. He believed that an
enlightened strongman, unconstrained by law or limits on power, could
solve the world's ills, which he otherwise deemed insoluble. That belief
has beckoned to many over the centuries and its appeal is once again
strong, as global complexities mount and expectations for the future
seem to grow darker. But Plato's Syracuse misadventure suggests that
we, like Shakespeare's Hamlet, might "rather bear the ills we have/than
fly to others that we know not of."

"Great men may make great mistakes," wrote Popper in his preface
to *The Spell of Plato*, generously declining to single out any one person.
"Some of the greatest leaders of the past supported the perennial attack
on freedom and reason." How terrible if he was right in his judgment of
Plato, and if he was, how dire for us if we remain under the spell. "If our
civilization is to survive, we must break with the habit of deference to
great men," said Popper, again referring to "men" when he mostly meant
Plato.[3] He wrote those words in 1943, when it seemed that civilization, as
it had long been defined, might indeed not survive.

This book tells a story that centers on Syracuse, a place name that American readers may first associate with upstate New York rather than ancient Greece. The Greek cities of Sicily and south Italy, the region I refer to as the Greek West, have gotten scant attention compared with their older, grander mother cities, places like Athens, Sparta, and Corinth. That's partly an accident of transmission and preservation, the process by which certain ancient texts were copied out of papyrus scrolls and into early books such that we have them today. Works that focused on mainland Greece, such as those of Herodotus and Thucydides, made that transition, while chronicles from the Greek West did not. Thucydides tells us something of Syracuse in the years 415 to 413 BC, because Athens, during its war against Sparta, tried, in a massive but disastrously bungled invasion, to capture the city; after that period, our information gets thin.

The fact is that in the first half of the fourth century BC, when Plato was writing *Republic*, Syracuse was the most powerful state in the Hellenic world. At its peak it boasted an army of a hundred thousand men and a fleet of over three hundred ships.[4] Its opulence was legendary. Athens and Sparta in the same era were diminished and only becoming weaker, each trying to hold its own against a resurgent Thebes; the "three-headed monster" was slowly destroying itself. The West, by contrast, had only one Greek superpower. If not for constant pressure by Carthage, its great non-Greek rival, Syracuse might have grown into what Rome later became.

The wealth and might of Syracuse was personified, in the eyes of the Greeks, by its towering rulers, a father and son both named Dionysius. The rumors and tales that gathered around these two men gave them an almost mythic stature, in contrast to their current obscurity. In the fourteenth century Dante Alighieri put "Dionysius"—perhaps an amalgam of father and son—right beside Alexander the Great in the circle of Hell to which he consigned all tyrants. Yet today when one googles "Dionysius," one gets thousands of hits for "Dionysus" instead; the search engine doesn't distinguish the god of wine from the rulers whose name has an extra "i" before the final "-us" (it rhymes with "-icious" or "issy-us" in English rather than "Isis").

Just as the rulers of Syracuse are unfamiliar today, so too is the story of Plato's involvement with them, the only part of his life we can recover in any detail. More so than other lives in that era, his has remained largely a blank. While biographies of Socrates appear reliably every few years, the past two centuries have seen only two lives of Plato in English, one of these a translation from a German original.[5] The lack of attention to Plato's life, in contrast to the prominence of his ideas, relates to the problem of the Platonic letters: Questions about their authorship have made them, for most historical writers, too hot to handle. And without them, we have very little to go on.

In addition, the spell of Plato has played its part in both of these silences. Syracuse in the time of the Dionysii is a place to which many wish Plato had not gone, and the letters are documents many wish he had not written. The latter wish is especially strong in the case of what is known as the *Thirteenth Letter*. This uniquely personal document seems to show Plato as a man of affairs, not an ethereal thinker, and to place him in a close entente with Dionysius the Younger. But before we get to the controversy over that missive, let us look at the entire group of thirteen and the centuries-long debate over which of the letters, if any, are Plato's authentic writings.

The Platonic letters, thirteen in number, come down to us in a collection of everything Plato wrote, compiled by one Thrasyllus, an ancient scholar, in the early first century AD. By that time a few look-alikes had gotten into the pool of Platonic texts—in some cases, works in Plato's style that got assigned to Plato erroneously, in other cases deliberate forgeries. Modern scholars labor to separate out the spurious works from the true ones in the Thrasyllan canon, and the letters have proven especially vexing. At least one of the thirteen is certainly not by Plato, as revealed by its style. Judgments about the other twelve have varied over the centuries and from one letter to another. In recent decades, these judgments have taken a strongly negative turn.

In 1987, the Platonist Luc Brisson tabulated opinions about each of the thirteen letters. He made a chart of thirty-two scholarly publications going back to 1484. He assigned numerical values to each scholar's belief in a letter's genuineness: a 2 for solid belief, 1 for uncertainty, and 0 for lack of belief. Between 1865 and 1947, according to Brisson's chart, the Platonic letter collection received an average composite score of over 15. From 1948 to 1983, by contrast, the score fell to just above 4. The shift toward skepticism is not the result of new information or methods; even the advent of the computer has not made much of a difference.[6] The main thing that has changed is the frame of mind of inquirers.

Attitude swings like this one are often found in scholarship, as each generation sets itself apart from the one before it. The oscillation in this case can be clearly seen in a celebrated twentieth-century German work, published in English as *A History of Autobiography in Antiquity*, by historian Georg Misch. In his first edition, in 1907, Misch omitted Plato's autobiographical *Seventh Letter* but added it in the second, in 1931. "The epistle is now regarded by the leading experts as genuine," Misch wrote in a footnote. "Forty years ago the opposite view predominated."[7] Thirty-five years further on, Ludwig Edelstein's *Plato's Seventh Letter* sought to again prove the letter a fake, and that view has had a long run.

Today it seems possible the pendulum is reversing. Several recent or forthcoming studies mount strong defenses of the *Seventh Letter* and some of the others.[8] But a 2015 book by two renowned scholars, to be discussed in chapter 12, announced its skepticism in its very title, *The Pseudo-Platonic Seventh Letter*.[9]

There *are* good reasons to be skeptical about Plato's letters—because they are letters. In antiquity personal letters were often forged for material gain, since libraries paid high prices for the papers of famous thinkers. There are other surviving "Platonic" letters that did not make it into Thrasyllus's canon and clearly are not by Plato, as well as letters falsely purporting to be those of Socrates, Aristotle, Diogenes the Cynic, and others. Pseudonymous letters were also created by rhetoricians in training, who honed their skills by way of impersonation. But amid the forgeries and impostures, we do have letters from Plato's era that seem to be genuine.[10] For centuries, the problem for scholars—anticipating what we all now confront in an age of "deep fakes"—has been how to distinguish pseudo-Plato from the real thing.

All the tests that scholarship can devise have been used on the Platonic letters. The primary target of inquiry has been the *Seventh*, because it's both very long—longer than all the others put together—and rich in detail. It also contains a philosophic excursus in which the author explains his theory of what reality is and how we can know it. So the letter gives ample scope for three lines of inquiry: those based on literary style, on historical accuracy, and on the "fit" of its concepts with Plato's philosophy. The results, in all three cases, have been inconclusive. Those who believe it is Plato's and those who believe it isn't have both claimed to find support for their views.

In debates over the authorship of ancient texts, a scrap of papyrus sometimes emerges from Mediterranean sands to help make the case. One such piece was uncovered in Egypt and published in 2008. The tiny, tattered fragment, with handwriting dated to the early third century BC, contains a few legible words of the *Eighth Letter*.[11] This lucky find allows us to set the date at which the *Eighth Letter* existed far earlier than it had previously been set, strengthening the case that Plato wrote *that* document, at least. Supporters of the authenticity of the letters argue that if *one* is genuine, others probably are; opponents argue the contrary, that one bad apple spoils the rest of the barrel.

In general it has been specialists in philosophy who have rejected the letters, while historians have supported their genuineness.[12] Philosophers look for consistency between the letters and Plato's other writings and claim not to find it. Historians look at the letters in the context of Plato's life circumstances, his relationships with his correspondents, and whether the events or people referred to can be cross-checked against other sources. Within that framework, most of these documents hold up well. The slips they contain—which I discuss as they arise—are remarkably few, well within the "margin of error" for a writer relying on memory for his facts.

The questions that need to be asked of the letters were best expressed by Glenn Morrow, who published *The Platonic Epistles* in the 1960s (a slightly revised edition of a 1935 study). Morrow, a specialist in Platonic political thought who taught at the University of Pennsylvania, shared his own method of inquiry: "Are the feelings the letter expresses those that the supposed writer"—Plato—"would naturally express under the circumstances? Are they expressed with sincerity? . . . Are the traits of the letter consistent with what we otherwise know of the character of the author?"[13] Features of this kind, as Morrow observed, are nearly impossible for another person to mimic, especially in an epistle of substantial length.

"The application of these criteria is seldom easy," wrote Morrow, "but any letter which satisfies them, and at the same time agrees in thought, style, and diction with the acknowledged works of its supposed author, and has moreover the weight of the literary tradition in its favor, must certainly be accepted as genuine." Applying this long and nuanced checklist, Morrow decided that the *Fourth, Seventh,* and *Eighth* Platonic letters must be authentic, and he leaned toward the same conclusion about several others.

Morrow's method does not have the rigor of scientific proof. It's more like the famous Turing test, in which subjects tried to determine, by way of a typed conversation, whether their interlocutor was human or a machine. Even when they couldn't quantify the signals they looked for, they knew when something sounded "off." If the conversation went on a long time and nothing tripped their sensors, they decided their correspondent was a real person.

The Turing test is a relic in the age of ChatGPT, when machines can perfectly replicate patterns of human communication. But ancient forgers had no such tools to create their illusions. The longer their texts, the more they give themselves away by making "mistakes" of style or content or both. The five Platonic letters I draw on are long, yet remarkably true to the language of Plato's time and to known historical facts. We can either imagine a forger who possessed AI-level skills, or, more plausibly, believe that the letters' author was Plato.

The three letters Morrow had most conviction about belong to a subset of seven I will here call the Syracuse letters. All are concerned with Plato's engagement in Syracusan affairs in the 360s BC, or the aftermath of that engagement in the following decade. All except one, the *Thirteenth*, are open letters, designed, as we can tell from both style and content, to be copied and widely circulated. Open letters were common devices in

Plato's time for putting forward one's views, in the way an op-ed columnist or Substack writer might do today.

Not all of the Syracuse letters can be defended. The group includes the obvious fake, the *First Letter*, addressed by "Plato" to Dionysius the Younger, and serious doubts have been raised about the *Second*, also sent by "Plato" to Dionysius. I have accepted the other four open letters as genuine writings of Plato. The *Third* is addressed to Dionysius, the *Fourth* to Dion, and the *Seventh* and *Eighth* to Dion's family and friends. These letters, according to details they contain, were written between the years 361 and 354 BC, and in the Thrasyllan collection, they form a chronological series, the *Third* being earliest. The *Seventh* is by far the longest and covers a range of topics, some going back half a century before the time it was written. It's the most important source for this book.

The *Thirteenth Letter* stands outside this sequence; it's the last of the group but earliest in its notional date (365 BC). It purports to be a *private* letter from Plato to Dionysius, not intended for circulation as the other four were. The *Thirteenth* has found few defenders and many opponents; it was the first of the letters to be decried as a fake, some six centuries ago. Yet opposition to it is rooted not in its style or content, but in the continuing influence of the spell of Plato. The letter breaks that spell by showing Plato dealing with mundane matters—money he's owed or needs to borrow, expenses he needs to meet—and working hand in glove with a notorious tyrant.[14]

The Italian Renaissance scholars who first studied Plato's works, and translated them into Latin, decided the *Thirteenth Letter* was unsuitable for publication. "I judged that the majesty of Plato should not be commingled with this letter," wrote Leonardo Bruni in 1420, explaining why he omitted it from his translations. Those words were echoed five centuries later by a revered Platonist, R. G. Bury, in his own condemnation of unlucky number thirteen. "The Plato disclosed to us in this letter," Bury writes, "is no longer the sublime philosopher, contemptuous of all that is sold in the merchant's mart, but a businessman engrossed in all the financial operations of the money market, buying and borrowing."[15]

Bruni's "majesty" and Bury's "sublime" show how the spell of Plato endures across the centuries. It has made the *Thirteenth Letter* a literary pariah. Yet this document gives more insight into Plato's unfiltered thoughts and personal life than anything else we possess. It allows us to see Plato whole, a figure *more* appealing because he's more real. "To me, it seems a very human document indeed," wrote John Burnet, one of the scholars of Plato who has gone on record defending the letter, "and it only increases my respect and admiration for the great Athenian."[16]

In chapter 6, I'll explain in greater depth my reasons for accepting the *Thirteenth Letter*. There can be no proof it is genuine, but despite determined efforts, no one has proved otherwise.

The other sources that I have drawn on include some of the most significant writers and thinkers from antiquity.

Plutarch's *Life of Dion*, an entry in his biographic anthology *Parallel Lives*, gives a detailed but biased account of events at Syracuse in Plato's time. Plutarch puts his subject, Dion, in the best possible light and tears down Dion's opponents; I have dealt with the problems raised by his bias at various points. Plutarch also looked often to Syracuse for *exempla* to use in his non-biographical works, a vast collection of ethical treatises grouped together today under the title *Moralia*.

The chronicler Diodorus Siculus—a Sicilian Greek by birth, as the second part of his name indicates—compiled a survey of all of Greek history in the first century BC. Like Plutarch he worked from primary sources, many now lost, but summarized these amateurishly and incompletely. His account of fourth-century Syracuse is especially incomplete; it becomes a bare trickle of information at a crucial point, around 356 BC, but is useful up to that moment. Justinus Frontinus, or Justin as he's more commonly known, was also a compiler of history rather than a historian. In the second century AD (or perhaps later) he summarized in Latin a long work written in Greek, the now-lost *Philippica* or "Events concerning Philip," and created what is called his *Epitome*. He presents a darker, more lurid picture of Dionysius the Younger than that found elsewhere.

Anecdotes and factoids concerning the two Dionysii appear in a wide array of sources. Aristotle preserves precious details, as does one of his students who composed a work in his style called *Economics*. A contemporary of Aristotle, Aeneas of Stymphalus (also known today as

Aeneas Tacticus), made several notes about Dionysius in his manual of military tactics.

In the Roman world of the first century BC, Cicero was fascinated by Dionysius the Elder as an avatar of monarchic power. A near contemporary of Cicero, the Greek geographer Strabo, presents only two substantive items about Dionysius the Younger, but they're both doozies (see chapters 12 and 13). Later in time, but reliant on earlier sources, are four authors who mined the historical record for entertaining tidbits: Athenaeus, Diogenes Laertius, Polyaenus, and Aelian, all Greeks of the second or third centuries AD, and the Roman Aulus Gellius, from the same era.

A word should be said regarding my handling of *Republic*. The work is vast in its scope; it includes many topics I won't deal with here, especially its theories about the effects of art and literature. My goal is to mark out a pathway into the work by way of its political themes and its connections to Plato's life. I've narrowed my focus to how the work deals with monarchic power—condemning one version, tyranny, as the greatest of evils while exalting another, philosopher-kingship, as the greatest of goods.

"Tyrants are wise by the company of the wise," wrote Sophocles in one of his plays, referring to the fondness of despots for keeping philosophers at their courts. This book will deal with that line's corollary: The wise can become more tyrannical by the company of tyrants.

# A NOTE ON THE LINE DRAWINGS

Each of this book's five "acts" is introduced by a line drawing made from the paintings on the Darius Vase, a much-debated Greek ceramic vessel found in southern Italy in 1851. The central panel of the vase depicts scenes from a Persian monarchal court, possibly that of Darius III, the ruler dethroned by Alexander the Great. Strangely though, the figures who converse with this Persian king, in postures that suggest disagreement, are recognizable as Greek by the style of their dress. It's been thought that the vase depicts scenes from a play, and the Greeks who appear there are warning the king against imperial overreach—a warning he ignores, to his woe.

The artist who created the vase, whose name is unknown, seems to have worked at Tarentum, in the heel of the Italian boot, around 330 BC. His childhood and youth almost certainly overlapped with the reign of Dionysius the Younger, a neighboring ruler known to have styled himself after the Persian kings. It's possible then that he had Dionysius's opulent court in mind, and the visits that Plato paid to it, when illustrating the vase. Certainly his city knew much about the last of those visits, having barely prevented it from ending in disaster.

No portrait busts have survived of either Dionysius the Younger or

A NOTE ON THE LINE DRAWINGS

his father. These sketches from the Darius Vase can allow us to imagine the two most powerful men of their times as they hosted visiting sages (Acts I, II, and III), as their agents collected taxes and tallied sums (Act IV), and as Greek observers watched in awe the spectacular fall of their dynasty (Act V), a drama in which Plato had played no small part.

# ACT I

## THE FIRST VISIT

*The driver of a four-horse chariot, the ultimate Greek symbol of wealth and status. Wall painting from a south Italian tomb of the fourth century BC.*

# CHAPTER 1

# TYRANTS AND KINGS

## (388 BC and before)

The quadrennial festivals held at Olympia, in the western Peloponnese, were always grand affairs in the Greek world, but the festival of 388* was especially grand. In that year a rising Sicilian ruler, Dionysius of Syracuse, later to be known as Dionysius the Elder, was doing his best to impress his fellow Greeks. As leader of a city of two hundred thousand, in command of a massive fleet and standing army, he had quickly become the most powerful Hellene the world had yet seen.[1] He now meant to show off his greatness.

The Greek cities of Sicily and south Italy, founded by colonists from mainland Greece, were not often in the front ranks of Olympic competition. But Syracuse, founded as a colony of Corinth, was an exception. It had raised itself above the other settlements in its region, in large part thanks to two earlier autocrats, Gelon and Hieron. During the decades they reigned, the 480s and 470s BC, these two brothers had sponsored winning chariot teams, then touted those feats as signs of magnificence. The coins they issued, the loveliest of any produced in their day, showed on one face a chariot team being crowned by Nike, the goddess of victory. Dionysius was hoping to rival those illustrious predecessors. He'd

---

* All dates are BC unless otherwise indicated.

*Four-drachma coin minted by Gelon. Later Syracusan coins show the chariot team driving right to left instead of left to right.*

shipped across the sea to the Peloponnese several four-horse teams to compete in the chariot race, Olympia's most spectacular event. He'd also sent bards and musicians trained to perform his own verses, for Dionysius fancied himself a poet as well as a sovereign. To prove he was an enlightened man, he'd named his first-born daughter Dicaeosynê, "Justice," and two later daughters got similar names: Sôphrosynê, "Moderation," and Aretê, "Virtue."

Though Dionysius himself stayed in Sicily, he made sure that the contingent he sent would display his power and wealth. The tents that the Syracusans put up were adorned all over with bands of gold and bolts of costly, colorful cloth. They looked like something a king would erect, though the Greeks had not known true kings for many an age. The monarchs who ruled Greek cities, often for short spans of time, were instead referred to as *tyrants*, a word that connoted one-man rule without a dynastic past. Dionysius, who'd risen to power *ex nihilo*, conformed to the type but avoided the title, perhaps instead dubbing himself archon, a less unsavory term.[2]

Despite its grandeur, the Syracusan cohort had a wretched Olympic outing. The costly chariot teams either ran off the track or fouled one another and crashed before reaching the finish line. Dionysius's poems, recited as part of a verse competition, were mocked as hack work and awarded no prizes. But the greatest embarrassment came from a riot sparked by an orator, Lysias, who'd come to Olympia from Athens for the purpose of denouncing Dionysius. This man, a Syracusan ex-pat, was determined to warn the Greeks that Dionysius's rise threatened all of their freedoms.

"I have not come here for logical niceties or wrangling over words," Lysias told his audience, vowing rather to speak about "the weightiest things." The cities of mainland Greece, he observed, had weakened themselves with endless infighting. Autocrats stood on either side of them, profiting from their divisions: to the east, the Great King of Persia, sovereign of a vast Asian empire, and, to the west, Dionysius. "The King possesses many warships, and so does the tyrant of Sicily," Lysias said, linking the two in a parallel structure that made Dionysius seem both fearsome and vaguely non-Greek.[3]

Having stoked his listeners' outrage, Lysias urged them to overthrow Dionysius and free the Sicilians, starting right then and there. "No opportunity in the future is better than what's before us," he said. He urged that the Syracusans be banned from the games, since competitors sent by a godless regime would pollute the sacred enclosure. Then he turned the crowd's gaze toward the gold and purple tents that stood a short distance away.

The crowd, enraged, rushed toward the tents and attacked them. They pulled down the poles and plundered the cloths and gold threads as though taking spoils in a siege.[4] The showy adornments they tore had been cast by Lysias as symbols of despotism, the arrogance born of excessive power and wealth. It seemed to the mob they were shredding the emblems of tyranny.

This was not the end of Dionysius's woes. The fleet that brought his defeated contingent back home was wrecked in a storm off of Italy. Crewmen straggling back to Syracuse spread a rumor that Dionysius's bad poetry had cursed the whole expedition. Courtiers made haste to comfort the archon, reassuring him with the thought that much great art had at first been received with scorn.[5]

At the very moment the ships were returning, or perhaps shortly after, Dionysius hosted an Athenian ethicist, Plato, who'd made a stop in Syracuse while touring the region. Plato's visit was to become the stuff of legend, for very good reason. It set in motion a chain of events that stretched across decades, into the era of Dionysius's sons and grandsons, and changed the course of history in the Greek West.

Those events would bring the destruction of much of what Dionysius had accomplished. They would give the lie to his daughter's name, Justice; for his regime, in its response to the turmoil, would perpetrate some of the worst *in*justice ever seen by the Greeks. But Syracuse's misfortunes would also guide Plato, part observer and part participant, on a search for Justice, the thing itself in its absolute form, a virtue pure and unchanging—the search that produced his masterpiece, *Republic*.

Plato had already written part of *Republic* before he visited Syracuse, and he continued to work on the treatise long after. The ideas it explored, about the kind of government Greek cities needed, were informed by Plato's contact with the greatest city of his day. But those ideas had also led him to make that contact, in a search for new models of rule. Plato's evolving political theories, and his role in political practice in Syracuse, are strands that intertwined through much of his life, each crossing over the other.

This book will follow the braid of theory and practice, showing both how Syracuse helped shape Plato and how Plato attempted to shape Syracuse. It's a story told in large part by Plato himself.

By the time of Plato's visit, in 388 or 387 BC, Dionysius had ruled Syracuse for nearly two decades. He'd come to power not by turning weapons against his people but by exploiting their fears, their anger and their mistrust of traditional leaders, persuading them to vote away their own freedom. Tracing how this transpired, how Syracuse first renounced one-man rule only to embrace it again, requires going back to the time of Gelon, the chariot victor, and to the long, intermittent conflict between the two peoples vying for Sicily, Greeks and Carthaginians.

Sicilian Greeks, unlike Hellenes elsewhere, faced a constant, and sometimes existential, threat from their non-Greek neighbors. Colonists from Carthage, a Phoenician (Punic) city on the North African coast, had settled in western Sicily and wanted the East as well. Under a towering general, Hamilcar, they'd invaded the eastern, Greek portion in 480

BC, but were stopped in dramatic fashion at Himera, on the north coast. Gelon, at that time tyrant of Syracuse, led the victorious Greeks in that battle and saw his power greatly increase in its wake. Many thousands of soldiers, gathered in an assembly, had hailed him as their *sôtêr*, "savior," and even as *basileus*, "king."

Gelon's model of one-man rule was nearly extinct by this time in the rest of Greece. Other city-states had expelled strongmen in previous decades and taken steps to prevent their return. Tyranny had been disappearing, replaced by oligarchies where nobles held sway and finally, in Athens, by a thriving democracy. The tide of history seemed to have turned—but on the island of Sicily, the old, waning system hung on. With his victory over his Punic foes, Gelon, together with his brother Hieron, had given it new life.

After his triumph Gelon built a giant shrine to the goddess Athena; its massive columns still stand today, forming part of the walls of the Siracusa cathedral. Gelon is also said to have minted a marvelous coin, the Damareteion, named for his wife Damaretê. According to one source,

*The columns of Gelon's Athena temple, visible in the walls of Siracusa's cathedral.*

she had played a key role in arranging the safe release of Carthaginian captives, and Carthage thanked her by bestowing a weighty gold crown. This object, plus the huge ransom Carthage paid, is said to have subsidized the new coin.[6]

The story has been doubted and the Damareteion traced to Gelon's successors rather than Gelon.[7] In either case, the coins of this era attest to the greatness of Syracuse under its tyrant brothers. They include the Greek world's first decadrachms or ten-drachma pieces, each containing about an ounce and a half of pure silver. Their larger surface could be embossed in greater detail than any previous issue. Syracuse used them to show the victorious chariot team, by that time the ruling regime's icon, but now put a lion, symbol of Carthage, under the horses' hooves. The image thus combined military triumph with older ideals of athletic prowess and wealth. The dramatically larger denomination—more than double the value of the largest Greek coin to that date—was scaled to the city's outsized ambitions.

The opposite face of these coins, like most of those minted by Syracuse, showed another national emblem, the profile of Arethusa, a virgin sea-nymph. According to legend, the city had first been founded on a small island just off Sicily's coast, a place called Ortygia, "Quail-land." In earliest times the place had been given by Zeus to his virgin daughter, Artemis, whose sacred bird was the quail. To welcome the goddess to her new property, the nymphs in her retinue, including the pure Arethusa, created a spring on the island. That spring, with its standing pool, took its

*A later version of the chariot-victory theme, on a ten-drachma piece minted by Dionysius the Elder. On the reverse, Arethusa surrounded by dolphins.*

name from the nymph, and is still today known as Fonte Aretusa. In it, in ancient times, swam eels and fish that were held to be sacred to Artemis and could not be touched.[8]

The coins minted under Gelon and Hieron depicted four dolphins leaping around Arethusa, a design that refers to the spring's miraculous nature—fresh water somehow flowing forth on an island surrounded by sea. Thanks to that strange phenomenon, Ortygia served the Syracusans as a strategic stronghold. If besieged by their enemies there, they had a steady supply of drinking water, as well as ready access to excellent harbors on either side of the island. Few places in the Greek world offered such natural assets.

As their city expanded, the Syracusans built a causeway connecting Quail-land to Sicily proper. Ortygia became a peninsula, but the people still called it the Island based on its early topography. It remained the nucleus of the city's ritual life, with its gleaming complex of temples, altars, and shrines. The tyrants made their home there in a palace called the acropolis; it wasn't built on high ground but, because of its fortifications, seemed to provide as much safety as if it had been.

The Carthaginian threat subsided after the battle of Himera and, as Syracusans grew more secure, their need for a strongman ebbed. When Gelon died and his less popular brother took over, the city began to resent its loss of freedom. Sensing discontent, Hieron acted in ways that anticipate later autocracies. He created a cadre of *Otakoustai*, "ear-listeners," to spy on gatherings and meetings, a secret police force—but this only bred more discontent.

In 466, after Hieron's death, amid dissension among the ruling clan, Syracusans rose up and took back their city. The last of Gelon's kin was driven out. Syracuse became a democracy.

The currents of history seemed to be flowing, as elsewhere in Greece, away from one-man rule and toward one-man-one-vote, the principle of the people's assemblies that governed democracies. For nearly sixty years Syracusans met in such an assembly and guarded their newly won freedoms, adopting harsh measures to deal with internal threats.

By referendum they could exile for five years anyone they deemed sufficiently undemocratic. Athenians cast similar votes on broken ceramic sherds, *ostraka*, in a process called ostracism; the Syracusans recorded their ballots on *petala* or leaves of wild olive. Hence their procedure got the charming name "petalism."[9]

Resistance to would-be autocrats was so intense that Syracuse even exiled a man who'd won a resounding victory. In 413 BC that man, Hermocrates, had marshaled Syracusan forces to defeat an invasion by Athens; he'd been instrumental in forcing an unconditional surrender. But his very success made him seem a potential threat. A short time later, while Hermocrates was off on an Aegean naval campaign, the assembly voted to banish him. But the move was controversial and some Syracusans, especially the wealthier class, were determined to get it reversed. If they couldn't do so by legal means they were willing to help Hermocrates force his way back.

Among that pro-Hermocrates faction was a young Syracusan, at this point in his early twenties, who clerked in a low-level government post—Dionysius.

Aiding Hermocrates' cause was the fact that Carthage was once again on the attack in Sicily, after decades of quiet. Its leader, Hannibal Mago—namesake of the Hannibal who would one day march on Rome—had made up his mind to avenge his grandfather, Hamilcar, for the defeat at Himera. In 409 BC Hannibal wreaked a terrible vengeance, executing three thousand Greeks on the very spot where Gelon had triumphed. Syracuse sent ships to Himera's aid but these arrived late; the troops they landed were soundly thrashed and had to depart in such haste that the bodies of the slain Syracusans were left to rot where they lay.

The unburied bones of the dead were still lying there two years later, and the Carthaginians were still advancing toward Syracuse, when Hermocrates landed in Sicily with a band of mercenaries. He had a plan to win his way back to his native city by helping it fight off its Punic foes. He dealt several quick blows to Hannibal's army, then collected the Syracusans' remains from the ruins of Himera. In a gesture of reconciliation, he loaded the bones in wagons and sent them to be buried in native soil. In Syracuse this prompted a fierce assembly debate, as pro- and anti-Hermocrates factions wrangled over the city's response. Finally Syracuse opened its gates to the wagons but kept them closed to Hermocrates. It stuck by its sentence of exile.[10]

Dionysius, who likely attended that debate, was watching and learning. There were fault lines within his city, divisions that an ambitious man could exploit. The wealthy and well-born wanted Hermocrates back, even at sword point. The less well-off mass of the population, the demos or *dêmos* as the Greeks called it, was mistrustful and angry, resistant to any leader who sprang from the ranks of the rich. That kind of class division, in earlier times, had often produced a tyrant who rose to power by championing the poor. Perhaps the same strategy might work again, especially if the demos was not only angry at the wealthy but fearful of Carthage.

The upper-class faction contrived a plan to slip Hermocrates and his troops inside Syracuse. They enlisted a group of supporters to open one of the city's gates, and Dionysius was part of that squad. On a prearranged day Hermocrates arrived at the gate as planned, but some of his soldiers had lagged behind; while Hermocrates waited outside the walls, word of the infiltration got out. An armed crowd gathered to stop it and battle was joined near the gate, with one Syracusan faction fighting to keep Hermocrates out, another to let him in. Hermocrates himself was slain in the fracas and Dionysius was wounded. The incursion was stopped; the democracy held its ground.

Syracusans who'd aided the plot were branded as rebels and subject to execution, but some of the wounded avoided that fate by having their families report them as already killed. Dionysius escaped punishment in this way. As he recovered, he had time to assess the current moment of crisis. Without Hermocrates' help against Carthage, the forces led by Syracuse were facing defeat. A new Punic leader, Himilco, had replaced Hannibal and was making steady advances; refugees from captured cities were streaming eastward. Many of these spoke loudly against the Syracusan commanders, who, they said, were failing so badly as to suggest they were taking bribes from the enemy. In that mistrust lay an opening for Dionysius.

At a heated assembly meeting, Syracusans debated what should be done about their *stratêgoi*, the military commanders elected to lead their campaigns. Since these *stratêgoi* came from the upper social ranks, often mistrusted by those lower down, the charge the refugees leveled against them—collusion with Carthage—found purchase. Debate proceeded along class lines, with commoners angrily voicing their accusations and higher-class speakers defending their peers. No consensus had yet emerged when Dionysius, healed from his wound and somehow clear of insurrection charges, stepped to the speaker's platform.

Channeling the rage of the demos, Dionysius urged the assembly to dismiss the *stratêgoi* on the spot and elect new commanders with better democratic bona fides. The proposal ran counter to constitutional norms, so officials in charge of the meeting threatened him with the relevant fine. But a staunch supporter stepped up and came to Dionysius's aid. Philistus, a wealthy aristocrat with strong monarchic leanings, had either been coached in advance or took the initiative in the moment. He vowed to pay whatever fee was imposed, even if Dionysius went on speaking and racking up fines all day long.

Philistus was about twenty years old and must have known Dionysius from boyhood; he'd judged that his age-mate had the makings of greatness. A few days before this assembly session, he'd witnessed a portent that seemed to confirm this judgment. Dionysius had been fording a river when his horse got stuck in an eddy and couldn't pull out. Dionysius had left the creature behind, but a little further down his path he heard a whinny behind him. There was the horse, with a swarm of bees in its mane. Philistus later wrote of this in a now-lost work of historical prose, depicting it as an omen of glorious rule.[11]

Relying, ironically, on Philistus's riches, Dionysius continued to rant against the perfidy of the rich. The generals, he claimed, had contempt for the demos and were willing to sell out all the Greek cities for gain. The assembly, its class-based resentments inflamed, at once dismissed the standing *stratêgoi* and appointed others, including this new firebrand, Dionysius, to take their place. The horse-and-bee sign had proven prophetic. The young cadet's bid for power was launched.

N{o}t content to be one among many, Dionysius made a show of spurning board meetings with the other *stratêgoi*. He suggested that these men, too, were in cahoots with Himilco. Amid the panic caused by the Punic advance, such rumors were all too quickly believed. At further assembly meetings, the Syracusans, now infatuated, voted to make Dionysius *stratêgos autokratôr*, a general empowered to act without oversight. In only a few months he'd risen from near anonymity to the equivalent of commander-in-chief. The Syracusan democracy, so stoutly defended against strongmen for decades, had opted to create one.

The generalissimo set about assembling a loyal cadre. He arranged the recall of exiles who'd supported Hermocrates; he had married Hermocrates' daughter and could count on the support of this faction. Then he marched off westward to Gela, a Greek Sicilian city allied with Syracuse. Here too, rich and poor were at odds amid a stumbling war effort. Again spurring class resentment, Dionysius persuaded the Geloan assembly to execute wealthy landowners, then seized their estates and used the gains to hire more soldiers. He got Gela's commanders cashiered on grounds that they too were collaborating with Carthage.

War-torn Sicily was by this point full of displaced persons and soldiers for hire from elsewhere. Dionysius built up a personal army, doubling pay to ensure its fidelity. He sought security not by changing the constitution but by displays of strength that made his rule seem inevitable. After an attempt on his life (which may have been staged), the Syracusan assembly granted him a bodyguard corps of six hundred; he promptly increased that number to over a thousand, carefully picking the landless and desperate and outfitting them with the finest armor and weapons. He gathered in mercenaries who'd arrived under Spartan command, veteran toughs who'd made a career by backing whoever paid the best. The weighty decadrachm coin was a powerful draw to such men, as intended by the tyrants who had first minted it.

Looking back to the model of Gelon, Dionysius knew his best chance at firming up power would come from victory over Carthage, yet he couldn't achieve it. Even when he led a vast, composite force, over thirty thousand strong, to confront Himilco at Gela, the attack miscarried. His many contingents, including non-Greek mercenaries, had trouble coordinating their movements; when some were cut off and destroyed, Dionysius was forced to withdraw within Gela's walls. Uncertain of how he would fare the following day, he evacuated Gela during the night and beat an embarrassing retreat.[12]

After that failure, a cohort of Syracusan nobles decided to rid their city of Dionysius. They tried to ambush him on the roads but found that the forces surrounding him were too strong. Instead they locked the gates of the city against him and seized his house and his wife, hoping to drive him away for good. But Dionysius burned down the gates and forced his way in. In a brutal night battle, he overcame the rebels and retook control of the city.

In his recovered home, Dionysius found that his wife, Hermocrates' daughter, had been gang-raped during the uprising. That was one blow that could not be overcome, no matter how many he killed. The traumatized woman, whose name is unknown, soon took her own life. Few of the wives of the rulers of Syracuse over the next five decades were to have peaceful deaths.

The rebellion against Dionysius had almost succeeded, and a second one followed soon after. This new revolt, and the failure of the Gela campaign, shook the confidence of the otherwise cool Dionysius. When things seemed darkest, he called a meeting of close advisors and told them he wanted a way to surrender his power. That meeting produced two apophthegms that came to embody the spirit of his regime.

A man named Heloris spoke first and delivered the first of these sayings: "Tyranny makes a fine shroud."[13] Better to hold onto rule even at the cost of one's life.

One of the tyrant's kinsmen objected, saying that Dionysius should ride to safety and live out his life in exile. That prompted a third advisor, one Megacles, to deliver another dictum that soon became famous. "One shouldn't gallop away from tyranny on a fast horse," declared Megacles, "but rather be cast out of it, dragged by the leg."[14]

Dionysius recovered his nerve and swung into action, using brute force to reestablish control. He'd made up his mind to rule at all costs. And the costs, he was finding, were huge.

A connoisseur of tragic drama and a playwright himself, Dionysius took to quoting a line from Aeschylus, from the play *Prometheus Bound*, to sum up his tenacity. In the opening lines of that play, the allegorical figure of Kratos, Force, gives orders that Prometheus be chained to his rock of punishment "in shackles of adamantine bonds." With surprising candor, Dionysius used the phrase "adamantine bonds" to describe what he sought to impose on his city.[15]

He continued building up loyal backers and quashing opponents. He confiscated the land and wealth of those who took part in the uprisings and parceled it out to supporters; some even went to the slaves he'd freed and dignified with the title of "New Citizens." He disarmed the populace, collecting shields and spears from their homes. If his people needed to wield these in war, he'd restore them, but only at a safe distance from Syracuse; then he'd confiscate them again when the battle was over. Perhaps at some point he stopped using any citizen troops in his army, finding that his mercenaries required less oversight.

The strongest of these adamantine bonds was Ortygia, the Island. Dionysius set up a wall and gate, the Pentapyla, to control the causeway and strengthened his palace complex, the so-called acropolis. The Island became an enclosed preserve for his family, his troops, and his inner circle; no other citizens lived there. An adjacent harbor was redesigned with sheds for sixty warships, walls to prevent attack from the land, and a floating boom that could narrow the entrance such that only one ship could pass at a time. With his fleet safe in this pocket of sea, Dionysius could not be starved out in a siege; the ships could bring his food in, while the spring, Arethusa, kept him supplied with fresh water.

Dionysius got busy building other walls, too, to protect Syracuse from invasion. The tract of high ground to the north, called Epipolae, had in the past been a route for attackers. Walling off this plateau required a vast labor force, so Dionysius enlisted sixty thousand able-bodied men, divided them into teams of two hundred, and set prizes for teams that worked quickest. Stones were brought from local quarries by the continuous effort of twelve thousand oxen. We're told that a section of wall three and a half miles long and perhaps eighteen feet high, complete with defensive towers, went up in *three weeks*.[16] While securing his city's environs and his own redoubt on the Island, Dionysius expanded his influence. He won control of eastern Sicily, then crossed the Straits of Messina

*The remnants of Dionysius's Epipolae walls.*

to begin annexing the toe end of the Italian boot. Here he could harvest resources, especially timber for his enormous naval buildup. Syracuse had a staunch ally on the toe, the city of Locri, but also a stern opponent, Rhegium (on the site of modern Reggio Calabria). When the Rhegians seemed intractable, Dionysius laid siege to their city, an operation that turned into the grimmest, most protracted ordeal of its era.

For eleven months Dionysius maintained a cordon around Rhegium, choking off its access to food. As their supplies dwindled, the Rhegians took to eating their horses, then to boiling their leather shoes, then to sneaking out of the walls by night to devour wild grasses. Dionysius soon brought in cattle to graze on the grass and reduce it to stubble, eliminating this last food source. Finally the city could take no more and submitted. By then the streets were littered with corpses. The emaciated survivors, six thousand in number, were deported to Syracuse, where those who could not pay a ransom were sold into slavery.

The poets of Greece lamented the sufferings of the Rhegians, especially those of their commander, Phyton. Dionysius had this man bound to one of the Syracusan siege engines, just as Zeus had Prometheus chained to his crag. A messenger was sent to inform Phyton that his son had been executed the day before. Then Phyton was flogged through the city streets while a crier followed behind announcing that he was paying the price for defiance. Even the Syracusan soldiers found this repugnant. Dionysius feared they would set Phyton free out of pity, so he had the man drowned in the sea along with his kin.[17]

Through cruelty abroad and repression at home, Dionysius had shown an unbounded will to power. No one had any idea how far he might go. When his ships crossed the northern Adriatic and landed troops in Illyria (modern Albania), ostensibly to support his Illyrian allies, it was thought he intended to plunder the oracle of Delphi, the wealthiest and most sacred of all Greek shrines.[18] In the end he made no move to do so, but it's startling that he was even suspected of such an audacious plan.

Small wonder then that Lysias, in his Olympic oration in 388 BC, denounced Dionysius as a threat to all Greece and an offense to the gods. Small wonder too that Plato, on his voyage to the Greek West, felt impelled to visit this potentate and see firsthand the mechanics of tyranny.

By 388, Plato knew what the grip of tyranny felt like, for he'd experienced it in his own city, Athens. After its defeat at the hands of Sparta, sixteen years before, Athens had briefly been ruled not by a single strongman but by an entire gang—the Thirty, or as they soon became known, the Thirty Tyrants. Twenty-four-year-old Plato had watched their progress with interest and initially, as he reports, with hopes for their success.

Installed by the Spartans and backed by Spartan arms, this junta embarked on a reign of terror in Athens, arresting, exiling, and executing their democratic opponents. Like ancient Savanarolas, they saw themselves as reformers and purifiers, cleansing the city of its excesses of freedom. They were led by one Critias, an Athenian who became infamous for his ruthless purges, "the first Robespierre" in one recent assessment.[19] Plato observed this man with particular care, for Critias was his cousin, the son of his grandfather's brother.

Plato had grown up in Athens during its long war with Sparta, a war that cost Athens much yet led to defeat. Born in 428 or 427 BC, just after the death of the great Pericles, he'd known only poor leadership, bad assembly decisions, and the ruin of a once-great empire.[20] In his teens he'd seen Athens take an enormous gamble, an invasion of Sicily, and lose its entire fleet plus thousands of lives. He'd watched this parade of errors through the eyes of a mentor, Socrates, who had no love for the city's democracy and who often challenged its leaders, questioning them in ways that exposed their ethical blind spots.

The installation of the Thirty seemed, to the youthful Plato, to promise a better day. "I believed that they would manage the city by leading it out of a certain unjust life, into a just way," he wrote of the Thirty decades later, reflecting on this moment of radical change.[21] He reveals in the same reminiscence, the *Seventh Letter*, that he was asked to join the regime; as a kinsman of Critias he was naturally seen as an ally. But despite family ties and his own high hopes, Plato held back to see what kind of body the Thirty would be. It was not long before he found out.

The *Seventh Letter*, a missive Plato composed late in life in part to explain decisions he'd made long before, supplies nearly all we know of Plato's youth, and that isn't much. It tells us nothing of Plato's love affairs, friendships, or recreations; it focuses exclusively on his role as an Athenian citizen. All who held that citizenship were expected to play their part in running the city, especially those who came from well-off families, as Plato did. In the letter Plato takes pains to account for his lack of participation. His need to explain is more urgent because, though he'd avoided politics at home, he had, by the time he composed the letter, become enmeshed in those of Syracuse, a city to which he had no natural ties. His tone in the letter makes clear that this choice did not sit well with his fellow Athenians.

The Thirty proved themselves far out of line with the "just way" Plato was seeking. Among its many crimes, the regime had antagonized Socrates, whom Plato in this letter—his only surviving comment, in his own voice, on the man who had changed his life—calls "a rather old man, whom I would hardly be ashamed to call the most just of those of that era."[22] The Thirty had called on Socrates, together with others, to arrest a leading dissident and bring him before them for execution. Socrates had declined to take part. He simply went home and did nothing. The others carried out the arrest, and the dissident, Leon of Salamis, was killed.

Leaders who might have steered Athens toward justice had in fact tried to make "the most just" Athenian act unjustly. The emphasis Plato gives in the letter to "justice," at both the public and personal level, is of a piece with his thought and writings elsewhere. Plato's greatest dialogue, *Republic*, bears the alternate title "On Justice"; neither title is Plato's own, but the secondary one is on some levels more fitting. The principal goal of this work is defining the nature of justice, in both the state and the individual soul, and to show how it leads to ultimate happiness.

Perhaps it was lucky for Athens that the Thirty moved so quickly away from justice, for their purges provoked a counterrevolution. Critias was killed in an uprising sparked by democratic insurgents; other members of the Thirty fled into exile. Democracy was restored, and Plato, as he writes in the *Seventh Letter*, was again drawn toward politics, "though more reluctantly this time," given how badly the Thirty had fared. But once again, things went awry, and once again Plato recoiled from how his mentor, Socrates, was treated by those in power.

"By a certain chance," Plato writes, "some men who at that time held sway brought this same Socrates, our friend and ally, into the lawcourt, leveling a most unholy charge that befit Socrates least of all people." The charge as given in the letter was "impiety" (it also included "corrupting the youth," as we learn elsewhere). Plato found it deplorable that this charge could be brought against a man who'd been "pious" by not giving aid to the Thirty. The conviction and execution that followed convinced Plato that, as he says with a sneer, "the laws, both written and customary, were falling to ruin at a truly amazing rate of progress."[23]

Not only in Athens, but everywhere Plato cast his eyes—in cities governed by popular assemblies and those ruled by wealthy elites—things seemed to be sliding downhill. Plato writes that his soul-sickness was like the queasiness one might get from gazing down from great heights. "Looking at all the cities that now exist, I realized that they were *all* badly governed, for their laws were in a condition that's nearly beyond cure, barring some miraculous contrivance accompanied by good luck," he laments.[24]

Plato goes on in the *Seventh Letter* to hint at what that miracle might look like. An "upright" philosophy—the kind that Socrates had embodied, a search for understanding of ethical truths—could reveal to those who pursued it "all of what's just, both in states and in individuals." Political life could be put on an entirely different footing, guided not by the shifting desires of mobs or the selfish interests of oligarchs, but by Justice itself, a shining beacon of truth. Plato began to conceive of a new kind of leader who'd been trained in this "upright" habit of mind and who knew what perfect Justice looked like.

Such thoughts occupied him in 388, he writes in the *Seventh Letter*, at the time he struck out for Italy and Sicily.

It's possible Plato had left Athens only one prior time, and had then gone only to nearby Megara. He was around forty now and had already written and circulated some of his dialogues, including an early and partial *Republic*. He doesn't say what prompted his voyage westward, beyond the connection he draws to his sickness of soul. Only philosophy, he now thought, could point the way toward good governance, so humanity's only hope was to have philosophers lead. Not coincidentally, in one of the places to which he was headed—the Greek city of Tarentum on the heel of Italy's boot—this hope was about to come to fruition.

Tarentum, or Taras as the Greeks called it, was a center of Pythag-
oreanism, a mystical, cult-like school of thought that deeply interested
Plato. Pythagoreans believed that numbers and their relationships held
universal truths; they immersed themselves in geometry and mathematics, as well as in music, the aural expression of math. Though they didn't
discover it, the theorem named for their school, a formula for finding
the length of a right triangle's hypotenuse, reinforced their belief in the
divine nature of ratios and mathematical laws. Astronomy too was one
of their studies, for the planets, in their view, were governed by perfect
numerical patterns and produced musical tones as they moved—what the
Pythagoreans called the harmony of the spheres.

Tarentum was democratically governed, but a Tarentine of exceptional wisdom, trained as a Pythagorean, would soon take on a nearly
monarchic role. Archytas had been nurtured on geometry, music theory, astronomy, and mechanics; he eventually published treatises in all
these fields. He also had a deep interest in ethics, political theory, and
military command. His versatile mind was as much at home in mathematic abstractions as in highly practical matters of weapons and battlefield tactics. He was widely admired, too, for his moderate nature and
emotional self-control. Once he became enraged at some misdeeds of his
slaves, and, after calming down, told them: "You wouldn't have gotten
away unpunished, had I not been so angry."[25] His emotions had been so
intense that he'd felt compelled *not* to act.

Archytas had already emerged as a leading Pythagorean, and perhaps
as a budding political leader as well, at the time Plato went to Tarentum.
Eventually he was elected to seven one-year terms as a *stratêgos* of the
city, one of its joint chiefs of staff. The constitution imposed a limit of
only one term, but Tarentines set the rule aside in his case. Eventually
he would play an even larger executive role in a league of Italian Greek
cities that Tarentum headed. Under his guidance, Tarentum was to enjoy
a golden age of prosperity and power.

Plato says nothing in his *Seventh Letter* of meeting with Archytas in Tarentum, but various hints in his dialogues, including *Republic*, make clear that he did. And, as later events reveal, the encounter
cemented an enduring bond. "They established a relationship of guest-
friendship . . . which obligated them to do their best to further each

other's interests," writes the classicist Carl Huffman in his book, *Archytas of Tarentum*.[26] That relationship was one day to save Plato's life.

Two of the thirteen letters in the Platonic collection, the *Ninth* and *Twelfth*, purport to be missives from Plato to Archytas, both apparently part of an ongoing exchange. Huffman considers the *Ninth* to be "probably spurious" but also writes "there is nothing . . . that makes it impossible to suppose that Plato wrote it."[27] In it, "Plato" speaks as a mentor to Archytas, advising him to obey the call to public service even against his own will. "We've been born, each of us, not for ourselves alone," the letter avers. If it *is* genuine, it must have been sent at a time when Archytas was entering public life and regretting the need to leave his studies behind. No proof of the letter's authenticity is possible, but, as Huffman conceded, there are also no grounds on which to reject it.

The *Twelfth Letter*, also from "Plato" to Archytas, is more problematic. It bears a copyist's note, in Greek, that questions its authorship: "There's contention that this is not by Plato." No one knows who wrote this or when, or whether its author had any relevant knowledge. There are other reasons, too, why experts reject this epistle, though Plato scholar A. E. Taylor was "rather inclined to think that it is genuine."[28] It's very brief, in any case, and its contents are not consequential; it looks like a "cover note" designed to accompany writings that "Plato" was sending.

Plato's stay in Tarentum came at about the same time as Dionysius's war against Rhegium. Tarentines were far enough east to avoid that fight, and anyway, they had no reason to oppose the Syracusans. Both peoples belonged to the Dorian branch of the Hellenes and spoke the Doric dialect, with different spellings and vowel sounds than the cities around them. Tarentum was also a fellow expansionist power, aiming at domination of the Italian heel just as Syracuse did of the toe. Tarentum, however, did not have call to fight other *Greeks*; its wars were against non-Greek peoples, Lucanians and Messapians, who had long been its foes.

To secure his claim on the toe, Dionysius started building another wall, the most ambitious yet of his fortifications. He meant to cut the foot of the boot in half at the place where it was pinched in the middle, making that east-west line the northern frontier of his realm. This astonishing project would have crossed more than twenty miles of rough terrain, a greater length than the entire circuit surrounding Epipolae. The

Greeks dwelling north of its course recognized what was happening and stopped it in time.[29] Otherwise a large chunk of their region, with its rich agricultural land and stands of timber, would have effectively become annexed to Sicily.

Did Plato learn of this building project during his stay in Tarentum? If so, he might have reflected on how the wall would demarcate two models of leadership. South of its course, a strongman held sway who relied on force, surrounded himself with paid troops, and rode roughshod over constitutional norms. To the north lay the home of a deep mathematical thinker who was gaining power by winning the trust and respect of his people. One leader wrote tragic dramas, replete with tempestuous passions and lurid crimes; the other, sober treatises on harmonics, mechanics, and optics.

The two men exemplified two different systems that Plato was writing about in *Republic* and that he'd spend much of his life pondering. North of the line stood the prospect of kingship, as Plato conceived of that institution; to the south, tyranny. If other political systems were failing, as Plato believed they were, then one of these two forms of monarchy would have to take their place. It was vital, in Plato's eyes, that the Greeks learn to tell them apart and choose correctly.

Syracusan rulers of earlier times had sometimes been hailed as kings, even if most Greeks considered them tyrants. Gelon, as we've seen, was addressed as *basileus*, "king," by his soldiers after his stunning victory at Himera. Later the Theban poet Pindar, celebrating a chariot race won by Hieron, sang in an ode of "the horse-loving king of Syracuse" who "wields the scepter of justice."[30] In Greece of the early classical age, the two terms, tyrant and king, overlapped.

What, in the Greek mind, distinguished a king from a tyrant? Clearly the first was the preferred title, for no one ever said "Oh tyrant!" in Greek when addressing a ruler, whereas "Oh king!" was common. Generally speaking, kings were thought to descend from dynastic lines, while tyrants were newcomers; thus the play we wrongly call *Oedipus the King* (or in Latin, *Oedipus Rex*) is more accurately *Oedipus the Tyrant*, since

Oedipus is a first-generation ruler. But this distinction, as Gelon's case shows, wasn't always observed.

Another inconsistent idea was that kingship belonged to the non-Greek world, whereas tyranny was homegrown. Barbarian rulers were hardly ever called tyrants. The historian Herodotus, discussing the rise to power of Gyges, a Lydian (from what's now western Turkey), calls Gyges a king even though he'd seized power as a usurper. In Greek usage, the phrase "the king," if not qualified, signified the Great King, the head of the Persian empire (based in what's now Iran). In Hellas, by contrast, kings were part of the world of the past, the mythic landscape of tragic dramas and epics. One exception was Sparta, but the Spartans broke all known patterns by having *two* kings, dyarchs rather than monarchs.

With the rise of Dionysius in Syracuse, the question of where to place the "wall" between tyranny and kingship became more pressing. In public Dionysius sought to look royal, going about in purple robes and a golden crown, much like the Persian Great King or the kings of the tragic stage.[31] Still, to most Greeks he was simply a tyrant, and Lysias called him that in his fiery speech at Olympia. Dionysius himself, as we have seen, may have avoided self-definition by using the vague title "archon."

Ethical thinkers in the era of Dionysius started taking a harder look at the two versions of monarchy. In one of his dialogues, Xenophon, a former member of Socrates' circle (as Plato was), puts the distinction thus: "Socrates thought that kingship was rule over subjects willing to be ruled and according to the laws, while tyranny was rule over the unwilling and not according to the laws but directed by the will of the ruler."[32] Plato makes a similar point in his dialogue *Statesman*, dividing kingship from tyranny according to whether they partake of "the forceful" or "the voluntary."[33] Both Xenophon and Plato write of a *basilikê technê*, a "kingly craft," by which a leader would benefit his subjects;[34] there was no corresponding "tyrannical craft," for tyrants sought only their *own* benefit, another important distinction.

Two notions of one-man rule, once overlapping, were drifting away from each other. But it was Plato's *Republic* that thrust them to opposite poles, good versus evil.

*Republic* explores the surprising idea that a city-state shares the same structure, on a much larger scale, as the human soul. Whatever virtues are seen in the city can also be seen, in miniature, in the soul, Plato maintains. The project for which *Republic* is famous—construction of a perfectly just city-state—is undertaken not for its own sake but in order to seek *individual* justice. Plato explains his procedure with an analogy: If words are too small to be read, we can first read the same words in larger versions; then, knowing the content, we can turn back to the smaller letters. The city-state with its larger font size can help us read the messages of the soul.

Pursuing this city-soul symmetry, *Republic* examines how different regimes correspond to different personality types. Oligarchy has the same qualities as the oligarchic man, democracy those of the democratic man, and so on. When one regime morphs over time into another, as Plato believes will always happen, the change is paralleled, at the individual level, by transitions from father to son; states and people both have lines of descent. And descent is indeed what occurs, for these parallel arcs, the political and the personal, both bend, in Plato's view, ever downward. Better regimes give way to worse and parents raise children whose flaws are worse than their own. At the bottom of the descending chain lie tyranny and the tyrannical man, the most wretched of both the civic and human conditions.

Plato's description of the tyrannical man, whom he also calls "the tyrant," is nightmarish—in a literal sense, since, as *Republic* maintains, he's driven in waking life by his harrowing dreams. "While the other part of his soul—the rational, gentle, and ruling part—is asleep," Plato has Socrates say, "the bestial and wild part dances about . . . It does not shrink from having sex with a mother, or with any other human, god, or beast; it butchers anyone it chooses, and holds back from no kind of food" (the last point implying gluttonous feasting but also, perhaps, cannibalism).[35] Such dream impulses become the tyrant's reality, for the rational part of his soul—the "ruling" part, at least in a healthy person—is permanently asleep.

In contrast to this dream-driven tyrant stands the man whom Plato terms "the king," the happiest man and head of the happiest state. In kings, the rational mind is truly and properly "ruling," and the promptings of dreams are kept under tight control. The king has healthier dreams to begin with, because he has nurtured his reason, "feasting it on noble arguments and inquiries" rather than food and wine, before going to sleep.[36]

Plato nowhere calls this rational ruler "philosopher-king"; that term is a modern concoction, first used at the end of the eighteenth century. But clearly it's the pursuit of philosophy that makes him royal. He looks upward to that which is "true" and "real"—eternal and unchanging things—rather than wallowing in the dross here below, the world of gross substance. In *that* world, Plato says with disgust, people "graze, stooped down toward the earth and toward their tables, getting fatted and rutting" much as herd animals do.[37] (The image of unphilosophic life as a feast at bestial "tables," as the next chapter will show, owes much to Plato's visit to Syracuse.)

*Republic* measures the gap between king and tyrant by a strangely precise mathematic equation. Looking at the descending chain of human types, and the descending regimes they are linked to, Plato has Socrates reckon up the distance between top and bottom. The figure arrived at is three to the sixth power, also expressed as nine cubed. To the amazement of those who witness this calculation, Socrates pronounces the sum by "bringing down," like a modern-day gavel, a stunning seventeen-syllable Greek word: The king, he reports, is happier than the tyrant *enneakaieikosikaieptakosioplasiakis*, by "729 times," and so too the states that they govern.

"An inconceivable reckoning!" exclaims an auditor, Glaucon, even while accepting the logic that led to this outcome. "And a true one, befitting human lives," replies Socrates, adding, in words that have mystified readers, "if indeed the days and nights and months and years befit them."[38] That opaque sentence in fact points toward Tarentum and its math-centered philosophic school.

The Pythagoreans, with whom Plato met in Tarentum while writing *Republic*, believed that numbers, especially potent ones like 729—the next number after 64 that is both a perfect square ($27 \times 27$) and a perfect cube ($9 \times 9 \times 9$)—were deeply embedded in the code of the cosmos. By a small astronomical fudge they reckoned the length of the solar year at 364.5 days so as to make the total of days plus nights come out to exactly that number. Then they went further, calculating the orbits of sun and moon—both of which, they believed, revolved around a fiery mass at the galaxy's center—in such a way that the cycles coincided once every 729 years. That very infrequent occurrence they dubbed the Great Year.

The universe, in the Pythagorean view, ran on a clock whose minute and hour hands both came full circle at that mystical number, 729. So when Plato used the same cosmic clock, in *Republic*, to "time" the gap between king and tyrant, he made clear how much he owed to the Pythagoreans and, we may guess, to Archytas of Tarentum. Certainly that man's later career would conform, as closely as anyone's did, to Plato's vision of the philosopher-king.


J ust as Plato's time in Tarentum inspired his thoughts about kingship, so too his next destination, Syracuse, would teach him about tyranny. Sometime in 388 or early 387 BC, he traversed that ideological wall and sailed across the Straits of Messina, headed for the court of Dionysius.[39] "Some divine chance" drew him on, he says in the *Seventh Letter*, as though he had had little choice in making the journey. Well he might say so, for by the time he wrote those words, more than thirty years later, it was clear that his going had been a dreadful mistake.

*Sujet d'un Vase de la même forme.*

A Greek banquet scene, depicted by nineteenth-century artist Benedikt Piringer
based on a vase of the fifth century BC.

CHAPTER 2

# SYRACUSAN TABLES

## *(388–387 BC)*

"When I arrived I was in no way and no manner pleased with 'the happy life,' as it is termed there," Plato writes in the *Seventh Letter*, of his first visit to Syracuse. "It's a life filled with Italian and Syracusan tables, where living means stuffing oneself two and three times a day, and never lying alone in bed at night."[1]

His dismay was rooted as much in politics as in personal morals. A state where the search for pleasure reigned, he believed, produced an unstable citizenry and itself became unstable. He thought of the hedonism of Syracuse, its emphasis on satisfaction of appetites, as linked to its tyrannical government. During his decades-long engagement with the city, he would stress again and again the need for sobriety and self-restraint as a path to larger reforms.

In part this high living was a regional trait. Plato's mention of "Italian and Syracusan tables" references a proverbial expression: "Syracusan tables," in Greek parlance, was shorthand for indulgence in food and wine. The rich soil of eastern Sicily, made fertile by Etna's eruptions, contributed to the bounty that appeared on those tables, as did the large stocks of fish that schooled in local waters. Great wealth such as Dionysius possessed heaped them up even higher. And along with rich foods and fine wines, as Plato noted, went easy access to sex, often from female musicians hired to "play" at the feasts.

The pleasures of Syracusan tables were enjoyed far beyond Syracuse itself; Greek cities in southern Italy, too, took part in the regional bounty. The city of Sybaris, on the arch of the foot of the boot, became legendary for sensuality in ancient times and remains so today through the adjective "sybaritic." What made Syracuse a unique case of overindulgence was the fact that its population belonged to the Dorian branch of the Greek family tree. Dorian Greeks elsewhere, especially in Sparta, were known for their self-control and moral rigor. If Dorians had given in to temptation, as it seemed the Syracusans had done, then, the Greeks reasoned, those temptations must be overwhelming—a problem for moralists but a magnet for those with a taste for the high life.

As earlier tyrants had done, Dionysius, the archon of Syracuse, relied on that magnetic pull to draw thinkers and men of letters to his court. He maintained them at his expense as a way to secure their allegiance, in hopes of boosting his cultural stature. Luminaries arrived from all over Hellas to take part in his feasts, writing and speaking well of him in exchange, even praising his verses—for Dionysius craved not only power but literary acclaim. One famous poet, Philoxenus, took up residence in Syracuse, no doubt drawn away from his native Cythera, an island off the Peloponnese, by the very lifestyle that Plato found repellent.

Philoxenus enjoyed a good meal and made sure to get his fill. Once, we're told, he noticed that Dionysius's plate had a fish much larger than his did, so he picked up his fish and held it close to his ear. When the tyrant asked why, he explained he was doing research for a poem, *Galatea*, about a sea-nymph; he wanted news of the undersea world, "but my fish knows nothing about it, since he was caught so young. Yours is older and has more to tell." Dionysius laughed at the witticism and ordered the bigger fish placed in front of his guest.[2]

In the competition for delicacies at the tyrant's table, it paid to be quick. We're told that Philoxenus accustomed his hand to heat by plunging it into hot water at public baths. That way, when a new dish emerged from the kitchen, he could grab a portion and eat it while others were forced to wait for the food to cool down.[3]

One of the poems of Philoxenus,[4] entitled *Dinner*, is thought to contain a description of Dionysius's banquets. The poem is lost but one long passage is quoted by a later writer. The passage begins with the setting-up of tables and hanging of lamps. Then a vast array of food is laid out: barleycakes in baskets; platters of eels, swordfish, squid, and octopus; wheat buns and honey cakes; pork loin, boar's head, and slices of goat meat; various cuts of beef; lamb, rabbit, partridge, and pheasant; honey, clotted cream, and cheese. Even allowing for poetic license, this feast was enormous. After the diners had eaten their fill, Philoxenus tells us, the tables were taken away still laden with food.

Those who enjoyed Dionysius's meals were expected to praise their host, but bold Philoxenus did not live up to the bargain. At one state dinner he spoke his mind and let Dionysius know how little he thought of his poems. Insulted, the tyrant had Philoxenus hauled away to the Latomiae, a set of hollowed-out quarries converted into a grim, rocky prison. A short while later, we're told, Dionysius relented and brought Philoxenus back, then asked him again, over another feast, to comment on his verses. This time the poet did not reply but surrendered himself to the guards standing near: "Take me back to the quarries," he said.[5]

The subject of Philoxenus's undersea poem, *Galatea*, was not idly chosen. The name Galatea belonged not only to a mythic sea-nymph but to a Syracusan woman the poet was smitten with. Unfortunately for him she was also a mistress of Dionysius (one of many, surely). Philoxenus tried to win her away from the tyrant, an attempt that landed him in the caverns for an extended stay. Unbowed, he found a form of revenge that has since immortalized Galatea, the object of his desire, in literature, music, and art.

While languishing in the Latomiae,[6] Philoxenus composed a genre-bending poem, *Cyclops*, a verse drama set to a dancing rhythm. Since he wrote the poem in a cave, Philoxenus took as his setting the most famous cave in Greek myth, the one in which, according to Homer, the man-eating Cyclops imprisoned Odysseus. He adapted that story to his own circumstances, recasting Dionysius as the monstrous Cyclops, himself as heroic Odysseus, and spinning a plot in which both were in love with the sea-nymph Galatea. The poem reenacted Odysseus's escape from the cave but brought Galatea into the story as the hero's deliverer. In the poem's conceit her intervention shows she prefers a human suitor over a one-eyed ogre.

How it must have galled Dionysius when *Cyclops*, in which he was made to look ugly and foolish, became a panhellenic sensation. The caricature of Dionysius as a violent monster harmonized with widespread fears about the man's growing power. The Athenian playwright Aristophanes spoofed the poem in his last surviving comedy, *Wealth*, in a way that suggests his audience was widely familiar with it. Later Greek and Roman poets picked up the theme of the lovelorn Cyclops scorned by the fair Galatea, sometimes omitting the Odysseus figure, sometimes swapping him out for a handsome young suitor named Acis.

Ovid wrings a new twist on the story in his poem *Metamorphoses*. He has Acis killed by a rock the Cyclops has thrown, but the murdered youth is then resurrected, by merciful gods, in the form of a river. That version later furnished the plot of operas by Handel and Haydn, and inspired paintings by Poussin and others. Galatea became an icon of feminine loveliness for early modern Europe.

The Latomiae quarries gave rise to another legend that lives on today, preserving the fame of Dionysius (though not in a way he might want). One of these hollowed-out limestone caves has an elongated shape that partly resembles an ear. The painter Caravaggio, when visiting the site in the early seventeenth century, imagined that Dionysius had chosen the place for a prison because the rock chamber amplified sound. The tyrant could stand at the top, he thought, and listen in on the whispers of prisoners. Ever since then the place has been known as *l'orecchio di Dionisio*, the ear of Dionysius.

Two further tales are told of the verbal wit and bold spirit of Philoxenus. When Dionysius asked yet again for a candid critique of his verses, Philoxenus gave an ambiguous one-word reply, *oiktra*. In Greek this could mean either "evoking pity," as good tragic drama should do, or "pitiful," that is, so bad as to cause one to weep.[7] Thus the poet avoided a return trip to the quarries and still did his duty to literature.

On another occasion, when Dionysius gave Philoxenus one of his dramas to edit, the poet promptly took up his stylus and crossed out every line from beginning to end.[8]

Along with the luminaries and gadflies he kept at his tables, Dionysius dined with his large family—doubly large, for it was really two families

*A sketch of the "Ear of Dionysius" by German artist Friedrich Gaertner (1819).*

in one. After the suicide of his first wife, Hermocrates' daughter, he had taken not one but two others, whom he'd wed simultaneously. Polygamy up to this point had been the prerogative of Asian monarchs, off-limits to Greeks, but in this, as in many things, Dionysius was breaking new ground.

One of these wives, a woman named Doris, had come from across the Straits of Messina, from the city of Locri on the Italian toe. She'd been betrothed to Dionysius as part of a pact of alliance, voted on and approved by the city's assembly. (A less tractable city, Rhegium, had declined such a pact by telling the tyrant that, if he wanted to wed a Rhegian, he could have the hangman's daughter. For this and other acts of defiance, Dionysius destroyed the place, as we've seen.) The second bride, Aristomachê, was a high-born Syracusan, daughter of a staunch regime loyalist. The first brought Dionysius support from across the Straits, the second from his own city—an ideal combination for an expansionist ruler.

Dionysius was careful to make no distinction between his Italian and local brides to avoid offending either of their homelands. He brought

Doris from Locri in the *Boubaris,* a fabulous ship he'd commissioned—
the first quinquereme, a larger and grander warship than the triremes in
use at the time. To fetch Aristomachê from her Syracuse home and spirit
her to the wedding venue, he sent a grand, gold-adorned chariot drawn
by four white steeds.[9] He kept a strict balance between the two wives,
wedding them on the same day and consummating the unions on the
same night, even keeping secret (perhaps from the brides themselves)
which conjugal rite had come first. Thereafter, we're told, they slept in
his bed on an alternating schedule.[10]

Syracusans waited to see who would be first of the two to conceive,
almost certainly placing their hopes in the native-born bride. But it was
Doris of Locri who gave birth first, and, crucially, to a son. Dionysius
made this boy his presumptive heir, the future archon, by giving him
his own name, another break with Greek custom; in most cases a man's
name was handed down to his grandson, skipping a generation. Later
Doris gave birth to a second boy, then the girl whom Dionysius named
Dicaeosynê, "Justice," to advertise the enlightened values he claimed.

Aristomachê, the tyrant's native-born wife, remained for years without child. The explanation some gave was that Doris's mother had fed
her drugs that prevented conception to ensure that the heir would come
from her own line. One source reports, perhaps too luridly to be believed,
that Dionysius killed his mother-in-law when this scheme came to light.[11]
Whatever transpired to change the pattern, at some point Aristomachê
began having children as well, ultimately giving birth to two sons and
two daughters.

The Great Kings of Persia had revealed many times the perils of
fathering sons with multiple wives. Even when the succession was fixed
by order of birth, Persian half-brothers had fought or killed one another
and mothers had schemed at getting *their* sons on the throne. Polygamy
had huge drawbacks that nearly outweighed its advantage: production of
multiple sons who could serve in high office and daughters who could be
married to powerful allies. In time, Dionysius would do his best to min-
imize the risks. He would adopt a scheme of intermarriage between the
two lines, splicing the family together across its seam. Marriage between
half-siblings who shared a common father was legal in some parts of
Greece, in particular Athens, so the issue of incest didn't need to arise.

Dionysius hoped to cement the family into a unified whole, which also meant welding the Italian toe, where Locri was situated, to his Sicilian homeland. But other familial problems were lurking that Dionysius had not foreseen and could not resolve by marital engineering. These stemmed from the unusual niche occupied by Aristomachê's brother, a young man named Dion.

Dion was not yet a teen at the time he became the ruler's brother-in-law. He grew to be an adept young man who offered important services to the regime. Dionysius began to seek his advice on matters of state and assign him critical tasks, including high-level diplomatic missions. He sent Dion to Carthage to negotiate with his great foreign foe; the young emissary was received there with honor. Back home in Syracuse, Dionysius granted Dion the right to draw freely from the treasury to meet his own needs, provided that an account was kept of the drawdowns. Dion grew rich and influential as a trusted aide at the tyrant's right hand.

But dynasties value blood ties above all other connections, and this was one asset Dion did not possess. Unlike Dionysius's brothers, who'd been given army commands, and his eldest son, who'd been given his father's name, Dion had no place in the line of succession. His outsider status made an uneasy combination with his superior talent for statesmanship.

Dion was an outsider in other ways, too. Abstemious in his lifestyle, he felt ill at ease at the Syracusan tables, where drinking and feasting strengthened political ties. Those who enjoyed the tables found him austere, a stranger to their easy camaraderie. "A few vices might have made him more popular," comments one recent scholar.[12] Out of place amid the ebullience of court life, he looked elsewhere for someone who shared his grave disposition. He found that person in Plato.

According to one extant source, it was Dion who first arranged for Plato's visit to Syracuse. The Roman biographer Cornelius Nepos claims that, "burning with desire to hear Plato's words," Dion convinced Dionysius to issue an invitation.[13] Plato himself does not confirm that account, instead describing his journey to Syracuse, in the *Seventh Letter*, as the work of destiny. A number of later, less reliable authors claim, improbably, that Plato went to Sicily as a naturalist, investigating the active volcano there, Etna.

Plato's arrival in Syracuse awakened something vital in Dion. According to the *Seventh Letter*, the two men formed an immediate bond. "He listened to my words more intently and keenly than any other youth I have ever met," writes Plato. "He opted to live the rest of his life in a different way than the other Italians and Sicilians, devoting himself to virtue as a thing worth more than pleasure."[14] Plato's recollection of this encounter, set down in writing much later, may have been burnished by time, but there is no doubt that Dion and Plato became profoundly attached, a bond that would endure throughout three decades.

Plato's discussions with Dion concerned not only personal ethics but ways in which Dion might influence policy. "I revealed to him the things I deemed the best for humankind, and advised him to put them in practice," Plato relates in the *Seventh Letter*. To put them in practice, in Dion's case, meant using his high position to bring about political change. Dion was only twenty years old, but his influence led Plato to hope for great things, not only in Syracuse but across the lands that Syracuse controlled. A chain reaction of reform might begin with a man of exceptional moral strength—a man like Dion.

Plato envisioned transformation on a grand scale. It seemed to him that the future of Hellas, perhaps the entire world, was at stake in Syracuse. The scope of his thinking is clear from the most famous sentence of his *Republic*, perhaps (as one scholar opined) the most famous in any of his writings.[15] "Unless philosophers become kings in the cities," he has Socrates say in that work, "or unless those now termed kings and rulers truly and fully practice philosophy . . . there will be no cessation from troubles for the cities or, I think, for the human race." Later, in the *Seventh Letter*, he repeated that thought, in similar words, in his own voice: "The human race will not cease from suffering until righteous and true philosophers take political office, or until those now ruling, by some divine stroke of luck, become philosophers."[16]

In Dion, Plato saw the chance that one of these possibilities might come to pass. As a convert to philosophy, Dion might someday take power in Syracuse, if the succession took unforeseen turns. Or, he might be the "divine stroke of luck" that could transform Dionysius, if not into a philosopher, at least into an ethical monarch who followed the rule of law—a king, not a tyrant. Whichever path seemed more likely, it was clear that in this one city, and in this one man, lay Plato's best hopes of achieving his grandest goals.

So began what we might call Plato's Syracuse project, an attempt to bend the arc of the world toward justice.

At some point during this visit to Syracuse—the first in a series of three, over nearly three decades—it's likely that Plato spoke with Dionysius, or even went on a trek with him to explore nearby Etna. A brief note in the work of Athenaeus, a late Greek collector of anecdotes, refers to a little-known expedition: "Plato went to inspect the lava flows, that time when he, together with Dionysius, were at grave risk." Somewhere Athenaeus had read of an outing in which the two men climbed Etna's slopes and, we can guess, got a little too close to danger.[17]

In his letters Plato says nothing of Etna or of any meeting with Dionysius. But our sources insist that such a meeting took place, and agree in general terms on what happened: Plato refused to flatter the tyrant and spoke his mind freely, too freely for Dionysius's liking; the tyrant reacted with anger. How much these tales can be trusted is difficult to assess. Suspicions are raised by the fact that they all conform, more or less, to a story pattern the Greeks found fascinating. Decades before Plato's time, the historian Herodotus depicted an Athenian sage, Solon, angering a king, Croesus, by telling Croesus he was not (as he thought) the world's happiest man. The scene is presented as fact but was almost certainly invented as a way to explore the contrast between power and wisdom. Our accounts of Plato's encounter with Dionysius may also be fabrications, but it's not unlikely that some such meeting took place.

The oldest version of Plato's meeting with Dionysius is found in the *Index Academicorum*, a history of Plato's philosophic school, the Academy, by a writer named Philodemus. This work was composed two millennia ago but has been known to the world for a much shorter time. The story behind its recovery deserves to be told, especially since that story is still evolving today in breathtaking ways. Its outcome may provide the biggest breakthrough in classical studies since Florentine scholars learned to read Greek at the start of the Renaissance.

Philodemus wrote a great number of works, including the *Index*, during the mid-first century BC. Like many Greek thinkers of his day, he emigrated to Italy, where he found admirers and patrons among the Roman elite. His particular friend was Calpurnius Piso, father-in-law of Julius Caesar, and he made a gift to Piso of some of his manuscripts, including his working copy of the *Index*. Piso added this papyrus scroll to his collection of Philodemus's works, which he kept in his sumptuous home in the city of Herculaneum.

The scroll of the *Index* was still in that home a century later, in the time of Piso's descendants, when Herculaneum and its neighbor, Pompeii, were destroyed by volcanic eruption. Piso's house was buried, along with the rest of the town, under hot ash in a series of scorching pyroclastic flows. Remarkably, the scrolls in the Pisos' home were not set aflame but carbonized into ashen lumps. In that condition they lay undisturbed as the eons passed.

In the eighteenth century Herculaneum's ruins were discovered, along with those of Pompeii, and excavations began. Over a thousand carbonized scrolls were brought out of the Pisos' house, but efforts to unroll and read them only destroyed them. Then an ingenious Italian priest who curated Vatican manuscripts, Antonio Piaggio, devised a machine to pry the layers apart very slowly and gently. In 1795 a scroll was opened by the machine to reveal Philodemus's history of the Platonic school—the *Index*. Portions of the tattered, blackened document—including the earliest surviving record of Plato's visit to Dionysius—could be read for the first time in over seventeen centuries. But the scroll was damaged by the unrolling, and Piaggio's machine was soon abandoned.

In our own era, technologies have emerged for reading the Herculaneum scrolls without unrolling them. In early October, 2023, news broke that a single word, *porphyras* ("purple"), had been read from inside one of Piso's scrolls by means of computer tomography, the same technology used in CT scans of the body. The image produced by the scan was enhanced by new artificial intelligence software. Only a few months later, the process of recovering text by CT scan and AI processing had already advanced by a quantum leap. A team of students used those tools

*The papyrus of Philodemus's* Index, *enhanced by digital imaging.*

to decipher over two thousand characters from inside a Herculaneum scroll, thereby winning a huge cash prize in an incentive program called the Vesuvius Challenge.[18]

For the scroll of Philodemus's *Index*, already unrolled but marred by holes and by charring, the modern world has devised other means of access. Computer enhancement of photographs of the text, followed by multispectral imaging, then hyperspectral imaging, have added bits and pieces of legible Greek over the course of decades. A very recent method has brought to light words written on the reverse side of the papyrus, inaccessible otherwise because the whole scroll was glued down to a board to keep it from falling apart.[19] The text on that back side turns out to be a first draft of what's on the front, augmented by edits and markups.

The account the papyrus gives, interrupted by breaks in its surface, runs parallel to the Solon-Croesus encounter described by Herodotus. "Plato spent time in the company of Dionysius (called 'the Elder')," Philodemus reports, "and when this man endured with annoyance Plato's freedom of speech, because when asked 'who seemed to him to appear happier,' he did not say . . ." There the papyrus is broken, but it's clear that Plato refused to gratify Dionysius by calling him "happier." The tyrant's "annoyance" evidently increased in a further exchange, from which only one word survives on the broken papyrus: "in irritation."[20]

Plutarch, in his *Life of Dion*, gives us a different view of the ruler-meets-sage conversation, while agreeing with Philodemus on its basic outlines. According to Plutarch, Plato was introduced to Dionysius by Dion, who naively thought the tyrant would be won over by Plato's ideas. Dionysius was cool to the meeting, so he squeezed it in "when he happened to have some free time." Admitted to the ruler's presence, Plato discoursed on the topic of courage, maintaining that tyrants possess the least amount of this virtue. Then he explained the doctrine of his *Republic*, that justice brings happiness to those who practice it, injustice, unhappiness. Dionysius grew angry at what he took as an insult, and also noticed that those at his court, spectators to this colloquy, were entirely too impressed by the sage.[21]

Finally, says Plutarch, Dionysius demanded of Plato: "What was your purpose in coming to Syracuse?" When Plato replied "I came to find a good man," Dionysius shot back: "By the gods, it seems you haven't yet found one!" His meaning seems to be that *he* was not "good" and might easily do Plato harm. The meeting ended, and Plato, now "eager" to be on his way, was conveyed by Dion's friends to a ship in the harbor. He'd barely gotten free from the tyrant's wrath, though the story will have a sequel.

Diogenes Laertius, who compiled his *Lives of the Philosophers* about a century later than Plutarch's *Parallel Lives*, presents yet a third version.[22] Diogenes agrees with Plutarch that Plato discoursed on *Republic*'s themes, condemning tyranny and insisting that rulers be guided by moral virtue. But the verbal duel that results plays out differently in Diogenes' work. Dionysius grew angry at the implied reproach and lashed out by coining a word to use as an insult: "Your words *elderize*," he declared, meaning they smacked of an old man's rants. Plato hit back with a made-up word of his own: "And yours *tyrantize*," that is, bear the stamp of a despot. Dionysius became enraged and wanted Plato killed but was dissuaded by Dion, together with some obscure figure named Aristomenes.

Several sources agree on what followed the encounter, though they diverge on details. The sequel I've referred to presents a bizarre, but plausible, plot twist, resulting in one of the central events in Plato's life, if it really occurred—a point that can't be determined. These ancient authors concur that Plato, at Dionysius's behest, was sold as a slave.

Plutarch supplies our most detailed account of the strange episode. He says that, after departing in haste from his meeting with Dionysius, Plato boarded a vessel captained by a Spartan named Pollis (a man known from other sources as a prominent naval commander). Before the ship set sail, Dionysius, still angry at being shown up in front of his court, called Pollis in for a secret conversation. He asked the seaman either to have Plato killed or else to have him sold as a slave in some port of call. "He'll take no harm," Dionysius sneered, turning Plato's own doctrines against him; "he'll be happy even in slavery, since he's a *just man.*"

Pollis, says Plutarch, disembarked Plato on Aegina, an island off Attica that was then at war with Athens, and Plato was duly sold. Since his focus is on Dion, not Plato, Plutarch drops the thread there and does not tell us how the philosopher got out of this jam.

Diogenes Laertius agrees with Plutarch that Plato was taken by Pollis to Aegina and sold there and adds a few piquant details. The laws of Aegina mandated death for Athenians, but Plato was spared when someone identified him as a philosopher. At the assembly meeting where this decision was made, Plato stood by impassively, awaiting the city's verdict. By chance a wealthy admirer of Plato, Anniceris of Cyrene, was present and intervened. He purchased Plato's freedom for the price of twenty *minae*, or about twenty pounds' weight of coined silver, and helped him to get back to Athens. Later, Diogenes says, the gods punished Pollis for his part in the plot: fifteen years further on, a tsunami that flooded Helicê, a city in the northern Peloponnese, overwhelmed his ship and drowned him.

The chronicler Diodorus gives a different version entirely,[23] though he agrees on the price of twenty *minae*. Neither Pollis nor Aegina play any part in *his* story. Dionysius acted entirely on his own, Diodorus asserts, and had Plato sold right there in Syracuse. A group of "philosophers" pooled their money and purchased his freedom. When they sent him back home, these sages offered advice with an adage that has a sing-song cadence in Greek: A wise man should spend time with tyrants either *hôs hêkista*, as infrequently as he can, or else *hôs hêdista*, taking care to be pleasant and not give offense. That was in essence telling Plato he should have played nice.

The account of Plato's enslavement found in Philodemus's *Index* also involves a Spartan ship and a landing on Aegina, but is otherwise out of step with the other versions. Philodemus recounts this tale in a chronological context at least a decade earlier than 388, the date of Plato's visit to Syracuse. To the great surprise of the team working on the papyrus—who in 2023 were still teasing out more letters in the relevant passage of text—the oldest of all our accounts presents Plato's enslavement as an independent event, with no connection to Dionysius the Elder.[24]

Which story, if any, contains the truth of Plato's departure from Sicily? Plato's silence about the reported enslavement, even in the detailed *Seventh Letter*, has convinced some scholars it never occurred. Others suppose, reasonably, that if he *had* been sold as a slave, Plato might have preferred not to mention the matter. With only late and diverging stories to go by, we're driven back on surmise.

If Dionysius did order Plato killed or enslaved, his motive may have had less to do with injured pride than concern for his regime's security. Something about Dion's bond with Plato may have made him want Plato out of his city, and out of communication with Dion, for good. By his own account Plato had seen that bond as a way to get his ideas put into practice. To an autocrat like Dionysius, whose only philosophy was pursuit of power, an alliance like that could easily have posed a threat.[25]

The question of Plato's enslavement bears closely on the next event in his life, the founding of what we now call his school. Sources tell us that Anniceris, the man who'd bought Plato's freedom, declined to accept reimbursement from Plato's friends, but instead used the funds they'd collected to purchase a plot of land for Plato's use. According to a plausible variant of this tale, the source of the money was not Anniceris but Dion, Plato's Syracusan acolyte. No ancient source imagines that Plato funded the purchase himself. By all accounts Plato had only a modest fortune and sometimes relied on wealthier friends, including Dion, to help him with major expenses.

The purchased plot adjoined a locale that was called Academia because a shrine of the minor god Academus was found there. In time the plot took on the name of the neighboring grove and is hence known today as the Academy.

The amount that was paid for the plot is given as either twenty or thirty *minae* of silver, that is, either two or three thousand drachmas—neatly enough, the same two figures reported as Plato's slave-purchase price. In real estate terms, this was a handsome but not a princely sum; a house in central Athens might sell for twice as much.[26] So we should imagine a modest parcel, hardly a grand or sprawling estate. Ancient sources often call it "the garden," implying perhaps it contained a small orchard. Those who wanted to study with Plato began to make their way there.

The idea of a gathering place for adult learners was a radical one in early fourth-century Athens. Athenian children received education, of course, sometimes in a tutor's home, sometimes in a *didaskaleion* or schoolroom, but "higher ed" was as yet barely a concept. It was one of Socrates' followers, a man named Isocrates, who first launched a course of adult instruction centered at a single locale—his own house. That institute was but a few years old at the time that Plato returned from the West and took the idea of a school one step farther, setting aside a tract of land for educational use. He created, in modern terms, the western world's first campus.

The Academia is today an urban park frequented by dog-walkers; in antiquity it lay outside the walls of Athens, about a mile distant. Before Plato established his school there, Athenians knew it as a place for strolling or running foot races, since it was shaded by a stand of twelve magnificent olive trees: the Moriai. Those trees, the Athenians said, had been bred from an olive first bequeathed to the city by Athena herself, hence the grove, like that olive, was held to be sacred. The oil squeezed from Moriai olives was also sacred, and vessels filled with it were given as prizes to victors in the Panathenaic games, an athletic festival held at Athens every four years.

Other gods besides Academus were worshiped in the Academia, including, uniquely, Eros, the mischievous lad whom the Romans called Cupid, the avatar of sexual desire. An altar to Eros—a god to whom Plato, in two of his dialogues, was to pay particular homage—served as the starting point for the race course that ran along under the shade of the Moriai.

The grove also had a large public building, in part a gymnasium, with half-open gathering places called *exedrae* along its outer perimeter. In earlier decades, Socrates had often carried on conversations in such civic spaces; more recently one of his followers, Antisthenes, had started doing likewise, holding colloquies at a gym called the Cynosarges. Athletic centers like these drew the sons of the upper class, young men with enough wealth to subsidize *scholê*, "leisure time" that could be devoted to learning. (That Greek word *scholê* became the root of English *school*, an etymology that bewilders modern students accustomed to think of "school" in terms of "school*work*.")[27] With their porticoes and places for bathing, gymnasia offered relative comfort in Mediterranean heat. And the sight of young wrestlers stripped down for matches, their bodies gleaming with olive oil, provided a background buzz of erotic attraction.

Plato's garden may have had a small building somewhere, but not one in which Plato lived. His home was elsewhere, most likely in a nearby place called Eiresidae. Any notions we might entertain of a grand research center, equipped with study rooms and laboratories, are pure retrojection from the modern "academy" (or, closer in time, from Aristotle's Lyceum, established some fifty years later). The garden's purpose was simply to allow men—and, in two specific cases, women—to meet in the open air for discussions and walks. "The Academy is more a state of mind than a place," writes Plato scholar John Dillon.[28]

It's hard not to picture a library of papyrus scrolls as part of Plato's Academy, but that too may be a misconception. Plato collected the works of fellow philosophers for his own use and is said to have paid a high price for scrolls of some Pythagorean thinkers. But "book" learning was not a goal his Academy promoted. Socrates, after all, had not written a single word in the course of his philosophic career. He posed questions *viva voce* and then followed up with further probes, the model for what modern educators call "the Socratic method." Plato reimagined those conversations in his dialogues, as did another who'd witnessed them, Xenophon, in a compilation usually titled *Memorabilia*.

The "curriculum" of the Academy was likely based on conversations, not readings. But Plato conceived of these as exchanges between *two* trained minds, rather than, as in Socrates' case, an interrogation by an enlightened person of one less enlightened. Seekers of philosophic truth,

*The foundations of the gymnasium building where Plato once taught.*

in Plato's view, could push one another forward by means of queries and challenges, until they arrived at insights that satisfied both. To this collaborative, give-and-take process Plato gave the name *dialectic*, perhaps making use of a term that was coined by a predecessor, Zeno of Elea.[29]

The garden provided an intimate space for Plato's closest adherents to conduct these conversations; larger, more diverse groups likely met elsewhere, such as in the *exedrae* of the gymnasium. The garden thus served to define an inner circle, "companions" as they were known. It's this set of seekers, likely no more than a score at any one time, that we usually mean when we speak of "the Academy." Others passed more briefly through Plato's orbit without committing themselves to his teachings. The core group, the true Academics, were defined by the length of time they spent with Plato and also by the specialized, difficult subjects they studied: mathematics, harmonics, and theoretical physics, among other topics.

The fact that Plato's institution occupied purchased ground gave it not only a fixed locale but also longevity. Unlike the school of Isocrates, based in the schoolmaster's house, the Academy was designed to endure beyond a single lifespan. Indeed Plato may have conceived it from the start as a continuing enterprise. His nephew Speusippus, the son of his sister Potone, entered the institution at an early stage and became one of its leading lights, despite holding beliefs that varied sharply from Plato's.[30] Later Plato would make Speusippus heir to the Academy headship, an office that came to be called that of scholarch, "school leader." Using family ties to establish a line of succession was the mark of a dynast who wanted his work to endure.

If this was indeed Plato's goal, he succeeded miraculously. The Academy would continue to meet in the garden for three hundred years, until a Roman general, Sulla, destroyed its grounds in 86 BC during a siege of Athens. Later, those who regarded themselves as Platonists reconstituted themselves, in Athens, as an "Academy," though not in the Academia. Their link to the original group was considered unbroken even though their doctrines had changed, as signaled by the name that was later applied, "Neoplatonists."

A small coterie of these distant descendants, supported by an endowment fund, was still discoursing and writing in Athens in AD 529, when a Byzantine ruler, Justinian, kicked them out in an effort to Christianize his empire. Even then a small Platonist school survived in exile, in Harran, in what is today eastern Turkey. Members of what had by then become an island of pagan belief in a sea of Islam were active as late as the tenth century AD, some thirteen centuries after the time of Plato.[31]

An anecdote found in numerous ancient authors claims that, at the Academy entrance, an inscription forbade entry to those who had not studied geometry.[32] The story dates from after Plato's time and is widely mistrusted, not least because it presupposes a building on which the words were inscribed. But like many spurious tales about Plato, this one at the least contains the germ of a larger truth. Geometry, with its perfect circles, polygons, spheres, and polyhedrons, all conforming to mathematical laws, exemplifies Plato's notion that objects worthy of study should be abstract, eternal, and unchanging, which is to say perfectly *good*.

A circle drawn with the hand, as we know, is only a shoddy version of a *real* circle. Even today, the most advanced software cannot generate a perfect circle, and even if it could, the medium of representation—a piece of printer paper, perhaps, or a computer screen—is subject to deformation and decay. No image can be made that constitutes a *real* circle, yet we know that "circle," or circle*ness*, exists. To grasp the *real*ness of intangible things, and to look away from imperfect, tangible copies, as one does when one studies geometry, was to take a first step in Plato's direction.

Plato believed philosophy's mission was studying things perceptible to the mind but not to the senses. Plato called these real-but-intangible entities *eidea*, a term that is usually translated "Forms" or "Ideas." Mathematical study could bring the trainee into contact with the most basic Forms, like that of circle or square, but others, harder to grasp, required far greater effort. Knowledge of ethical Forms, like Courage and Justice, could not come from study of earthly examples or historical precedents. Such *eidea* had to be glimpsed as pure essence to be understood.

Philosophers needed to spend fifteen years training the mind, according to a scheme that *Republic* lays out, to begin to catch such glimpses. Their advanced education would start at age twenty with mathematics, geometry (both planar and solid), and theoretical astronomy, subjects to be pursued for ten years. At age thirty, they would move on to dialectic, the capstone of philosophic study, which would occupy five more years. After that, Plato implies, their mental quest would continue, self-motivated, by way of dialectic, until, at age fifty, they at last became capable of beholding "the Good itself," the highest of Forms.[33]

Plato's language in *Republic* is rich with metaphors as he describes this program and the goals it strives for. He speaks of lifting or turning the "eye" or the "sunbeam" of the soul, of escaping the "barbaric mud" of the physical world, or of waking from dreams into reality. The things that can be perceived in this new, waking life are variously called "the beautiful and the good," "the truth," "that which is," "the invisible realm." Their precise location is vague but clearly lies aloft or on high, for the mind reaches them by traveling *up*. Plato's stress on upward movement would later make his system of thought congenial to early Christians, who likewise thought of the soul's quest for the divine as an ascent.

The grandest metaphor in *Republic*, however, derives not from flying into the sky but climbing up out of the earth. Humanity dwells in darkness as though in a cave, Plato claims in the work's most famous image. The things we take to be true are in fact only shadows, cast on the wall of our cave by the light of a fire. We base our judgments on the shapes of those shadows and the sequence in which they occur, coming to wrong conclusions about where happiness lies or what we should strive for.

Outside our cave lies a different and beautiful world, the realm of the Forms, lit up by a brilliant sun. After a long course of training and mental effort, a philosopher might learn to exit the cave and step into that sunlight. His eyes would be blinded at first, but in time he'd adjust and even look right at the sun—the Form of the Good, the sovereign Form that imparts goodness to all the rest in the way that the sun imparts light. The happiness that this vision would bring him would be pure and intense.[34]

The Academy's emphasis on invisible Forms confused or amused those outside its ambit, for whom eyes and ears were more to be trusted than mental conceptions. Comic playwrights in Athens tried to get laughs from audiences by pulling Plato's airy philosophy down to earth. "I told you not to marry but to enjoy life," says a confirmed bachelor to his friend in a play by Philippides; "this is the Good that Plato speaks of."[35] Cratinus the Younger presents one character telling another, "You're clearly a human being, so you have a soul, according to Plato," to which the other replies (perhaps while patting his body as though checking for it) "I don't know, but I *guess* I've got one."[36]

A third comic dramatist, Amphis, presented a dialogue between a slave and his master, concerning some plan the two are concocting, no doubt in pursuit of a sexual tryst. The master has an idea to seek a woman's help in the plan, but the slave has his doubts. "Whatever good you'll get by involving *her*, I understand even less than the Good of Plato," says the skeptical slave, as the master prepares to explain himself more fully.[37] The joke, of course, is that no one "gets" Plato's Good.

Perhaps this mockery was prompted in part by the one occasion we know of when Plato tried to address the general public, on a topic announced as "the Good." Athenians understood that term to refer to things *they* found good, such as health, wealth, and strength, but instead heard a talk that was focused on the Academy's central pursuits: geometry, astronomy, mathematics, and a hard-to-grasp notion that "the Good" was a single entity, whole and complete. The listeners, as we're told, muttered to one another in scorn and dismay. Plato's attempt to bring them inside his charmed circle, to share with them discourse heard in the garden, had failed.[38]

In Plato's terms those disenchanted listeners were *philotheamones*, "sight-lovers," a word that first occurs in *Republic* and may well have been coined for that work. Socrates explains its meaning: "Sight-lovers delight in beautiful colors and shapes ... but their mind cannot see or delight in the nature of Beauty itself."[39] The passage is meant to give a jolt to Athenian readers (as it does to modern ones), who considered enjoyment of art, or of beautiful bodies, a high form of pleasure. To Plato such pleasure paled before the far greater joy that would come from abstract thought. Those settling for sights and sensations—the vast majority of humankind—pass their lives in illusion. Only those who strive toward the Forms, in Plato's view, could perceive true essence and gain true happiness.

Plato never implies that he himself, or anyone that he knew, had beheld the Form of the Good. His system requires a leap of faith, a belief that a higher plane exists and can be accessed with studious training and effort. The cave passage in *Republic* is a fervent attempt to convince us to make that effort, but Plato knew that few of his readers would do so. His school, part system of thought, part mystic religion, was not for the masses. Yet *Republic*, and other dialogues, are Plato's way of reaching out to seekers; they open doorways through which newcomers might enter.

Those who most flourished at the Academy were specialists in theoretical subjects, mathematics and a discipline closely related to math (for the Greeks), astronomy. Eudoxus of Cnidus, a pioneer in both fields, held the Academy's goals so high that Plato, when called away from Athens, reportedly made him substitute scholarch. The same honor went, on a different occasion, to the astronomer Heraclides, who tried to explain the movements of stars by way of Earth's rotation rather than that of the celestial dome.

Other Academy members pursued more terrestrial goals in the spheres of politics and personal ethics. It's these more pragmatic, even activist, thinkers who will concern us in what lies ahead. Chief among them, we'll see, was Plato himself.


The cave has become the most well-known illustration of Plato's thought, the first thing that comes to most people's minds when they hear Plato's name. The finale of the cave allegory is less widely known, but crucial for assessing its meaning. Once they've left the cave and beheld the Forms, Plato says, philosophers must abandon the sunlit world they have reached and return to the dark.

At age thirty-five, Plato says, after these searchers have mastered geometry, math, and dialectics, "they'll have to descend back again into that cave, and they'll be compelled to take charge of military affairs and the offices young people hold, so that they won't be lacking experience compared with others."[40] To their theoretical training they must add pragmatic and civic pursuits to prepare themselves for leadership roles in their city-states. By age fifty, if they go back to the cave, they'll have matured as political actors while also completing ascent toward the highest objects of knowledge.

Plato admits that reentry into the cave will be painful. The philosopher's eyes will again be temporarily blinded, and what's worse, the cave-dwellers, believing that the shadows before them are real, will fear and mistrust anyone who considers them false. The philosopher's life may even be in danger from those in the cave—an allusion, most believe, to the fate that befell Socrates, though perhaps there are other levels. Nonetheless, *Republic* maintains, philosophers *must* return to the dark in order to lead their societies in a just manner. They must become, to employ that latter-day term, philosopher-kings.

Plato knew that his readers would find the idea of philosopher-kings hard to swallow. At its first appearance in *Republic*, it's compared to the third, most destructive wave of a three-wave tsunami sequence, which, Socrates predicts, "will swamp us with floods of mockery and disbelief."[41] The metaphor is not idly chosen: as mentioned earlier, the Greek city of Helicê, in the north of the Peloponnese, was destroyed by tsunami in

372 BC, at the time when *Republic* was being composed. The idea of rule by philosophers, Plato implies, might have as much power as that monstrous wave. Existing systems might need to be "drowned" in order to build better ones.

Plato presses his case with another analogy, developed at greater length. Invoking the trope of the ship of state, familiar in his day as in ours, he describes the chaotic condition of "seafaring"—that is, politics—in the Greek world. The ship's captain, in his allegory, is both deaf and nearsighted, unable to keep a straight course. The crew sense his weakness and overthrow him, then set about feasting, getting drunk, and killing off other crewmen who want to steer in a different direction. They exalt as their greatest pilots those who seized the helm from the captain. They fail to see that what the ship needs is a steersman who trains his eyes high above, who navigates by the stars. They regard that type as a useless *meteôroskopos*, a "sky-gazer."

Keeping one's mind on distant, eternal things—the Forms, here reconfigured as stars—is the defining task of Plato's philosophy. Ingeniously reworking the ship of state theme, Plato asserts that the best political leaders are those with their eyes on the heavens. Just as stars guide good pilots, so the Forms give rulers direction in all their decisions. Problems can be more justly resolved by looking at Justice in its pure form than at instances of what has worked in the past or is working elsewhere.

It's not at all clear from *Republic* why a thinker who finds his way out of the cave would ever agree to go back. Plato has Socrates speak of a vague "compulsion" that leads a wise person to rule despite the desire not to. Perhaps, as a recent scholar asserts, this "compulsion" results from self-interest: To decline to rule means accepting that someone with less insight will do so, and therefore that one's homeland will be less just than it could be.[42] Plato may not have fully resolved, in his own thinking, the question of the philosopher's motivation.

Some Academy members seem to have followed Plato's directive to return to the cave. Several went off to Greek cities, after their study with Plato, where they framed laws and counseled rulers; Plato himself, we are told, was recruited to draft the laws of Megalopolis, founded around 370. (He declined, goes the tale, but dispatched a student to write the laws in his place.)[43] Several of the shorter Platonic epistles, especially the *Fifth* and *Sixth*, appear to show Plato giving direction to "operatives" placed at monarchal courts. If these could be proven authentic (they can't be), they would show definitively that the Academy was, as one scholar terms it, "the RAND corporation of antiquity."[44]

Any path that explores this view must pass through Syracuse, the city of Dionysius—a place that was famous for caves, the dreaded Latomiae. It was there that Plato would make his descent from the airy realm of theory into practical politics. He would bring Academy members, including Speusippus, along as he took this step. By his own report in the *Seventh Letter*, he hoped to show the Greek world that his teachings, although they relied on an abstract notion of Justice, could make an actual city more just.

So it is to Syracuse that our story returns, just as Plato himself did, not once but twice.

*Dionysius having his beard singed by his daughter. Canvas by Baroque artist Simone Brentana.*

# CHAPTER 3

# "ADAMANTINE BONDS"

## *(387–367 BC)*

I n Syracuse, Dionysius continued to write tragedies, then stage them in a grand stone theater that comfortably seated twenty thousand spectators. His productions were one of the primary means he employed for projecting the image of an enlightened ruler. "Tyranny is the mother of wrongdoing," he wrote in one of his dramas, an antimonarchic line that survives in a chance quotation.[1] But this must have sounded to many Syracusans more like a confession than a moral critique. Dionysius, even as he wrote plays and hosted philosophers, was doing a great deal of wrong—or at least, so our sources attest.

Some of the stories those sources tell are so bizarre, and so damaging to Dionysius, that one modern scholar assumes they cannot be true. Classicist Lionel Sanders devoted a 1987 book, *Dionysius I of Syracuse and Greek Tyranny*, to blaming these stories on a rumor mill, run by those—philosophers above all—who found it useful to blacken the image of tyrants. This "hostile tradition," as Sanders termed it, relied on the testimony of a certain Timaeus, who wrote a history of Sicily, his native island, in the early third century BC. Sanders argued that this tradition depended too much on Timaeus, who had an antimonarchic agenda, and ignored the works of Philistus, the Syracusan aristocrat, who in *his* writings—now lost—painted a more positive picture of Dionysius.

To be sure, those two chroniclers held starkly opposing viewpoints. Philistus, as we've seen, had helped Dionysius take power and hold it. He served the tyrant in top posts and, even when exiled, for reasons we'll come to, stayed loyal. Timaeus, for his part, grew up the son of a monarch—his father, Andromachus, was ruler of Tauromenium (modern-day Taormina)—but he and his family were driven out of that seat by a crueler and fiercer monarch, a Syracusan named Agathocles. Timaeus landed in Athens and spent the rest of his days there. His life experience made him allergic to tyrants, especially Syracusan ones.

The question of whom to believe, when perspectives radically differ, is one that has always bedeviled political life. Some commentators want to see the best in their leaders, others, the worst; both seek out sources who lend support to their bias. Divergences were especially great in ancient Greece, where stories flew from mouth to mouth and the chance of fact-checking was slim (a problem replicated, in digital form, on today's internet). Timaeus and Philistus each selected the stories they favored, and later writers selected one source or the other according to *their* inclinations. Each tradition got distilled over time. In the end, the antityrannical views of Timaeus won out, in part because they were largely adopted by Plutarch.

How much of a despot was Dionysius? Complicating our efforts to answer that question is the length of his reign—nearly four decades—and his degree of success. He enjoyed "the greatest and most long-lasting tyranny of any recorded in history," according to Diodorus Siculus.[2] Achievements like his give an impression of virtue, as seen in the appellation "the Great," awarded to builders of empires. But *moral* greatness, as the modern world knows all too well, does not always go hand in hand with great achievements. Power can be sustained through cruelty and repression as well as beneficent leadership.

A second problem is that some of the tales told about Dionysius seem too good—or rather, too evil—to be true. Tyrannical cruelty fascinated the Greeks, and their stories about it often resemble myths; thus Phalaris, an early tyrant of Syracuse, was said to have tortured his foes by roasting them inside a hollow bronze bull. But our own age should teach us that truth can be stranger than fiction in the cases of those who wield absolute power. If we'd read in an ancient source that a dictator had a holy book written out in his blood (Saddam Hussein), or executed an uncle by feeding him to starving dogs (Kim Jong-Un), or surrounded himself with a bodyguard of virgin women trained in the martial arts (Muammar Gaddafi), we'd dismiss those stories as fables. It's likely that *some* of what's told about Dionysius is true, and we can't know how much.

A third problem for historians dealing with Dionysius is the fact that the tyrant named his son after himself. Ancient writers sometimes use the name "Dionysius" to refer to both father and son, without adding "the Elder" or "the Younger." (The custom of assigning Roman numerals to leaders who share the same name did not develop until modern times.) So it's sometimes hard to tell who is meant in accounts of how "Dionysius" behaved. A difference of emphasis, revealing a difference of character, can help sort out which tale belongs to which tyrant, but there's still overlap. Stories surrounding the Younger tend to focus on drunkenness, sexual debauchery, and relations with toadying courtiers. Those surrounding the Elder deal with loftier themes: abuse of power, paranoia, fear of assassination.

Opinions about Dionysius the Elder were already sharply divided by the 380s BC, especially among Athenians. The view that Lysias expressed in his speech at Olympia—that Dionysius presented a threat—was echoed by Isocrates, teacher of rhetoric, in the first of his many political essays, *Panegyricus*. There he wrote, without naming names, that "Italy has been ravaged and Sicily enslaved," referring to the destruction of Rhegium and Syracusan expansion.[3] (He'd later reverse himself and lionize Dionysius, as we'll see.) But Athens also had a pro-Dionysius faction, led by a poet named Cinesias. In 393 BC this bard—a man whom Lysias detested—sponsored a measure to praise Dionysius in a public inscription. The stone containing that tribute was set up near the Athenian acropolis; it survives today.[4]

Which side of that dividing line did Plato fall on? In his letters he says very little about Dionysius the Elder, though he had much to say about that man's son. We must look instead to *Republic* for vague indications of how he perceived the archon of Syracuse. In Books 8 and 9 of that work, near its end, Plato, speaking through Socrates, sketches the type he calls "the tyrannical man" or "the tyrant." It's a composite sketch that incorporates features of several historical figures, but those of Dionysius stand out most clearly.[5]

Plato makes clear that he drew on first-hand experience when he composed this portrait, in a sentence so self-referential as to break the fourth wall of the dialogue. His created character, Socrates, asks the people with whom he's conversing whether it wouldn't be best "that all of us listen to the man . . . who has lived with a tyrant in the same house, has been beside him in his domestic life."[6] The group agrees that this *would* be best, and so the account of "the tyrant" proceeds, with Plato, the unseen author, laying claim to its insights.

"The dialogue form is strained almost to the breaking point in this remarkable sentence," wrote James Adam in his 1902 commentary on *Republic*. "We are all to be silent and listen to Plato himself."[7]

Plato had been repelled, as he says in the *Seventh Letter*, by his first glimpse of feasting at Dionysius's court, the home of the infamous Syracusan tables. He thought that such banquet halls, with their surfeits of food, wine, and sex, must inevitably lead to bad governance: "Those in power" in cities where feasting prevails, he writes, "can't bear to hear even the name of a just and fair constitution."[8] It's striking then that he makes gluttony and improper eating prominent features of Books 8 and 9 of *Republic*, the books that contain his sketch of "the tyrant." He introduces the theme in a story that traces the start of a tyrant's reign to an act of cannibalism.

Long ago in the ancient Greek land of Arcadia, writes Plato, the people made sacrifice to Zeus on the slopes of Mt. Lycaeon, "Wolf Mountain," and their offerings included a single human being. When the meat of the animal victims was roasted and served to the worshipers, one bit of human flesh was mixed in. Whoever ate that bit was instantly transformed into a wolf. Plato turns the myth into a political allegory: "Doesn't the leader of the masses act in the same way," he has Socrates say. "Gaining control of an easily led mob, he does not refrain from shedding the blood of his fellow citizens. . . . Isn't it necessary, and meted out by fate, that such a man either be destroyed by his enemies or else rule as tyrant and become a wolf instead of a man?"[9]

The tale, unique to Plato, presents tyranny as a form of predation involving consumption of human flesh. The passage fits with other parts of *Republic* where tyranny is linked to cannibalism. We have already seen that Plato depicts the tyrant acting out in waking life the stuff of his nightmares, including dreams in which he "refrains from no kind of food," a phrase that seems to refer to anthropophagy. Later on in *Republic* Plato goes even further in this gruesome direction. He claims that those who choose the life of a tyrant will be impelled someday to *eat their own children*.[10]

Other Greeks, too, had linked Dionysius with cannibalism. Philoxenus's landmark production, *Cyclops*, reconfigured Dionysius as Polyphemus, the one-eyed ogre who, in Homer's *Odyssey*, devours Odysseus's crewmen two at a time. *Cyclops*, as we've seen, became a hit across Greece, reinforcing the link between Syracusan tyranny and cannibal feasting.

A second feature shared by Plato's generic tyrant and the ruler of Syracuse is reliance on mercenaries, especially soldiers of non-Greek extraction. Speaking through Socrates, Plato describes how a tyrant employs a host of armed guards, comparing these to a swarm of drone bees who hover around their "king" (the Greeks believed that the monarch of a beehive must be a king, not a queen, and that drone bees had stingers). He uses unusual terms to describe these drones, calling them "motley," "diverse," "ever-changing," and, in one instance, *xenikoi*, "foreign." "They'll fly to him in great numbers, without any prompting, if he furnishes pay," he has Socrates say.[11] By the time Plato arrived in Syracuse in 388, Dionysius had indeed assembled an army that was both "motley" and "foreign." He had formed a uniquely diverse mercenary corps, drawing on peoples of Italy, the Iberian peninsula, and even the Balkans—the farthest-flung recruitment effort any Greek leader had yet attempted.

Some of these soldiers came from the northern peoples of Europe who were, at this moment, migrating south. Shaggy-haired Gauls had crossed the Alps in the early part of Dionysius's reign and poured into Italy; they'd made their mark on Roman history by sacking Rome (at that point a mid-sized regional power, not a world empire).[12] Dionysius had been in southern Italy then, making war on the Greek city of Croton; Gallic ambassadors came to him and proposed an alliance. "Our nation can be of great service to you, either by fighting head-on against your enemies or by attacking them from the rear when you've engaged them in battle," a source quotes their envoys as saying.[13] Dionysius accepted their offer and took them into his service.

Other nations who'd migrated into Italy, or who'd long been established there, likewise found it useful to ally with Dionysius. The Lucanians had warred with vigor against Italian Greek cities, inflicting great harm, but the city they hated most, Thurii, was also an enemy of the Syracusans. Dionysius helped the Lucanians storm and take Thurii, cementing a bond that brought him more recruits.[14] Like his alliance with the Gauls, this Lucanian pact aligned him with a "barbarian" race against fellow Greeks; that no doubt caused a certain discomfort, but not enough to make him pass up a huge military resource.

Some of the foreign fighters hired by Dionysius had reached his doorstep thanks to the Carthaginians, their previous employers. Campanians from the foot of the Italian boot had taken part in Himilco's sack of Himera in 407 but then felt cheated by their commander when he divided the spoils.[15] Recognizing both their cupidity and their ferocity, Dionysius bought their allegiance with handouts and entered them into his army.

Similarly, Iberians—expert horsemen—had been brought by Carthage to Sicily, from what's now Spain and Portugal, to aid in an assault on Syracuse. The attack fell short after Punic troops contracted a virulent illness, and Dionysius cut off and killed some of those who withdrew. To escape that fate, the Iberians sent Dionysius a message saying they'd gladly switch sides. Dionysius accepted their terms, thus gaining a powerful cavalry.[16] Iberians used a novel device that helped them stay on their horses: a saddle, something not yet in use among Greeks.

Dionysius reached ever farther in his recruitment drive. From the eastern side of the Adriatic came tough, hardy folk of the Balkans, both Greeks and non-Greeks: Illyrians, Molossians, and the Epirotes who claimed descent from Achilles. From southern Greece, from the Peloponnese, Dionysius acquired his most potent troops, Greek infantry trained by the Spartans or experienced in disciplined Spartan-style warfare. These men had had lands destroyed or vocations wrecked in the wars of the previous decades; they had no better way of making a living than fighting, for whatever city or cause paid the most.

Dionysius housed this multinational force in barracks he'd built on the Island, where they served as both his standing army and his security force. Plato surely observed them there on his visit in 388. The languages he must have heard there, the array of clothing, footwear, and weapons, the range of ethnicities, were unlike anything he could have encountered elsewhere. One day he would find himself in the midst of these men and at their mercy, when many among them decided they wanted him dead.

Not only will the generic "tyrant" gather his "bees" from abroad, Plato says in *Republic*, he'll also create a domestic supply by freeing his city's slaves; for freedmen, in their gratitude, will be his most loyal troops.[17] The resulting inversion of hierarchies, Plato writes, will make freeborn citizens servants of their former servants. "As the saying goes, the people, in fleeing from the smoke of enslavement to the free, fall into the fire of subjection to their slaves," Plato has Socrates say—using "smoke" where the modern expression instead has a "frying pan."[18] Here, too, Plato seems to be shaping his portrait of tyranny out of material gathered in Syracuse.

On at least two occasions, Dionysius freed Syracuse's slaves to bolster his armed forces, and apparently also relied on freed slaves as his household staff.[19] In a third case he created a garrison force out of freedmen to whom he had offered a strange kind of bonus. The evidence for this bizarre plan comes from two sources, one of them nearly contemporaneous and therefore credible or else we might never believe him. Having captured a city but lacking the forces to guard it, Dionysius freed the slaves who belonged to its leading citizens, then allowed them to marry the daughters and sisters of their former masters. Some even wed their masters' wives, presumably after Dionysius had pried the women away from their husbands. "In this way," our source reports, "he thought the slaves would be more hostile to their masters and more faithful to him."[20] The strategy must have worked; it was later adopted by other expansionist rulers.[21]

To provide for his hired army, Plato says in *Republic*, "the tyrant" will need a huge revenue stream. He'll start by snatching precious objects from temples, a ready source of wealth for those who needed to borrow, or were willing to steal, from the gods. Then he'll plunder the estates of his executed or banished opponents. He'll try to avoid imposing broad taxes, since the common people form his base of support; but finally, Plato predicts, he'll have to tap the demos as well as the rich. That will lead to a breakdown of trust, with the demos attempting to rid itself of the tyrant, and the tyrant turning his drones—his security force—on the demos.[22] All this follows closely the fiscal policies of the tyrant he'd seen at first hand.

Tales of the ways Dionysius raised money are recounted by several sources, including Roman Cicero. Dionysius robbed the shrines of the gods with abandon, says Cicero, often following up his thefts with scornful comments to show his disdain for taboos. When sailing away from Locri, where he'd plundered Persephone's temple, he noted that the ship was being borne by favorable winds. "My friends," he sneered to his shipmates, "do you see what a fine voyage the immortal gods have bestowed on us 'unholy' men?" In another such tale, Dionysius took a gilded bronze cloak that clothed a statue of Zeus and replaced it with one made of wool, then quipped that the god would be warmer in wintertime. After robbing temples, Dionysius would auction off the sacred goods he'd stolen, then announce that the objects were contraband and must be returned to their shrines—so that he could steal them again. In this way, Cicero says, he outraged both gods and mortals at the same time.[23]

Taxation and currency manipulation were other ways Dionysius increased revenue. The Greek treatise *Economics*, likely by one of Aristotle's students, claims that under Dionysius a person's entire net worth could be consumed by taxes within the space of five years.[24] From both *Economics* and the numismatic record, we know that Dionysius used his mint to create fiat wealth. He issued bronze coins in place of silver, then paid off his debts with these at a steep discount. Reportedly he demanded an assembly decree that all such coins were to be accepted at the higher valuation.[25]

Dionysius's most audacious financial move involved both extortion and false valuation at the same time. He borrowed money from wealthy citizens; then, when the loans came due, he demanded, at sword point, that these rich men turn over more of their silver. He minted this new reserve into coins of one-drachma weight but stamped them to show a value of two drachmas. Then he gave his creditors back their inflated

*A bronze coin of the type minted by Dionysius.*

money, declaring that he'd paid off both debts at once.[26] The fleeced Syracusans were powerless to protest.

A wolf-man feeding on prey, a cannibal, a "king" bee who sends his drones to attack—with these metaphors in *Republic*, Plato presents the tyrant as dangerous to his people. He examines various motives that lead a tyrant to kill: the need for money, the fear of revolt, or sheer, untrammeled bloodlust. With deft psychological insight, he also adds a further factor, the hatred that springs from envy. The tyrant, writes Plato, eliminates the most upright among the citizen body, simply because the virtues of good men highlight the ones that he lacks.

"The tyrant must take a close look to see who is brave, who is proud, who is wise, who is rich," Plato has Socrates say, "and, whether he likes it or not, he must of necessity"—in order to boost his own stature—"become the enemy of all these and plot against them, until he purges the city."[27] If Plato was indeed sold into slavery by Dionysius, he knew whereof he spoke: In our accounts of that episode, Dionysius acted when made to look small by Plato's devotion to justice. In Plutarch's version, the tyrant had mocked that devotion when sealing the sage's fate, a sure sign of envious spite.

Dionysius was reportedly galled not only by thinkers but also by writers whose talents surpassed his own. He was troubled by the lack of success of his plays at the Athenian drama festivals; they never won first prize in those competitions and indeed often came in last (in third place), if they were even produced. Two reports tell us he bought the effects of great Athenian playwrights—the writing-tablets of Aeschylus and the harp and tablets of Euripides—as though to acquire inspiration by purchase. When he tried composing on the tablets of Aeschylus, "he nonetheless wrote even sillier stuff than before," scoffs our source.[28] He reportedly had Euripides' tablets inscribed with his own name next to that of their famous previous owner, then put on display in a temple of the Muses.[29]

As we've seen, Dionysius sparred often with Philoxenus, whom he admired as a poet but could not abide as a rival and critic. After twice getting out of the caverns, Philoxenus left Syracuse for good, landing in Tarentum. Dionysius reportedly sent a letter begging him to come back, to which Philoxenus sent a reply of a single Greek "o" repeated several times, signifying a very brusque "no." That rejection gave rise to a proverbial phrase, "a Philoxenus letter," used to denote a message that slams the door shut on an offer.[30]

Less fortunate than Philoxenus was another bard, Antiphon, an orator and author of tragic dramas, whom Dionysius brought from Athens as a collaborator. During a mealtime discussion of sculpting materials, Dionysius is said to have asked this man, in an idly curious way, what was the best kind of bronze. "That from which the statues of Harmodius and Aristogeiton are made," the free-spoken Antiphon replied. He had named the famous Tyrannicides, young Athenian men who'd helped bring down an autocratic regime. Dionysius, we're told, had the courageous writer flogged to death.[31]

As the threats, real or imagined, posed by free thinkers increased, so too did Dionysius's vigilance. Taking a cue from his forerunner Hieron, who'd established the "ear-listeners," Dionysius recruited as spies the courtesans who slept with the city's elites. These informants, according to Aristotle, got the name *potagôgides*, "tale-bringers."[32] Another source, Polyaenus, relates that Dionysius promised the women pay for their service but then had them tortured instead to get (as he thought) the most reliable information.[33]

Even successful businessmen struck Dionysius as problems (as Plato perhaps acknowledges when listing the rich among the tyrant's targets). Aristotle tells of a Syracusan speculator who cornered the market on iron ore from the region's valuable mines. When buyers arrived to purchase the ore, the man leveraged his monopoly and doubled his investment. Dionysius got wind of the ploy and ordered the man to leave Syracuse, on the grounds that "he'd discovered a revenue stream that was disadvantageous to Dionysius's own undertakings."[34] Wealth could be used to purchase armed force, as Dionysius well knew, having done that himself.

While eliminating the talented and the best, Dionysius is said to have also promoted the worst. He favored drunkards and gamblers who'd gone into debt, advancing them so they'd provide models for others and dissolution would spread.[35] In a moment of unusual candor, Dionysius reportedly said, when he heard complaints that he'd promoted a villain, "I want there to be someone who's hated more than I am."[36]

Within his inner circle however—meaning, in large part, his family—Dionysius seems to have valued talent, and, of course, loyalty. His need of capable right-hand men explains the high stature of Dion, who maintained an upright, temperate lifestyle yet somehow never fell from the tyrant's favor. Under the *next* Dionysius, the Elder's son and successor, Dion would not be so lucky.

More fearsome to tyrants than unfavorable comparisons was the threat of assassination. Dionysius went to great lengths to protect himself, as seen in two lists of tales, one supplied by Plutarch, the other by Cicero. Some of these anecdotes may be apocryphal, but, as we've noted, the lengths to which modern despots have gone to protect life and rule have often blurred the line between fact and fantasy.

Cicero tells us that Dionysius would not allow barbers to use a blade on his hair or beard, lest it also be applied to his throat. He trained his young daughters to groom him, says Cicero, but when the girls grew up, he didn't trust even them; instead of a razor, he made them use heated walnut shells, or coals, to singe off his whiskers.[37] The tale sounds outlandish, but a Greek comedy of Dionysius's time, now lost, employed a compound word that lends it support: *dionusokouropurônôn*, "Dionysio-flame-barbering."[38] The tyrant's contemporaries already had the idea that he'd found some bladeless way to get shorn and shaved.

Plutarch gives other examples of Dionysius's fear of blades. Everyone, even the tyrant's brothers and sons, was required to change their clothes, or shake out the ones they were wearing, before being admitted to his presence. One day, Plutarch says, when Leptines, the tyrant's brother, was illustrating a point of strategy, he took a spear from a nearby guard to draw a sketch in the sand. Horrified at the security lapse, Dionysius had the guardsman executed.[39] The threat posed by Leptines troubled him too, as seen in his later actions.

Wives and consorts were no more trusted at Dionysius's court than brothers and sons, for they too could hide daggers. Dionysius reportedly devised an ingenious way to enjoy "safe sex" in his chambers. We're told that he had some sort of moat dug around his bed, with a bridge that could be disassembled. After a woman had crossed the moat to join him in bed, he removed the bridge. The woman thus knew that she'd never escape were she to do harm to her lover.[40]

The ever-present danger of blades was no joking matter, as two Syracusans discovered to their woe. According to Cicero, Dionysius, in a pattern common to men of his times, took as a lover a beautiful boy named Leon. One day, while attended by Leon, Dionysius stripped off his tunic and sword and prepared to play a ball game, one of his favorite pastimes. He handed the sword to Leon to hold, prompting a snide bystander to make an unfortunate joke: "At least to *him* you entrust your life!" Even more unfortunately, Leon laughed at the sneer. Dionysius demanded that *both* be killed, though the prospect of losing Leon pained him greatly. Cicero says he rescinded the order three times, reinstating it each time with tears of remorse. Finally he declared the decision final: "Leon, it is not possible for you to live."[41]

If jests could get a Syracusan killed in the era of Dionysius, so, according to Plutarch, could dreams. A trusted palace insider, one Marsyas, carelessly told a friend that he'd dreamed of killing the tyrant; word got back to Dionysius, who ordered the man's execution. A woman of Himera was reportedly arrested, and later killed, for a shout she'd let out on account of a prophetic dream. It seems she'd once dreamed she'd gone to Olympus and beheld Zeus on his throne; beneath the throne a red-haired man was chained, of whom Zeus said "This is the Scourge of Italy and Sicily; if he ever gets loose, he'll ravage the lands." Later, when the woman came to

Syracuse and spotted Dionysius, she recognized the red-haired man of
the dream. Her scream of terror attracted the tyrant's attention, and that
was the end of her. The tale was later reported by Timaeus.[42]

One clever fellow found a way to capitalize on Dionysius's fears. He
went about telling the Syracusans that he knew of a fail-safe way to detect
conspiracies. Dionysius learned of the claim and had the man brought
to the palace. When asked to explain his method, the man requested to
speak to Dionysius in private. Courtiers and guards were sent out of the
room, whereupon the man explained that his trick was already in force:
All those who had left would think that the secret detection method *had*
been revealed, and that any plots they might hatch would be suicidal. The
stratagem delighted Dionysius, who sent the man away amply rewarded.[43]

Dionysius used a similar ploy on a lieutenant named Andron. When
he went away on campaign he put Andron in charge of the treasury, a
vast stash of coin. One of Andron's comrades urged him to steal from the
hoard; Andron refused, but also declined to inform on his friend when
Dionysius returned. Knowing nothing for certain but suspecting much,
the tyrant falsely told Andron he'd heard of a plot to betray him and
wanted particulars. Andron quickly told all, but told it too late. Because
he'd withheld information, he was sent to his death, as was, of course, his
larcenous friend.[44]

According to Polyaenus, Dionysius on several occasions tested his subjects' loyalty, then executed any who failed the test. One time he sailed
off to Italy, then had word sent back that he'd been killed on the voyage;
his agents took down the names of any who celebrated. Another time,
when his warships were about to set sail, he gave the ships' captains
sealed tablets that, as he said, revealed their as-yet unknown destination. The tablets were not to be opened until the fleet was at sea, so that
no one could leak. He went on board his own vessel and made ready to
sail, then abruptly called off the departure and had the writing tablets
collected. They were in fact blank, but any captain who'd broken the seal
was deemed a traitor and killed.[45]

Suspicion poisoned all Dionysius's relationships, even, perhaps,
that with his son, the young Dionysius. Plutarch reports that the Elder
declined to educate his son or allow him to talk with intelligent men, fearing the boy would conspire with them against him. The young Dionysius

kept to his rooms, or was kept there, untutored and solitary, passing his time carving wagons and miniature pieces of furniture out of wood.[46]

Dionysius seems to have been generally displeased by his eldest son and namesake, a socially awkward youth. Walking into his son's rooms and noting the large collection of gold and silver cups, Dionysius rebuked the boy for making no friends despite having wealth to attract them. "You have no mind for tyrannical rule!" he exclaimed.[47] Yet the young Dionysius remained, by virtue of order of birth, his presumptive heir.

In *Republic* Plato several times links the mindset of tyrants with madness and with delusional states like nightmare or drunkenness. Dionysius is said to have had a spell of madness himself in the early 380s BC, brought on not by Plato's visit but by the poor showing his verses had made at Olympia.[48] Whatever the cause, the tyrant's mistrust of his underlings apparently grew at that time into full-blown paranoia.

Dionysius had always rewarded his brothers with high commands until, in 389, he stripped one of them, Leptines, of his position. Leptines had captained the fleet ever since Dionysius's early days in power. But while away in Italy on a mission, Leptines had displeased his brother, brokering an end to a war when Dionysius had wanted a fight to the finish. Dionysius removed Leptines from command and entrusted the fleet to his other brother, Thearides.

Dionysius knew that Leptines was held in high regard by the people, too high for his comfort. He tried to neutralize his brother by dispatching him to a remote outpost, the small guard station at Himera, and ordering him to remain until sent for.[49] But even at a distance Leptines troubled his mind. In 386, Dionysius learned that his brother had secretly let Philistus, another naval commander, marry his daughter. That move seemed to hint at a larger conspiracy.

Enraged, Dionysius had the daughter put in shackles and banished both Leptines and Philistus from Sicily. Then, in a general purge, he killed off Syracusans he had on his enemies list. It's hard to judge the scale of the bloodletting: Plutarch puts the number of victims at *ten thousand* over the course of Dionysius's reign, but the Greeks often used "ten thousand" to signify any large, indeterminate number.[50] At least a few heads must have rolled on this occasion.

Philistus, now in his fifties, withdrew first to Thurii, on the instep of the foot of Italy's boot, then northward to Tuscany, to a Greek and Etruscan town called Adria (the origin of our "Adriatic"). There he started composing a history of Dionysius's reign, a work now lost but once highly regarded. Fragmentary remains show that Philistus wrote without rancor about the sovereign who'd banished him, as well he might, for he still had hopes of a recall. Those hopes, as we'll see, were not to be disappointed. Philistus would yet have a part to play in the drama of Syracuse, a role that would make him Plato's antagonist.

Leptines spent a short time in exile, then Dionysius brought him back and restored him to favor, giving him the ultimate gift, the right to marry his daughter, Dicaeosynê. Like despots and dynasts everywhere, Dionysius needed his family members even more than he feared them. Blood ties and marital bonds were his most reliable form of allegiance, and his best strategy was to have kinsmen linked by *both* blood and marriage— which accounts for his family's convoluted genealogical chart. Weddings were carefully orchestrated to strengthen bonds to the patriarch and to knit his two lines together, that of Aristomachê, his Syracusan wife, and that of the Locrian, Doris.

The tyrant's eldest son and presumed heir, the young Dionysius, was paired with his half-sister, Sôphrosynê, in exactly this way. He was the child of Doris, she of Aristomachê; half-siblings were permitted to marry, by Greek law, so long as they shared a father and not a mother. Their union was intended to head off a rivalry over succession. Aristomachê had borne two sons of her own, and in other amphimetric families— those with two maternal lines—the murder rate between half-brothers ran high. But if the half-brothers were also brothers-in-law, that risk was reduced; after all, what brother wants to face a sister after killing her husband?

By a similar strategy, a brother-in-law might be more tractable, and less inclined to disturb family peace, if he also became a *son*-in-law. Dionysius's brother-in-law was Dion, the brother of Aristomachê. The question of what match *he* would receive, as a loyal regime insider, must have puzzled the tyrant, after he'd given away all three of his daughters. But then Aretê, his daughter by Aristomachê, became free when her husband was killed in battle. She was Dion's full niece but avunculate marriage did not strike the Greeks as a problem, any more than marriage between paternal half-siblings. Aretê and Dion were wed sometime after 380 BC. They soon had a son, Hipparinus, and Dion at last became connected to the tyrant's bloodline.

Dionysius was planning carefully for the future, building a tyranny held together "by adamantine bonds," as he liked to say—in this case, bonds of kinship. Still, the threat of betrayal was always looming, a sword of Damocles over the tyrant's head. In fact it was Dionysius himself who gave us that time-worn expression, as told in a legend related by Cicero.

Damocles, Cicero says, was a courtier who envied Dionysius's life of wealth and luxury. When the tyrant heard of his jealousy, he traded places. Damocles was permitted to feast and drink on the tyrant's elegant dining-couch, attended by beautiful servants. But Dionysius also suspended a sword above the man's head, affixed to the ceiling by a single hair from a horse's tail.

Damocles found he could not enjoy the food or the wine, or even cast a glance at the lovely attendants; his eyes and mind were always trained on that sword. He quickly renounced the swap and returned to his former status, unwilling to live with a tyrant's fears in order to taste his pleasures.

Cicero adds his own comment to this iconic story. Dionysius, he says, was condemned to live beneath that same sword—and also to use his sword against his own people. "It was no longer open to Dionysius to return to the path of justice, or give the citizens back their freedom and rights," Cicero says. "For, as a young man, with youthful lack of foresight, he'd ensnared himself in such errors and committed such crimes that he could no longer be *safe* if he took to becoming *sound*."[51] The wolf-man, that is, was trapped in its lupine form.


Warfare is the foremost arena in which *Republic*'s generic tyrant resembles the one who ruled Syracuse. Plato asserts that this typical tyrant relies on threats from external foes to keep his subjects dependent. "He is always stirring up some war or other, so the people may be in need of a leader," Plato argues, in words that are framed as a hypothetical case but also seem to point to the leading exemplar.[52] Dionysius was known throughout Greece for his conflict with Carthage, a conflict that some-how—by design, some believed—remained unresolved for decades.

Dionysius had first come to power in 407 BC, during, and largely because of, the invasion of eastern Sicily by Himilco. In that campaign the Carthaginians had nearly captured Syracuse, but a plague forced Himilco to abandon his siege. The war was resolved by a treaty that gave Carthage sovereignty over portions of Sicily and also confirmed Dionysius in power. Thereafter the two sides skirmished on several occasions, with Syracuse winning small victories but never dealing Carthage a knockout blow. Some Syracusans held Dionysius to blame for the stalemate, claiming that, since warfare increased his power, he kept on prolonging its course.

A story arose—whether by way of accusation or excuse is unclear—to explain the unending conflict. It was said that the gods had sent Diony-sius a prophecy that he'd die when he defeated those better than he was. The archon, the rumor alleged, assumed that the "betters" the prophecy spoke of were his Carthaginian foes. Thus he'd always held back when the hour of victory neared, lest he bring on his own demise.[53]

Himilco mounted a second eastward campaign in 397, assembling a massive armed force and a fleet of hundreds of ships. He besieged Syr-acuse by both land and sea in 396 and the city again appeared doomed. Dionysius sent money to mainland Greece in an urgent recruitment effort while Himilco gathered food and supplies for the men in charge of his siegeworks. At this moment of crisis, Syracusans' suspicions about Dionysius burst into public view and nearly led to the tyrant's overthrow. The episode is described by the chronicler Diodorus, based on what he had found in the work of Timaeus.[54]

Dionysius was briefly away from the city, having sailed with a squad-ron of ships to intercept Himilco's shipment of food. While he was gone, the remaining fleet, manned by the Syracusan demos, engaged the Punic attackers and, to the surprise of both sides, emerged victorious. Return-ing to the city in triumph, with Dionysius still off the scene, the Syra-cusans started to talk of revolt. They asked why they tolerated a tyrant when they'd shown they could win their battles without him.

Amid these discussions, Dionysius returned with his convoy and called an assembly. He tried to regain control by vowing that he would soon bring the war to an end. Then a man named Theodorus—who otherwise does not appear in surviving sources—took the speaker's platform. The accusation he made sounds much like what Plato describes, in theoretical terms, in *Republic*: The conflict with Carthage was still going on because it enabled the tyrant to stay in power.

"Dionysius is just as wary of peace as he is of war," Theodorus inveighed, according to Diodorus. "He believes that, because of our fear of the enemy, we Syracusans will not attempt action against him, but that once the Carthaginians are beaten, we'll take back our freedom."[55] With keen-eyed precision, Theodorus recalled two prior occasions on which Dionysius had failed to close a trap on the Punic foe and let him escape to fight another day.

"Victory, for us, would be no better than defeat," Theodorus then told the assembly, referring to the ongoing war. "For if we conquer the Carthaginians, we'll have, in Dionysius, a harsher master than they are." He went on to say that rule by the tyrant was really no different from foreign occupation, given how many non-Greek soldiers Dionysius relied on. The acropolis—a fortified palace that occupied part of the Island—was little more than a fortress, claimed Theodorus. It had been set up to besiege the city, just as the Carthaginians were besieging it at that moment. What was worse, it was "guarded by weapons of slaves"—hired soldiers—who had in turn made the citizens slaves. (Enslavement to slaves—one of tyranny's consequences in *Republic*.)[56]

Some of those mercenary "slaves" were at the assembly session where Theodorus was speaking. Among them were Spartans whom Dionysius had recently hired from the Peloponnese and a Spartan commander who led them, a man named Pharacidas. Theodorus, in the account of Timaeus, looked to this man and his troops for support, since Sparta had long been renowned for dislike of tyrants. In his closing words, Theodorus made an appeal for help by suggesting that Sparta might take control of the city once it was liberated from Dionysius.

Pharacidas then stepped to the speaker's platform as Syracuse held its collective breath. "Everyone expected he was going to be the initiator of freedom," our source, Diodorus, reports, but the Spartan's words dashed those hopes.[57] Pharacidas declared himself firmly behind the tyrant. He'd been sent to fight the Carthaginians, he said, not to overthrow a Syracusan. The Spartan troops standing by took their cue and formed up around Dionysius, prepared to meet any resistance. The opportune moment, in which the demos might have succeeded in throwing the tyrant out, had passed.

Diodorus says nothing of what became of Theodorus, an omission that casts some doubt on whether the speech was actually delivered.[58] Perhaps Timaeus, Diodorus's source, composed it himself as an antityrannical diatribe, then put it in the mouth of a character he'd invented. Regardless, the speech's insights are valid, echoing what was doubtless talked of in Syracuse. An endless conflict served the needs of Dionysius the Elder. As he'd learned from the start, a city that lived in fear would look to a strongman for safety.

For a second time, plague in his ranks forced Himilco to call off his siege of Syracuse. Another negotiation led to another stalemate, with Sicily again divided between two powers. Ashamed at having twice fallen short of his goal, Himilco, according to Diodorus, bricked himself up in his house in Carthage and starved himself to death. The long-running struggle between Syracuse and Carthage continued to fester but, for a time, as a cold war.

In 369 BC, Dionysius, in his mid-sixties, seemed to want to settle the conflict once and for all. He moved westward through Sicily with an enormous force: thirty thousand infantrymen, three thousand horsemen, and an astonishing three hundred warships with which to confront the powerful Punic navy. Along with this vast armada and army came new artillery weapons driven by springs of twisted bundles of hair. Dionysius had hired engineers to develop these torsion devices, revolutionary innovations for their time.[59] The four-decade, on-again-off-again war seemed about to conclude.

Carthage was weakened at that moment, ravaged by more outbreaks of plague and rebellions of allies. In addition, a strange mass delusion, we're told, had caused its people to run madly into the streets and fight one another as though fending off invaders.[60] Even so, the Carthaginians had a formidable leader, Hanno, sometimes called Hanno the Great, and a navy of two hundred ships—fewer than those of the Greeks, but that would soon change.

Hanno had overcome a political rival, a man named Suniatus, who'd worked against him as a double agent. In secret letters written in Greek, Suniatus had told Dionysius about Hanno's plans, hoping to bring about his rival's defeat and his own ascendance. But one of these missives got intercepted and the plot was exposed. The Carthaginian senate had Suniatus killed, then took the remarkable step of forbidding the study of Greek. From that time forward, as their decree proclaimed, all communications with Hellenes had to be translated by state-appointed interpreters who could monitor their content.[61]

Back in mainland Greece, and especially in Athens, Dionysius's decision to move against "the barbarian" was highly regarded. The idea of a Greek crusade against a non-Greek people held enormous appeal at a time when Athens, Sparta, and Thebes were mostly at war with each other. Alliance under a single leader, even a tyrant, to combat an alien foe seemed a possible remedy for the decline of Hellas. That was the cure, at least, prescribed by Isocrates, the Athenian teacher of rhetoric who by now had become Plato's determined rival.

At around the time that Dionysius was taking the field, Isocrates sent him an open letter, a document that survives in incomplete form. In the portion of the letter we have, Isocrates looks to Dionysius as a kind of superman, capable of "the salvation of the Hellenes." He addresses the tyrant in hagiographic tones: "the foremost person among our race and holder of greatest power."[62] He'd use similar hyperbole many times in the years to come in letters he'd send to other hoped-for redeemers.

Isocrates used such open letters as vehicles for publicizing his views. He lacked the strong voice and confident manner required of orators, so he took to writing rather than speaking. He framed his first published pamphlets as though they were speeches, then turned his hand to expressing his thoughts in epistles. The letter form gave the illusion of intimacy yet also allowed for the kind of rhetorical tropes that Isocrates specialized in. He came to rely on this form as a method of swaying opinion. Plato would one day adopt it as well, perhaps in imitation of his competitor.

Isocrates starts his letter to Dionysius by expressing regret that he can't make a personal visit, being too old for the journey (he was then around eighty). He feels he could achieve more in a face-to-face meeting than in a letter, especially since written words can often be misunderstood. He's heard, too, that Dionysius may not be inclined to listen to counsel, though he, Isocrates, claims to know better. He alludes cryptically to the source of the rumor: "Some people who've spent time with you have tried to warn me off, saying that you honor flatterers and scorn those who offer advice."[63] If it was Plato he meant by "some people," then he was currying favor with Dionysius at his rival's expense.

The letter goes on to speak of "serious matters" that closely concern its addressee. Isocrates asks Dionysius to involve himself in mainland Greece and fill its power vacuum, since the Spartans, Greece's traditional leaders, have been overthrown (he means by Thebes at the battle of Leuctra, some three years before this). He vows that his native Athens will gladly follow the banners of Syracuse. Earlier, in a "speech" known as *Panegyricus*, Isocrates had urged *Athens* to lead the Greeks, but a decade or more further on, with Athens still in decline, that seemed a vain hope. Having seen other cities lose direction and Greece lose cohesion, Isocrates was ready to turn to the strongman of Syracuse.

In *Panegyricus*, Isocrates had proposed a campaign against the Persian Empire as a way to unite the Greek cities. No doubt he saw in Dionysius's campaign against Hanno a template for what the Greeks might achieve against the Great King. In his open letter, he likely proposed that Dionysius lead an invasion of Asia after he'd finished the conquest of Sicily. But the letter breaks off at just the moment the plan was to be introduced.

Athens generally was taking a brighter view of Dionysius, as a result of foreign policy shifts. Now aligned with Sparta instead of against it, and therefore more open-minded about authoritarian rule, Athens voted in 369 to award honorary citizenship to both Dionysius and his two sons by Doris. According to a surviving inscription, all three were given golden "crowns" with a value of a thousand drachmas apiece—not, in this context, a marker of royal status, but a standard way in which Athens forged foreign friendships and recognized merit.[64]

The following year, as another inscription attests, Athens made a defensive alliance with the Syracusan regime, a pact in force "for all time"—an unusual clause, since other such treaties came with expiration dates. This second decree, which also survives, proclaims Dionysius to be *agathos*, "a good man."[65] That word, bestowed by high-minded Athens, conferred an invaluable moral legitimacy. Dionysius had come far indeed.

The war against Hanno began well for Dionysius. His troops conquered several Sicilian cities controlled by Carthage and advanced to Eryx (modern Erice) at the western end of the island. Dionysius stationed 130 ships in the harbor there, then sent the others, more than half, back home to Syracuse. It was said that he reduced his fleet after hearing that the Carthaginian navy had been destroyed in a fire.[66] If that was the case, he fell victim to disinformation; in fact Hanno's navy was waiting to pounce as soon as he let down his guard.

In a naval battle in the harbor of Eryx, Dionysius, taken by surprise,

*A closeup of the Athenian stele recording Athens's treaty with Syracuse.*
*Dionysius's name (ΔΙΟΝΥΣΙΟΣ) can be seen in the fifth line from the bottom.*

suffered a crushing defeat. He was forced to call off the western campaign and sign yet another treaty dividing Sicily between Syracuse and
Carthage. Since he'd started the war, he had to agree that Syracuse would
reimburse its costs, meaning he'd need to squeeze more money out of his
overtaxed citizens. These surely wondered whether, as Theodorus had
charged, the tyrant was keeping the conflict going in order to keep them
in thrall.

As Syracuse reckoned up its new debts, a man arrived at the tyrant's
fortified palace. A choral dancer from one of Dionysius's plays, *The Ran-
soming of Hector*, had hastened home from Athens so as to be first with
the news: The drama, based on the final book of Homer's *Iliad*, had
received first prize at the Lenaea, one of two yearly Athenian festivals.
The honor that Dionysius had sought for decades was his at last.

After heaping rewards on this chorister, Dionysius held a celebratory
feast. He drank deep at that banquet, perhaps too deep, for soon afterward he fell ill and began to decline. Within a short time, the archon of
Syracuse, the most powerful ruler in the Hellenic world, was dead. Syracusans muttered that he had finally defeated his "betters"—the better
poets of Athens—and so sealed his doom.[67]

Ancient writers disagree on whether foul play was involved in the
archon's death. Three assert he was murdered, including Cornelius
Nepos, who claims that the heir apparent, Dionysius the Younger, asked
the court doctors to give his ailing father a toxic drink. The son, according to Nepos, had feared that his father would change the plans for succession. Plutarch in part supports that account but puts the blame on the
doctors, not on the heir. A third source says simply that Dionysius was
killed by conspirators, without saying who. However, a fourth source,
Cicero, asserts that the tyrant died of natural causes—a shame, Cicero
thought, since that way he'd escaped divine retribution.[68]

Yet another source, Diodorus, attributes Dionysius's death to overcon-
sumption of wine at the drama-victory banquet.[69] The tale has the mark
of a parable, a warning about getting what you wish for (in this case, literary acclaim), but it may still be true. Wine had always flowed freely at the
Syracusan tables, and Dionysius may have fatally overindulged. Alcohol
poisoning cannot be ruled out—nor, for that matter, can poisoned alcohol.

A magnificent funeral was held by the Royal Gates, at the causeway that led to the Island. Philistus, in his now-lost history of Dionysius's reign, gave an account of this rite that made a deep impression on Plutarch. Deploying the time-honored metaphor of public life as a stage play, Plutarch called these obsequies "the grand finale of the great tragic drama that was the tyranny of Dionysius."[70]

Dionysius had been a theatrical figure indeed, who not only wrote for the stage but went about wearing its costumes and props in hopes of inspiring awe. Yet his thirty-eight-year reign was only Act I of a larger drama, the tragedy of the fall of Syracuse. A second act was set to begin, that very year, with Plato's return to the city.

# ACT II

## THE SECOND VISIT

*The complex figure of Dion, as portrayed by Johann Heinrich Füssli in a 1787 print.*

# CHAPTER 4

# "WOLF-LOVE"

## (367–366 BC)

In proposing the idea of philosopher-kings, Plato was conscious that he was straining credulity. In *Republic* he envisions "the many," *hoi polloi*, greeting this and his other ideas with anger or scorn. He's conscious that his innovations will seem like prayers, not valid proposals, unless a clear path could be shown leading toward their fulfillment. Then he allows Socrates to point out that path. "Will anyone make this contention," he has Socrates say (implying that no one will), "that the offspring of kings and rulers could *not*, by chance, be born philosophical in their natures?" Such philosophical princes, Socrates concedes, could only with great effort be saved from "corruption"—the rot that afflicts those raised in a palace. But if that effort succeeded in only one case, the payoff would be immense. "*One* would suffice, if he had an obedient city, to accomplish all the things that now seem beyond belief," Socrates proposes to his auditor, Glaucon, prompting Glaucon's affirming response: "Yes, one would be enough."[1]

As Dionysius the Younger ascended to the archonship, Plato had reason to wonder whether the object of these "prayers"—a ruler's son with philosophic leanings—had emerged in Syracuse. His devotee there, Dion, was sending him letters, asserting that the young man—in his late twenties at that point—was eager to learn from Plato, as Dion himself had done two decades before. "Now, if ever," Dion wrote, "any hope that exists, that the same men will turn out to be both philosophers and rulers of powerful states, will be brought to pass. What more opportune moments will we wait for, than these which have arisen by some divine fortune?" Dion urged Plato to hurry to Syracuse, before "certain others" arrived and drew Dionysius away from the best sort of life.[2] At least, that is Plato's account in the *Seventh Letter*, but that document may not represent the whole truth.

Was it too late to save this prince from "corruption"? Dionysius the Younger had grown up at the Syracusan tables, or else sequestered in his rooms with his whittling projects. He'd become an alcoholic and rumor had it that the effects of drink and rich food had damaged his eyesight; according to the Roman historian Justin (summarizing the work of an earlier writer), his bloodshot eyes could not stand the brightness of day.[3] Plutarch, with his talent for metaphor, compares him to a palimpsest scroll that scribes had only partly erased before writing over the previous text; the set-in ink and "stains" from the old text made the scroll unusable.[4] That judgment, though, was the product of hindsight; at the start of the young man's reign, there was room for hope.

Apart from the high-minded motives the *Seventh Letter* attributes to him, Dion likely had his own reasons for summoning Plato. His position at court had weakened with the death of Dionysius the Elder; his abstemious ways and aloofness, long perceived as a kind of contempt, were more resented than ever, as the court became more dissolute. "Dion's nature contained a certain haughtiness and a harshness that made him hard to approach or deal with," Plutarch concedes. "Many of those who were close to him . . . held his social manner to blame."[5] His temperament was a political handicap, but with Plato by his side, he might appear serious rather than severe.

It's possible Dion sought not just a more secure footing at court, but a foothold for reaching the top. Two sources claim that, in the last days of Dionysius the Elder, Dion had tried to gain an audience with the dying archon in hopes of getting the plans for succession revised. He'd reportedly wanted the sovereignty, or a share of it perhaps, to pass to his preteen nephews, the children of Aristomachê, rather than to the elder son of Doris. Such a change would have brought Dion great power, perhaps the position of regent.[6] According to Plutarch, the Elder's doctors had intervened to prevent the deathbed colloquy, in order to win the future ruler's favor.

Did Dion bring Plato to Syracuse in hopes of mounting a coup? If he did write the words Plato quotes, expressing his hope "that the same men will turn out to be both philosophers and rulers," was he talking about himself? This dark view of Dion's summons to Plato has had strong supporters among modern scholars, as well as determined opponents. "Dion was pursuing in secret the design of expelling Dionysius from the throne to gain power for himself or for his nephews," wrote one of Dion's detractors, the historian K. J. Beloch, in 1923. "To pave the way for this, Plato was summoned to Sicily, and came . . . without any suspicion that he had been made a tool in a political intrigue." H. D. Westlake however called Beloch's view "untenable," largely on grounds that Plato could not have been so thoroughly "hoodwinked."[7]

But Westlake's argument collapses if Plato was aware of Dion's intentions. Beloch, while accusing Dion of plotting to overthrow his brother-in-law, absolves Plato of collusion (he "came . . . without any suspicion"). But as we shall see, Syracusans who mistrusted Dion also mistrusted Plato and believed the two men were in cahoots to depose Dionysius. That possibility can't be dismissed. When he'd first met Dion, in 388, Plato had urged the spirited twenty-year-old to work toward political change: "I revealed to him the things I deemed the best for humankind, and advised him to put them into practice," he recalls in the *Seventh Letter*.[8] Twenty years later it may have been Dion, more than Dionysius the Younger, whom Plato saw as the fulfillment of the "prayers" of *Republic*.

We have only Plato's testimony, in the *Seventh Letter*, that he went to Syracuse reluctantly, at the urging of Dion. Could it be that the voyage suited his own intentions better than he admitted? That seems not unlikely, given that letter's labored discussion of why he made the journey.

Plato speaks at length in the letter of the internal conflict he felt on receiving Dion's summons. On the one hand, he had misgivings about Syracuse's new ruler, "for the wishes of young men are flighty and liable to reversals." But on the other, he recognized that this might be his best chance to put his political theories to the test. "If ever anyone could try to realize his ideas about laws and government, *this* was the time to make the effort," he writes. "For by convincing only one man, I would have sufficiently accomplished all good things."⁹ That thinking, says Plato, led to his decision to go.

Plato then lists a second reason for making the journey to Syracuse: a sacred bond between himself and Dion. He says he dreaded betraying Dion's *xenia* (very roughly, "hospitality")—the kindness Dion had shown him during his previous visit. He imagines a speech of reproach that Dion would make if, for lack of Plato's support, he'd gotten banished from Syracuse by the new ruler or even killed. "How have you not betrayed philosophy, the thing you are always exalting?" he hears Dion saying. "Do you think you would ever escape from a charge of cowardice, if you now put the blame on the length of the journey and the scope of the voyage and labor? Far from it."¹⁰

"So I went," Plato continues in his own voice, "in as rational and just a manner as one could ever find in human life, for reasons such as I've said." The superlatives are noteworthy; Plato becomes emphatic as he reaches a crucial point. "I left behind my customary pursuits, which are not unseemly, to live under a tyranny, a system not fitted to either my words or myself," he writes.¹¹

In this lengthy discussion Plato claims noble and urgent motives for going to Syracuse, but those around him had alternative theories. "I departed with *this* intention . . . and not the one that some have supposed," Plato writes in the *Seventh Letter*. Who those "some" were and what they suspected are not specified. Plato's tone shows he felt stung by the talk of these critics; evidently they'd seen something discreditable in the Syracuse project. We cannot be certain that they were wrong to do so.

In Syracuse, the hardliners who stood firmly behind the new ruler were certain that Dion was up to no good. As Dionysius the Younger consolidated his power, they began to spread rumors of plotting on Dion's part. With the wedges these courtiers inserted, the rift between the family's two lines, though carefully bridged by marital ties, began to gape wider. It was noted that Dion had control of the fleet, the regime's best way of keeping the Island supplied; those same ships, used against the regime,

could mount a naval blockade.¹² Then too, Dion was known to have
friends in Carthage. Was he capable, the court wondered, of conspiring
with Syracuse's mortal enemy?

Dion sought to dispel this last notion at a meeting of the council of
state. As senior staff member, he gave a report on the conflict with Carthage, halted by truce the previous year. Then he made a striking pledge
of good faith. If Dionysius desired a permanent peace, Dion said he'd go
to Carthage himself and work out a treaty on the best possible terms.
But if it was war the new sovereign wanted, Dion vowed to draw on his
own vast fortune to outfit fifty fast warships and pay for their upkeep
and crews.¹³ This offer greatly impressed the young Dionysius but further
dismayed Dion's rivals at court, who saw a bid to surpass them. The idea
of Dion going in person to Carthage, a place he'd been warmly received
on an earlier mission, doubtless raised eyebrows as well.

The hardliners were especially irked by Dion's outreach to Plato,
which they saw as another effort to undermine them. Their own strategy
was to provide the young archon with pleasures, carousing with him at
banquets and drinking parties, diverting him with desirable women and
boys. Dion was making appeals to a different side of his nature, his aspirations to high repute as a leader. A battle was underway for the soul of
the young Dionysius.

Dion promised his brother-in-law that Plato could make him a king,
not a tyrant, an object of admiration. "It's dishonorable in a ruler" Dion
reportedly told Dionysius, ". . . to adorn his dwelling with luxurious fur-
nishings . . . but not to outfit the palace of his soul in a manner worthy of
royalty."¹⁴ The visions Dion instilled, of a glorious reign surpassing that
of the Elder, hit their mark. Dionysius was fired with an ardent love—an
erôs—to hear Plato's teachings, writes Plutarch. For reasons we'll come
to, he selected with care that potent word erôs, "sexual desire."

Dionysius joined Dion in writing to Plato to urge him to come at once,
according to Plutarch. But he also issued a second summons, this one
to the banished hardliner and senior statesman, Philistus. The former
naval commander, kicked out by Dionysius the Elder nearly two decades
before, had stayed faithful to the tyrant-house during his exile; he'd published a historical work that showed the Elder's regime in a positive light.
Now, under the Younger, he was granted a pardon and asked to return.

Most likely the hardliners played a part in this move: No one was better positioned than Philistus to counterweight Dion, and Plato too, if the sage was headed their way.

It's not clear which counselor was summoned first, Philistus, the hard-nosed authoritarian, or Plato, who stood for ethical limits on power. Dion, in his letter to Plato, had warned that "others" might get to the new ruler first, before Plato arrived; if those were indeed his words, he may have already caught wind of Philistus's recall. But things may have gone the other way: The hardliners might have heard of the invitation to Plato and demanded a standard-bearer of their own. In any case, two very different advisors, with starkly opposing political views, must have arrived in Syracuse at nearly the same moment.

Since Dionysius had summoned both men, it seems he was undecided about which direction to turn, kingship or tyranny. The best path of course was to have the second but make it seem like the first by keeping moral philosophers at one's side.

The day in 367 that Plato's ship landed was a festive one in Syracuse, according to Plutarch. Dionysius the Younger came to the docks in one of his father's magnificent chariots, a vehicle adorned with silver and gold and pulled by white steeds. As Plato disembarked, the tyrant made sacrifice to the gods in thanks for such a great boon. Then he took the chariot reins, normally held by a driver, to convey his guest to the palace. He wanted the city to see as he drove that he'd "landed" the foremost philosopher of the age.

Plato attests, in his *Third Letter*, to the pride Dionysius took in having a distinguished sage at his court. He describes a state banquet that took place not long after his arrival. Plato says he was seated far down from the head of the table; at one point, Dionysius got up, came over to him, and made a witty remark (that Plato does not relate). The person at the next place overheard and said admiringly, "It certainly seems, Dionysius, that you've had much profit from Plato in your pursuit of wisdom." "Indeed I have, and in many other things too," the young ruler replied. "From the moment I sent for him, I began to profit right away from the very fact of my sending for him." The exchange, if correctly reported, shows Dionysius basking in the glow of Plato's high stature.[15]

The more open-minded members of court fell in with the pro-Plato mood. Plutarch paints an amusing picture of life in the palace during these heady days: The air, he says, was filled with dust as courtiers drew polygons in the sand, making a show of their passion for geometry.[16] But the hardline faction, Philistus and his crew, looked askance at Plato's arrival. Philosophy, they felt, could only enervate Dionysius and turn him away from the forceful actions that his position demanded. Plato and Dion seemed to them bent on reducing the tyranny to something milder, a limited monarchy—in their eyes, a weak institution. They used rumor and innuendo to discredit both men.

An incident occurred some days after Plato landed that highlighted what was at stake. Dionysius was making a sacrifice to the gods on the palace grounds. An attending official offered the usual prayer at the start of the rite, that the tyrant might have an undisturbed reign for many more years. Dionysius greeted the prayer with an unaccustomed reply: "Stop calling down curses on me!" The jest, equating tyranny with misfortune, was no doubt meant as a tribute to Plato, who must have been in attendance. But others took the joke seriously, seeing it as a sign the young man might well step down.[17]

Philistus's faction redoubled its efforts to vilify Dion and Plato. They harped on Dion's self-interest: If the archonship became vacant, then Dion's nephews, now approaching their teens, might next occupy it. In that scenario, Dion would be the power behind the throne, or might even take the throne from them.

Aiding the hardliners' case was the fact that Plato was an Athenian. It had been almost fifty years since Athens invaded Sicily with massive force and besieged Syracuse. Athens had been beaten after two years of bitter fighting, suffering horrific losses. Recently, Athens and Syracuse had struck a pact of alliance, but memories of the old conflict died hard. Could it be, Dion's enemies asked, that Plato had come to their shores to avenge his city's defeat? Could a single Athenian "sophist," as they termed Plato, achieve, without armor or weapons, what a massive armada and army had failed to?[18]

Plato became aware that, in coming to Syracuse, he'd walked into a vipers' nest. "Upon my arrival," he wrote years later in the *Seventh Letter*, "I found that everything surrounding Dionysius was full of factionalism and slanders about Dion. . . . I fought these off to the degree I was able, but I accomplished little."[19] The situation was difficult. By standing up for his friend, Plato could only arouse more suspicion that the two were somehow conspiring together.

Still, Plato had to make the attempt, for it was largely on *his* account that Dion was in such disfavor. From the moment he'd landed in Sicily twenty years earlier and formed an attachment to Dion—an attachment that aroused the mistrust of the court—he'd become, in part, responsible for Dion's fate. That sense of responsibility was destined to haunt him for twenty more years.

A further factor may help explain Plato's protective impulses. There's some evidence, though partial and controversial, that he and Dion were lovers.

In pursuing this question, we have to jump forward in time fourteen years, from 367 to 353 BC, a time when Dion had recently died and Plato had reached his seventies. According to several ancient sources, Plato composed a six-line poem in tribute to his deceased friend; one writer claims (no doubt wrongly) that the poem was inscribed on Dion's tomb. The poem is preserved, and its plaintive last line expresses a passionate, perhaps sexual, longing. In this line Plato addresses the dead man as "Dion, you who drove my soul mad with *erôs*."[20]

The problems this poem presents to scholars are like those surrounding the Platonic letters. Its authorship cannot be proven. There are many poems preserved under Plato's name, some of which are clearly *not* by Plato, while others are often accepted as genuine. Most of these poems are expressions of love for a young man or, in rarer cases, a woman. A famous couplet addressed to a young man called Astêr, "Star," is thought by some experts to be Plato's work:[21]

*You're gazing at stars, my Star; Oh might I be*
*the sky, to look down at you with thousands of eyes.*

Arguments for or against assigning these poems to Plato are based, first, on their style, and second, on what appears plausible about Plato's emotions and romantic partners. Hellenists agree that the Dion poem passes the style test; it has no nonclassical usages and reads like the work of a capable, though not brilliant, writer. As to the poem's emotional content, we find ourselves on trickier ground. We know little about Plato's romantic life, but inferences have been made from his two discussions of *erôs*, in the dialogues *Symposium* and *Phaedrus*. Those works speak of *erôs* as an intense attraction between an older and younger man (women are largely left out of the picture). It has a physical basis but, in the best kind of bond, leads not to a sexual act but to joint contemplation of philosophic truth—the so-called Platonic love, a term coined in the Renaissance.

Is it plausible then that Plato had *erôs* for Dion, whether he meant that word in the chaste or the sexual sense? Scholars have answered that question based on their notions, often highly subjective, about the course of romantic love in long human lives.

The classicist Denys Page denounced the poem as spurious on the grounds that the passion it describes would have passed its expiration date. "It is downright absurd," Page wrote, with complete self-assurance, "to suppose that Plato at the age of seventy-five, mourning the death of [Dion] at the age of about fifty-two, made the climax of his poem a strongly-worded reference to their homosexual relations in the very distant past (presumably some thirty-four years earlier, when Plato first met Dion in Sicily)." Historian Peter Brunt made a similar argument. "If Plato was the [poem's] author," he wrote in 1991, "he must surely have been recollecting passion he had felt for Dion at their first meeting; it would have been bizarre if *erôs* persisted in long years of separation until 353 when Plato was about 75 and Dion about 57."[22]

Both Page and Brunt have skewed the argument over the poem by assuming that Plato's *erôs* for Dion, if it existed, was "long years" in the past by the time the poem was written. But Plato's first meeting with Dion, in 388, was followed by others; the two men were together in 367, for much of the six years thereafter, and a third time in 360. In any case, even if the years of separation were long, who would presume to assign a shelf life to erotic emotions? Brunt himself apparently carried a torch for six decades after a woman rejected his marriage proposal in the late 1940s.[23]

Brunt and Page call attention to the ages of Plato and Dion at the time the poem is set, suggesting a further, equally biased, source of their skepticism. The point they hint at is made more explicit by Platonist A. E. Taylor: "It is, perhaps, hardly likely that Plato, writing after seventy to a friend who was over fifty, would use the word *erôs* to describe the attachment."[24] *Erôs*, in other words, may exist between men but not those who've passed the days of youth and mid-life—another assumption belied by experience.

The longest discussion in English of the poem's authorship, by Maurice Bowra, comes to very different conclusions than those of his colleagues. Avoiding assumptions about how older men experience love, or how long passion endures, Bowra analyzed the poem in light of both Dion's career and Plato's other writings on *erôs*. His conclusions are carefully hedged but nonetheless strongly in favor of Platonic authorship: "The poem is most easily understood if we assume Plato wrote it." Bowra goes on to say that, if we make that assumption, the poem "becomes a document of some relevance for [Plato's] biography," without spelling out the obvious point, that it gives us a new understanding of what knit Plato and Dion so closely together.[25]

If the poem is indeed genuine, then another question arises. Did Plato base his descriptions of philosophical *erôs*, the Platonic love extolled in his dialogues, on his relationship with Dion? His *Phaedrus* seems, to some eyes, to give evidence that he did so, but again the point is contested.

In his discourse on love in *Phaedrus*, Plato has Socrates classify lovers' souls according to which god they most resemble. Combative lovers belong to the cohort of Ares, artistic ones to that of Apollo, and so on. The loftiest souls are those that resemble Zeus, for just as Zeus is both wise and kingly, these souls belong to philosophers who are also political leaders. Such souls seek others of their own kind as lovers, as Socrates says: "Those that belong to Zeus look for someone Zeus-like in soul to be their beloved; and they examine whether he is inclined in his nature toward philosophy and leadership, and when they find him, they fall in love and do all in their power to see that he become such a one"—that is, a fellow Zeus-soul.[26]

This sentence sounds like a veiled description of Plato's first encounter with Dion, for Dion was indeed "inclined in his nature toward philosophy and leadership"; Plato had seen this unique combination and had done "all in his power" to make him more Zeus-like. And, lest we miss the parallels, Plato supplies a verbal cue that seems to flag them for us. In Greek the words "from Zeus" and "Zeus-like" are *dios* and *dion*, near homophones for Dion's name (the sound of the vowel "o" differs slightly, long in the name and short in the other two words). Plato deliberately structures the sentence so the two Zeus-words are juxtaposed: "Those from Zeus (*dios*) a Zeus-like (*dion*) person seek...." The juxtaposition highlights the homophony and winkingly references Plato's connection to Dion. At least, that is how philosopher Martha Nussbaum interprets the passage, though others have disagreed.[27]

Together with the funeral poem, the *Phaedrus* passage suggests an erotic (though not necessarily sexual) bond between Plato and Dion. Neither text is conclusive, but the two reinforce each other, as Bowra recognized. Both, moreover, cohere with the *Seventh Letter*, where the intimate friendship that Dion strikes up with Plato springs from their shared "Zeus-like" quality, the union of philosophical learning with political leadership.

In following this twisting trail, we have already gone several steps beyond what some scholars might think prudent. But Plutarch's account of the machinations at Dionysius's court, following Plato's arrival, impel us to take one giant step further. Plutarch indicates that, after some months of instruction by Plato, *Dionysius likewise* developed erotic feelings. Indeed, he suggests that the tyrant's attachment to Plato was just as ardent as that of Plato for Dion, and that his mistrust of Dion arose out of jealousy.

We have already seen that Plutarch uses the strong word *erôs* to describe how Dionysius longed for Plato's arrival. Later Plutarch repeats that word and compounds its force with two verbs derived from it. In recounting how the tyrant grew close to Plato, Plutarch says "Dionysius loved (*êrasthê*) a tyrannical love (*erôs*) and thought it right that he alone be loved back (*anterasthai*) by Plato." This heaping-up of *erôs* words is impossible to ignore or explain away as mere rhetoric, and Plutarch adds to the heap in the very next sentence. He describes how the tyrant flew into fits whenever Plato showed himself partial to Dion—"just as tormented lovers (*duserôtes*) do."[28]

Plutarch had a lively interest in the sex lives of his subjects and often gives intimate details not found in other sources. He alone tells us, for instance, that Cleopatra and Mark Antony reconciled, after they lost the battle of Actium, with "make-up sex" on board Cleopatra's flagship.[29] It's not often clear how much such details can be trusted since they come from texts that have since been lost. In the case of Dionysius's attraction to Plato and malice toward Dion, something Plutarch had read convinced him that *erôs* was at play. He depicts a dynamic that can best be described as a love triangle.

Plato's *Third Letter* adds a further suggestion that love played a part in what went on in the palace. Plato there uses an opaque word, *lukophilia*, "wolf-friendship" or "wolf-love," to describe Dionysius's relations with him at this juncture.[30] The compound word does not occur elsewhere in classical Greek and it's not at all clear what Plato means by it. As we've seen in *Republic*, Plato employs the wolf as the animal avatar of "the tyrant" or the tyrannical man. In a later work, *Laws*, he cites an Aesopic fable involving the rapacity of wolves, who fall on defenseless sheep after bribing the sheepdogs that protect them.[31]

It seems that Plato must want the *luko-* of *lukophilia* to signify something like "predatory" or "based on superior force." That would fit a pattern well known to Plato's readers, by which tyrants coerced sex from, or raped, whomever they fancied. Later in life, as we'll see, Dionysius would become infamous for doing exactly those things. The "wolf-love" that Plato felt from his host likely involved coercion, whether specifically sexual or more broadly emotional.

Further than this we dare not go in the realm of speculation, but one more word deserves to be said. Unusually for a man of his era, Plato never married, nor was he linked as an adult with any romantic partner other than Dion. If we trust the evidence collected here, inconclusive though it must be—the coded allusion to Dion's name in *Phaedrus*, the last verse of the funeral poem, Plutarch's report that Dionysius felt jealous of Plato's connection to Dion, the idea of "wolf-love"—then a line that connects these points would lead us to one conclusion: Dion was the great love of Plato's life, a love he cherished for decades.

With that, let us leave the fog of uncertainty and return to where the skies are clearer, the city of Syracuse in 367 BC.

"Give me a city ruled by a tyrant," says Plato's spokesman in *Laws*, the last work he is known to have written. Such a city, the speaker asserts, would be the easiest kind to reform, for everything in it flows from the ruler; if *his* nature can be improved, then so can that of society as a whole. If a tyrant comes to power who's young, noble in spirit, and educable, *Laws* proposes, and if at the same time a lawgiver "worthy of praise" arrives on the scene, then the stage will be set for a transformation that might in turn transform the entire world.[32]

The pairing Plato imagines in *Laws*, of wise lawgiver and teachable tyrant, is what he must have hoped would occur when he joined Dionysius the Younger. But *was* Dionysius teachable? That was the question Dion and Plato faced as they set about to reform Syracuse, and indeed the Greek West, by reforming one man.

We have seen that Dion, in his invitation to Plato, expressed confidence that Dionysius was eager to learn (though not so eager as his own nephews). Plato's assessments of Dionysius as student, found in his letters, present a more measured view. His most explicit statement comes in the *Seventh Letter*: "He [Dionysius] was not without a natural aptitude for learning," Plato writes there, "and he had a remarkable desire for honor"—the honor that came from being taught by a sage.[33] So Dionysius, in Plato's eyes, was hardly an ideal tutee but also not hopeless. Plutarch later took Plato's cue and delivered a mixed verdict on Dionysius: "He was not by nature one of the worst class of tyrants."[34]

The fact that Dionysius was nearly thirty posed a challenge for his would-be teachers. The educational scheme of *Republic* mandates ten years of geometry and math before that age is attained; Dionysius was off to a very late start. Then there was the problem of whether his notorious drinking problem had rotted his mind as it had reportedly weakened his eyesight. Plato considered wine in excess a deterrent to higher thought, and portrayed Socrates, his model philosopher, as someone who never got drunk.

Plato and Dion worked together to tap whatever potential their student had, according to the *Seventh Letter*. The first step the two men urged on the tyrant was a change in behavior, "to live day by day in a way so as to become master of himself"—to cease his pursuit of pleasures and show himself to be a serious person. This step required *sôphrosynê*, sometimes translated "self-restraint," ironically also the name of Dionysius's wife. But Dion's example had shown where *sôphrosynê* might lead: estrangement from those at court who bonded over wine and feasts, and abandonment of the celebrated tables.

But estrangement from court life was just what Dion and Plato felt was needed. The two men told Dionysius his current friendships were unhealthy and counterproductive. They said he "must get friends who are in harmony with him in respect to virtue; and he must be in harmony with himself. It was this," Dion and Plato hinted, speaking in indirections so as not to offend, "in which he was remarkably lacking."[35] True friendships were rooted in shared respect for virtue, they counseled. Only with help from friends of this kind could Dionysius achieve his political goals.

High on the list of those goals was restoration of eastern Sicily, the portion of the island under Syracusan control. The cities there, victims of multiple wars, were in a ruinous state; many were either empty or claimed by non-Greek peoples, among them the Celts and Iberians brought to the region to serve as mercenaries. Plato and Dion blamed the decline on Dionysius's father, the Elder, who, they said, had based his friendships on shared debauches and therefore lacked trusted men to send into the field. Unable to count on allies or even his own brothers, he'd hollowed out the lands to his west and absorbed their populations into Syracuse—"uniting all Sicily into a single city," as Plato says in the letter—rather than rebuilding.[36] (The Elder had in fact depopulated these places in order to then give their lands as rewards to his troops.)

With better friendships, the young Dionysius could gain a reliable staff and re-Hellenize Sicily, Plato and Dion urged. They presented him with the example of Darius, the Persian Great King of the previous century, who'd relied on seven loyalists to help run his empire. That strategy made Darius seven times stronger than Dionysius's father had been, the two argued. An Asian potentate who'd launched an attack on Greece made for an odd role model, but longevity of empire was their principal point. Under the "laws" Darius established, the Persian state had kept its vigor long after the ruler's death.

Then Plato and Dion invoked another example, from closer to home. If Dionysius could achieve wisdom and temperance, they promised, "he would be ready to impose a much greater servitude on the Carthaginians than that which had been imposed on them in the time of Gelon."[37] The great military prize his father had sought—defeat of Carthage in Sicily—could be his, if he could only rein in his appetites and sober up. An unwarlike man who had never yet (that we know of) been on a battlefield could hope for a glorious victory to rival what Gelon had won at Himera.

Geometry must have seemed an odd place to start this program of self- and civic reform. But that is where Plato seems to have urged that Dionysius begin.[38] Plato believed, as we've seen, that contemplation of unchanging things was the basis of all education. Even the "eye of the soul" of this nearsighted youth might perhaps be directed upward, away from the "tables" that Plato scorned in *Republic*, where people who lack philosophy feed like beasts at a trough. Dionysius's hopes of seeing the Forms were vanishingly small, but contemplation of perfect circles and squares could benefit even a tyrant, perhaps turn him into something nobler—a king.[39]

The hard men at court, led by Philistus, fought back against Plato and Dion with all their rhetorical weapons. They mocked Plato's educational goal as "the Good that's shrouded in silence," which made his highest ideal seem not only obscure but sinister. If Plato and Dion had their way, they suggested, Dionysius would chase after happiness in the Academy's gardens, while Dion and his nephews enjoyed *true* happiness—power, wealth, and the bounty of the proverbial tables. Bit by bit they eroded Dionysius's trust in his brother-in-law.[40]

Negotiations with Carthage were then underway as part of the stalemated struggle for Sicily. Dionysius, though new to such parleys, would be expected, as sovereign, to oversee them. But Dion, as senior advisor, feared that the new monarch might not be up to the task. He wrote to the Punic envoys, asking them to be sure that *he* was included in any future discussions. He did not reckon with the tyrant's network of spies, men for whom news of a letter like this would lead to ample rewards.

One of these spies intercepted the letter and brought it to Dionysius. The tyrant in turn took it straight to Philistus, who put its contents in the worst possible light. The letter seemed to confirm suspicions that Dion had secret contacts with Carthage. Dion, Philistus said, was a traitor; he could not be allowed to remain in the palace or even in Sicily.

To banish a man of Dion's high standing was no easy affair. Dionysius and Philistus stationed a light skiff, manned by a reliable crew, in the harbor. Dionysius then invited Dion to walk with him down by the docks, feigning that he'd moved past his mistrust and was now on good terms with his brother-in-law. When they neared the skiff, Dionysius produced the intercepted letter and accused Dion of treachery. Before any allies could intervene, Dion was put aboard the boat, which set off at once for Italy.

In the space of an hour or two, the extraction had been completed. Dion was gone from the island. Philistus had won.

Was the charge of treachery justified? Views of Dion, both ancient and modern, diverge on this question, as they do on that of Dion's tyrannical ambitions. In fact the two questions are intertwined, for if Dion *was* planning a coup, he'd likely have used his contacts in Carthage to line up support. Philistus, with his keen political sense, may have sniffed out a very real threat to the crown. Alternatively, he may only have seen a good pretext to get Dion off the scene and take his place as senior advisor.

Dion's supporters were outraged when they learned of Dion's exile. Some were even hopeful the move would spark a reaction and lead to Dionysius's overthrow. The women of Dion's household, including his wife Aretê—the tyrant's half-sister—made a display of grief by appearing in public in mourning clothes, contributing to the sense of a family rift. Dionysius was forced to make concessions and offer excuses. He claimed that Dion had been sent away for his own good, lest his arrogance provoke the regime into doing him harm. There may have been truth in this; he may have hoped, at this point, that Dion could be brought to heel and recalled, as Leptines had been in the days of his father.

To placate Dion's family—who were also his own extended family—Dionysius gave them the use of two ships to convey to Dion in exile whatever he needed, including money (we're told that Dion possessed a hundred talents of silver, a staggering sum). He gave better treatment than most exiles got, at some risk to himself, for riches meant power in an age when soldiers for hire were everywhere. In messages to Dion, Dionysius warned against recruiting mercenaries or spreading loose talk to sway Greek opinion against him. He also kept control of enough of Dion's estate that noncompliance would be extremely costly. Dion's wife and young son, Hipparinus, could serve as hostages, too, if things came to that.

The banishment of Dion revealed to Plato how badly he'd erred in coming to Syracuse. Instead of strengthening Dion's faction at court, he'd greatly weakened it by provoking the opposition. Though he'd taken no part (that we know of) in Dion's outreach to Carthage, his very presence had helped create the air of mistrust in which Dion's missive had seemed a treasonous act.

Plato found his own position at court becoming precarious. He and his allies—the friends and supporters of Dion, including two prominent figures we'll soon meet again, Theodotes and Heraclides—feared they'd be implicated and punished in turn. Plato heard of rumors going around that *he* was to blame for Dion's alleged betrayal and that Dionysius had put *him* to death.[41]

For his part, Dionysius feared that a rupture with Plato, either real or perceived, might create further strife between factions. He entreated Plato to stay in the city and show himself not only alive and well but an ally of the regime. "Nothing good would come to me from your leaving," he told Plato, "but it *would* come from your remaining."[42] The sage's departure now, Dionysius knew, would be an implicit protest against the exiling of Dion. He could not risk such a high-level defection.

Plato discovered he had no choice about staying or going. "A tyrant's requests are mingled with compulsion," he writes in the *Seventh Letter*. At Dionysius's behest Plato's quarters were relocated to the palace complex on the Island, the fortress that served as the ruler's own residence. Plato interpreted this as a sealing off of escape routes: In his new home

he would have no contact with mariners nearer the shore who might conduct him to Athens, or to Dion in Italy. Dionysius's grip on the Island was
such that Plato could not even walk by himself toward its gate; to do so,
he says, would have resulted in his immediate arrest.[43]

Despite the tensions, Plato continued to offer the tyrant instruction. "I
held fast to the original intention of my coming there," he writes, "to see
whether he would come to a desire for the philosophic life." This tenacity
was later portrayed in unflattering terms by Plato's critics, who saw it as
an attempt to curry favor. The question of whether Dionysius was educable therefore became a crucial one, and Plato returns to it several times
in his letters. He's careful to explain that, at this juncture, the young man
still gave him hope. Dionysius *wanted* to learn, he claims, but kept drawing back, half-trusting the rumors of an attempt to dethrone him.[44]

Tensions rose when Plato used the tutorial sessions to try to get Dion's
sentence of exile reversed. Dionysius disliked these efforts, regarding
them as a kind of rejection. "As time went on he grew more attached,"
Plato says in the *Seventh Letter.* "He wanted me to praise him more than
Dion and regard him more particularly as his friend." The tyrant even
offered Plato "honors"—the Greek word, *timai*, could also mean political
offices or titles—as well as, intriguingly, "money," to take his side in the
family rift and attest that Dion's exile was justified.[45] Plato makes clear
in the letter that he refused, but as we shall see, not all of his contemporaries believed him.

Plato's phrase "grew more attached" hints at the bond that Plutarch
paints more colorfully. As we've seen, Plutarch compares Dionysius
to *duserôtes*, lovers tormented by jealousy. He describes tempestuous
scenes in which the tyrant raged over Plato's closeness with Dion, a bond
that excluded *him*. His anger, says Plutarch, would reach a crescendo,
then give way to tearful apologies and attempts at reconciling. Dionysius at one point became so desperate, Plutarch claims, that he offered
to hand the reins of government over to Plato, if only he could gain the
sage's favor.[46]

This astonishing portrait of a young man's infatuation is difficult to
assess. It may have been based on some primary source, now lost, but it's
hard to imagine how anyone gathered such information from behind palace doors. The picture fits Plutarch's general impression that the tyrant's

attraction to Plato was sexual at its core, though that idea, too, comes from sources unknown, or perhaps from Plutarch's reading of Plato's letters. Those letters hint only vaguely at the nature of the tyrant's "wolf-love."

The tense encounters of ruler and sage might have gone on indefinitely, but war broke out and changed the equation. Syracuse marshaled its armies against their former allies, the Lucanians. For reasons that neither Plato nor Plutarch make clear, Dionysius saw this conflict as reason to send Plato home. Perhaps he needed support from his hardline faction, who'd long resented Plato's presence and would be only too glad to see him gone from the city.

To lessen the impact of Plato's departure, and perhaps because of his own "attachment," Dionysius pressured Plato to promise he'd soon return. The tyrant's insistence on this point gave Plato a certain leverage. He'd had half a year or more to brood on the fate of Dion, and he recognized now that he had the means to improve it—and also that Dionysius had the means to make it far worse. In a parley with Dionysius that Plato describes as "difficult"—unquestionably an understatement—he worked out a deal: He and Dion would *both* come back to Syracuse, at Dionysius's summons, once a peace was concluded and things settled down. With that arrangement agreed on, Plato set sail for Athens.

Plato had spent the better part of a year in Syracuse and accomplished little, except to aggravate tensions within the tyrant-house. He'd been displayed by Dionysius as a kind of trophy, a mark of the regime's enlightened values, but had not altered those values in any significant way. The court was still dominated by Philistus and the hardliners, men who regarded Plato—rightly or wrongly—as a threat. Yet Plato had not given up on the Syracuse project, or on Dionysius.

Back in Athens, Plato returned to the Academia, where the banished Dion had also arrived or soon would. Perhaps *Republic* was largely complete by this time, though it's more likely the work was still in progress. That question will be taken up in the following chapter, as we turn to a closer exploration of Plato's masterpiece.

Assuming Plato *was* at work on *Republic*, he had more to write about now than before. Once again he'd witnessed tyranny at close range, so close that he'd nearly become one of its victims. "The man we should listen to," he has Socrates say in *Republic,* "is the one who's lived with a tyrant in the same house." Now he had lived with *two* tyrants, and he wanted the Greek world to listen to what he had learned.

*A manuscript illustration of the late fourteenth century shows Plato pointing and gazing upward, as if toward the Forms. Socrates, engrossed in writing, seems not to notice.*

# CHAPTER 5

# ONE NIGHT IN PIRAEUS

I n the mid-eighteenth century, poet and classicist Thomas Gray, author of the much-recited "Elegy Written in a Country Church-yard," proposed a theory concerning Plato's *Republic*. Gray surmised that, when Plato wrote of saving the world by saving *one* prince from corruption, he referred cryptically to the younger Dionysius. Gray even sought to date the passage in question to 367 BC, just as Plato was making his way to Syracuse at Dion's invitation.[1] That correlation may be too precise, but less uncertain is that Dionysius the Younger was on Plato's mind, and the minds of his readers, when *Republic* proposes a single king's son as the path to redemption.

Was *Republic* already written and in circulation when Plato made his second voyage to Syracuse, or did it appear afterward? It seems both are partially true. The research into this question follows a series of twists and turns that began more than two centuries ago.

Plato wrote philosophic works over much of his eighty-one years, starting perhaps in his early twenties and continuing up to his death. But he set these works at a time when his mentor, Socrates, was alive and in his prime, often several decades before his own time. He hardly ever included references to contemporaneous events; as a result it's hard to say at what age he composed any one dialogue. But enormous efforts have been expended, by both man and machine, to put his works into a chronological sequence, such that they trace an arc of a life and the development of a thinker.

The painstaking ways this problem has been approached can inspire admiration or dismay, perhaps both at once. In one type of study, minute shifts of Plato's language, such as the differing manners in which a respondent says "I agree"—the sort of thing said hundreds of times in Plato's works—have been carefully compared, in an effort to find a meaningful progression. The same approach has also been applied to the Greek words for "really" or "truly," another frequent locution that Plato, probably unconsciously, seems to have varied slightly as he matured.[2]

In the late nineteenth century the Polish scholar Wincenty Lutoslawski, who had experienced a kind of religious conversion while reading Plato's *Symposium*, isolated no fewer than *five hundred* features of Platonic language that seemed to him to shift over time, assigning numerical values to each based on what he judged to be their importance. But all these labors pale next to that of the *clausula*-counters, scholars who sought to distinguish earlier from later Platonic works based on the rhythm of *clausulae* or endings of sentences. In an era before computers, these researchers spent innumerable hours recording the metrical sequence of the last five syllables of *every Platonic sentence*, on the assumption that Plato's rhythm preferences follow an evolutionary pattern.[3]

In his 1982 monograph *Studies in Platonic Chronology*, classicist Holger Thesleff compiled one hundred thirty-two such attempts to determine the sequence of Plato's dialogues.[4] The number of person-hours behind these attempts is terrifying to contemplate, and more have accumulated since Thesleff wrote. The aggregate of these studies has produced a broad grouping of early, middle, and late dialogues, with many arguments still going on about which works belong where, or at what date the groupings begin or end. But however the scheme is laid out, *Republic* has always been the most difficult work to situate within it.

Unlike other dialogues, *Republic* is widely acknowledged to be a composite, added to and revised by Plato at different stages of life. "He had to return to its issues again and again," was Thesleff's conclusion. "It was constantly present to Plato, from the early 390s down to the 350s, when, I presume, it was finally 'published' as a complete whole."[5] Thesleff, like many others, posits a "proto-*Republic*" or a "manifesto," already in circulation in Athens by 392 BC, when the playwright Aristophanes parodied it in his comedy *Assemblywomen*. But in the very books of *Republic* where that core segment is found, Thesleff detected features of Plato's *late* style, a sign of revisions nearly a half-century later. Put simply, according to Thesleff, Plato never stopped work on *Republic* from the moment he started.

In fact, we have ancient testimony to suggest that *Republic* occupied Plato right up to the day of his death. An anecdote repeated by several writers claims that, just after Plato's demise, his followers found, among his effects, a wax-coated writing-tablet, the kind that gave writers freedom to erase and rework. On it, Plato had been revising the opening words of *Republic*, spoken by Socrates: "Yesterday I went down to Piraeus with Glaucon, the son of Ariston." As with most biographical tales, we have no way to confirm or refute the story, but its point is nonetheless valid: *Republic* was seen as the acme of Plato's craft, a work produced with consummate care.[6]

One marker of *Republic*'s composite nature is a distinctively Sicilian turn of phrase. It seems, to judge by surviving texts, that the emphatic question *ti mên*, "why indeed?," and other expressions involving the Greek word *mên*, were used by Sicilian Greeks in the fifth century BC but not by Greek speakers elsewhere.[7] In the 1880s German scholar Wilhelm Dittenberger noted that several phrases of this type appear rather often in some of Plato's dialogues, including those assigned to his later life, and not at all in those thought to be written early. Dittenberger deduced that Plato learned the jaunty expressions on his first visit to Syracuse and liked them well enough to sprinkle them into his prose.[8] Later it was observed, by those investigating *Republic*, that these phrases appear several times in each of that work's ten books except for the first, where they do not appear even once.

That finding accords with other stylistic gaps that separate Book 1 from Books 2–10, and with the fact that the characters who converse with Socrates in the first book, principally a man named Thrasymachus, fall nearly silent in subsequent books as other speakers come forward. These discontinuities seem to show that Plato wrote Book 1 of *Republic* not only first but well before all the others, probably as a separate work that was then grafted onto the whole. The presence or absence of *ti mên* and similar phrases reveals the seam and also suggests, according to Dittenberger, that the *Thrasymachus*, if we can so call what later became Book 1, was written before Plato's Syracuse journey in 388 BC, the rest of *Republic* after.

No other Platonic dialogue contains splices, seams, and stylistic shifts of these kinds. Other works were likely revised or enlarged but on a much smaller scale. In *Republic* Plato created a vessel for his most cherished ideas and thus couldn't put it aside, at least not for two or three decades after he'd started. If the work sits on a pedestal today, it's for a good reason, and much in line with Plato's intentions for it.

We have already looked at a portion of *Republic*'s contents: its dark portrait, in the eighth and ninth of its ten books, of tyranny and the "tyrannical man." It's time to turn the pages back and start from the beginning, indeed from the very opening words, so meaningful as to make us believe that Plato was still trying, on his deathbed, to get them just right.

"Yesterday I went down to Piraeus with Glaucon, the son of Ariston." Socrates speaks those words, but to whom is he speaking? Right away we're confronted with one of the features that make *Republic* intriguing. Plato had different ways of opening dialogues; in most cases he simply raises the curtain and characters start to talk, their identities revealed by how they address one another. A few dialogues, however, are "framed," that is, recounted by someone who heard a previous conversation and then recounts it to others. In only three cases, of which *Republic* is one, the man in that frame is Socrates himself, and we—Plato's readers—are the people he speaks to.[9] The technique is intimate and enigmatic. We have the sense of being Socrates' confidants, as we do in modern-day first-person fiction or in films in which the narrator opens the story by speaking direct to the camera.[10]

Another point that makes *Republic* unique lies in its third and fourth words—"to Piraeus." Plato has set his scene several miles from the walls of Athens, the only instance in his surviving dialogues where Socrates ventures so far.

Piraeus, the harbor town serving Athens, lay a two-hour walk from the city and stood even farther away in cultural terms. Its high proportion of foreign and immigrant residents made it a zone of ferment and innovation, a fitting place to contemplate radical thoughts. Ships came and went constantly, bringing with them new customs and new ideas. In fact, as we learn before *Republic*'s first sentence concludes, Socrates has come to this bustling port to witness a novel religious rite, a festival for a goddess imported from Thrace. This day, he tells us, marks the first time that the rite had been introduced—a moment propitious for change.

Piraeus also has political meaning as a setting for *Republic*. In the civil war that took place in 403 BC, as the Thirty Tyrants fought against democratic opponents, Piraeus had been a key battleground, in part because of its prodemocracy leanings. Indeed the faction that ousted the Thirty came to be known as "those from Piraeus" because their leaders and principal forces were based there. It was in Piraeus, in bloody hand-to-hand fighting, that Critias—Plato's kinsman, leader of the Thirty, and architect of its reign of terror—was killed and the junta's power was broken.

The surviving leaders of the Thirty were granted safe conduct away from Athens, but the wounds they'd inflicted still festered many years later, long after democracy was restored. Plato set his *Republic* at a time before the trauma of the Thirty began, but most of his Athenian readers had lived through that trauma. By setting his dialogue in Piraeus, Plato signals one of the levels at which *Republic* will operate: It will deal with his city's recent encounter with authoritarianism.

The next words of the opening sentence, "with Glaucon son of Ariston," give readers a further cue to sit up and take notice, for Glaucon was one of Plato's two older brothers. *Republic* is the only work in which Plato made one of his siblings a leading character.[11] Glaucon will be the principal figure with whom Socrates will converse in the discussion to come, followed closely, in terms of the size of his role, by Plato's other full brother, Adeimantus (whom we'll soon meet). By giving such prominent parts to his nearest kin, Plato shows us how deeply invested he is in this dialogue above all the others he wrote. (We have twenty-eight or perhaps a few more, depending on which ones are counted as genuine; it seems that none Plato wrote have been lost.)

Glaucon seems to have been a year or two older than Plato, Adeimantus a bit older still. Both are depicted in *Republic* as old enough, and brave enough, to have fought against Spartan-led forces at Megara, perhaps in a battle of 409 BC. But Plato has scrambled *Republic*'s chronology such that we cannot reconcile historical time with the ages of the *dramatis personae*, or fix on a date when the dialogue took place.[12] It's clear, anyway, that Glaucon is at least twenty, old enough for military service in the war against Sparta that's still going on at this time. He's several decades younger than Socrates, whose exact age is also hard to assess from the dialogue's cues.

As Socrates continues to tell us of his walk in Piraeus, we find he is at a point when the festival of the Thracian goddess has paused; a procession, something like a modern parade, has just ended. It's a hot day and Socrates and Glaucon have a long walk to get back to "the city," meaning Athens. They start to head homeward, but a slave comes up from behind and pulls on Socrates' cloak. The slave, as Socrates learns, belongs to a man named Polemarchus; he's been sent by his master to stop Socrates from departing. In the next minute, Polemarchus himself appears on the scene, attended by several friends who had marched in the procession. Two of these friends are named: the aforementioned Adeimantus, and Niceratus, the son of a great Athenian general.

A small drama now takes place that summons up ghosts from the days of the Thirty—an era that ended close to the spot where these conversants are standing. (Again, in *Republic*'s temporal setting, those events have not yet occurred.)

Polemarchus has stopped Socrates in order to keep him from leaving Piraeus, presumably because he enjoys the sage's company. But Socrates has already started for home and wants to continue on. Polemarchus then hints that his group will use force to prevent him from going. "You see how many we are?" asks Polemarchus. "You must either be stronger than we are, or else stay here."[13] Socrates says he'll perhaps persuade the group to let him go on his way, but Polemarchus vows he'll refuse to listen.

The standoff is becoming tense when Adeimantus steps in as a mediator. He points out that later that evening, a novel spectacle, a horse race in which the riders will pass lighted torches to one another, will be held in Piraeus—an event worth sticking around for (as noted in the introduction). Glaucon, either enticed by this prospect or impressed by the strength of the gang, induces Socrates to give in. "It seems that it's necessary to stay," he says, to which Socrates consents.

The whole party moves off to Polemarchus's house, where the dialogue proper will shortly begin. The conflict that loomed in this little vignette has been averted, but a sense of disquiet lingers. We have briefly entered a world in which might makes right, where the will of a weaker, older man can be thwarted by those more numerous and physically stronger.

Lurking behind this encounter are painful memories of the crimes of the Thirty. Both Polemarchus and Niceratus, historically, were arrested by that regime and forced to drink toxic hemlock, the standard Athenian method of state execution. In both their cases, wealth was part of their downfall, for the Thirty sought money to bolster their power and plundered homes and estates, more easily done if the owners had been killed. At the point we encounter these two in *Republic*, their fates lie several years in the future; the mock arrest they enact anticipates, in a bitter dramatic irony, what they themselves would soon undergo.

The historical Polemarchus was in fact arrested in the streets of Piraeus—exactly where his fictional self conducts the "stop" of Socrates. A man named Eratosthenes, one of the Thirty, made that arrest, during a round-up of men who owned large estates and thus offered tempting prizes. Polemarchus's younger brother, Lysias—the man who would later denounce Dionysius the Elder at the Olympics of 388 (see chapter 1)—was also seized in the round-up, but survived, as he describes in his courtroom speech, *Against Eratosthenes*. In attempting to bring one of the Thirty to justice, he recounts, for an Athenian jury, the day that led to the death of his brother and the theft of the family business, a thriving shield factory.

Lysias's speech helps fill in the backdrop to Plato's *Republic*, for it shows what life was like for those at the mercy of tyranny.

As he describes in the speech, Lysias had been entertaining at home in Piraeus when agents of the regime appeared at his door and told his guests to leave.[14] The agents put him in the custody of one of the Thirty,

Peison, then went on to the shield factory to make an inventory of its assets. In another part of Piraeus, Eratosthenes and his henchmen were at that moment arresting Polemarchus, along with six other rich men and two poorer targets (who'd been put on an enemies list for appearance's sake, as Lysias thought).

Left alone with Peison, Lysias tried to bribe his way out of danger. He offered Peison a talent of silver (six thousand drachmas), and Peison swore an oath that he'd let Lysias go free for that sum. But when Lysias went to his money-chest to get the needed silver, Peison observed him and commandeered the whole chest, which contained several times that amount. Peison then turned Lysias over to other captors and disappeared, promising to return and fulfill his end of the bargain—a promise he clearly never meant to keep.

Lysias was held under guard in the home of another prisoner but spotted a doorway that somehow wasn't sealed off. He dashed through it and made for the home of a shipowner friend, whose vessels could convey him safely out of the region.

Before he departed, Lysias sent the shipowner to try to rescue his brother, but the man soon returned and told him the situation was hopeless. Lysias sailed the next day for Megara, where he learned of Polemarchus's fate and that of the family business. Polemarchus had been arrested and condemned to death without judicial proceedings. After his execution, the Thirty forbade his family to lay out his corpse in their homes or to use a cloak from his wardrobe for funeral garb (since his property had been appropriated by the regime). In a last outrage, a member of the Thirty strode into the dead man's house and plucked the gold earrings from the ears of his widow.

All the rest of the family estate was seized, as was the factory, including seven hundred shields that were ready for purchase and a cohort of a hundred and twenty slaves. Lysias had survived, but he was bereft of his brother and impoverished. When the Thirty fell and he returned to his home, he took to writing courtroom speeches to make a living, a profitable trade in litigious Athens. The speech *Against Eratosthenes*, written on his own behalf rather than for paying clients, was likely his first effort in this new line of work.

During the trial Lysias asked Eratosthenes, the man who'd arrested his brother, a round of questions. Their exchange is recorded in the speech. Under interrogation Eratosthenes claims that he, too, is a victim of the Thirty, or rather, of those higher up in its ranks than he was. In words that would echo millennia later in Nuremberg and The Hague, he claims that he had had no choice but to follow his orders.

"Did you arrest Polemarchus or not?" Lysias asks, hoping to secure a conviction and sentence of death. "I acted on the instructions of those in power, out of fear," Eratosthenes answers. Lysias turns to the jury and asks in outraged tones, "From whom will you ever exact punishment, if it's permitted to the Thirty to say that they acted on the orders of the Thirty?"[15] Whether he won his case is not known.

Plato includes Lysias, as well as Polemarchus, in *Republic*. When Polemarchus brings his group, which now includes Socrates and Glaucon, to his Piraeus home, he finds his brother Lysias there, talking with friends, as well as his aged father Cephalus, who's in the midst of sacrificing to the gods. Over the course of the evening to come, Lysias won't speak a word, but his presence is nonetheless meaningful, as is that of Niceratus, another mute figure who (as we readers know) will soon be arrested and killed. These men bear witness to the Thirty's practice of putting to death wealthy men whose riches could then be seized to fund the regime. Plato deliberately stocks the cast of *Republic*, an inquiry into justice, with future victims of extreme *injustice*.

There's more backstory behind Polemarchus's family that makes them meaningful presences in *Republic* and Polemarchus's house a meaningful venue. Uniquely among Plato's huge cast of dialogue speakers, Polemarchus and his family were natives of Syracuse. Cephalus left that city when Polemarchus was young, invited to Athens by Pericles, according to one account, but in another, sent into exile by the tyrant Gelon.[16] We can't be sure which tale to trust, but if Gelon (or his crueler brother Hieron) did in fact chase Cephalus out, then the family of Polemarchus was a two-time loser to autocrats, once in the father's generation and again in the time of his sons.

However those events played out, the fact that *Republic* takes place among Syracusan ex-pats reminds us that much was at stake for Plato in the progress of one-man rule in Syracuse. The reign of the Thirty at Athens was over, if hardly forgotten. Other cities in mainland Greece had long since kicked out their tyrants in favor of oligarchies or democracies. It was in the Greek West, in Syracuse, that tyranny was once again raising its head, and morphing into a new and more potent form.

Cephalus, father of Polemarchus and Lysias, interrupts his religious rite to greet Socrates, and *Republic* begins to close in on its central question. He and Socrates move from small talk about old age and the loss of sex drive, to the topic of Cephalus's wealth, which seems considerable. In answer to Socrates' questions, Cephalus avers that the best part of having money is being able to pay people back and not deceive anyone, and so live a life of justice.

But, says Socrates, is *that* what justice is, telling the truth and paying back what one owes? Old Cephalus is not quite prepared to pursue such a difficult question, and he shuffles off to complete his sacrifice to the gods. He hands the discussion off to his son Polemarchus, who's eager to joust with Socrates, and the inquiry into justice gets more intense.

Watching these two first exchanges is a man we have yet to meet, though he's about to become the star of *Republic* Book 1. Thrasymachus, whose name means "reckless fighter," is an orator and a teacher of rhetoric, what the Greeks called a sophist—sometimes a term of reproach. Sophists were mistrusted for their reliance on language to win legal cases or build political influence. Their emergence on the scene, in late-fifth-century Athens, had challenged traditional values; since they used words to change or create perceptions, they were seen as shysters or moral relativists. Critics charged them with making inherently weaker reasons defeat stronger ones, thereby inverting notions of right and wrong.

Such tactics could easily serve the cause of a tyrant, for the sophists could strip away moral constraints by depicting them as mere artifices. That act of stripping away might leave nothing behind except power and force. The gods themselves, a sophist might say, are only fantasies, conjured up by some evil genius to inspire fear in the masses. In fact, a play written by Critias, head of the Thirty Tyrants, features a character who makes exactly that case.[17]

Thrasymachus looks on with mounting impatience as Polemarchus and Socrates conduct their inquiry into the nature of justice. He objects not only to the path the argument takes but to the polite tones in which it's conducted. With his turbulent soul, he's exasperated by niceties, and by the time he finally breaks in—the others had long held him back—it's with furious force: "What garbage is this you've been foisting on us, Socrates? And why are you two idiots bowing and scraping to one another?" Plato compares his outburst to the pounce of a bloodthirsty wolf—the animal that will serve later on in *Republic* as the avatar of the tyrant. "I think that if I had not seen him before he saw me, I would have been struck dumb," Socrates says of Thrasymachus, in a reference to a folk legend concerning wolves. Even the imperturbable Socrates is afraid of this violent man. He addresses him "while trembling slightly," a rare instance in which the sage admits to being intimidated.[18]

When given a chance to define justice, Thrasymachus offers a strange formulation: "the advantage of the stronger." What he means is that rules and laws, the apparatus of justice, are formulated by rulers to keep their subjects in line. The absolute ruler, the tyrant, exemplifies this idea. He obeys no law but forces his subjects into complete compliance, thereby reaping the greatest advantage and becoming most "just." In this moral system—where rulers are shepherds who care for their flocks only in order to eat them—the words "just" and "unjust" seem to swap meanings, exactly the kind of inversion for which sophists were sometimes reviled.

Then Thrasymachus drops the pretense and, his passion rising, delivers an ode to *in*justice, the art by which the tyrant shucks off all restraint:

> Turn to the example of the ultimate injustice, which makes the wrongdoer most happy and those who are wronged and who refuse to do wrong most wretched. This is tyranny, which seizes others' property by stealth and by force, not little by little but all at one go.... When someone not only steals the citizens' wealth but ransoms and enslaves the people themselves, instead of ... shameful names, he's called "happy" and "blessed." ... Thus it is, Socrates, that injustice, if it grows sufficiently great, is stronger, and freer, and more lordly a thing than justice.[19]

After throwing down this gauntlet—a grotesque justification of what would befall Polemarchus—Thrasymachus tries to leave, but the others block his exit. He must stay and submit to cross-examination.

There follows some brilliant dramaturgy in which Plato explores how Socrates might handle a hostile witness. Thrasymachus quickly gets fed up with Socrates' questions, which he feels are designed to entrap him. He sullenly vows he'll agree to everything, insincerely, so as to get the ordeal over with. Socrates then demolishes his position, but, since the conversation has been one-sided, the question of justice has not been fully explored. Socrates' method of question and answer, it seems, does not work without a cooperative partner. A tyrannical man cannot play the part—a lesson Plato was learning in Syracuse.

The cowing of Thrasymachus brings *Republic*'s first book to a close. Like an overture in an opera, it has introduced the motifs of the larger work, especially the problem of tyranny. Those who populate its first half were known to Plato's times as tyranny's victims; in its second half, a violent man, configured as a ravening wolf, bursts in and delivers an ode to tyrannical power. In the books that follow, Glaucon and Adeimantus, thus far silent onlookers, will take up the questions Thrasymachus drops and lead the inquiry forward. We shall look at *their* connections to tyranny, especially that of Glaucon, in chapter 7.

The name of Syracuse has not been uttered in this first book of *Republic*, and it will be mentioned only once in the rest of the work (in the phrase "Syracusan tables").[20] But Plato's choice of Syracusans as hosts of the night's discussion is surely not happenstance. It is one of several links that he makes between the concerns of the text and his own dealings with the Greek world's most prominent tyrants.

Those dealings had been interrupted when Plato departed from Syracuse a second time, in 366 BC. But as he left he vowed to return, and soon he'd be called on to fulfill that promise.

*Archytas of Tarentum. An engraving from Thomas Stanley's seventeenth-century History of Philosophy.*

# CHAPTER 6

# THE DIONYSIOFLATTERERS

## *(366–363 BC)*

With Dion and Plato both gone from Dionysius's court, spaces had opened at the Syracusan tables, and volunteers eagerly stepped up to fill them.

As his father had done, Dionysius the Younger made sure to surround himself with writers and ethical teachers, to project an enlightened image to other Greeks. According to Plutarch, he used to tell confidants that he fed and housed "sophists," as he termed his coterie, not because they impressed him but because they made him impressive.[1] No one, of course, could make him more impressive than Plato, but for the moment that trophy thinker remained out of reach.

Collectively the new courtiers were known across Greece as the *Dionysokolakes*, the "Dionysioflatterers," and were said to go to great lengths to stay in the tyrant's good graces. Stories abounded of the depths to which they stooped in this quest. It was said that, knowing Dionysius to be nearsighted, they pretended to be nearly blind, boosting the tyrant's ego by seeming worse off than he was. At the banquet table they'd grope about for their food, then allow the beneficent tyrant to guide their hands to their plates.[2] Whether true or not, the story attests to the vanity of the ruler and the self-abasement of those who gratified it.

But dining with learned men was not merely a way to seem learned.

Unlike his father, Dionysius the Younger actually wanted to learn—to continue the philosophical training he'd begun under Plato. He'd developed an interest in ethics, along with his widely known predilections for wine and high living. Fortunately for him, the latest arrivals at court were specialists in letting him have things both ways. This new group of teachers led the young man on the path of hedonism, a path opposite to the one urged by Plato and Dion. Their school of thought gave moral approval to drinking, feasting, and sexual self-indulgence on the theory that physical pleasure was the highest human good.

Chief among the new thinkers was Aristippus of Cyrene, like Plato a former student of Socrates. Socrates had seen in Aristippus a weakness for food, drink, and sex and had tried to reform him. In one of their conversations, according to Xenophon, Socrates had told Aristippus about the mythical choice of Heracles. In this allegory, Heracles had been faced with a choice of two roads, one rugged and steep, the other smooth and lined with comforts and pleasures. The hard road was watched by a spirit named Aretê, "Virtue," the soft road by a figure called either "Happiness" or "Vice." Heracles, a hero famous for rigor, of course selected the hard road of ethical striving.[3]

Aristippus was evidently impressed by the tale, since he later named his daughter Aretê—also the name Dionysius the Elder had given to one of *his* daughters. Nonetheless Aristippus chose the softer road for himself. He founded the philosophic school that came to be named for his native North African city, Cyrene—the Cyrenaics.

Hedonism put Aristippus squarely at odds with Plato, his former fellow Socratic. The two men came to resent one another as their approaches diverged and as the words of Socrates faded with time, lending themselves to different interpretations. "Our comrade never said anything like *that*," Aristippus once told Plato, when the latter was holding forth.[4] Aristippus derided Plato's most valued pursuit, mathematics, on the grounds that it didn't produce benefits that could be measured, as, say, shoemaking did.[5]

Plato, for his part, disliked Aristippus for charging his students fees—the first of Socrates' followers to do so. Plato showed his disdain by banishing Aristippus entirely from his dialogues, save for a single mention in *Phaedo*. In that dialogue, while describing how Socrates died surrounded by acolytes, Plato has one of his characters note that Aristippus was absent from the gathering.[6] That sole call-out was a bigger insult than if Plato had never mentioned Aristippus at all.

Born poor, Aristippus lined his pockets by cadging money from friends and charging exorbitant rates for his lessons, reportedly asking a thousand drachmas of one student. When the student's father balked at the price, saying he could buy a slave for that much, Aristippus replied "Don't hire me then, and you'll have *another* slave."[7] His wealth meant he could enjoy the high life of Athens, but he made his way west to Syracuse where the living was even higher. When challenged about this move, he punned that he'd gotten *paideia* (learning) from Socrates, but now sought *paidia* (fun times) from Dionysius.[8]

Aristippus fit in well at court on account of his versatile nature. "He was always well situated for whatever chance might occur," remarks his biographer, Diogenes Laertius, in comments that sum up the ideal courtier. "He readily adapted himself to the time, the place, and the part he had to play."[9] Plato saw him in a similar light, having once reportedly told Aristippus, "You alone are able to wear both the robe and the rag," that is, to play the nobleman or the beggar with equal facility.[10]

Dionysius made Aristippus rich, such that the man could afford to pay fifty drachmas—the earnings of nearly two months for an average worker—to buy a rare and delicious fowl for his dinner. An observer of the transaction reacted with horror, so Aristippus asked the man if he'd pay a mere obol—one-sixth of a drachma—to purchase the bird. The man said of course he would do so. "Well, my fifty drachmas mean the same to me as your obol does to you," Aristippus replied.[11] In a similar exchange with Plato, who'd objected to a huge outlay for a purchase of fish, Aristippus reportedly said "It's not that *I'm* a gourmand, but that *you* are a miser."[12]

Living off the largesse of a tyrant made Aristippus what Greeks called a *parasitos*, someone who "dines alongside" his meal ticket. The word gives rise to the English "parasite," but its tone in Greek was more humorous than harsh. Comic dramas made light of the shamelessness of these figures; the satirist Lucian wrote an essay praising parasitism as the highest of all the arts. Aristippus, Lucian asserted, was a virtuoso, so talented that Dionysius sent the royal cooks to him every day for instruction. By contrast, writes Lucian, Plato, in Syracuse, had shown he had no knack for the craft. "After freeloading off the tyrant for just a few days, he lost his place as a parasite for lack of aptitude," snarks Lucian.[13]

As leader of the *Dionysokolakes*, Aristippus was forced to put up with degradations, but always came up smiling, sometimes with a jest on his lips. When begging Dionysius for money and meeting resistance, he groveled at the tyrant's feet, prompting an observer to mock him. "It's not my fault," he said in response, "but that of Dionysius, who has ears in his feet."[14]

On another occasion he was jeered at for allowing Dionysius to spit in his face. His reply blended worldly wisdom with wordplay. "Fishermen tolerate being splashed with seawater, in order to catch the goby," he said, "so why should I be ashamed to be splashed with phlegm, in order to catch a blenny?" In Greek the word for blenny, *blennos*, also refers to the fish's mucousy slime, so *blennos* was a double entendre for the man who had "slimed" him. To "catch" such a fish, in this trope, meant putting Dionysius "on the hook" for money and delicacies.

Not only fine dining but sexual pleasure abounded in Syracuse. Dionysius once offered Aristippus his choice of three courtesans, surely selected from his own harem. Joking that the mythic Paris had only brought trouble by making a similar choice—the contest of beauty that led to the Trojan War—Aristippus walked off with all three.[15] Despite the bounty of court life, Aristippus decamped for two months of the year to the island of Aegina, where he lavished money on Laïs, a famously lovely hetaera renowned for her décolletage. To those who reproached him for this dalliance, he made a thoughtful reply. "I keep her, but am not kept *by* her," he said. "The best thing is to master pleasure and not be conquered, rather than to avoid the experience."[16]

Sex was a prime example of the "smooth motion" that Aristippus regarded as the source of pleasant sensation, a principle he likened to a gentle wind blowing at sea. A wise man, he said, should experience this but avoid the passions of *erôs*, for those entailed pain and "rough motion," like a sea storm. He put this in practice in his liaison with Laïs. It did not bother him, he claimed, that Laïs took other lovers, for, as he said, a passenger in a ship does not mind if others sail in it before or after. When someone told him that Laïs did not love him, he replied that neither did a vessel of wine or a plate of fish, yet he partook of both very gladly.[17]

For Aristippus, life at Dionysius's side meant striving to keep self-respect while enjoying the tyrant's largesse and enduring his scorn. The peculiar bond of ruler and parasite is neatly summed up in an exchange where each quoted lines from Sophoclean drama.[18] Dionysius first offered a couplet that belittled Aristippus:

> *Whoever sojourns to a tyrant's home,*
> *even if free, becomes the tyrant's slave.*

Unbowed, Aristippus recalled another verse:

> *But if he goes there free, he is no slave.*

That rejoinder asserted, in an elegant paradox, that one could live a servile existence and still be autonomous, provided one did so by choice. Such were the convolutions by which ethical thinkers—philosophers in their own eyes, mere spongers to others—made themselves at home with a decadent despot.

A close colleague of Aristippus and fellow traveler on the soft road was Aeschines of Sphettus, another former student of Socrates. He'd come to Syracuse in an impoverished state but promptly won a place at the famous tables by giving Dionysius a set of his works and reading aloud from one called "Miltiades."[19] This must have taken place at a time when Plato was present, for two stories are told, of opposite tenor, about Plato's reaction to Aeschines' arrival. According to Plutarch, Dionysius at first ignored Aeschines until Plato convinced him the newcomer was a model of virtue; the tyrant then welcomed Aeschines and renewed his friendship with Plato, with whom he had earlier been at crossed swords. Another source gives the more likely account that it was Plato, not Dionysius, who ignored Aeschines.[20]

A shadowy figure named Polyarchus was also part of the tyrant's hedonist circle. His total devotion to pleasure, in both his thought and his lifestyle, got him the nickname *Hêdupathês*, "the Luxuriator." Dionysius employed him on diplomatic missions to Archytas of Tarentum, with whom Syracuse had forged an alliance. In the shrines and stoas of Tarentum the two men of opposing creeds—Archytas the sober Pythagorean and Polyarchus the sensualist—would walk back and forth, debating ethical questions, especially those concerning desire and sensation. A record of what Polyarchus said, or perhaps *could* have said, during one such debate has survived.[21]

Polyarchus makes the case that Nature had given its blessing to the hedonist creed. "Nature, whenever it speaks with its own voice, orders us to follow pleasures, and says that to do so is the mark of the wise," he asserts. To refuse Nature's bidding is equivalent to "enslaving" desire. He adduces as examples the Great Kings of Persia, who, with the power to do whatever they wish, make pleasure their principal goal. These monarchs, he says, have even instituted rewards for inventions of new kinds of pleasure, since novelty magnifies pleasure's impact. Thus the Persians are always devising new dishes, new incenses and perfumes, and new types of bedding for more luxurious rests. The Kings, too, maintain a harem so ample as to provide a new partner for every night of the year.

The conjunction of pleasure and power seen in the Great Kings brings Polyarchus to the subject of Dionysius. If the Persian King is the happiest man on Earth, he says, then Dionysius takes second place, only because he has fewer lands and less wealth to furnish sensations. But, he claims, the growth of Syracusan power means that Dionysius is catching up. Expansion, in Polyarchus's view, is driven by the quest for more and newer pleasures; each imperial power in turn seeks to gain a monopoly. Soon, he implies, the time will come when Syracuse, and Dionysius, will dominate the pleasure market.

Polyarchus ends his sermon with the most daring assertion of all. The very idea of justice, he says, has been invented by lawgivers jealous of unrestrained pleasure to ensure that no one can claim too great a share. Poets write odes to justice, and others speak of it as something divine— a reference to Plato's *Republic*?—but their real agenda is to protect whatever few pleasures they have. Only the monarch who stands above such illusions, Polyarchus implies, lives in true freedom, enjoying full pleasure, living as people were meant to live.

Polyarchus thus introduces a chilling new way of defining autocracy: the ultimate form of harmony with Nature. Dionysius, in his view, exemplified what a human being could become, if not held down by absurd ideas about *justice.*

Archytas doubtless made strong objections to speeches like these, as we can guess from reports of his views on pleasure. Put simply, he was against it. "Archytas used to say that no other, more ruinous plague had been given to humankind than bodily pleasure," writes Cicero. "There is no crime, no evil deed, that desire for pleasure does not drive us to undertake." Pleasure, Archytas argued, is the enemy of rational thought and therefore "snuffs out the light of the soul."[22] As proof of this point he mentioned sexual pleasure; no one, he noted, can use the rational mind in the midst of the sex act. Opposition to pleasure, however, did not keep Archytas away from Dionysius's court. In fact, it was Plato who helped put him there, having brought him into an *entente cordiale* with the tyrant in 367.

Archytas was by this time proving himself an accomplished geometer and theoretician, worthy of the Academy's respect. Various ancient accounts credit him with solving the doubling of the cube, a mathematical problem in which Plato had taken a personal interest.

The problem arose when the inhabitants of Delos, an island sacred to Apollo, were struck by a plague, and the Delphic oracle told them they could recover their health by doubling the size of their cube-shaped altar. The Delians doubled the length of each side, but that produced an altar of eight times greater volume; then they consulted Plato. In some versions of the story, Plato himself solved the problem, but in those told by Plutarch, Archytas, along with one or two others, devised the solution when Plato was unable. According to these accounts, Plato was scornful of Archytas's solution because it made use of drawings and models, the stuff of the physical world, rather than pure theory.[23] Modern geometers are more generous, praising Archytas's solution—which has been preserved—as a *"tour de force* of the spatial imagination."[24]

Archytas had other talents, too, of a kind not often found in Academy circles. According to Aristotle he invented a child's toy called a *platagê*, "clapper," designed to keep little hands busy lest they break things in one's home.[25] This seems to have been something like a pair of castanets, though doubtless more diverting. Archytas also contrived a wooden dove that was made to fly through the air by "a puff of wind concealed inside"— some sort of pneumatic device.[26] However this automaton worked, it was so original that our sole source, the Roman tale collector Aulus Gellius, seems not to have had the language to describe it.[27]

It would seem out of character for this brilliant, abstemious man to take a seat at the Syracusan tables, yet Plato reports in the *Seventh Letter* that, shortly after he left Syracuse, Archytas arrived there. He implies that Archytas engaged Dionysius in conversations about ideas, just as he'd tried to do himself. Somehow these talks convinced Archytas that the tyrant was eager for liberal learning—or at least Archytas was willing to make that claim, for the sake of luring Plato back to the city. The *Seventh Letter* attests that he regarded Plato's presence as vital to sustaining his new alliance with Syracuse.[28]

"Letters kept coming from Archytas and those in Tarentum," Plato says of the years that followed his return to Athens, "praising Dionysius's philosophical study to the skies and saying that, if I didn't come, I'd completely ruin the friendship that had arisen, through me, between themselves and Dionysius—a friendship that was of no small importance to their state interests."[29]

Archytas had a political stake in depicting the tyrant as studious. But Plato also had reasons to want to believe his report. He was trying to see the best in Dionysius at this moment and was still committed to keeping the Syracuse project going. We know this from another of his epistles— a private letter he sent to the tyrant from Athens, likely in 365.

It seems that, soon after he left Syracuse and around the time that Archytas arrived there, Plato was writing to Dionysius, hoping to further the tyrant's education. One of these efforts at "remote learning" has miraculously survived. I refer to the *Thirteenth Letter*, a fiercely contested document, as discussed in the introduction. Largely suppressed since it first reached Western eyes in the Renaissance, this fascinating epistle needs to be brought out into the full light of day.

Plato—as I shall call the *Thirteenth Letter*'s author since I believe that's who wrote it—begins by using a shared recollection to assure Dionysius the letter comes from *him* and not some impostor. He recalls the banquet at which Dionysius rose from his place, came to where Plato was dining, and paid him an extravagant compliment (see chapter 4). Of all the moments that might have served to establish identity, this one is uniquely intimate. "This must be preserved," Plato writes, referring to the spirit of that exchange, "so that the benefit we have from one another may always increase."[30] The opening sets a friendly tone, accenting the best side of former relations and ignoring the worst—that is, the tension over Dion's exile.

The letter makes clear that Plato still hopes to educate Syracuse's ruler. He has sent Dionysius some philosophic treatises: Pythagorean works and something called "distinctions," perhaps exercises in classification of the kind the Academy practiced. A tutor, too, will soon be arriving in Syracuse, a man named Helicon, whom Plato says he has carefully vetted. The dispatch of this fellow was agreed upon "by us, back then," before Plato left Sicily. Helicon is not all that Plato might wish, but "he's not without charm and he doesn't seem bad-natured." Plato cautions Dionysius to keep a close eye on him, for human nature is shifty and changeable.

Plato acknowledges that Dionysius may be too busy to study, referring obliquely to his ongoing war. Helicon can give instruction directly to Dionysius if the tyrant has time, but if not, he can teach someone else at court—perhaps Plato was thinking of Archytas—who can later teach Dionysius. In this way teachings that Plato approves may reach Dionysius at second hand, "so that, learning at leisure, you may become better and gain a good reputation, and so that the benefit you have from me may not cease."[31] Then Plato moves on to his next topic, for us a surprising one: items he has purchased on the tyrant's behalf.

The first of these buys, a statue of Apollo, had been at the request of Dionysius. Plato relates that he commissioned it from one Leochares (known from other sources as a brilliant Athenian sculptor, just starting out at this time) and has sent the completed work to Syracuse by way of an envoy named Leptines (a different person than the tyrant's uncle). While browsing in the sculptor's shop, Plato writes, he spotted another piece he admired and purchased it as a gift for Sôphrosynê, Dionysius's wife—"for she took good care of me both when I was well and when I was sick," a reference to some illness he'd contracted during his recent visit. For the couple's four children, Plato has sent twelve jars of "sweet wine," a drink more sugary than alcoholic, and two jars of honey from Attica's famous bees. Plato says he would have liked to send preserved figs or myrtle berries as well, but he arrived home too late for fig season and the berries had soured. "We will manage better next time," he writes.[32]

Thus far the *Thirteenth Letter* shows Plato playing multiple roles in relation to Dionysius: teacher, grateful house guest, and purchasing agent abroad. All are amicable, to a degree that disconcerts those who prefer to see Plato as Dionysius's foe. The warmth of the letter however makes sense from a more pragmatic perspective. "There is every reason to suppose that . . . [Plato] endeavored to remain on good terms with the tyrant, as the best way of influencing him toward the recall of Dion and the philosophical reform of Syracuse," writes one modern scholar, Glenn Morrow, in his study of Plato's letters.[33]

There was much that Plato could gain, both for Dion and for the Greek West, by preserving friendly relations with Dionysius. In the letter's next section, where he deals with financial matters, Plato reveals he has interests at stake of his own.

Plato reports he has kept an account of money he has received from Dionysius by way of the go-between, Leptines, and what he has spent on the tyrant's behalf. Expressing himself politely and delicately, he indicates that he got sixteen *minae* (sixteen hundred drachmas) via Leptines, reimbursement for what he'd paid out for passage to Athens by ship. Strangely, he feels compelled to account for how he is using the money, writing as if it still belonged in part to Dionysius. "I will make use of your money, as I used to tell you back then, in the same way I do that of other close friends; I am using as little as possible, just as much as seems needful and just and fitting, both to me and to whomever I get it from." It seems that Plato had other sources of funds besides Leptines, "close friends" who, almost certainly, included wealthy Dion.

Plato then begins a new discussion in which he distinguishes "your money kept at Athens"—the funds the tyrant dispenses through agents—from "my money." Regarding the latter, Plato makes a list of upcoming expenses. He has four grandnieces, ranging in age from one to teenage years, for whom "I and my close friends" will need to supply dowries (their parents, evidently, were either dead or not well off). The oldest, already betrothed to her cousin Speusippus—Plato's nephew—will need thirty *minae* at the time of her wedding (a moderate sum for a gift of this kind).

Another ten *minae* will be required, at some point soon, for a funeral monument for Plato's mother (at this point no doubt about ninety). The fact that these expenses fall in the "my money" section shows that Plato intends to pay them from his own resources. He mentions them here "as an explanation of his own frankness in reminding Dionysius that he was in Plato's debt" for costs incurred by the visit to Syracuse, as Glenn Morrow observes.[34] To invoice a tyrant, as Plato had effectively done when discussing his travel expenses, required a certain tact.

Plato then turns from his own funds to the tyrant's—"the expenditure of your money held at Athens"—and the question of what he is saying becomes rather tricky. He anticipates that he will need to pay for a *chorêgia*, the public duty of fitting out a chorus for a performance, or some other obligation of the kind that Athens imposed on the well-to-do. Historically, Plato was rich enough to incur such expenses but not rich enough to afford them with ease; we're told by Plutarch that Dion, a very rich man, stepped in and paid for a *chorêgia* on Plato's behalf.[35] So when Plato writes to Dionysius, "you have no agent who will give [the money to meet this expense], as we assumed," he seems to be worried that funds will not be forthcoming to pay for the *chorêgia*—perhaps the same one that Dion then subsidized.[36]

It's possible to suppose that the *chorêgia* for which Plato seeks funding was not his own burden but that of Dionysius, who, as an honorary Athenian, would incur such obligations. That is, Plato will spend the money "on your [Dionysius's] behalf," a phrase that one scholar, John Harward, inserted into his translation of the letter, setting it off by parentheses.[37] But it's just as likely that, in this sentence, Plato expects Dionysius to take the *chorêgia* expense off *his* shoulders. That possibility has bothered Plato scholars enormously—one says that the letter's author seems a "contemptible cadger of money"—and has helped get the letter thrown out as a fake.[38] But we need not judge harshly if Plato looked toward patrons for help, as many in his era did. "If we had the full details before us," writes Glenn Morrow, "we should find nothing disturbing or undignified in Plato's attitude here."[39]

There is more on matters of finance as the letter continues. It emerges that Dionysius's credit in Athens is not very good, and Plato has had trouble securing loans on the tyrant's behalf. A banker named Andromedes, whom Dionysius had thought would provide advances, had recently offered only a small sum since he'd had trouble recovering previous loans. By contrast, Leptines, Plato writes, has been open-handed in supplying whatever was needed. It's clear that *this* money, at least, is not for Plato's own use; it merely passes through his hands as he fills the tyrant's purchase orders (such as the one for the Apollo statue) or meets his fiscal obligations in Athens.

In contrasting the quick and the slow moneylenders, Plato realizes he's elevating the former at the expense of the latter. He sees this as part of his duty toward Dionysius. "I must report to you things like these [Leptines' readiness to lend] and the opposite, however each person appears to me in connection with you," he writes. He has taken on yet another role here, that of consultant to the regime on personnel matters. He seems to be finding agents who will best serve the tyrant's needs and weeding out those who will not.

"I'll speak candidly to you about money matters," Plato goes on, "for that's just, and also because I can speak from my knowledge of those who surround you." Plato now plays the whistleblower, pointing out that the tyrant's agents, fearful of displeasing their sovereign, have been downplaying the costs of his policies. He gives Dionysius stern advice: "Accustom them and compel them to tell you this, and other things too; for you ought to know all. . . . This will be the best thing of all in regard to your power."[40]

Misleading estimates of costs have hurt the regime's credit rating, Plato implies, perhaps because they have led Dionysius into making unwise commitments. His tone is judicious, sagacious, nearly paternal. He is seeking, with evident good will, to help a young monarch who does not know whom to trust.

Plato now changes the subject and devotes a single, opaque paragraph to the subject of Dion.

Dion, as we know from Plutarch's biography, was residing in Athens

at this time and frequenting the Academy. While in the city he lived at
the house of another Academy member, a man named Callippus, but he'd
also bought a country estate for himself, drawing on money sent from
Syracuse. With these funds he was able to live quite well and, as we've
seen, to pay at least one of Plato's major expenses. There's every sign that
he and Plato stayed close, whether or not there was *erôs* between them as
the contested funeral poem would suggest.

In the *Thirteenth Letter* Plato tells Dionysius that he's expecting to
hear from him soon about Dion. We'd give a lot to know what was in
the message he was anticipating. Dion's exile and promised recall was
the principal issue on the table; perhaps Plato was hoping for guidance
on when this recall, and his own return to Syracuse, would take place.
Meanwhile, he had some news to convey to the tyrant, on a subject that,
as he evidently had been instructed, he left unexpressed.

"Regarding those things that you would not permit me to mention to
him [Dion]," Plato writes, "I didn't mention or bring them up, but I tried
to determine whether he would find them easy or hard to put up with,
were they to happen. It seemed to me he would be not a little aggrieved,
should they take place. In other respects Dion seems to me to be even-
tempered toward you in both speech and action."[41] And with those mysterious words, Plato passes on to other topics.

No portion of the *Thirteenth Letter* has troubled modern scholars
as much as this one, for it gives the impression that Plato was working
against his friend as a kind of spy. That's not a wholly mistaken view, but
the situation needs to be charitably assessed. The rift between Dion and
Dionysius was deeply painful to Plato, who had reason to think that he'd
caused it. He no doubt felt bound to heal it in any way that he could. Presumably, supplying the information the tyrant wanted might have led to
such healing, though it seems that what Plato obtained was not what was
hoped for. An awareness of Plato's position—caught between estranged
branches of the Greek world's most powerful family—should help miti-
gate our discomfort.

What was it that Plato had learned Dion would not tolerate? The letter gives no clue, but Plutarch supplies a possible answer. He claims that
Dionysius arranged with Plato, before Plato's departure from Syracuse,
to sound Dion out about divorcing his wife, Aretê. The tyrant's plan, later

enacted, was to find Aretê a husband more loyal to his regime. Plutarch adds that Dion was thought to be unhappy in his marriage, so Dionysius had reason to think he might leave it.[42] Clearly the tyrant had much to gain if the bond could be severed and Dion excised from the family. Plutarch refers specifically to the *Thirteenth Letter*, claiming that the mystery subject mentioned there was the idea of divorce.

It's unclear what Plutarch's source could have been for this statement. The collusion that he refers to, between Dionysius and Plato, was meant to be kept confidential, though perhaps Philistus learned of it and wrote about it. More likely Plutarch guessed at the secret topic, based on what later took place: The marriage of Dion and Aretê *was* dissolved, and Aretê was remarried to a regime loyalist. But Dionysius managed all that without either partner's permission; he had no need to sound Dion out, so Plutarch's guess doesn't seem right. We simply don't know what topic was so important to Dionysius that Plato discreetly tried to learn Dion's views.

In its final section, the *Thirteenth Letter* addresses a wide range of "housekeeping" matters, fascinating in their mundanity and detail. Plato suggests that Dionysius send small gifts to two Academy members, men whose good will can benefit the Syracusan regime. He mentions a Syracusan diplomat then visiting Athens, Philagrus—"the one who back then had a problem with his hand"—who, he takes pride in conveying, is extolling the virtues of Dionysius's rule and the support that Plato has lent it. He reminds Dionysius of a confidential signal he'll use when sending letters to the tyrant on behalf of those seeking favors. Since he does not like to give offense by refusing to write such letters, he says he will use as his opening line "with the help of the gods" (a standard formal heading) if he'd written out of politeness; if the letter has his true endorsement, he'll instead use the singular, "with the help of god."

In his sign-off Plato again expresses hope for Dionysius's moral improvement. "Be well and pursue philosophy," he writes, "and turn the other young men in the same direction." He wants his greetings conveyed to the tyrant's *susphairistai*, his "sphere-buddies"—a word found nowhere else in surviving classical Greek. It's usually taken to mean the men with whom Dionysius plays some sort of ball game (one translator charmingly renders it "tennis-club").[43] But the term could just as easily designate a group of people who joined the tyrant in the contemplation of spheres. Since Plato's educational program centered on geometry and astronomy—the movements of the celestial spheres—this second meaning is the more likely one. If it's correct, it again underscores that, from Plato's perspective, the Syracuse project was still very much underway.

Plato ends the *Thirteenth Letter* by urging Dionysius to "save this letter or a summary of it, and take it to heart." It seems that somehow the letter *was* saved, despite its personal contents, to be added later to the dozen open letters in the Platonic collection, like the unlucky thirteenth guest at a fairytale banquet.

The *Thirteenth Letter* is the most revealing of the Platonic epistles and, largely for that reason, the most controversial. British classicist Reginald Hackforth wrote in 1913, just as he assumed a Cambridge professorship, that it depicts "the philosopher in undress"—a sight that many prefer not to see. Hackforth replied to a list of sixteen points a German colleague, Constantin Ritter, had made to discredit the letter as a fake, refuting each one in turn; in a footnote he stated the crux of their disagreement. "It is clear that Ritter's desire to prove the letter spurious is due to his belief that it shows Plato in an unfavorable light," Hackforth wrote.[44]

In this book's introduction and in what I have written elsewhere, I have used the *Thirteenth Letter* as an exemplary case of the letters debate generally and of larger questions of how we imagine Plato.[45] *Republic* gives us a portrait of an idealized philosopher, a being who trains his mind on transcendent Forms. Almost inevitably, that portrait has fused with our image of Plato himself. An ethereal figure has taken shape, a platonic Plato, who doesn't seem capable of fretting about expenses, monitoring moneylenders, or picking out thoughtful gifts for a tyrant's wife. To accept the *Thirteenth Letter* requires us to give up the phantasm and behold a real person instead.

Because it's the only private missive in the Platonic collection, the authorship of the *Thirteenth Letter* demands a unique investigation. In other cases where letters are thought to be fake, the imposture has been attributed to some ancient student of rhetoric, honing his skills, as

speakers in training did, by impersonating the great. But that explanation can't apply here; rhetorical exercises dealt with grand public questions, not with minutiae like souring myrtle berries and overripe figs. So
we'd have to imagine a different reason this letter got created if it is not
by Plato. That proves a difficult task.

The most likely forger would have been seeking to sell his work to a
library, as many Greek forgers did. But profiteers, as we know, kept their
letters short and vague to avoid missteps. The writer of the *Thirteenth
Letter* goes on at great length, naming names and giving details, yet com-
mits no detectable errors. He includes banal subject matter of little interest to paying collectors. What's more, he refers to a crucial matter that
would have held *great* interest, but keeps it veiled—the secret question
concerning Dion that Plato had tried to get answered. Any buyer would
be on the hunt, in the case of a Plato letter, for Dion-related content; a
forger looking to make a sale would want to supply it. Why would this
writer, with the freedom to freely invent, keep Dion consigned to a single,
opaque paragraph?

But perhaps profit was not the prime motive of our hypothetical
forger. Some have supposed that the letter's author was seeking to deni-
grate Plato by showing him taking money from Dionysius. Perhaps Dionysius himself, it has been suggested, sponsored the letter's creation—to
get back at a man by whom he felt slighted.

Fake letters *were* sometimes designed to harm reputations, but if *that*
was our forger's intention, he's done a poor job. The letter might easily have shown a ventriloquized Plato asking Dionysius for handouts.
Instead it depicts a man who keeps close accounts so as *not* to rely on
a patron unless he has to and who speaks with self-possession and dig-
nity. "There is a noticeable absence of purely personal motives," writes
Morrow, the letter's most careful interpreter. "Nothing . . . would justify
us in classing the Plato described here with a man like Aristippus."[46] A
character assassin would have framed an entirely different epistle, not to
mention a much shorter one.

Or did a propagandist create the letter to boost Dionysius's reputation
as an enlightened man? Here, too, the letter falls far short of what we'd
expect. It concedes that Dionysius may have no time for ethical thought
and may have to put it off for a later occasion. It places Dionysius in the

position of needing advice from Plato, of failing to spot the lies of his courtiers, and of having his credit downgraded by lenders in Athens. The portrait it paints is one of mixed tones, neither as bright as the tyrant's supporters would make it nor dark enough to please his opponents.

In short, our hypothetical forger would cut a very peculiar figure. It's clear he possesses exceptional talent, yet he's put that talent to use for no practical purpose, other than for the sake of deception itself. As Hackforth reasoned, applying Occam's razor, it's harder to think that such a person existed than to believe that the letter is what it claims to be, the writing of Plato.[47]

To accept it, though, we have to accept that the platonic Plato, a shining creation shaped from the dialogues, didn't really exist. We'd have to be willing to see a sage in a state of undress.

The *Thirteenth Letter* raises the question of how Plato met his expenses. The Academy did not take fees from its students, yet it likely could not have gotten by on Plato's resources alone. Its property, by report, had been purchased with outside funds, and its operations—including frugal, but frequent, common meals—also required subsidies. Small hints in the sources, the truth of which is hard to assess, suggest that both Dionysius and Dion helped underwrite the Academy. One source specifies a staggering amount, claiming that Dionysius gave Plato more than eighty talents; unfortunately that source, a certain Onetor, is virtually unknown apart from this one factoid, so we cannot assess his reliability.[48]

The Greeks were by nature suspicious of anyone dealing with a wealthy ruler. It seemed to them (and they may have been right) that interactions with potentates would always involve self-interest. A truly virtuous man would avoid such entanglements, as Socrates reportedly did by refusing to join the court of Archelaus, king of Macedon. The fact that Plato did what Socrates hadn't—accepted a monarch's invitation—weighed against him in the scale of public opinion. Barbs and jests in the agora made him out to be another compromised devotee of the Syracusan tables.

This cynical view was espoused by the man for whom the word "cynic" was coined, Diogenes of Sinopê. Diogenes had arrived in Athens shortly before Plato's sojourn with Dionysius the Younger. Attaching himself to Antisthenes, a former member of Socrates' circle, he developed ethics entirely different from those of Plato's school and took a strong dislike to Plato himself. In the tales surrounding Plato's Syracuse project, Diogenes serves as spokesman for dark interpretations of motive, giving voice to what many suspected—perhaps with some justification.

Diogenes had left Sinopê, a Greek city on the north shore of what's now Turkey, under a cloud of familial shame. His father, a wealthy banker, had been put in charge of the city's mint and had been charged with a crime involving falsely struck coinage. Diogenes consulted the oracle of Delphi and was told to "deface the currency"; this sounded like an echo of what his father had done, but the Greek word *nomisma*, "currency," also meant what was "current," that is, social customs. Exiled from his home and stripped of his family's wealth, Diogenes landed in Athens, where he followed the Delphic command in this second sense. Through his strange way of life and his fearlessly candid pronouncements, he challenged Greek values and mores or even held them up to ridicule.

Diogenes took the template of Socrates, who had disdained wealth and power, and pushed it into the realm of asceticism. He went about clad in a ragged cloak, carrying only a battered pouch that held a dry crust of bread and a cup for drinking water from public fountains. When one day he saw a young boy scooping water with his hands, he dashed his cup on the ground and cursed his luxuriousness. Where Socrates had gone barefoot in all seasons, Diogenes sought out greater discomforts, rolling in hot sand in summer and hugging frozen bronze statues in winter. He slept for years in porticoes and storage sheds, then finally took up residence in an enormous clay pot, displaying his freedom from even the need to be housed.

What else but contempt could such a man have for refined, aristocratic Plato, with his two well-appointed homes and his coterie of rich students? Diogenes stood for everything the Academy wasn't. He declared his "doggish" existence (in Greek, *kunikos*, later "cynic") to be the "short-cut to virtue," requiring none of the decades-long study that Plato endorsed. Truth, for him, lay not in apprehension of distant, abstract Forms but in simple lifestyle choices: shedding of material comforts, embrace of the lowly and mean. The idea of an organized school, with a master holding sway over devotees, looked, from his point of view, like a circle of self-regard. "What serious thing has that man accomplished," he supposedly said of Plato, "if he's practiced philosophy for such a long time, yet caused no one pain?"[49]

Plato had equally little esteem for Diogenes, whom he reportedly called "a Socrates gone mad." He deemed the Cynic's primitivism merely an act designed to attract attention. A reported exchange between the two men underscores the divide between them. Interestingly, it is set at a moment when Plato was hosting some guests "from Dionysius"— people who, like the agent Leptines, passed between Athens and Syracuse, bearing money or messages. Somehow Diogenes turned up at the party. Finding the setting far too posh, he stamped his feet on the soft carpeting, declaring loudly "I trample on the pretentiousness of Plato." His host replied, according to one account, "Yes, Diogenes—with a different pretentiousness."[50]

Diogenes obtained his only needs—scraps of food to stave off hunger—by asking passers-by for handouts. When someone reproached him for begging when Plato did not do so, Diogenes' reply was characteristically barbed. "He begs too, but," said the Cynic, quoting a line from Homer, *"he holds his head close so that others do not notice."*[51] At two points in the *Odyssey*, that verse describes how one character whispers conspiratorially to another. Plato's begging, Diogenes implied, was just as real as *his*, but more surreptitious.

The person Diogenes thought that Plato was begging from, in all likelihood, was Dionysius of Syracuse. The Cynic had made up his mind that Plato's recent visit to the tyrant had been motivated by money and the rich fare of the famous tables. A raft of stories preserved in our sources attest to this jaundiced view, a view shared by others as well. I relate these tales not to claim they're historically true—undoubtedly most are not—but because they reveal thoughts entertained by Plato's contemporaries or those who followed soon after.[52] Diogenes, and other free-speakers, were convenient mouthpieces for wider suspicions about the Syracuse project.

In one anecdote, Plato passed by as Diogenes was washing a head of lettuce in a public fountain. Plato scorned the humble meal, saying "If you were paying court to Dionysius, you wouldn't be rinsing lettuce." Unfazed, the Cynic shot back: "And *you*—if you were rinsing lettuce, you wouldn't be paying court to Dionysius."[53] (It seems that in an earlier version Aristippus was the butt of the jest; Plato was likely swapped in by someone who thought that he too was nothing more than a Dionysioflatterer.)

Another reported exchange between Diogenes and Plato also raised the question of parasitism. At a banquet where both men were dining, Diogenes noticed that Plato was eating only olives and leaving more delicate dishes untouched. "How is it," he asked, "that you, the sage who sailed to Sicily for the sake of tables like these, aren't enjoying them now when they're set before you?" "By the gods, Diogenes," Plato replied, "even *there* I was all for olives and things like that." "Then," said Diogenes, "why did you need to sail to Syracuse? Wasn't Attica producing olives at that time?"[54] He implied that Plato was lying to conceal his Sicilian gourmandizing.

In yet another reported exchange between Diogenes and Plato, the Cynic made ingenious use of a legend concerning dogs. Just as we say today that dogs return to their vomit, the Greeks evidently believed that, once sold to new masters, dogs would return to the place where the sale was concluded. So when Plato called Diogenes a dog for ignoring a lecture he was delivering, Diogenes had an ingenious comeback. "But *I* don't go back to where I was sold, like dogs do," he rejoined. His comment was based on the tale, quite possibly true as we've seen, that Plato had been sold as a slave on the orders of Dionysius the Elder. To revisit the scene of *that* crime, the Cynic suggested, would be the mark of a *true* dog.

According to ancient sources, Diogenes, too, was sold as a slave, after being captured by pirates and taken to Crete. The stories of his enslavement pose a sharp contrast to what's reported of Plato. Standing on the auction block in Crete, the captive Diogenes was asked what skills he possessed; to general amazement he answered, "Ruling men." He bid the crier announce that reply to the crowd, "in case anyone wants to purchase a master." A wealthy Corinthian named Xeniades bought him and took him to Corinth. After realizing that he'd purchased someone far wiser than the average slave, the man put Diogenes in charge of teaching his sons.

When friends later sought to ransom Diogenes, as Plato's admirers had done for Plato, Diogenes refused to be freed. Lions are not slaves to their feeders, he said, but the other way round—implying he was the lion.[55] He refused to be humbled by servitude, another way he "defaced the currency" of social convention.

Diogenes was not alone in questioning Plato's motives for visiting Sicily. Rumors insinuated that Plato had bought or obtained Pythagorean books in Syracuse from which he had then plagiarized, especially in his dialogue *Timaeus*. In versions of this rumor, Dionysius played a supporting role, either by giving the books to Plato or by giving him money to pay for them.[56] A rhetorician named Alcimus made the case that Plato had stolen all his most central concepts, including the theory of Forms, from a Syracusan playwright named Epicharmus.[57]

A biographer named Satyrus records that Plato wrote to Dionysius, requisitioning Pythagorean books at a cost of one hundred *minae* (ten thousand drachmas). The exorbitant sum makes Plato seem desperate to get the books and extravagantly wealthy as well; a second biographer adds that he'd gotten the money from Dionysius to start with.[58] Thus, in a single slander, Plato was cast as a plagiarist, fat cat, and parasite all at once.

In such ways Plato's Syracuse journey became a source of reproach, as Plato acknowledges in his *Seventh Letter*: "I departed with *this* intention . . . and not the one that some have supposed."

Athenians set great store by their *euthuna* procedure, an audit they imposed on public servants whose jobs involved handling money. Their assumption was that, absent such audits, anyone who had the chance would skim off funds and enrich themselves. That assessment of human nature colored the way they regarded Plato's visits to Sicily, where the deepest coffers in all of Hellas were found.

We can't audit Plato from a distance of 2,400 years, nor perhaps should we. What we can know is that his Sicilian sojourns looked suspicious to many in Athens. It seemed to them that Plato had stuck his hand in the ultimate honey jar, or feasted at a tyrant's tables, or both. Those suspicions became more intense when Plato went back, for a *third* time, to Syracuse, his second visit to Dionysius the Younger.

We'll soon follow his footsteps there, as he made a new effort to educate the Greek world's most powerful ruler. To change the world by changing one man—that was Plato's own account of his reason for going to Syracuse.

Not coincidentally, Socrates has much the same goal in *Republic* when he sets out to educate Glaucon, Plato's brother. That fictional teacher-student bond, to be explored in the chapter that follows, reflects, though in a distorting mirror, the outlines of the Syracuse project.

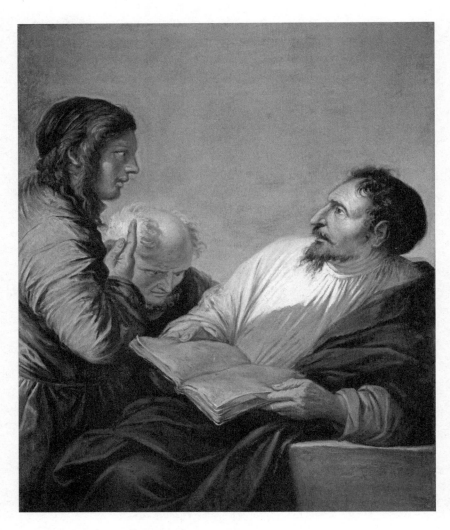

Plato's Academy, *an oil painting by Salvator Rosa (1615–1673).*

CHAPTER 7

# THE EDUCATION OF GLAUCON

As Thrasymachus argues in *Republic* Book 1 that tyranny brings the ultimate happiness, Plato's brother Glaucon, who'd accompanied Socrates down to Piraeus that day, is watching with fascination. As Book 2 of *Republic* begins, Thrasymachus falls silent and Glaucon takes up the argument, insisting that Socrates offer a fuller defense of justice. "Thrasymachus seems to me to have been charmed into submission by you, as one charms a snake, sooner than what was needed," Glaucon protests.[1]

Glaucon vows to "reinvigorate" the argument for tyranny and injustice. Though he claims he doesn't believe it himself, he concedes that he's "at a loss" when he hears the words of Thrasymachus, as well as "thousands of others," pounding in his ears. He seems to be under a massive assault by defenders of tyranny. Without a counterargument, this young man might well fall under the spell of authoritarianism, convinced that only *in*justice will bring him fulfillment.

It falls to Socrates to prevent that disastrous outcome. The next few books of *Republic* form a pedagogic drama, an effort to win the struggle for Glaucon's soul (and, less crucially, the soul of his younger brother, Adeimantus).

Plato, of course, was taking part in his own pedagogic drama—the education of Dionysius the Younger—during the time when *Republic* was (almost certainly) under construction. His age when he went to the Younger's court in 367 BC, about sixty, was close to that of Socrates in *Republic* (insofar as Plato's vague chronology allows us to guess); Dionysius, just shy of thirty, was perhaps slightly older than Glaucon. The stakes of both projects, moreover, are similarly high. Glaucon, as portrayed by Plato, has the right stuff for leadership, so if Socrates can turn him toward justice, he'd give Athens hope of political renewal. Dionysius was already a leader, so if Plato got through to *him*, he might save Syracuse. The fate of both cities depends on how much headway a teacher can make with a student.

The parallels aren't perfect. Glaucon is given qualities in *Republic* that less resemble those of Dionysius than an Athenian adventurer, Alcibiades, who'd been kicked out of Athens for his perceived tyrannical leanings. Socrates, in *Republic*, moreover, is no mere stand-in for Plato. Nonetheless the Piraeus project, as we might term *Republic*, resembles the Syracuse one in that it shows Socrates acting as mentor, guiding a youth who stands at a crossroads in life. And, as in the case of Syracuse, the alternative path for the student, if his teacher does not succeed, is tyranny.

All this impels us to take a closer look at Glaucon, the puzzle at the heart of *Republic*. It is Glaucon who leads the dialogue's cast in its central task, construction of a hypothetical city, and that city is largely designed to satisfy *him*. By way of that city, Callipolis, Plato confronts a problem he also encountered in Syracuse, the problem of pleasure.

Little is known for certain about the historical Glaucon, beyond the fact that he sought political power. Xenophon makes that point clear in his *Memorabilia*, a collection of Socratic dialogues that are shorter and more matter-of-fact than Plato's. In one such dialogue, Xenophon shows the young Glaucon, not yet twenty years old, brashly explaining to Socrates that he intends to become leader of Athens. None of Glaucon's friends, says Xenophon, had been able to stop the youth from making a fool of himself with this headstrong ambition. Socrates undertakes to bring

Glaucon down to earth, showing him, point by point, that he has no idea what to do as a head of state. The little vignette, likely based on Xenophon's personal knowledge, shows Glaucon so eager to get to the top as to skip over all the preliminaries.[2]

Glaucon's will to power made him an apt choice for the foremost supporting role in *Republic*'s cast (Socrates as usual plays the lead). Plato portrays his brother as a talented, spirited youth with strong autocratic leanings, as well as a strong sex drive—two impulses that, as we've seen, are closely connected in Plato's system of thought. The link between them is underscored at the start of Book 2 of *Republic*, when Glaucon, in the work's longest speech, tells a story involving an Asian monarch who came to power with help from a magic ring.

Long ago, in Lydia (western Turkey), says Glaucon, a nameless shepherd, tending his flocks, found a ring that, if turned a certain way on his finger, made him invisible. Using the ring, he inserted himself into the palace guard corps, seduced the queen, and, with her help, assassinated the king. In this way he made himself ruler of Lydia and founded a dynasty that later included a king named Gyges (a figure well known to the Greeks through the writings of Herodotus).[3] The shepherd's path to monarchy does not run straight to the throne room—where he might have done the murder unassisted—but takes an erotic detour into the queen's bedroom. The lust for power, in Plato's view, walks hand in hand with physical, sexual lust.

The conjunction of the two drives, for power and sex, emerges again as Glaucon imagines what a just man would do if he too could become invisible.[4]

> If there should come to be two rings of this kind, and the just man put on one, the unjust man the other, it seems there would be no one of such adamantine nature as to remain by the side of justice and have the strength to refrain from the belongings of others and keep his hands off them, when he could take from the marketplace anything he wished, without fear, and go into houses and lie with whomever he wants, and to kill, or release from bonds, whomever he wants, and to behave in other ways, among humans, as the equal of a god.

The rewards that Glaucon imagines for owning the ring include unlimited rape, reminding us that Plato, in his discussion of tyranny in *Republic* (see chapter 2), speaks of "erotic and tyrannical appetites" as though the two forces were one.

As *Republic* continues, we learn more about Glaucon's sex drive, which seems to be directed at men more than women. Socrates calls him an "erotic man" and notes that he takes a romantic interest in beautiful boys of all kinds.[5] At a certain point in *Republic*, Glaucon responds very warmly to a suggestion that soldiers get kisses as a reward for bravery, and insists that they also be given the right to kiss anyone they please without fear of rejection.[6] (A scandalized scholar refers to this as "almost the only passage in Plato that one would wish to blot."[7]) That sounds like a milder version of what Glaucon had earlier imagined the invisible ring-wearer would do: "go into houses and have sex with whomever he wants."

Erotic appetites define the soul of the tyrant, so Glaucon's have the potential to lead him toward tyranny. But philosophy is likewise an erotic activity, as Plato conceives it. In his two dialogues that explore *erôs* most directly, *Symposium* and *Phaedrus*, Plato shows how the libido can lead two seekers of truth—imagined as male, in those works—not toward the bed but toward contemplation of eternals and ultimately of the Forms. Socrates is made to embody this philosophical *erôs*—Platonic love as it later came to be called—in that he's desired by younger men but channels their urges away from sex and toward dialectical inquiry.

Plato does not create any "heat" between Glaucon and Socrates in *Republic*. He instead lets us know, through hints dropped by Socrates, that Glaucon has younger "boyfriends" (*ta paidika* in Greek) and also an older male lover. In Greek terms he's both an *erastês* and an *erômenos*, pursuer and pursued, no longer a youth but not yet fully adult.

Plato's mention of Glaucon's *erastês*, an older man who remains unnamed, has attracted much interest from scholars. Nearly two centuries ago the German Platonist Friedrich Schleiermacher hypothesized that Glaucon's *erastês* is none other than Critias, leader of the regime of the Thirty Tyrants. The idea has intrigued many other experts and some have endorsed it; Debra Nails, author of *The People of Plato*—a meticulous reference work—lists "lover of Glaucon" among the roles she assigns to Critias.[8] The connection can't be proven but makes good sense, in that Glaucon and Critias belonged to the same social class—indeed the same extended family—and thus presumably shared political values. The unnamed *erastês*, moreover, is portrayed as an occasional poet; the historical Critias is known to have dabbled in verse.

Whatever we make of Schleiermacher's thesis, the ghost of Critias lurks behind *Republic* and the problem posed by tyrannical *erôs*. For Critias, as head of the Thirty, had behaved very much like the owner of the ring of invisibility, usurping royal power, killing and thieving at will (see chapter 5). He was infamous too for his sexual appetite. A jest of Socrates, recorded by Xenophon, compares Critias, in his urgent pursuit of a man named Euthydemus, to a pig that can't help rubbing itself against stones.[9] He had an "itch," in Xenophon's view, that compelled him to scratch.

As we've seen, the opening segment of *Republic* is set in the streets of Piraeus, on the very spot where Critias died while attempting to hold onto power. At the end of this chapter we'll come to the question of whether the historical Glaucon died there with him.

Looking ahead to Book 9 of *Republic*, the depiction of tyranny and the tyrannical man, we find that a tyrant's *erôs* pursues not only sex but all kinds of pleasures, especially those of the feast. *Erôs* is compared there to an enormous bee, with other desires swarming around it—"bees" that have fed fat on incense, festal garlands, and wine. The big bee, *erôs*, stings the soul of the tyrant and stirs up a swarm of other desires, inducing a kind of madness. Plato lists "courtesans," female sex workers, among this swarm but gives them no particular emphasis. *Erôs*, as Plato conceives it, transcends the libido; it includes appetites of all kinds.

Glaucon's desires, too, extend beyond sex to fine foods and luxury goods; he's unwilling to go without feasts. We learn this when Plato turns, in *Republic* Book 2, to the principal task of the dialogue, the building of a just city-state.

Recall that *Republic*'s main goal is to find the nature of justice within the human soul, and to do that it posits a parallel between the soul and the city. Whatever can be seen in large "font" in the city can be "read" in smaller letters within the soul. So Socrates leads Glaucon and his brother,

Adeimantus, in a giant thought experiment. Together the three set out to build a virtuous state, in an effort to find where justice lies within it. Once they have found justice there, they hope, they can look to the smaller unit, the soul, and find justice in the analogous spot.

Construction begins with Socrates working beside Adeimantus as Glaucon looks on in silence. The state that the two men build is a largely agrarian commune, designed to meet the most basic needs but little beyond that. Its workers produce houses, clothes, and shoes, while its farmers grow modest foods and grapes to make wine. Merchants and traders play a small part since even this simple society needs a few imports. Begetting of children, and by implication sex, is kept to what's needed for population replacement; any growth in numbers will create a need for expansion, here regarded as something to be avoided. This happy state has no "bees" to stir up desires.

Socrates paints an idyllic picture of a festival meal in this city, with citizens stretched out on reed mats eating barley gruel and wheat cakes. That pleasant idyll, however, causes Glaucon to at last raise his voice, in objection: "It seems you make those who are 'feasting' go without delicacies." Socrates proposes to add cheese, olives, greens, fruits, and nuts to the commune's diet, but Glaucon protests that these are foodstuffs for pigs, not people. At his insistence, Socrates abandons the subsistence city, which he regards as the "healthy" one, and creates a new one that is "fevered."

This second city has luxury goods, fine foods, and *hetaerae*, women who make themselves available for sexual pleasure. The "fevered" city serves as the basis for all the state-building that follows throughout the first half of *Republic*. The "city of pigs" as Socrates calls it—ironically, to modern ears, since we think of pigs as gluttons—is left behind for good, as Glaucon's demands become the dialogue's driving force.

The state-building project has progressed from modest to luxurious feasting. Ascetics like Socrates, Plato seems to be saying, might be content with a whole grain diet and, for recreation, communal hymns to the gods. But the drives of an "erotic man," Glaucon, must be satisfied too, if *any* city is to succeed. Its builders must take account of desires for embroidered couches to dine on, fine goblets to drink from, food that gives more than nutrition, and sex that does more than replace the population. Yet the stings of the *erôs* bees, which goad the erotic soul toward tyranny, must be avoided.

All this connects with Plato's Syracuse journeys, though it also, of course, goes much further. In his visit to Dionysius the Elder, Plato had glimpsed gluttonous eating and drinking and promiscuous sexual mores and drew back in disgust. In his visit to the Younger two decades later, he tried to teach sobriety and restraint as the path to kingship. Much of *Republic* was written between those two journeys and revision was still in progress after the second, according to our best attempts at dating the work. *Republic* thus reflects, in its central concern with finding the right kind of feasts, what Plato encountered in Syracuse in 388, what he failed to achieve on his second visit in 367, and what he might still hope for if he returned.

To satisfy its desires the "fevered" city needs many more people than the "city of pigs": producers of all kinds of goods and suppliers of services. Its demographics require expansion of territory, and expansion (in the Greek world at least) means warfare, so the city also requires an army. *Republic* turns next to recruitment and training of soldiers, or "guards" as it calls them. That topic occupies much of its next three books.

Plato seems not to have fought in the war between Athens and Sparta, though it's not clear why he did not. Scholars have sometimes revised the year of his birth, from the consensus date of 428 BC down to 424, on the assumption he must have been still too young for service, that is, less than twenty, when that war ended in 404. In any case, his two older brothers, Glaucon and Adeimantus, not only fought in the war but won glory in one of its battles, at least according to *Republic*. Glaucon's *erastês*, be that Critias or some other person, is said to have written a poem extolling their heroism, a claim that *Republic* backs up by quoting the opening lines.

Glaucon's warlike spirit, like his eroticism, makes him a promising student for Socrates. It turns out that, for Plato, the part of the soul that seeks victory, honor, and glory—what he termed *thumos*—motivates not only soldiers but also philosophers. Indeed, in the city under construction, soldiers will *be* philosophers, and vice versa. Socrates brings the two roles together in the analogue of the guard dog, a creature that has the aggression to bite its foes but also the wisdom to know whom to bite. With his combination of intellect and highly active *thumos*, Glaucon exemplifies this "dog-like" caste, the Callipolitan guards.

Just as dogs must be properly trained by their masters, these guards must be educated by the master *they* serve, the state. So Plato lays out an educational program for the guard class, focused not only on their soldierly role but also on their souls and minds. The proper training of their children requires censorship of literature, including the banishment of the Greek world's most treasured texts, the poems of Homer and Hesiod. Guard children cannot be taught that the gods behave in the way that Homer's gods do, committing adulteries and rapes and taking petty revenges; they must have better role models. "All people will go easy on themselves when they are bad, if they're convinced that 'the offspring of the gods' did and still do such things," Socrates argues. Since poetry in the Greek world was often set to music, Plato also deals with the music the guards are exposed to; certain kinds have the wrong effect on their souls. They must only hear, or perform, hymns to the gods in uplifting musical modes.

Thus far it has been assumed that the guards form a homogeneous class, but toward the end of Book 3 it emerges that some will be better than others at serving the state. Socrates and Glaucon agree to a sorting process, conducted by unspecified observers. Young guards who show fidelity to the city, in whom education has had the desired effect, will be distinguished as "rulers," the others as "ruled." This is the first time *Republic* has broached the question of rule, and it doesn't say much. The rulers seem to be a meritocratically chosen committee rather than a unitary executive. Those who do not make the cut, the ruled, are henceforth labeled *epikouroi*, "auxiliaries," a word that implies subservient military support.

At this point the state-building project of *Republic* becomes increasingly bizarre, as signaled by Socrates' trepidation in putting proposals forward. The guards, he says, must be convinced that in their prenatal state they took shape within the earth, then were born out of the earth and not from a mother's womb. This "noble lie," as *Republic* terms it, will ensure that the guards treat one another as brothers and the land as a mother that they must protect at all costs. They must also be convinced that the earth, when creating them, infused them with metals of different kinds: gold in the souls of the rulers, silver in the auxiliaries, and iron or bronze in the population at large. Thus each guard will feel that his social role is immutably fixed by his birth (or *her* birth, for it later emerges that women, too, can be guards).

What will prevent these armed and trained guards from preying on fellow citizens? *Republic* solves this problem with other fantastical measures. The guards will not be allowed to have property, land, or wealth. Their food will be supplied by the laboring class (those of bronze and iron); they'll eat together in groups and keep the doors of their dwellings open to all who want to enter. Despite the fact that their natures are gold or silver, they won't be permitted to own or even handle those precious metals. Should they ever gain access to wealth or land, Socrates claims, they'll cease to be guards of the state and become its "masters and enemies."[10]

The problem of predatory guards is framed in *Republic* by a twist on its guard-dog analogy. Shepherds, says Socrates, breed dogs to be their helpers—the term *epikouroi* appears here again—and keep the flocks safe; it would be horrific if these dogs turned out more like wolves, attacking the sheep they are meant to protect. (The idea that guards might need to be bred, as dogs are, will be further explored in chapter 9.) The contrast thus drawn, between the benevolent dog and the menacing wolf, evokes the conceit of Book 1, in which Thrasymachus is said to pounce like a wolf, and also looks ahead to the legend Socrates later tells of the tyrant as werewolf (see chapter 2). Perhaps it also casts a sideways glance at the tyrant Plato knew best, the one he had charged with *lukophilia*, wolf-love.

Glaucon has agreed to all the proposals thus far, but now it is Adeimantus who steps in with an objection. The guards don't seem very happy to him, since they're stripped of so many things he too, like his brother, associates with the good life. Socrates answers by pointing out that the task of the city builders was not to make any one class, or one individual, happy, but the entire state:[11]

Don't force us to attach the kind of happiness to the guards that will make them into anything other than guards. We could wrap farmers in purple robes and adorn them with gold, and tell them to work the soil when they choose. We could stretch potters out on couches before the fire, passing the drinks around from left to right and banqueting, and put the potter's wheel by their side so they may throw pots when the mood takes them . . . but don't advise us to do this, since, if we concede this, the farmer will not be a farmer nor the potter a potter.

Pleasure-seeking becomes an end in itself and replaces one's proper task, a particular danger in the case of the guards; once they cease to be guards, the state is truly at risk. A society of "happy feasters," as Socrates mockingly calls the seekers of pleasure, would "not be a city but a festival."[12]

Correct education, *Republic* affirms, will convince the guards that the tradeoff they make is the right one: By giving up private property, and avoiding the stings of desire, they keep the city safe and collectively happy. And, adds Socrates, casually dropping a bombshell, they must also give up monogamy and childrearing. "The possession of wives, and marriages, and the raising of children must be constructed, insofar as possible, according to the saying 'friends share all things in common,'" he says, blithely proposing the end of all family relations.[13] Discussion of that huge topic then gets postponed to Book 5 (and, in our case, to chapter 9).

The three city-builders agree that their construction is now complete; Callipolis has been founded. Socrates and Glaucon scrutinize their creation to find where its justice lies. After a search that eliminates other virtues, they discover the city is perfectly just when constituent parts each do what they're meant to do, without deviation. Potters throw pots, farmers farm, guardians guard, and rulers rule, ensuring the happiness of the whole. To abandon one's role or take on another's means harming the city, and that is *un*just. So justice has finally been defined, in fulfillment of the quest that began in Book 1. It consists in the principle of "one person, one job," a strict division of classes and social duties.

*Republic* now moves to the search for *individual* justice, for the city was built as the "large-type edition" of qualities found in the soul. Just as the city has three "metals" or classes—the gold, silver, and the conjoined iron and bronze—so the soul, in Plato's analysis, also contains three parts. Examples of internal conflict, when a person is torn over what to do, prove this is so, since such conflicts result from parts of the soul tending in different directions. *Republic* plays out its grand parallel by matching each of the city's three classes to the three parts of the psyche.

We have already looked at two parts of the Platonic soul: the seat of the appetites, including *erôs*—what Plato calls *to epithumêtikon*, "that which desires"—and the drive toward victory and honor, *thumos*. *Thumos* is easily matched with the silver class of the city, the guards, for their soldierly role is defined by that quality. The match between the desires and the iron/bronze class is more problematic, since laborers surely do more than experience appetites. But *Republic* takes little interest in this bottom-most class, and the fit seems close enough for its purpose. That leaves the highest part of the soul, corresponding to the gold or ruling class in the city. Plato calls this *to logistikon*, "the calculating part;" it's the reasoning or rational mind, the seat of philosophic inquiry.

Plato has used the word *epikouroi* when discussing the silver race in Book 3, a word that elsewhere in Greek refers to auxiliary troops. In Book 4 the aptness of the term comes into clearer focus. In healthy souls, *thumos* obeys the reasoning mind and eagerly does its bidding, in the manner that conscripts or hired armies obey a commander. With *thumos* as its ally, reason has strength to restrain or overcome the desires, which otherwise might overwhelm it. It prevents the swarm of *erôs*-bees from stinging the soul into frenzy.

If each element sticks to its role and does its own job, and if *thumos* behaves like a true auxiliary force, the soul remains just, like Callipolis. If, however, *thumos* diverges from its role and allies instead with the seat of desire, the result is the most *un*just kind of soul, the soul of the tyrant.

The building of Callipolis was first launched because Glaucon was at a crossroads, tempted by the views of Thrasymachus but wanting not to heed them. *Republic* depicts him making the right choice and opting for

Socrates and the path of justice. He's so convinced by the end of Book 5 that he does little else throughout the rest of the work except agree with everything Socrates says. First-time readers sometimes find him a tedious yes-man from this point forward—but there may be a darker truth that's not apparent to them and has only been recently hinted at by experts.

We have no historical record of Glaucon's later life, and nothing is known for certain about his activities under the Thirty. Yet in a 2000 book, classicist Mark Munn surmised that Glaucon supported Critias when he led that regime and died in battle alongside him, fighting to preserve the iron grip of the junta. Partial evidence comes from *Republic*, where Glaucon's prowess in battle is praised by an older male lover, a man often identified as Critias, as we've seen. A further hint comes from Plato's account of Socrates' trial in *Apology*, where Plato and Adeimantus are both said to be present as spectators but Glaucon goes unmentioned. There's no good way to account for the omission except to suppose that Glaucon was dead by that time—just five years after the fall of the Thirty. Perhaps, as Munn suggests, he died in the streets of Piraeus, defending authoritarianism.[14]

Munn's idea that Glaucon might well have allied with the Thirty inspired Jacob Howland, who's studied *Republic* for decades, to completely revise his view of the work. In a 2018 book, he writes: "I now strongly suspect something that would have shocked my earlier self: . . . that Glaucon *did* choose tyranny over philosophy."[15] He mounts new arguments for this notion, suggestive but not conclusive. As with so many points in the biographical study of Plato, we must be content with intriguing possibilities.

Howland gives close attention to a passage of *Republic* Book 6 in which Plato examines why promising students sometimes go wrong. A youth with the best kind of soul, Plato has Socrates say, will be assailed by flatterers and manipulators, giving him high hopes of political power. If a teacher tries to tell him he needs to acquire wisdom, he may not listen, and if he does, the flatterers will dissuade him, for fear of losing his "companionship." They'll also try to block his teacher by means of private plots and public ordeals.

The passage has often been taken as a covert description of Alcibiades, the student of Socrates who had gone most clearly astray. Howland proposes it should instead be read as referring to Glaucon, on the assumption that Glaucon, too, had turned away from philosophy and grasped for the wrong kind of power.[16]

Glaucon may indeed have been at the front of Plato's mind if Munn and Howland are right. But the specter of Dionysius the Younger—the man who'd been pulled away from his teacher by plotters and flatterers—is surely lurking behind this passage as well, and behind *Republic*'s abiding interest in various versions of feasting.

Our story now returns to that monarch who'd continued to feast in Plato's absence but who also still wanted Plato's support and, perhaps, his affection.

# ACT III
---
# THE THIRD VISIT

*A detail showing Plato's idealized portrait, from Raphael's fresco* The School of Athens *in the Vatican Apostolic Palace.*

CHAPTER 8

# RETURN TO CHARYBDIS

## (363–360 BC)

The war that had broken out in Sicily was over, and Dionysius deemed it was time to call Plato back.

The understanding he and Plato had reached in 366 BC called for Plato's return to coincide with that of Dion. Now, though, a few years later, Dionysius was seeking to change the terms. He wanted Plato to join him immediately, but he put off Dion's recall for one additional year. It behooved him to keep Dion's restoration as a bargaining chip, to induce Plato to support him more fully.

Despite the breach of the understanding, Dion, who was living in Athens and also spending time in Corinth, urged Plato to accept the new deal and make the voyage. He hoped that his recall might happen more swiftly if Plato advocated in person on his behalf. He'd been advised to this effect by his sister, Aristomachê, and his wife, Aretê, both of whom were in Syracuse, living at close quarters with Dionysius. Plato, however, declined to go, telling both Dionysius and Dion that he was too old for the trip, while also insisting that the original terms be adhered to.[1]

Dion was living off his enormous wealth, buying property in various places while also sharing, in Athens, the home of Callippus, an Academy student. Perhaps he was also buying up mercenaries, for at one point he toured the Peloponnese, where experienced soldiers for hire were in ample supply. He stopped at Sparta during this tour, a city still reeling from its defeat at the hands of the Thebans eight years before. The Spartans were deeply impressed by Dion; his sober habits were in line with their own, where Athenians tended to find him aloof and prickly. Dion was given Spartan citizenship, a surprising honor given that Sparta risked offending Dionysius, an ally in its fight against Thebes.[2]

Plato remained determined not to give in to pressures from Syracuse, but then a vessel arrived in Athens, sent by Dionysius. The tyrant had cleverly stocked the ship with men Plato trusted: Pythagorean sages from Tarentum, associates of the revered Archytas. These Tarentines repeated to Plato what Archytas had already said in a letter: Dionysius was making philosophical progress; there was hope after all for his enlightenment. They also seconded Archytas's concern that Plato's continued absence was harming the new alliance between their city and Syracuse. Plato felt obliged not to desert this alliance, since he had helped engineer it.

The ship also carried a message from Dionysius, according to Plato's report in the *Seventh Letter*. "If, persuaded by me, you come to Syracuse," Dionysius had written, "first of all, the situation concerning Dion will be arranged in whatever way you want; for I know what you want is reasonable and I will agree to it. But if you don't come, none of the matters concerning Dion, whether related to other things or to the man himself, will turn out as you intend."[3] If these were the tyrant's words, he implied that he meant to hold hostage Dion's estate and family and might even someday strike at "the man himself."

Pressure was building on Plato from another quarter, public opinion. If Dionysius *was* inclined to improve his education, and Plato refused to teach him, the Greeks would see the Academy, and all of its talk of philosopher-kings, as so much wasted breath. Plato discusses this concern in his *Seventh Letter*, recalling his state of mind after hearing from the Tarentines. "It occurred to me that there was nothing remarkable if a young man receptive to learning . . . came to have a passion for leading a better life," Plato writes there, referring to Dionysius as "a young man receptive to learning." "And so I thought it was necessary to test how this matter stood and in no way to abandon it or to become the cause of very great reproach."[4] He dreaded being seen as a *logos*, a man of mere words, if he failed to respond to an earnest outreach.

But the danger of being blamed for not going had to be weighed against the opposite danger. Suspicions regarding Plato's ulterior motives, of the kind later put in the mouth of Diogenes the Cynic, had likely already arisen. A second visit within five years to a man of enormous wealth and power could only fuel those suspicions. And so Plato stayed put for a year, as letters streamed in from Dionysius and others in the Greek West.

At some point Plato wrote to Dionysius explaining his reluctance to go, in words that he later paraphrased in the *Third Letter*. He'd become aware, he said, that Dionysius's riches had attracted a flock of flatterers and rumor-mongers; he suspected these men would fend off any rival. He expressed his concern to Dionysius that "you will not be able to hold out against those who use slander and want us to come into enmity."[5] He feared both the damage that Philistus and the hardliners could do, by whispering that Plato's teachings were part of a coup attempt, and the cold reception he'd get from the hedonists, who regarded him as an ideological foe.

In short, Syracuse still presented a maelstrom of perils to Plato; the crosscurrents he'd dealt with poorly on his previous visit had only become more treacherous. In the end, though, the urgings of Dion and the Tarentines, and the hope that Dionysius was bent on philosophy, won out. "With many fears and poor prophecies," Plato writes, "I blindfolded myself" into thinking that all might be well.[6]

Maelstroms and crosscurrents were indeed on Plato's mind as he boarded Dionysius's trireme and set off for Sicily. The Greeks had identified the island as the setting for portions of Homer's *Odyssey*, including the episode of the whirlpool, Charybdis, that sucked ships down to their doom. In the *Seventh Letter* Plato quotes a verse from Homer's poem that occurred to him as he contemplated his choice: *"so that I'd remeasure the distance to dire Charybdis."*[7]

In that verse Odysseus, shipwrecked and alone, describes how he'd drifted on a raft made of wreckage toward dangers he'd barely survived on an earlier passage. For Plato, making a second Sicilian trip within six years' time, the quotation was all too apt. He, too, was bound on a path through hazardous straits—the turbulent narrows of a tyrant's court.

In Syracuse, the hardliners made ready to take advantage of Plato's return. They had devised an ingenious plan by which Plato could be blamed for things that went wrong in Dionysius's reign. Before, they had claimed to the tyrant that Plato and Dion meant to overthrow him; they'd succeeded in getting Dion exiled with that ploy. Now, they could claim to the public that failures in Syracuse, or in the broader arena of Sicily, were all Plato's fault. In a strategy used by autocracies everywhere, they sought to support the sovereign by finding a fall guy.

Some things were indeed going wrong for Dionysius. The cost of his standing army was huge, and his treasury was depleted, as seen in his trouble borrowing money abroad (see chapter 6). He had himself helped create this crunch by proclaiming a tax holiday for the first three years of his reign, a measure designed to win the love of his people.[8] Foreign affairs had suffered as a result of the shortfall, since projecting power abroad required full coffers. The cities of eastern Sicily remained in danger of losing their Greek identity, the outcome Plato dreaded. Publicly the tyrant's regime supported re-Hellenization, but it also needed lands and homes to award to its veteran soldiers, most of whom were non-Greek.

On his previous visit Plato had made the case that the tyrant had to reform his own nature before undertaking efforts at larger reform. He surely hadn't expected to turn Dionysius into a true philosopher; his principal goal was changing his lifestyle, then, if that worked, persuading him to accept restraints on his power. But on his return, Plato raised expectations of what the tyrant might strive for. Soon after arriving he gave his student a test, as he describes in his *Seventh Letter*—a test that he must have supposed Dionysius would fail.

Plato devised the test based on what he knew of his better students, who had shown an ardent desire for philosophy. Some had journeyed to Athens from far away or had given up previous lives; a woman from the Peloponnese, Axiothea, is said to have disguised herself as a man in order to study with Plato.[9] Those less devoted however had behaved, in Plato's memorable simile, like people seeking a suntan; they wanted a veneer of learning without great exertions. Plato decided that Dionysius must show which class he belonged to.

Upon arriving at Syracuse in the Spring of 361, Plato, as he says in the *Seventh Letter*, revealed to Dionysius the effort required to reach the highest goals of philosophy. Predictably, the reaction was disappointing. "He made out that he himself knew sufficiently much of this, and the most important parts, through hearing from others," Plato writes.[10] The dismissive response convinced Plato not to continue the teaching sessions begun on his previous visit. The high hopes he'd formed for Dionysius, based on reports he'd received, were already dashed.

No sooner had the lessons been discontinued than teacher-student relations went swiftly downhill. Observers at court, including the hedonist Aristippus, were hardly surprised by the slide, as seen in an exchange that took place in mid-May. A sage named Helicon—the man sent by Plato years before to offer the tyrant instruction—had predicted a solar eclipse in that month, and when it occurred, Dionysius awarded the man a talent of silver. Aristippus, ever alert for handouts, announced, winkingly, that he too could predict an event. When urged to reveal what it was, he said, "I predict that in a short time, Plato and Dionysius will be enemies to one another."[11] It turned out to be a safe bet.

Dion's estate once again became a bone of contention between Plato and the tyrant. For five years Dion had been receiving its proceeds, on condition he did not use the money to hire soldiers. Suddenly, soon after Plato arrived, Dionysius ordered the shipments of funds to be stopped. He claimed the estate belonged not to Dion but Dion's son, Hipparinus, and that the boy—his own nephew—was legally *his* ward, not Dion's. He meant to stiffen Dion's sentence from what the Greeks called *metastasis*, loss of homeland without loss of property, to *phugê*, loss of both. "I saw perfectly clearly what zeal Dionysius had for philosophy," Plato remarks with a sneer.[12]

What provoked Dionysius to make this move, an obvious slap in the face to Plato? Perhaps he had gotten word that Dion was using his wealth to recruit armed force; indeed Dion's tour through the Peloponnese might have had exactly this goal. Perhaps the coldness the tyrant had felt from Plato, or the cutting off of his lessons, prompted him to give up on staying friends with the sage, as he might have done by better treatment of Dion. A third explanation, undoubtedly part of the picture, is simply that Dionysius needed the money.

To show his displeasure over the tyrant's decision, Plato declared his intention to leave for home. His outrage was such that he even thought of making straight for the harbor and getting on board the readiest ship, at risk of being arrested. Instead he confronted the tyrant face to face, telling him "it was impossible for me to remain when Dion was being spattered with mud in this way." He knew, as Dionysius did, that his sudden departure would badly mar the regime, as would any attempt to detain him by force. Already he was under a thinly concealed house arrest; the gatekeeper of the royal complex in which he was housed would not let him pass without orders from the palace.[13]

Dionysius tried to convince Plato to stay, then agreed to arrange his departure. But the next day he took a different approach, speaking to Plato in coaxing tones. "Let's get Dion and his property out of our way, you and I, so they will no longer be the cause of our frequent disputes," Dionysius said, in words Plato quotes.[14] He proposed a trusteeship for Dion's estate with Plato to serve as trustee and to guarantee good behavior. The moveable wealth could be taken by ship to Dion's new homes, in Athens and the Peloponnese, and placed in escrow there, such that Dion could draw on the interest but not on the principal sum, unless Plato approved.

The tyrant proposed that Plato accompany Dion's money and goods to Athens to ensure their safety. By taking on this oversight role, he predicted, Plato would earn Dion's gratitude. But, he implied, the shipment could not be got ready until the following year. If Plato wanted to help his friend, he'd have to stay where he was.

Plato agreed to think the matter over. That night in his rooms, he pondered his dilemma, in thoughts he recollects in the *Seventh Letter*. He understood by now that any bargain he made with the tyrant might be revoked, but he was wary as well of a disinformation campaign. If he refused the deal and insisted on leaving, then *he* might be blamed for Dion's plight, as a result of letters and rumors that Dionysius could generate. How terrible if the Greek world at large, but especially Dion, saw *him* as a faithless friend! In any case, Plato reasoned, he could not depart Syracuse without permission, which the tyrant might now withhold no matter what Plato did. If he gratified Dionysius and stayed for the year, he at least had a chance that the deal would hold up and he'd leave for Athens as promised. In the meanwhile he could write to Dion explaining the situation.

The next day, the tyrant and sage met again. Plato agreed to the terms of the year-long stay, with one further condition: that he and Dionysius send a joint letter to Dion, outlining the trust arrangement and seeking approval. Evidently Plato felt that a written proposal, undersigned by the tyrant, would have the force of a contract, especially if it landed in Dion's hands. Plato also asked that no further harm come to Dion while the letter and Dion's reply were in transit. Whether that letter was sent, Plato does not say.

Plato stayed on in Syracuse as autumn arrived and stormy winds started to blow. As soon as the sailing season had closed, Dionysius announced a new plan. He would *sell* half of Dion's estate and keep the proceeds in trust for Dion's young son. Plato was staggered but realized the futility of protest. Lamely, he told Dionysius they ought to write to Dion again describing this new arrangement. He must have known that all correspondence had become meaningless.

Plato had been outplayed and entrapped, even more completely than on his previous visit. In striving to better Dion's fate he'd made it far worse, and lost his own freedom of movement into the bargain. It was going to be a long winter.

While Plato settled in for his stay on the Island, his nephew, Speusippus, was meeting the public in other sectors of Syracuse. Speusippus had accompanied Plato on this voyage; he too had become a close friend of Dion during Dion's sojourn in Athens. Plato had encouraged that friendship, in hopes that the strait-laced Dion might loosen up through contact with Speusippus, who was said to be good with a joke.[15] The confiscation of Dion's estate, however, was no jesting matter. The rift in the tyrant-house was becoming distressingly wide.

As he talked with the Syracusans he met, Speusippus raised the question of action against the Dionysius regime. Those he approached were hesitant to speak freely, fearing that their loyalty was being tested. Over time, though, Speusippus won their trust and drew out their candid opinions. The consensus view, as reported by Plutarch, was that, if Dion returned to Syracuse in arms and offered himself as their leader, they'd rise up as one to overthrow Dionysius. In fact, they said, Dion wouldn't need soldiers or weapons; if he merely rowed alone, in a dinghy, to Sicily's shores, they'd line up behind him and form an army of revolution.[16]

It's not clear whether Plato approved of his nephew asking the sort of questions that opened the door to revolt. In the *Seventh Letter* Plato opposes the overthrow of standing regimes. "A person of sense," he writes, "must not use force against his own land in order to change the government, if the land seems to him badly governed. . . . He should stay inactive and pray that good things may result for himself and his city."[17] But this passivity, as he no doubt understood, was exactly what tyrants relied on. If no one risked bloodshed in a city under an autocrat's boot, how could things ever change?

Plato had grown up among Athenians who lionized "the Tyrant-slayers," Harmodius and Aristogeiton, who'd helped liberate their city a century before. He'd walked many times past the statues that showed the pair preparing to strike with dagger and sword at the two brothers who then ruled Athens (they killed one of the two). In a popular ditty sung at drinking parties, young Athenians vowed to emulate Harmodius and carry a blade concealed in a bough of myrtle, as he had done, to slay any tyrant. Plato, no doubt, had heard it sung many times.

When Plato was in his teens, Athens instituted an oath, administered in a solemn rite, that deputized all citizens to take up arms against tyrants. The oath-taker vowed: "I shall kill, by both word and deed, by my vote and by my own hand, anyone who overthrows the democracy at Athens."[18] The oath included a promise that anyone who murdered a tyrant would be amply rewarded and would not incur blood-guilt. Remarkably, when Athenians in 403 BC overthrew the Thirty—who had not yet been dubbed the Thirty Tyrants—they did not execute surviving junta members but allowed them to go into exile. Still they continued to sing the Harmodius song and recite the oath.

Elsewhere in Greece, in the era of Plato and Dionysius, tyranni-cide was becoming increasingly common. Evagoras, the ruler of Greek Cyprus, was struck down by a dagger in 374 BC, though in his case the

*The Athenian tyrannicide oath, inscribed on a stele of the late fourth century BC. The scene at top shows Democracy crowning the people.*

motive may have been personal, not political. Four years further on the Greek world was shocked by the killing of Jason of Pherae, a warlord who'd come to control much of Thessaly thanks to his mercenaries. A group of seven conspirators approached him as he drilled these troops, pretending to argue among themselves, then stabbed him to death. A few years later, Timophanes, who'd seized power in Corinth with the help of hired toughs, was killed in a plot engineered by his brother, Timoleon (whom we shall meet again at this story's close).

The new emphasis on assassination as a way to overthrow tyrants attests to the threat that autocracy posed in mid-fourth-century Greece. More so than before, strongmen could arise out of nowhere, profiting from the disorders of previous decades: Wars and upheavals had created a pool of dispossessed men, experienced soldiers whose best hope lay in service as mercenaries. Money could buy an army and an army could seize a city, then form a protective wall around the man who led them. Dionysius the Elder had set the template, and Jason had followed suit; other caudillos would emulate their spectacular successes.

Plato never endorses assassination as a means to fight tyranny, and in the *Seventh Letter* he explicitly rules it out. But tough times called for tough measures. Academy students were to become assassins on at least two occasions, in 360 and 353, as we'll see in chapter 12. In Syracuse another Academy member, Speusippus, was raising the question of the toughest measure of all—violent regime change.

Behind the walls of Dionysius's palace, where Plato dwelt (as he says) like a bird looking out of a cage, life went on as though nothing untoward had happened. Since the tyrant had seized only half of Dion's estate, Plato had reasons not to offend, lest Dion lose the other half, too. Then one day, without consultation, Dionysius snipped the cord by which he'd held on to Plato's good will. Behaving "like a headstrong youth," as Plato describes him, he sold off the *entire* estate, on any terms and to any buyers he chose.[19] As guardian of Dion's son he could keep control of the proceeds.

Plato raised no objection; there was no point any longer. The terms of the deal under which he had stayed had been completely revoked. He must have wondered whether his departure the following year would also be canceled, since nothing Dionysius had promised had yet come to pass. But soon, new troubles arose that put him in more immediate danger.

Financial shortfalls were catching up to the tyrant. The taxes he had once remitted had been reinstated, but even so, the budget gap could not be closed. Dionysius foolishly tried to close it by cutting the pay of his hired guards. This precipitated a crisis.

The mercenaries gathered en masse on the Island to protest the pay cut. Dionysius locked the gates of his palace, but this only further enraged the soldiers. They started to storm the acropolis walls, raising war-cries in their various non-Greek tongues. Terrified, Dionysius backtracked. He not only withdrew the cuts he'd imposed but even increased the salary of his peltasts, the light-armed troops who formed his crack security corps. Only after extracting this bribe did the soldiers stand down.

The crisis passed but the tyrant had been humiliated, and a scapegoat had to be found. Blame for the uprising fell on a man named Heraclides, a friend of both Dion and Plato. As a guard commander, he may have had a hand in provoking the mutiny, but his connection to Dion also made him a target. In going after Heraclides, the tyrant was casting further disgrace on his brother-in-law and, by association, on Plato as well.

On learning he was being pursued, Heraclides went into hiding. Dionysius called in Theodotes, the wanted man's uncle, to get information. The two were conversing in the palace's open-air courtyard when Plato happened to pass nearby. In a scene recounted by Plato in the *Seventh Letter*, Theodotes called out to the sage, recognizing him as an ally. Plato had at this point opted out of politics but could not ignore a friend in obvious need. He walked over to the pair and became enmeshed in their parley.[20]

Theodotes called on Plato to witness his effort to save his nephew's life. He'd been trying to strike a deal with the tyrant: Heraclides would leave Sicily forever and move to the Peloponnese, and take no action from there against the regime, if his life could be spared. Perhaps influenced by Plato's presence, Dionysius agreed to this trade-off. "Even if Heraclides is found in *your* house," he told Theodotes, "he'll suffer no ill treatment that's out of line with what we've discussed." Thus was the matter resolved—for the moment.

The very next day Plato answered a knock on his door to find Theodotes in an agitated state, accompanied by a certain Eurybius. Despite what the tyrant had promised, Theodotes said, peltasts were on the hunt for Heraclides, who was hiding nearby and might be discovered at any moment. Plato agreed to go with the men and once again confront Dionysius. The scene that resulted is memorably evoked in the *Seventh Letter*.

Theodotes and Eurybius, terrified, silently wept in Dionysius's presence, leaving the more composed Plato to speak on their behalf. "These men are afraid lest you take some action against Heraclides, contrary to what was agreed yesterday," Plato said. Dionysius flew into a red-faced rage, prompting Theodotes, still weeping, to take his hand and beg for his kinsman's life. "Take heart, Theodotes," said Plato admonishingly, "for Dionysius won't dare to do anything other than what was agreed to yesterday."

Dionysius looked straight at Plato and spoke "like a tyrant," in Plato's recounting. "I didn't agree to anything with you, either large or small," he declared.

"By the gods you did," Plato insisted. "You promised the things that this fellow here is begging you not to do." And with that, he turned and walked out of the room. A show of outrage was his only counter. He'd seen once again how little sway a philosopher had when dealing with autocrats.

In desperation, Theodotes contrived to send his nephew a message: There was no hope left; he must run. Heraclides made it safely to Carthaginian territory just an hour or two ahead of the tyrant's troops.

Plato and Dionysius became even further estranged. The tyrant used an upcoming religious rite, a time when the palace grounds would be needed by female celebrants, as a pretext to remove Plato from his lodgings. Plato was relocated to the home of a Tarentine, Archedemus. All he could do now was wait for the weather to turn.

Back in Athens, several of Plato's fellow Socratics—those who'd once followed Socrates as Plato did but had since taken different paths—were trying, each in his own way, to correct the excesses of autocratic regimes. Xenophon and Isocrates, contemporaries of Plato, were publishing open letters, speeches, and dialogues in the 360s BC, addressing themselves to great monarchs past or present. Neither made mention of Plato, but both seem to have been influenced by what they were hearing about the Syracuse project. If one-man rule was to be a way forward for Greece, and if ethical thinkers were guiding rulers, then they, too, wanted to play their part.

Xenophon, in fact, chose Syracuse for the setting of a meditation on monarchy, a dialogue today known as *Hieron*. The titular figure is the tyrant Hieron, who, in the fifth century BC, had succeeded his brother Gelon as tyrant of Syracuse. Xenophon imagines Simonides, a poet who'd come to live at court, questioning Hieron about the life of a tyrant, then advising him on how to become a better and happier ruler. The scenario bears a striking resemblance to Plato's visits to Dionysius the Younger, especially since the work was composed, as it seems, just after those visits took place.[21]

In Xenophon's dialogue, Simonides starts by asking Hieron to describe the pleasures a tyrant's life brings. He's surprised to hear that there are none. Hieron complains that he cannot enjoy his food, since there's always so much on the table that he never gets hungry; he can't enjoy sex since his partners are too compliant; he's not gratified by the honors paid him, since these, as he knows, spring from fear, not true admiration.

Hieron goes on lamenting, in words that seem based on the Dionysius regime. He complains that he's forced to undermine worthy men in order to head off threats and instead to elevate toadies. He must plunder shrines and shake down the rich to raise money and pay his troops, or else perish—"as though there was permanent war." He claims he'd gladly put aside power and become a private citizen, but even this is denied him, for if he once relaxes his grip, his victims and foes would destroy him.

Simonides hears out this unhappy tale, then, in the dialogue's final segment, offers a remedy. He tells Hieron that by basing his power on the love of his subjects, rather than on their fears, he can have the pleasures he seeks. Hieron, he says, should assign to others—he doesn't say whom— the unpleasant tasks of punishing, forcing, and pressuring Syracusans, but reserve for himself the awarding of prizes and honors. He should offer prizes liberally, for inventions, for upright behavior, for new institutions of all kinds (including for "some painless way of raising revenue," an expedient Hieron will clearly need). As for the tyrant's bodyguard, Simonides concedes that the troops must be kept in service ("for there are villains in cities, as we all know") but detailed to protect the citizen body as well as the ruler. Hieron's mercenaries can, in effect, serve as his city's police force.

Xenophon's prescriptions for moderate rule, delivered through the words of Simonides, overlap with advice that Plato and Dion were giving, at nearly the same moment, to Dionysius the Younger. Those men, too, were urging a Syracusan monarch onto a path that would win him true allies and loyal supporters in place of mere lackeys. But the place where that path began, for Plato and Dion—geometry and abstract notions of virtue—was a place that hard-headed Xenophon never would choose as a starting point. His path toward a happy monarchic state was instead paved with handouts and economic advancement.

Xenophon might have picked any monarch as the audience of his lessons, so it's interesting that he chooses a Syracusan. Some scholars suppose, reasonably, that he meant to aim *Hieron* directly at Dionysius the Younger,[22] offering him a different kind of reform than the one preached by Plato. The idea has merit, given *Hieron*'s emphasis on pleasure: Simonides' goal is to steer the tyrant toward better *enjoyment* of power. Dionysius would have been highly receptive to a guide for getting the most out of food, drink, and sex.

While Xenophon looked westward in composing his *Hieron*, another Socratic, Isocrates, was looking to the East. On Cyprus—an island contested, as Sicily was, between Greeks and Phoenicians—a ruler named Nicocles had come to power in 374 BC, succeeding his father Evagoras. Pinning on this young man similar hopes to those that Plato would pin on Dionysius, including the hope of Greek pushback against a non-Greek foe, Isocrates addressed three essays, in the form of fictional speeches, to Nicocles during the 370s and 360s BC. His trilogy is known today as the Cyprian orations. To no other ruler did Isocrates give such attention, though he wrote letters and dedicated speeches to many, including, as we have seen, to Dionysius the Elder.

Nicocles was only a little past twenty when he took over the throne of his father, who'd been a popular king but nonetheless died by an assassin's hand. Isocrates was then in his seventies; he'd been teaching at Athens for more than two decades, even longer than Plato. There's no evidence that Nicocles sought advice from him, but Isocrates was not one to wait to be asked. In *To Nicocles* he assails the young monarch with long lists of precepts; their overriding message, like Xenophon's in *Hieron*, is that a true king must earn love from his subjects, not inspire fear. In another part of the trilogy, *Evagoras*, he eulogizes Nicocles' dead father for his success at this strategy, holding him up as a model for the son.

At various points in the Cyprian orations Isocrates contrasts himself, implicitly, with Plato, as well as with other teachers of "philosophy." Different schools follow different approaches, he tells Nicocles, yet all concur that, in the end, the goal is to make good decisions. So the question to ask of teachers is whether *they* have made good decisions and how they have handled problems they have encountered. Since Isocrates prided himself on achieving success in practical terms, in contrast to the airy Academy—"gymnastics of the soul . . . a training that's of no help in the here and now either toward speaking or doing"[23]—this advice was a kind of self-promotion. His efforts evidently bore fruit, for Isocrates admits in a later oration that Nicocles bestowed on his school a large sum of money.[24]

In *Evagoras*, Isocrates makes the surprising claim that Nicocles is "the first and only one of those in monarchic power . . . who has undertaken to study philosophy."[25] The date of the speech is difficult to determine but two experts put it at 365 BC, just after Plato's first sojourn with Dionysius the Younger.[26] If that date is correct or nearly so, then this claim of priority constitutes yet one more way of one-upping Plato. Whatever was going on in Syracuse, Isocrates may have been saying, was not philosophy but only "gymnastics of the soul."

Isocrates' Cyprian project came to an end when Nicocles was killed, probably in battle, in the late 360s. But the indefatigable orator reached out to other rulers who had recently ascended their fathers' thrones. He wrote didactic letters to Archidamas of Sparta (356 BC), to the children of Jason of Pherae (354), and to Timotheus of Heraclea (345), all of whom were young and untried and had taken the places of towering patriarchs. He sensed that the accession of such junior monarchs gave an elder sage like himself a natural opening—much the same judgment that Dion and Plato had made.

The spate of efforts by ethicists, in the second quarter of the fourth century, to give instruction to tyrants coincides with the increase in Greek esteem for tyrannicide slayings. Both trends can be seen as responses to the rise of strongman rule as other political systems deteriorated. Some Greeks were hoping the new autocrats could be trained to rule moderately, while others thought they simply had to be killed.

Everyone kept a watchful eye on Syracuse, for it was not yet clear which of the two paths might work there. Or were the adamantine bonds that Dionysius the Elder had forged too strong to be either bent or broken?

A few months had passed of the year that Plato had promised to spend in Syracuse, and the rift between him and Dionysius was wider than ever. The two kept up an appearance of amity, but the pretense was wearing thin.

Was the dismal outcome inevitable? Any teacher who's become estranged from a student has had to confront this question. Perhaps with a different approach, more indulgent and less demanding, Plato might have brought out the good side of Dionysius, the side that Archytas had seen. Perhaps if Plato had let go of his favored curriculum, the one that began with geometry, and moved straight to practical matters as Isocrates did, his lessons might have gained purchase. Perhaps if he'd shown less concern over Dion.... The question of Dion's estate had driven a wedge between sage and ruler, and the gap grew larger as the estate grew smaller. Plato had felt that he must stand up for his friend's right to use his own wealth, but Dionysius had feared—perhaps for good reason—that Dion's wealth was being used against *him*.

There are signs that, even after the Heraclides affair, Dionysius still cherished hopes of winning Plato's allegiance. But the aftermath of the episode opened another breach between ruler and sage.[27]

A messenger came to Archedemus's home, where Plato was now residing, and delivered a message. Theodotes, consumed with rage at the way he'd been lied to, was asking Plato to pay him a visit. He needed to vent his anger to the one person who understood what had happened, who'd seen first-hand the arrogance of the tyrant. Plato went to visit with Theodotes and lent a compassionate ear. His comings and goings, though, were at this point being observed by Dionysius's spies.

A short while later, when Plato had returned to his lodgings, another messenger arrived, this one from Dionysius. The man asked Plato tersely if he'd been to see Theodotes, and Plato replied that he certainly had done so. "In that case," the messenger said, "he bid me tell you"—there was no need to specify who was the "he" of that sentence—"that you are in no way acting well, always preferring Dion and the friends of Dion to *him*." The petulant tone is revealing; Dionysius still had enough at stake to feel hurt.

Plato was now removed to a less hospitable home, in the sector of the Island where mercenaries were housed. Among these hired soldiers was a squad of Athenian rowers, men sympathetic to Plato on account of their shared homeland. They confided in Plato the talk that they'd heard from other troops in the barracks: Plato, the soldiers were saying, was pushing to limit Dionysius's power and bring about the dismissal of his armed forces. Fearful of losing their livelihood, they were talking of killing Plato if they had a good chance.

There were still months to go before the constellation Pleiades rose above the horizon and signaled the start of the sailing season. No ships were leaving for mainland Greece or arriving from there, but a shorter crossing, between Sicily and Italy, was still possible. Somehow, despite Dionysius's spies, Plato got a message onto a vessel making this crossing and reached out to Archytas of Tarentum. Archytas acted with all the speed the situation required. On pretext of a diplomatic mission, he sent a thirty-oared ship to Syracuse, under command of one Lamiscus, with orders to exfiltrate Plato.

A letter purporting to be a message that Archytas sent with that ship is preserved by one of our sources.[28] It has been dismissed as inauthentic by the few scholars to offer opinions, even though "nothing in it is anachronistic or *per se* suspicious," as Carl Huffman comments in *Archytas of Tarentum*.[29] Huffman lists the letter as one of the "Spurious Writings," those wrongly assigned to Archytas, on grounds that "it looks very much like an elaboration on the story told in the *Seventh Letter*" of Plato. As often in authorship debates, the argument cuts two ways: Consistency with Plato's account could be taken as a mark of genuineness, not the opposite. Huffman also notes that the letter speaks of a second envoy, Photidas, sent with the rescue ship, and that this man is not mentioned by Plato—the kind of extraneous detail one does not expect from a forger.

In the letter, Archytas addresses Dionysius courteously but firmly. "You would do well to remember the zeal with which you bid us all to arrange his [Plato's] arrival here," says the letter-writer, whether Archytas or an impersonator. "Remember also that his arrival meant much to you and that from that point you cherished him more than anyone else at court. If some unpleasantness has now arisen, you must act with humanity and give the man back to us unharmed."

Apart from the promptings of "humanity," Dionysius could no doubt see practical reasons for allowing Plato to leave. If any harm came to Greece's most revered thinker, the tyrant's reputation would suffer a grave setback. Perhaps Dionysius welcomed the Tarentine ship's arrival as a way out of an unpleasant standoff. His acquiescence is noted matter-of-factly by Plato, without any hint of vainglory: "He concurred [with Lamiscus] and sent me away, with a grant for travel expenses."[30] The Syracuse project was over.

During the preparations for Plato's departure, a final, tense encounter took place between the sage and the tyrant, as recorded by Plato in his *Third Letter*.[31] The setting was the garden within the palace compound, where Plato had no doubt been summoned for some sort of parley. Dionysius was attended by two learned men, Archedemus and another respected thinker. He wished to make clear, in the presence of these witnesses, what had gone wrong in the past six years and who was to blame.

"Do you remember when you first arrived here, you advised me to resettle the Greek cities?" the tyrant asked, referring to Plato's re-Hellenization plan for eastern Sicily. The question was posed as a taunt; the plan was at that point seen as wrongheaded, perhaps because of the strain it would put on the budget.

Plato replied that he did remember, and that this still seemed to him the best course of action. "But," he asked, like a teacher quizzing his student, "did I say anything else in addition to that?"

With a forced and bitter laugh that derided the long-ago lessons, Dionysius said, "I remember well; you told me to get educated first and *then* do these things, or not do them."

"You have an excellent memory," said Plato.

"Then did you mean, get educated in *geometry*—or what?" The question dripped with ridicule.

There was much Plato could have said in reply, but he was aware that his leave to depart could easily be revoked. He kept silent, and the two men parted. The breakup of the "wolf-friendship"—as Plato termed their strange bond, casting Dionysius as wolf and himself, presumably, as prey—was complete.

Plato sailed from Sicily three weeks later. He'd once been told he could bring Dion's wealth with him when he left, and he seems to have held out some hope that this still might occur. But nothing was proffered and Plato did not inquire. Presumably he sailed for Tarentum, there to await fair weather for crossing to Greece.

In his second round of skirmishing with Dionysius the Younger, Plato had fared even worse than during the first. His entry into practical politics had been a colossal failure. "In the machinations of the Syracusan court Plato was little better than a child," writes historian Peter Brunt.[32]

Brunt compares Plato's Syracuse misadventure to a prominent passage of *Republic*. As we've seen, in the cave allegory, the philosopher whose eyes have beheld the sun—the light of the Forms—is obliged to return to the cave but finds himself blind and helpless when he reenters. As he stumbles and gropes in the dark, those who have never left the cave regard him as a madman and seek to harm or kill him. The troubling passage is usually read as a covert allusion to the execution of Socrates.

Brunt adduces this part of *Republic* as his own analogue for the Syracuse project, not one intended by Plato. But there's every reason to take that further step. Syracuse was well known for its caves, the Latomiae caverns in which its prisoners were held. In lamenting the blindness of the returning philosopher, Plato may well have been writing about himself.

Texte

*In a fifteenth-century manuscript, the god Cronus presides over the golden age of the world.*

# CHAPTER 9

# THE EVILS OF CHANGE

The Greek word *neôterizein*, literally "to make new," might seem to have a positive tone, but in fact it was almost always something to be avoided. By the start of the fourth century BC the word had come to mean "carry out a revolution," and, since that was usually done by force, a secondary meaning, "use violence," also emerged. The Greeks of Plato's day had seen many cities convulsed by change; few had stayed stable or evolved peacefully. Whatever was "new" in civic life was seen as destructive and bad. The happiest regime was one that kept its status quo for the longest time.

Greek cities cast about for ways to freeze their constitutions in place. Athens adopted a parliamentary move called *graphê paranomôn*, "writ of illegality," designed to instantly quash a proposal that seemed out of line with the standing order. A person who made an assembly motion risked a steep fine, or even loss of citizen rights, if this charge was leveled against him and then upheld by a court. In two Greek cities in Italy, Locri and Thurii, a citizen who wanted to change a law had to propose his change with his head in a hangman's noose. If the change was approved by an on-the-spot vote, the proposer went free, but if not, he was instantly hanged. At Thurii this measure was so effective that only three revisions, we're told, were ever proposed; at Locri, only one in two hundred years.[1]

Sparta was widely considered the best-governed state in that it had seen the fewest innovations. Its unique governmental structure and social customs, supposedly first prescribed by the oracle of Delphi, were thought to have endured for centuries.[2] The lawgiver who'd transmitted the oracle's mandates, Lycurgus, had helped ensure with his death that the city would never change. Before going off again to consult Delphi as to whether his system was good, he'd reportedly made the Spartans swear that they'd leave things as they were until he returned. After getting the oracle's blessing for his law code, Lycurgus, according to legend, starved himself to death there in Delphi. Since he never returned to Sparta, the oath he'd extracted remained in effect forever.[3]

By class and family background, Plato was predisposed to laconism, or admiration of Sparta; the Greek upper classes, to which he belonged, skewed that direction. His kinsman Critias—the man who headed the Thirty—published a tract that effusively praised the Spartans, including even the shoes they wore and the cups they drank from.[4] Spartan social strictures overlapped to a great degree with Plato's own morals. Spartan males dined frugally, as students and teachers at the Academy did; Spartan drinking habits and sexual mores were famously restrained. The Spartans exemplified what Plato praised, in both *Republic* and the *Seventh Letter*, as the "Dorian" lifestyle, the temperate habits to which he'd converted Dion but failed to convert Dionysius the Younger even with Dion's help.

What most attracted Plato to Sparta was its resistance to change. Its constitutional fixity aligned with Plato's ideas, especially his notion that true and knowable things—the Forms—never change, while their copies, things found in the physical world, inevitably deteriorate. A circle drawn with the hand is imperfect and also impermanent; its image will fade or the surface on which it is drawn will warp. By contrast "circleness" stays always the same. Just so, the Form of a city-state would always remain as it is; any change would be for the worse.

In *Republic* Plato set out to create an unchanging city. Just as the Forms stand outside space and time, in a realm that does not know decay, the city of *Republic*, Callipolis, stands outside history. So long as it keeps to a strict set of guidelines, and to a strange mathematical formula by which they are said to be governed, it escapes the gravitational pull that drags other states ever downward until they become the worst type of regime, tyranny. Once a city had reached that bottom, to lead it back upward was tremendously difficult, as Plato was learning in Syracuse.

For his unchanging city-state in *Republic*, Plato leaned heavily on the Spartan model. But in laying down rules for the guards of his city—the silver race—he out-Sparta-ed Sparta in quashing personal freedoms and giving the state control over private life. The most private arena of life, in fact, sexual relations, is the one that Plato regarded as most in need of control, as we shall see.

The statist design of Callipolis has opened Plato up to some of the harshest attacks leveled at any philosopher, ancient or modern. Within the past century he has been charged with a fascist agenda, with supporting "the totalitarian class rule of a naturally superior master race," and even with seeking to make *himself* an all-powerful dictator. The sharpest of these attacks emerged in the middle of the twentieth century, when the advent of European fascism colored many readings of classical texts, but they cannot be dismissed as mere historical relics.

Did Plato go so far wrong in *Republic* as to justify the very despotism he seems to despise? Is it possible that Callipolis, "Beautiful City," is in fact distressingly ugly?

We have already seen (in chapter 7) some aspects of state control of private life in *Republic*. The guards, also called the auxiliaries or the silver race, will have no private property or luxury goods, and their education will come through heavily censored music and literature. The segregation of the silver and gold races from each other, and of both from the iron and bronze—the laborers who produce their food and other essentials—will be strictly maintained, in part by the "noble lie," as it is called in *Republic*. By propagating the myth that its people are born from the earth, the leaders of Callipolis seek to prevent any mixing of silver into gold or of iron or bronze into silver—that is, to prevent any crossing of "racial" lines.

Plato makes clear the importance of such separation by the amount of space he gives to it in *Republic* and the severity of the work's proposals.

If a silver child is born to golden parents, the baby must be demoted to the silver class, just as a golden child born to silver parents must be elevated. (Presumably these "off-race" births result from adulterous unions, though Plato does not specify.) If a child born to gold or silver parents has an admixture of iron or bronze, this child must be "pushed out" into the farming and manufacturing cohort. Plato admits (through the voice of Socrates) that such demotions will require those who carry them out to suppress their feelings of pity. Fixity requires unflinching resolve.[5]

Plato's proposals for keeping the metals distinct discomfit many modern readers in light of the way racial theories have been put to use by fascist dictatorships. Two important attacks on Plato and especially on *Republic*—Richard Crossman's *Plato Today* and Karl Popper's *The Spell of Plato* (the first volume of *The Open Society and Its Enemies*), both written during the 1930s and 1940s—focus on its enforced divisions of classes/metals/races. Crossman, in a chapter that compares *Republic*'s philosopher-king to a fascist dictator, equates the "noble lie" with the Nazis' anti-Semitic propaganda. Popper, who took inspiration from Crossman, refers to the "noble lie" as "the Myth of Blood and Soil," invoking the infamous nineteenth-century phrase embraced by Hitler and his regime.[6]

But the "noble lie" is not the only falsehood that Plato's state needs to safeguard its "racial" boundaries. The leaders of Callipolis, says Plato, will have to invent an oracle predicting that "the city will be destroyed when a bronze or iron man acts as its guard," that is, performs the job of the silver race.[7] Preserving "racial" purity will thus be portrayed as essential to survival.

Book 5 of *Republic* introduces another path toward prevention of mixtures: state-controlled sex lives. "It is necessary," Plato has Socrates say, in one of *Republic*'s most chilling sentences, "that the best men must have intercourse with the best women as often as possible, and the worst with the worst least often; and that the offspring of the former be reared, those of the latter, not, if the flock is to reach its acme."[8] The word flock is meant to startle the reader; it transforms the guards, in essence, into an animal herd. Plato amplifies the point by using other terms derived from animal husbandry and evoking the analogue of horse- and dog-breeding. Greeks of his time were familiar with the use of prize horses for stud; *Republic* dares to apply that method to human reproduction.

How are "the best" to be selected and paired with one another? *Republic* empowers its rulers to arrange these eugenic unions, but directs them to conceal their supervisory role lest anyone contest their choices. Mating lots will be drawn on special festival days to make the assignment of sexual partners appear a matter of chance. In fact, the lots will be rigged by the rulers, based on which guards have given outstanding service or shown the most loyal support of the state. These "best" men will, by means of fake lots, be given more chances to procreate than other, less desirable guards. The use of fake lots will also permit population control, for the rulers must not allow the city to grow too large.

When Plato says that the offspring bred by the best will be reared, but those by the worst will not be, he's being deliberately vague about the fate of the latter. *Republic* goes on to clarify that children born to the worst will be removed at birth "and hidden in a secret and unseen place, as is fitting." Most scholars agree that this cautious language refers to infanticide. Whereas in Book 3 allowance was made for reassignment of "off-race" babies, with the bronze class absorbing those cast out from the silver, here it seems that unworthy infants must simply be destroyed.

The killing of substandard infants is justified, in *Republic*, because it ensures the survival of the state. In Book 8 of the work, Plato reveals that the fictional prophecy he had earlier proposed, "the city will be destroyed when a bronze or iron man acts as its guard," isn't fictional after all; mismatches in sexual unions will indeed usher in the fall of Callipolis. These mismatches occur when the city's rulers ignore a mathematical calculation, termed by modern scholars the Nuptial Number, that ought to govern eugenic pairings. "This entire geometric number is the master of better and worse procreations," Socrates declares, in words that have bewildered generations of readers. "And once your guards ignore these, brides will cohabit with bridegrooms out of season, and their children will be neither well-born nor lucky."[9]

As they mature, these children of poorly matched parents will no longer maintain the strict educational system prescribed for the guards; they'll fail to keep the "races" apart, thus allowing even more "off-race" guards to be born. A feedback loop will set in, leading to strife and violence. "The intermixing of iron and bronze with silver will breed dis-similarity and a discordant unevenness," Socrates predicts, "and once these arise, wherever they arise, they always beget war and enmity."[10]

Once tipped into the realm of change, Callipolis will inevitably slide down the slippery slope of regimes until it reaches the bottommost, tyranny. Ultimately this slide cannot be prevented, *Republic* concedes, "since decay belongs to everything that comes into being." Plato's goal is to hold off the start of deterioration as long as possible. This delay of decay is achieved by use of the Nuptial Number, "the master," as *Republic* terms it, "of better and worse procreations."

Plato's description of how to determine the Nuptial Number is perhaps the most obscure passage in all of his writings. Not only does it involve brain-numbing calculations, bringing together geometry, algebra, and theoretical astronomy, but it's also expressed in extremely opaque Greek. Already in the first century BC, Cicero considered it an outstanding example of obfuscation.[11] James Adam, in his 1902 commentary on *Republic*, devoted a sixty-page appendix to it, as well as footnotes on the passage itself that nearly crowd the Greek text off the page. Many other investigations have been made since Adam's time, none of them considered definitive.

The efforts to find the Nuptial Number are not our concern here, nor would the Number itself have much meaning if we were sure what it is (for the record, the most likely candidates are 216 and . . . 12,960,000). It is, however, worth asking why Plato made this passage so difficult, especially since the Number is vital to the health of the state. In another mathematical passage, in which Socrates measures the happiness gap between the just king and the tyrant, *Republic* delivers up the sum, 729, by a fairly straightforward reckoning (see chapter 1). Why does Plato now speak of "a basal four-thirds wedded to the pempad," "two harmonies at the third augmentation," and "the other dimension of a hundred cubes of the triad"?[12]

As part of his attack on Plato in *The Spell of Plato*, published in 1945 and reissued several times, Karl Popper drew attention to the difficulty

of this passage. In a three-page footnote Popper takes issue with interpretations made by Adam and other scholars, claiming that these "arise
from the tendency to idealize Plato." In his view, the Number's importance in maintaining the state, and the opacity of the way it is calculated,
are merely part of *Republic*'s racist, eugenicist, and authoritarian goals,
which, according to Popper, include Plato's bid to promote *himself* as
absolute ruler.[13]

"Philosophical breeding," Popper writes, referring to the Callipolitan
scheme of arranged sexual unions, "plays its main part in counteract-
ing the dangers of degeneration. In order to fight these dangers, a fully
qualified philosopher is needed.... Only he who knows the secrets of
mathematical eugenics, of the Platonic Number, can bring back to man,
and preserve for him, the happiness enjoyed before the Fall"—meaning,
before the descent from ideals into historical change.

Popper gives a dark twist to the famous sentence of *Republic* concerning the need for philosopher-rulers, a sentence he calls "the key to the
whole work." Plato claims there, as we've seen, that without the union
of philosophy and political power "there will be no cessation from troubles for the cities or, I think, for the human race." As Popper reads these
last few words, the idea of evils in the "human race," more literally "the
race of humans," refers not to some global view of human salvation but
to "the evil rampant in the members of the race of men, i.e. *racial degeneration*" (emphasis in original).[14] The Greek word *genos*, here translated
"race," can also mean "lineage" or "descent," so Popper assumes that
Plato refers, in this famous sentence, to the eugenic scheme of Callipolis
and to the Nuptial Number.

Putting the two key *Republic* passages together—Plato's call for
philosopher-rulers to save the "race" of humans, and his obscure account
of the calculation that, alone, can prevent the adulteration of "race"—
Popper arrives at a startling conclusion. "Nobody but Plato himself knew
the secret of, and held the key to, true guardianship," through his exper-
tise in higher math. "But this can only mean one thing. The philosopher
king is Plato himself, and the *Republic* is Plato's own claim for kingly
power—to the power which he thought his due."[15]

Popper uses other passages of *Republic* to support his view of Plato's
self-crowning agenda. One such passage, as we have seen, has often been

taken as alluding to Dionysius the Younger: the idea that "sons of kings," if they have avoided "corruption," can help bring about a philosophic regime (see chapter 4). Popper thinks it unlikely that Plato would give so much credit to Dionysius the Younger while also reviling the Elder, who, in his view, stands behind the nightmarish portrait of "the tyrant" in Books 8 and 9. Popper cites a note in an ancient biography of Plato, claiming that the sage could trace his lineage back to Codrus, a mythical Athenian king. Taking the word "sons" in the phrase "sons of kings" to mean "descendants," Popper sees Plato proposing himself as the uncorrupted prince who bears on his shoulders the future hopes of Greece.[16]

Popper's sometimes strained interpretations arise from a very dark view of *Republic* and of Plato. But in his final comments on the idea that Plato longed for dictatorship, Popper chose to make the sage seem foolish rather than menacing—largely because the Syracuse project had proved such a dismal failure. Popper reports feeling "a little sorry" for Plato, "who had to be satisfied with establishing the first professorship, instead of the first kingship, of philosophy." He compares Plato to Tono, the canine hero of a 1938 children's story, *The Ugly Dachshund*. Tono, a Great Dane raised among dachshunds, thinks that he sees, in visions, a deity he calls Great Dog. In the story's denouement, Tono realizes he has been looking into a mirror. The comparison of *Republic* to an animal fable, and Plato to a benighted dog who imagines himself a god, belittles both the work and its author.

"What a monument of human smallness is this idea of the philosopher king," Popper concludes. "What a decline from this world of irony and reason"—the world of Socrates—"down to Plato's kingdom of the sage whose magical powers raise him above ordinary men; although not quite high enough . . . to neglect the sorry trade of every shaman—the selling of spells, of breeding spells, in exchange for power over his fellow men."[17]

Looked at through Popper's eyes, the very definition of justice put forth in *Republic* is nothing more than a roadmap for authoritarian rule. If justice consists in each class or race keeping to its position, there can be no moves from below to displace those on top—who are, of course, Plato's own caste, philosophers.

"If anyone should hold that 'justice' means the unchallenged rule of one class, then I should simply reply that I am all for injustice," says Popper.[18]

Many cultures cherish a myth of Eden, a golden age that existed before the onset of change and decline. The Greeks identified this world with the reign of Cronus (Roman Saturn), the father of Zeus. In the time when Cronus ruled the cosmos, humanity was thought to dwell in perfect justice and harmony, without need of laws. In that age the earth itself brought forth its plenty spontaneously, so no one had any thought of owning land or hoarding wealth. But Cronus was overthrown by his son, historical time began, and human life, according to most Greek accounts, began to get worse.

In various dialogues, especially those concerned with politics, Plato embraces this lapsarian scheme or constructs his own myths along parallel lines. Perhaps the most famous of these myths is the tale of the island kingdom Atlantis, composed by Plato to serve as a follow-up to *Republic*.

The two dialogues in which Plato spins the Atlantis tale, *Timaeus* and *Critias*, are set, in Plato's carefully plotted chronology, on the night that follows the one when *Republic* took place.[19] *Timaeus* begins with Socrates summarizing much of the first half of *Republic*—recalling, for his three auditors, what had been discussed on the previous evening. *Critias* then immediately follows as though the conversation begun in *Timaeus* had simply kept going. It too is in some sense a sequel to *Republic*, a "night-after" dialogue.

Plato evidently intended a third dialogue to be part of this "night-after" series.[20] The people gathered with Socrates on this night, Timaeus, Critias, and Hermocrates, were apparently meant to have one turn each at leading the evening's discussion, creating a trilogy. For some unknown reason, Plato left the second installment, *Critias*, unfinished—the work as we have it breaks off in mid-sentence—and omitted the third altogether. The missing third dialogue would have been of great interest here, since the speaker it would have featured, Hermocrates, is a famous Syracusan—the exiled leader whose cause was embraced by Dionysius the Elder (see chapter 1).

*Critias* is tightly tied to *Republic* not only in time but also in its insistence on a sharply divided class structure. The main speaker, Critias—not the head of the Thirty Tyrants but (probably) that man's grandfather—describes Atlantean society in a way that anticipates that of Callipolis, though set nine thousand years in the past. The Atlantean soldier class is said to have been split off, by the intervention of "godlike men," from the farmers and laborers; thereafter these soldiers lived a life apart from the rest and were not allowed to own property. "They engaged in all those practices that were talked of yesterday, the things we discussed in connection with the hypothetical 'guards,'" says Critias, referring to the silver race of *Republic*.[21] Atlantis, it seems, has a silver race too, as well as "divine men" (in place of *Republic*'s ruling elite) to keep it from mingling with the common herd.

Like *Republic*, *Critias* endorses a eugenic scheme in which the adulteration of this higher race leads to destruction. As Plato imagines, the rulers of Atlantis, a board of ten kindred "kings," had sprung from five sets of twins born to the god Poseidon and a mortal woman named Clito. Thanks to their divine blood, the original ten were able to govern wisely and not be corrupted by the great wealth their empire produced. They did not "get drunk with luxury," but rather, by "staying sober," saw to it that their society focused on virtue, not prosperity.

But Atlantis was doomed, much as Callipolis is, to slide toward ruin through genetic decline. After begetting a first generation of kings, Poseidon took no further part in siring the royal line; the next generation was only one-quarter divine, the third, one-eighth. "When the portion of the god in them grew faint, having been mingled often with a great deal of mortality, and when the human element won out, they became unable to bear their prosperity and started to be unseemly," writes Plato. These degenerate Atlanteans could not resist "getting drunk" on what wealth could obtain. They angered the gods with their overindulgence and brought on the earthquake and flood that sank their island forever.

In *The Spell of Plato* Popper took strangely little interest in the Atlantis story. Yet the meanings later assigned to the legend support that book's startling assertion, that Plato, with his eugenic ideas, planted a seed that took root in twentieth-century fascist regimes. The Nazis, especially Heinrich Himmler, adopted the Atlantis myth as one of their theories defining the Aryan "master race;" Atlanteans, they asserted, escaped the flood that destroyed their island and passed on their wisdom to the Aryans. Nazi-sponsored archaeological teams hunted for years for Atlantis in an effort to find the homeland from which the ideas of the Germans, and other "superior" peoples, had sprung.[22]

Looking beyond the "night after" sequence that follows *Republic*, we find myths in two more of Plato's political works, *Statesman* and *Laws*, that follow a similar scheme: A superhuman race once governed the world in its golden age; then humans took over and introduced change and decline. Both myths take place during the reign of Cronus, a benevolent deity who appointed *daimones*, semidivine spirits, to be "shepherds" over mortal "herds."

According to *Laws*, Cronus himself arranged this *daimon*ocracy out of a sense of human inadequacy. He put "more divine and better" beings in power, as far above those they ruled as shepherds are above their flocks. Plato doesn't say how the reign of these *daimones* ended, but he does reveal extreme pessimism about the era that followed—our own times. "This story tells us, and truthfully," his spokesman interprets, "that any city in which a mortal rules, rather than a god, gets no escape from evils and sufferings. The story's meaning is that we must try by every possible means to imitate what's called the life of Cronus."[23]

Since *daimones* can no longer govern us as they once did, Plato in *Laws* proposes a second-best alternative. With an anagrammatic wordplay he substitutes a *dianomên*, or "distribution," made by human intelligence for the *daimones* of the myth. Plato equates that "distribution"—carried out with the help of philosophy—with law, the primary mechanism of social organization. A code of justly "distributed" laws, Plato implies, will serve as the latter-day god of the fallen world.

In *Statesman* Plato constructs a golden-age myth that is longer and more complex than that of *Laws* but hews to the same basic pattern. Long ago a benign deity, loosely identified with Cronus but often called simply "the god," set *daimones* over the "herds" of humans, to govern them as shepherds govern their flocks (the same analogue as in *Laws*). This imagined era had no need of constitutions for it knew no injustice. It also had no need of sex, since human beings were born spontaneously out of the earth—just as claimed in the "noble lie" of *Republic*. But then "the god" withdrew from the world and abandoned his governing role, causing massive upheavals. Into the fallen world came clothing, agriculture, technology, and all the other benefits of civilization, as well as all of its ills.[24]

The pattern established by these golden-age myths, in *Critias*,

*Statesman*, and *Laws*, reveals Plato's dread of historical change and explains his determination, in *Republic*, to freeze a city in time. He had come of age amid the political failures of Athens, then he had watched as other cities experienced misgovernance and economic decline. He saw Hellas sliding downhill toward what he felt sure would be a wretched condition. Small wonder that the prelapsarian world seized his imagination. In *Republic* he lays out a plan by which it might be restored.

Nowhere was the problem of history more apparent to Plato than in Syracuse. That city had in his youth descended into tyranny, the bottommost stage of decline in the scheme of *Republic*. Plato seems to have been in mind of this transformation when he placed Hermocrates in the "night-after" group whose discussions make up *Timaeus* and *Critias*. At the point in time this night-after conclave is set, perhaps the 420s BC, Hermocrates was as yet a statesman in a stable democracy, elected by Syracusans for his talent and insight. Ahead of him, as Plato's readers well knew, lay banishment and violent death, the preludes to the rise of Dionysius the Elder.

What would Hermocrates have said, in the dialogue Plato intended to center around him? We cannot know, but we can speculate, with philosophy scholar Mary-Louise Gill, that he would have provided a picture of Syracuse in *its* golden age, before the tumultuous sequence to come— invasions by both Athens and Carthage, the end of democracy, the reigns of two tyrants, the exile of Dion, the breakdown of order, descent into civil war.

If that guess is correct, then *Hermocrates*, had Plato composed it, would have hinted at yet another Fall, the one taking place at the moment when Plato was writing. "Like Atlantis and Athens," says Gill, explaining her view of Plato's unrealized intentions, "Syracuse too awaits the punishment of Zeus."[25]

# ACT IV

## REVOLUTION

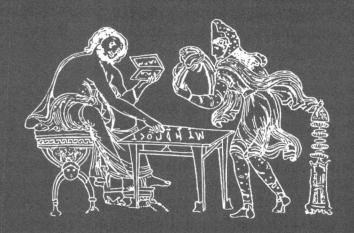

*Phintias, sometimes called Pythias, sentenced to death by Dionysius. Pen and ink drawing by Giovanni Francesco Barbieri (1632).*

# CHAPTER 10

# "DRUNKEN AND SOBER TYRANTS"

## (360–356 BC)

Plato left Sicily in the ship sent by Archytas, "filled with hatred for my Syracusan journey and my bad luck," as he writes in the *Seventh Letter*.[1] Especially hateful was the news he'd have to report to Dion when the two were reunited: Dionysius had laid claim to Dion's estate, then sold much of it off; he meant Dion's exile to be a life sentence, including permanent separation from his wife Aretê (by now his ex-wife) and his son Hipparinus.

Dion had been living in Athens but spending much time in Corinth, the mother city from which Syracuse had long ago sprung. He'd also traveled through the Peloponnese, drumming up support for his cause. That region was home to dissidents who'd been banished from Syracuse or had fled voluntarily—potential allies in any attempt at a coup. But first, Dion had to convince these men that he was a solution for Syracuse rather than part of its problem. Many had known him in his former role, chief minister of the regime that had driven them out of their homeland.

Dion had likely already conceived, by this time, a plan for invading Syracuse and ousting Dionysius. The obstacles would be enormous, but small bands of exiles had, in past decades, beaten huge odds in liberating their cities. He counted on local support to swell his numbers as soon as his return became known. Had not Speusippus been told that all

Dion had to do was row onto Sicily's shores in a dinghy, and the citizenry would fall in line behind him?

The quadrennial festival at Olympia offered an opportune venue for advancing such plans. Wealthy and powerful men from across Greece gathered at the site, in part to watch the games, in part to talk politics and form or strengthen alliances. Dion was attending the festival in the summer of 360 BC, no doubt engaged in maneuvering of this kind, when Plato arrived on his way east from Italy. A version of their conversation is recounted by Plato in the *Seventh Letter*.[2]

Upon learning that he'd been stripped of homeland, family, and wealth, Dion, writes Plato, declared that the die had been cast. He called upon Zeus to witness the righteousness of his undertaking, the overthrow of the Dionysius regime. He made clear he expected the help of Plato and other Academy members who'd been involved in the Syracuse project. They too had been victimized by Dionysius, he claimed; they had suffered what he called "guest deception," meaning they'd been used as pawns by a man who'd feigned benevolent motives for calling them in.

Plato made clear he did not see things the same way. "It was you, along with others, who forced me, in a way, to share bread and board with Dionysius and take part in religious rites with him," Plato told Dion. "He perhaps thought, due to the slanders of many, that I was plotting with you against him and his tyranny; yet he did not kill me, but acted with respect."[3] Countering Dion's charge of "guest-deception," Plato praised the tyrant for not using force when he might have. He even blamed Dion for creating a bond of *xenia*, guest-host obligation, that prevented him from acting against Dionysius. It was Dion, after all, who'd brought Plato to Syracuse and made him a guest at the tyrant's palace and table.

Plato went on to say he wished to remain "common" to both sides, an intermediary should they wish to repair their breach and "do something good." And, he claimed, he was too old for staging coups (he was then in his late sixties). As long as Dion and Dionysius longed for "evils," Plato bid his friend "summon *others* to help you." He refused to involve himself.[4]

Though by his own report he classed the coming conflict as "evil," Plato also takes pains in the *Seventh Letter* to show that Dion was aiming at good. Dion's goal in trying to oust Dionysius was not sole power, Plato writes—for that path brings only trouble and woe—but "settled government and the establishment of the best and most just laws, brought about with the fewest deaths and banishments."⁵ Nevertheless, as Plato well knew, Dion's double link to the tyrant-house, as brother-in-law to both the Elder and Younger, made his motives suspect. He had high enough dynastic rank to claim the tyranny for himself, and some in Syracuse thought that he'd wanted it all along.

Was it a lawgiver's passion for good governance, as Plato insists in the *Seventh Letter*, that made Dion decide to invade his homeland? Or was it what the hardliners saw: a desire for the power and pleasures of autocracy? The former view held greater sway in ancient times; it's enshrined not only in Plato's letters but in Plutarch's *Dion*, one of the more admired biographies in his *Parallel Lives*. But modern interpreters have often been skeptical, with good reason. They have noted that Plato, as Dion's mentor and ally, was defending himself by defending Dion, and that Plutarch, writing some five centuries later, had his own reasons for defending both.

As a young man, before composing his *Parallel Lives*, Plutarch had studied in Athens under a Platonist named Ammonius. Thereafter he considered himself a member of the Academy, still in his day a thriving institution though no longer in its old home; he wrote philosophic dialogues that took inspiration from Plato. Plutarch thus had a vested interest in defending Plato's legacy by burnishing the repute of Plato's most famous protégé, Dion. He was predisposed to trust Plato's letters, which strongly endorsed the idea that Dion had been a crusader for justice.

Historian Lionel Sanders, who, as we've seen, wrote a book in 1987 defending the reputation of Dionysius the Elder, later published an even longer volume, *The Legend of Dion*, attempting a similar move but in the reverse direction. Sanders argues that Plato and Plutarch have scrubbed Dion's record to erase his tyrannical leanings. Then he takes a leap forward in time and claims that some modern scholars who've endorsed these whitewashed accounts have themselves been defenders of tyranny. He writes of "the likelihood that modern apologists for Dion . . . are not merely unsympathetic to democracy but actually nurse a covert sympathy for tyranny as manifested in the career of Dion." In a footnote, he calls attention to the place and time of one of these pro-Dion studies, Germany in the early 1930s—seemingly drawing a link between the Platonist view of Dion and the rise of Nazism. (In fact, the scholar responsible for that study, Renata von Scheliha, fled from the Nazi regime.)[6]

Sanders's view is perhaps extreme, but the question of Dion's motives will trouble us at many turns in what lies ahead. Even Plutarch, Dion's greatest defender, had moments of doubt, as seen in a remarkable passage of *Parallel Lives*.

In that famous work Plutarch arranges biographies in pairs, matching a Greek to a Roman life, and prefaces each pair with an essay discussing the parallels. He matches Dion's life to that of Brutus, the deep-thinking Roman senator who led the conspiracy that killed Julius Caesar. In his comparative essay Plutarch at first holds Dion in higher regard than Brutus, because Dion had not betrayed a friend whereas Brutus had stabbed a man who trusted and loved him (*"Et tu, Brute"*). Rather, "after being banished from his homeland, wronged regarding his wife, and stripped of his wealth, Dion embarked openly on a war that was lawful and just."

Then, as though glimpsing the implications of what he'd just written, Plutarch rethinks. "Or does this turn things back in the other direction?" he asks, seemingly of himself. Suddenly the contrast does Dion *dis*credit. Brutus's hatred of tyrants was "unalloyed and pure . . . from no personal cause," whereas "Dion would not have gone to war if he himself had not been mistreated. . . . He made war out of anger."[7] Plutarch concedes that Dion's self-interest diminishes his moral standing. In the *Life of Dion* that follows, he does his best to assuage these qualms, but he nonetheless put them on record.

The problem of Dion's motives runs deep, even deeper than Plutarch acknowledges. For while Plutarch finds Dion's anger to be an ignoble *casus belli*, he nowhere suspects an even more troubling impulse, the will to absolute power. Yet some of Dion's moves, in the five years that followed his meeting with Plato at the Olympic games, suggest that he felt that impulse. If he did aim at tyranny, as Sanders believes, he had an excellent stalking horse: Plato's Academy.

The forces that Dion assembled as he prepared his campaign were oddly composed. Though he'd failed at recruiting Plato, he recruited several

Academy members, including Callippus with whom he'd shared living quarters in Athens. The presence of such men by his side implied that he aimed at a constitutional state with a ruler subject to law—the system that Plato promoted. But the troops supporting this leadership team were mercenaries Dion had hired, soldiers fighting for pay and not for a cause. It was not a good look for a liberator, but Dion had failed to attract Syracusan ex-pats in significant numbers. Out of more than a thousand Syracusans who'd landed in the Peloponnese, only two dozen or so agreed to join the expedition; the rest shrank back "out of cowardice," Plutarch claims, but mistrust of Dion also no doubt played a role.[8]

Recruitment and preparation consumed three years, from mid-360 to mid-357. Part of this time was spent acquiring weapons: Dion amassed thousands of sets of infantry gear to be given to his supporters once he reached Sicily.[9] Ships and supplies also needed to be procured. Dion settled on cargo vessels; warships would have raised greater alarm as they entered Sicilian waters. He suspected the tyrant's navy would be on the watch for his crossing, even though he kept his plans secret even from his own troops. The tyrant's spies and informants were everywhere and he could not risk leaks.

During this time Dion must have had discussions with Heraclides, who'd landed in exile in the Peloponnese. With his military background and high standing as an opponent of Dionysius, Heraclides had much to offer the expedition and plenty of motivation for taking part. But for reasons not entirely clear, he and Dion did not join forces. Heraclides too raised an army and ships but ended up setting sail some weeks or months after Dion. Plutarch says that he and Dion had quarreled, implying perhaps Heraclides had chosen to mount his own, separate campaign.[10] But Plutarch consistently denigrates Heraclides so as to increase the luster of Dion. It's possible the separate departures were part of a plan for a two-wave attack, the second one to be launched once the first gained a foothold in Syracuse.

Dion's force, said to be eight hundred men, set out in the merchant ships in late summer, 357 BC.[11] At Zacynthus, off the west coast of the Peloponnese, Dion at last revealed to his troops that his objective was Syracuse. The men flew into a rage, claiming they'd been tricked into a suicide mission. Dion calmed them down by explaining his thinking: The

Dionysius regime had grown so corrupt and enfeebled that a small push would topple it; the people of Syracuse would rally to Dion's banners. An officer named Alcimenes, trusted by many recruits, stepped forward to endorse Dion's plan. The unrest subsided.

Before the small contingent set sail, strange signs were observed, a matter of grave concern even to hardened soldiers. On the night of August 9, as the troops enjoyed a banquet that Dion provided, the moon went into eclipse, causing widespread alarm. A prophet named Miltas offered a benign explanation: The tyranny of Dionysius had been as resplendent as the full moon, but now it was due to be darkened. Then, swarms of bees were seen amassed on the sterns of Dion's ships. Miltas this time had a less positive message. Just as bees feed on flowers that bloom but then quickly wither, he said, the campaign would meet with initial success but would soon thereafter lose ground.

It was nearly autumn before the ships left Zacynthus, and storm winds were already brewing. The expedition set off on the crossing to Sicily. As it left port Dion made a bold proclamation, recorded by Aristotle in his work *Politics*. "However far I am able to advance," Dion reportedly said, "will suffice for me to have taken part in this venture. Even if it befalls me to die just after making landfall, that death will suit me quite well."[12]

Aristotle—who was at this point an Academy member—quoted these words as the mark of a man who seeks glory from ousting a ruler rather than the chance to be ruler himself. That was a generous reading of Dion, but one the Academy deeply hoped was correct.

In Syracuse, Dionysius, too, had seen portents and signs, most of them grim. An eagle had snatched a spear from a guardsman and dropped it into the sea, a clear indication that the regime was endangered. A litter of pigs had been born without ears, forecasting, according to seers, that the Syracusan people—here equated with piglets—would soon no longer listen to commands. At the docks of the Island, the water of the Great Harbor turned from salt to fresh for the span of one day. The seers predicted that the life of the citizenry, made bitter by despotism, would soon take a turn for the better and become sweet and comfortable.[13]

Life was already sweet for Dionysius, if not for his people. His Diony-sioflatterers had stayed on after Plato's departure, delighting the tyrant with their obsequiousness. Aristippus continued to fawn and cajole; he even, according to one report, put on purple robes at a dinner and danced about grotesquely at the tyrant's direction.[14] Other courtiers were equally obliging. One man, a certain Democles, was standing by when Dionysius announced he'd received a letter from his commanders abroad. "By the gods, they've done well, Dionysius," exclaimed Democles. The tyrant sensed fakery and put Democles on the spot: "But how do you know if the letter has good news or bad?" "By the gods, you do well to rebuke me," said Democles in the same cheerful tone.[15]

Six years in power, surrounded by lackeys and toadies, had made Dionysius willful and arrogant. He lied when he chose and was fond of saying that men were cheated by oaths just as children were cheated by dice.[16] When a famous *cithara*-player performed at his palace, Dionysius vowed to pay the man a talent of silver, but the next day turned him away empty-handed. He said that since he'd given delight for a day with the promise of riches, he'd paid the man back with pleasure equal to what he'd received from the music.[17]

As in the time of Dionysius the Elder, sages and thinkers who showed too much spirit got extra helpings of monarchal contempt. A philosopher called Philoxenus—the same name as the free-spoken poet jailed by the Elder—had come to the Syracusan court from Athens. Soon after arriving, Philoxenus made the mistake of besting Dionysius in a disputation. When he boasted of his achievement, the tyrant put him in his place. "Perhaps you refute me in words, but *I* refute *you* by your deeds," Dionysius retorted. "For you left behind what was yours to come here and pay court to me and what's mine."[18] The pull of the Syracusan tables gave him another win.

Dionysius was by this time drinking more heavily. He'd become so addicted that, when he briefly had to give up alcohol, he fell ill and only recovered when he started drinking again.[19] A now-lost work by Aris-totle, *The Constitution of the Syracusans*, claimed that the tyrant at one point held a wine-soaked banquet that lasted for ninety days, during which time the palace doors remained closed to official business.[20] It was this drinking habit, according to Aristotle, as much as abuse of power, that roused Dion to oust his brother-in-law.[21]

Dionysius was living up to his name, which connected him to Dionysus, god of wine, even while he promoted the myth that he'd been sired
by Apollo. An inscription he commissioned, a line of flowery verse, identified him as "son of Doris, begot by Phoebus's beddings".[22] He'd reinforced that idea by naming his eldest son Apollocrates, "strength of
Apollo," though the boy, now in his teens, was proving to be another devotee of the wine god, as were his half-brothers, the sons of Aristomachê.[23]

Life at court had taken the opposite path from the one that Plato and
Dion had charted a decade before. Plato had urged self-improvement,
including sobriety, as a means to gain reliable friends, and friends as a
means to enact political change. True friendship, based on shared love of
virtue, was key to any reform, yet the tyrant had settled for cheap adu-
lation and the fellowship of the cup. Even so, he yearned for something
authentic, as seen in a now-famous story told of his reign. In a cruelly
devised encounter with two Pythagorean sages, Damon and Phintias (or
Pythias, as he's more widely known), Dionysius reportedly glimpsed the
kind of friendship that Plato had preached but also learned it was something he could not have.[24]

The story concerns an argument at Dionysius's court. Two factions
there took different views of the Pythagoreans and their reputation for
inner peace. One group claimed that this serenity ran deep and true, the
other, that it was all a facade. A test was devised to resolve the dispute.
Phintias, apparently selected at random from among the Pythagoreans in
Syracuse, was hauled before Dionysius and accused of conspiring against
the tyrant's life. Lying courtiers corroborated the charge, and Dionysius
pronounced a sentence of death. Then all stood back to see how the subject would handle adversity.

At first surprised by the accusation, Phintias quickly recovered his
calm. He accepted his fate but made a request of the tyrant. He said that
he lived with a man named Damon, an intimate friend (a lover perhaps)
with whom he shared household affairs. He wanted leave for a day to
settle domestic details on Damon's behalf. To guarantee he'd return and
submit to his sentence, he said that Damon could take his place and serve
as a hostage. Dionysius expressed disbelief that Damon would do such a
thing, but when Damon presented himself and agreed to the terms, the
tyrant had to admit he was wrong on that score.

As Phintias went off on his errands, Damon endured the mockery of the court. Those who'd insisted that Pythagorean detachment was only a sham were sure that Phintias had made his escape and left Damon to die in his stead; they called Damon a dupe. But then, around sunset, Phintias reappeared, and the skeptics fell silent. The court stood amazed at a love between friends that transcended fear of death.

No one was more deeply moved than Dionysius. With a sudden onrush of longing, the tyrant embraced the two men and asked to be included in their bond as part of an intimate troika. It was as though he'd "gotten" Plato's lesson that friends who share a commitment to virtue cannot be parted. He'd seen that kind of ethical friendship in Plato's devotion to Dion, but never experienced it. Now that he'd glimpsed it a second time, he desperately wanted a share.

But Damon and Phintias would not let the tyrant join in their fellowship. No matter how much Dionysius begged, the pair held aloof. They could not open their arms to the man who had callously used them as guinea pigs, even if, as we presume, he'd revoked Phintias's sentence of death.

The tale of Damon and Phintias is found in numerous ancient versions. In some, it's Dionysius the Elder, rather than his son, who plays the lead role. The version recounted here, however, seems to have come from the mouth of the Younger himself. According to the source who preserves it—a philosopher named Iamblichus—the tyrant, late in life, told the story to one Aristoxenus, a sage from Tarentum. If that is indeed how the tale was passed on, one imagines that Dionysius was making a kind of confession to Aristoxenus, who is known to have greatly admired the Pythagoreans. He seems to have wanted to share his regret for what might have been.

Friendlessness had been a theme of the Younger's life, beginning in boyhood. When his father had seen that he'd made no friends despite having wealth, he'd spoken contemptuously. "You have no talent for tyranny," the Elder had said—prophetically, as it turned out.[25] When Plato had first come to court, in 367, the Younger had attached himself in a needy way, demanding the sage's affection, if Plutarch's account can be trusted.

Loyal friends were essential to anyone ruling a state, Plato and Dion had taught. Now, Dionysius was going to need friends more than ever, as he faced a ruler's ultimate test—armed invasion.

Dion's ships ran into a storm on their voyage to Sicily.[26] They got blown so far south that they had to use punting poles to push off from the African coast. But then the wind shifted and bore them northward again. At Dion's direction they made Sicilian landfall at Heraclea Minoa (near modern-day Agrigento), a port controlled by Carthage; the Punic commander there, Synalus, was a friend of Dion's despite the enmity of their respective peoples. Plutarch makes out that this landing was accidental, but it looks prearranged, to judge by its outcome: After a clash in which no one was hurt, Synalus fell in line behind Dion's invasion. Dion gave him the task of carting the spare suits of armor eastward while he led his army forward at faster pace.

As he made his way toward Syracuse, Dion lost the element of surprise, as he knew he eventually would. But, by extraordinary good luck, Dionysius was just then away from Sicily, managing his Italian forts and garrisons. His subordinate in Syracuse, Timocrates, sent off an urgent message calling him back, but by a second stroke of luck, it failed to arrive. It's said that the messenger, on his way north, came upon a sacrificial feast and put in his pouch a chunk of roast meat the celebrants gave him. While he slept by the side of the road, a wolf smelled the meat and seized the pouch, making away with the message it contained. When the messenger awoke and saw his pouch gone, he ran off and aborted his mission, fearing the tyrant's wrath if he'd had to admit to the mishap.

On the march across Sicily, Dion gained fresh recruits from the cities he passed. Most of these cities, as we have seen, were no longer Greek but had been claimed by veteran soldiers belonging to other nations, the tyranny's former guardsmen. These veterans knew well how much wealth had been stored on the Island and how much they stood to gain by sacking the place. By the time Dion reached the river Anapus, a short distance west of Syracuse, his original force of eight hundred had swelled to nearly six thousand, according to Plutarch, or more than three times that size by Diodorus's count. Many of these, no doubt, were hoping for plunder more than political change.

Inside the city, aware of Dion's approach, a long-oppressed people began to rise up, taking revenge against those who'd helped keep them down. Syracusans who'd served as spies and informants were being stopped in the streets and beaten to death.

The tyrant's armed forces could have stopped these reprisals, but instead they stayed in their bunkers on the Island, leaderless and lacking orders. Timocrates, their commander, had been cut off from them in the melee and, rather than fight his way through, he took to horse and fled the city. Meanwhile some of the troops who were manning the outer walls, who might have prevented Dion's entry, deserted their posts. Dion had sent out a false report that he meant to attack the nearby towns where they lived, and they made haste to protect their families and homes. The magnificent circuit wall, the most extensive one built by any Greek city, stood undefended and useless.

Dion assumed the air of a liberator as he approached the westernmost gate, riding in front of his column in brilliant armor. He was flanked on one side by his brother, Megacles, a man of whom we know little, and on the other by the Academy student Callippus; all three wore garlands atop their heads as though in a festal procession. A squad of a hundred mercenaries followed behind Dion, described by Plutarch as his personal guard. The sight must have given pause to those who had seen Dionysius the Elder, half a century earlier, secure his power with a bodyguard much like this one.

Dion entered the city to the sound of trumpets as cheering crowds lined the streets, setting out food and wine for the troops as they passed. A herald announced the conqueror's lofty goals: the overthrow of the tyrant and restoration of freedom to Syracuse. In the marketplace, where an impromptu assembly had gathered, Dion climbed atop a raised sundial, a monument erected by Dionysius, to make himself heard. He spoke in grand terms of the defense of liberty, and the people responded with ardent cries of support. They voted on the spot to make Dion their *stratêgos autokratôr*, commander with sovereign power, together with his brother Megacles. It was the same title they had once given Dionysius the Elder.

Dion seemed aware of this unfortunate echo. He requested a broader governing body than just himself and his brother, and twenty Syracusans were chosen to serve by their side. Ten of these were selected from Dion's small cadre of exiles, the rest, from the city at large. This meant that Dion's partisans did not have a clear majority. Dion was trying, in the revolution's first phase, to check his own power.

In his first acts as new head of state, Dion directed his troops to secure the Latomiae, the tyrant's grim caverns, and release the prisoners they held. Then he ordered a wall built across the isthmus, to seal off the Island from the rest of the city. The troops dug in there would eventually have to be dealt with, but for now Dion would simply keep them contained. His own forces were as yet unable to fight them; the infantry gear he had brought, with which to outfit a militia, was slow in arriving. Even slower to come were the ships and men Heraclides had mustered in the Peloponnese. The revolution had thus far succeeded on land but would need to win on the sea if it was to survive.

Dion sent a terse message telling Heraclides to hurry, encrypting it in case it was intercepted. He'd devised a code by which he could write in consonants only and use groups of dots, in prearranged patterns, to represent missing vowels. Miraculously, his message has been preserved by a military writer of the day, in a discussion of secret communications. The message reads (in transliteration) DNSS KLS RKLDS KT, with various patterns of dots separating the letters.

Classical scholars, though lacking the key that matches the patterns of dots with vowels, have gradually broken the code. The message is an urgent summons: *Dionysios kolos, Heracleidas hêketô,* "Dionysius has had his horns docked; let Heraclides come." That clipped call to arms perfectly fits the moment in early September, 357 BC, when it seemed Dionysius was on the run and the way was clear for a second wave of invaders.[27]

But Dionysius was not on the run, nor had his horns been docked. His delay in getting the news of Dion's arrival had given a false impression of weakness. In fact, once fully informed, he'd resolved, as his father once had, to hold onto his seat or make his enemies drag him away by the leg. He set sail in haste for his native city, while urging Philistus, who'd gone farther north with a part of the fleet, to do likewise.

A week after Dion's arrival, Dionysius rowed into the Island's fortified harbor, disembarked, and made his way to the acropolis, his palace and armory. Behind the isthmus wall Dion's men had erected, he marshaled his forces and planned for the coming struggle.

The Greek noun *stasis* derives from the verb "to stand," giving rise to the English word for a "standstill" condition. To the Greeks it denoted a "station" or a "position" but also a political faction made up of those taking a "stand," or a conflict between such factions. In this last sense it's often translated—ironically, to the modern ear—as "civil war" or "revolution," but neither word gives the right meaning; "class war" comes closer. Typically, *stasis* involved a clash between the more and the less well-off, since the former favored oligarchic regimes that better served their interests, the latter, a more democratic diffusion of power. When both groups decided they *must* have control, passions could burn white-hot and lead to appalling violence.

The historian Thucydides gives a chilling account of one such *stasis*. During the Peloponnesian War, on the island of Corcyra (modern Corfu), a pro-Athenian, poorer faction squared off against pro-Spartan rich who had tried to seize power. With Athens supporting one side and Sparta the other, the two parties entered into a life-or-death struggle, each going to any lengths to attain victory. In a final orgy of killing, the commoners, having gotten the upper hand, began executing a group of the rich who had fled to a temple of Hera for sanctuary. Those trapped in the shrine, seeing their fate was sealed, began murdering one another and hanging themselves to avoid the worse deaths their enemies would have dealt them. The carnage continued, Thucydides says, for an entire week.

"Every form of death took place," Thucydides writes of the Corcyra *stasis*. "Father killed son, and men were dragged from the altars or slain upon them, and some were even walled up inside the temple of Dionysus and died there."[28] He does not state how this second group of suppliants perished; one wonders whether they too killed one another, or whether those who'd imprisoned them stood guard for days while they slowly perished of thirst.

Thucydides used Corcyra to illustrate *stasis* generally, since he saw the affliction spreading widely throughout the Greek world. *Stasis*, he writes, was producing "every form of viciousness" across Hellas, leading to a perversion of moral value. He dramatizes the high cost of factional strife in the hopes that future generations might learn to avoid it. But the decades that followed the Peloponnesian War showed that the Greeks had learned nothing. *Stasis* continued to rage in the era of Plato and Dionysius. Indeed, the worst *stasis* ever recorded (according to its chronicler, Diodorus) took place in 371 BC, in the city of Argos, just a few years before Plato's first visit to Dionysius the Younger.

This Argive *stasis* was known to the Greeks as the *skutalismos*, "the affair of the clubs," because of the way the killings were carried out. It began, like the one at Corcyra, with the rich attempting to subvert democracy. Their plot was uncovered before it went into motion, and a captured plotter gave the names of thirty confederates, all leading men. These thirty were put to death, but the masses, consumed by fear and urged on by demagogues, lashed out at all those they regarded as oligarchs. The number of victims swelled, eventually reaching twelve hundred in Diodorus's count, fifteen hundred in Plutarch's. When the demagogues drew back from the slaughter, fearing that things had gone too far, they too became victims, for the mob would no longer tolerate lack of resolve.[29]

One sickens to think of over a thousand men beaten to death with clubs, yet episodes nearly as bad were commonplace in this era. "*Stasis* was a vicious circle with no solution," writes historian M. M. Austin about the fourth century BC.[30] At Corcyra, the disaster of 427, so memorably described by Thucydides, was only the first of a series; further outbreaks of *stasis* took place in 411, 374, and 361. In the last of these episodes, the wealthy faction seized power in a false flag operation: Soldiers supporting the rich cut their own flesh with blades and made bruises by cupping, then rushed to the market proclaiming they'd been attacked. Citizens who were in on the plot seized weapons, calling out that the democrats were to blame. Before inquiries could be made, the soldiers had rounded up those on their enemies list.[31] The political order had been overturned yet again.

This final Corcyraean *stasis* is recounted by Aeneas of Stymphalus, also known as Aeneas Tacticus, the same author whose military handbook, *Life under Siege*, preserves Dion's dot-vowel code. As it happens, Aeneas wrote his work just after Dion's revolution, though he does not discuss that event; his focus is on central Greece and the cities of Asia Minor, not the Greek West. But the view he offers of a disordered political landscape adds sobering context to the story of Syracuse.

In the Greek world surveyed by Aeneas, *stasis* lurks everywhere (except perhaps in Athens, a place Aeneas ignores). Conflict between the classes threatens at every turn to erupt into warfare. Tricks and subterfuges are constantly being devised or improved by both sides, so no one can ever feel safe. Even the quotidian has come to seem sinister: Lamps lit at night in private homes give rise to fears that insurgents outside the walls are receiving signals. It's the nightmare world that Thucydides had decried in his meditation on the Corcyra *stasis*, seemingly normalized some six decades later.

Since the root cause of *stasis* was economic inequality, Aeneas urges financial measures as ways to preserve the peace. The debts of the poor must be reduced or even canceled, he writes, and welfare funds provided to those without means. Yet these measures must somehow avoid offending the rich, who own the debts and pay the bulk of the taxes. To learn the secret of threading this needle, Aeneas tells us, a different book is required: "The revenues from which this outlay may be funded are clearly laid out in my work *On Finance*," he says.[32] Since that work is entirely lost, or perhaps was never written, the cross-reference gives a modern reader an impression of hopelessness. One cannot imagine what magical resource Aeneas recommended, since no Greek city succeeded in finding one.

Syracuse had escaped the problem of *stasis* so long as the Dionysii had kept a tight rein on the city. But that was about to change with Dion's return and the ouster of Dionysius the Younger. *Stasis* would soon break out there as well, but in a form more complex than the bipolar struggle of rich against poor. Both Dion and Dionysius were backed by professional armies rather than by class-based political factions. Both belonged to the same family, an extremely wealthy one. This symmetry left the demos confused and disenchanted, ready to follow another leader, should one enter the fray—as one soon would.

The struggle for Syracuse was to involve *three* contestants, or even, at times, four or five. "Dion launched a campaign against Dionysius and stirred up all against all," was one ancient writer's assessment.[33] For that kind of conflict, Aeneas of Stymphalus had no advice in his handbook, nor could Plato offer solutions, though he would try.

Syracuse was now two adjacent cities, each unable to make headway against the other. Dion could not storm the Island, and Dionysius, it seemed, could not move his forces out from the Island and retake the mainland. Between their two realms, on the causeway that formed the isthmus, stood the Pentapyla, a five-gated structure, and, inland from that, the wall set up by Dion to keep the tyrant contained. By sending messengers back and forth through these barriers, the brothers-in-law opened a negotiation.

Dionysius began by offering mild concessions, but Dion refused these and insisted on abdication. Then, miraculously, Dionysius agreed to step down, in exchange for safe passage out of the region. He invited Dion's envoys to come to the Island to discuss these terms and firm up an agreement. But when the men arrived, in the secrecy of his enclave, he had them arrested.

Unaware of this move, Syracusans on the mainland feasted and drank, thinking they'd soon be rid of the tyrant's regime. Dionysius had counted on this, knowing that his bibulous ways were shared by much of the demos. His scouts had seen that the towers on Dion's wall were not well guarded; after a night of drinking, they'd be even less so. At dawn the next day, he launched a surprise attack.

The immense armed force on the Island, said to number more than ten thousand, poured onto the causeway, shouting the war cries of various non-Greek nations. The first armed clash of the civil war had begun.

The tyrant's troops broke through Dion's wall and slaughtered its garrison force, then streamed into the marketplace beyond. A chaotic battle took shape. Dion was by now on the scene and attempting to form up his forces, but panicked civilians kept running into their midst, shouting loudly. Dion's orders were swallowed up in the din. Either because he could not be heard, or because he was eager to claim a personal triumph, he advanced alone toward the causeway, now crowded with enemy soldiers. Spears jabbed at him and stones struck his armor, until, with his right arm wounded, he sank down on the ground.

Dion's men saw their leader fall and pushed forward urgently, into the "heavy" formation of Dionysius's army. According to Diodorus, they turned the tide of battle with this determined push and forced the tyrant's men to withdraw to the Island. Plutarch, by contrast, gives more credit to Dion: The wounded man mounted a horse, Plutarch says, and rode to another part of the city to rally fresh forces. This second wave of attackers sent the tyrant's men fleeing when it arrived on the scene.[34]

Whatever role Dion played, his troops, in league with some Syracusan supporters, had carried the day. Dion set up a trophy to mark the spot where his foes had been turned, then collected the bodies of those who'd died in his service, some seventy or eighty in number.

Dionysius, for his part, had lost hundreds. He was given permission to gather the fallen under a truce. If we can trust a surviving report, the tyrant, drawing on his store of luxury goods, had each of the corpses wrapped in a purple cloth and crowned with a golden wreath; he meant to show the rest of his men how highly he valued their lives. He bestowed further gifts on survivors who'd distinguished themselves in the fighting. Not long before, he'd tried to cut the pay of these men, but he ended up giving them bonuses; he'd have to spend even more freely now to buy loyalty.[35]

Dionysius went back to seeking negotiation. Dion stalled for time while his wall was being repaired; he knew that a breakdown in talks might lead to another attack. When the breach was securely sealed, he sent his envoys across the causeway to offer a deal. He insisted that Dionysius abdicate but allowed that "certain honors," unspecified by our sources, might be continued thereafter. This provision did not tempt the tyrant, who was starting to show he believed in his father's maxim, "tyranny makes a fine shroud."

Digging in for a protracted struggle, Dionysius organized raiders to forage for food and sent out his ships to buy grain. He needed to store up supplies while he still had control of the seas. Effectively, the Island was under siege.

The standoff between the brothers-in-law entered a new phase, a battle for public opinion. This battle was fought not with shields and spears but rumors, reports, and letters, especially letters designed to be widely read. As it happens, two of these letters, from opposite sides, are known to us today. One, from Dionysius to Dion, is preserved in summary form by Plutarch and Polyaenus. The other, from Plato to Dionysius, survives intact—the *Third Letter*.

Dionysius's missive to Dion was included in a packet of letters sent out from the Island. Most of what the packet contained came from the wives of prominent Syracusans; evidently the tyrant had seized these women as hostages when the conflict began. Their letters, begging for rescue, were read aloud in a solemn assembly meeting. Among them were pleas sent by Dion's wife, Aretê, and his sister, Aristomachê, who were also penned up in the palace that had been their home.

Then a letter purporting to come from Dion's young son, Hipparinus, was unsealed. The assembly advised Dion to scan this message in private, but Dion, seeking transparency, insisted it too be read aloud. It soon became clear that the letter was not from the son at all but from Dionysius.

The tyrant addressed Dion in tones that were far too familiar for the assembly's liking. He invoked Dion's previous service to the regime, even while reviling the current invasion and threatening to harm Dion's family. Then he delivered the master stroke: In words heard by the assembled citizenry, he offered to step down and let Dion take over in order to preserve the dynasty. "Don't set free a people who hate us and who remember their sufferings," the letter implored, deploying a first-person plural that made Dion the tyrant's confederate. "Rule them yourself, for thus you will safeguard your friends and relations." That last clause suggested that Dion, as ruler, would see to it that a deposed Dionysius escaped retribution.[36]

Dion had been done in once before, a decade earlier, by an indiscreet letter, his own communication with Carthaginian envoys. He must have recalled that episode now as the tyrant's letter was read out in public. The suspicions that many harbored of Dion's motives seemed to have been confirmed, and to them was added the fear that, given the chance, Dion would pardon the tyrant or even reward him.

Both Plutarch and Polyaenus, relying on some common source, present this letter as a trick cooked up by Dionysius to tarnish Dion's image. But that source could hardly have known what the tyrant's intentions were. It's not unlikely the message was a sincere outreach by one brother-in-law to another, stressing common interests and family solidarity. Dion's later defenders did not want to acknowledge those interests and therefore assumed the letter was a clever set-up job.

The letter undermined not only Dion's image but Plato's as well. The Syracusans were well aware that these two were allied, and in the past few weeks they'd seen a student of Plato, Callippus, riding beside Dion at the head of an army. If Dion was only another tyrant, but dressed in a philosophic disguise, then Plato, who'd helped create that disguise, could be seen as his coconspirator. The hardliners at Dionysius's court had seen him that way all along.

The regime's need to discredit Plato had greatly increased now that Dion had launched his attack. At the time of that launch, it seems that Dionysius was giving out nasty reports about Plato to envoys who came to his court. He'd started saying that Plato, while visiting Syracuse, had stood in the way of reforms that *he* had intended. He sought to make Plato the fall guy for shortcomings of his regime: its slowness in re-Hellenizing the cities of Sicily, and its failure to rein its own powers in as a limited monarchy.

Plato struck back in the document now called the *Third Letter*. In it, Plato protests that Dionysius is turning things on their head: Plato had urged Dionysius to change *himself* first, and *then* attempt larger projects, but that advice was now being cast as a block on reform. Plato summarizes what he has heard about Dionysius's slanders: "You say I prevented you from doing these things, though you were very eager to, and that now I'm instructing Dion to do the same things, and that we're using your own intentions to strip you of your power."[37]

Evidently the tyrant was painting Plato as Dion's puppet master, working behind the scenes to help the invasion succeed. It was a cunning slur, more effective because, to all appearances, it contained a grain of truth.

Unlike the private *Thirteenth Letter*, the *Third* was written for wide circulation; much of what it relates was well known to Dionysius but served to establish a public record. To that end, Plato conducts a review of his involvement with Dionysius over the preceding decade. His tone has changed markedly from that of the chummy *Thirteenth Letter*, written some seven or eight years before. The *Third Letter* is suffused with anger and outraged pride. Even Plato's salutation, normally a pro forma matter, is laced with contempt for its addressee.

"Plato bids Dionysius 'rejoice'. . . . or should I rather write 'fare well'?" Plato asks, comparing two standard openings of the day. "Fare well," Plato says, is the one he usually uses, but in contemplating a change to "rejoice," he raises the ethical problem of pleasure—a problem, he knew, that the tyrant had not managed well. He recalls a recent occasion when Dionysius had sent envoys to Apollo's oracle at Delphi. Dionysius had bid the envoys address the oracle with a line of hexameter verse: "Joy to you! and preserve the pleasure-filled life of the tyrant."[38] That greeting makes no sense, Plato says, since gods have a constant nature, removed from pleasure and pain, and so cannot "rejoice."

In just the same way, Plato continues, "rejoice" should never be wished on a human being, "for pleasure and pain give rise to much harm, begetting in the soul an inability to learn, and obliviousness, and foolishness, and arrogant pride."[39] These failings loom large in Plato's assessments elsewhere of Dionysius's nature. He seems to be calling the tyrant out as a man who's been morally damaged by excess of pleasure. The quote that Plato provides from the message to Delphi—"preserve the *pleasure-filled* life of the tyrant"—helps drive the point home.

Plato has highlighted flaws he sees in the Dionysius regime in his very first sentences. He comes out swinging to show the Greek world how much distance there was between that regime and himself, since many were sensing there was not enough. His final comment in this opening segment displays a remarkable coldness. "Take this however you choose, when you read it," he says snippily, then moves on to the substance of his message.[40]

The charges Dionysius is making, Plato writes, have been heaped on top of older ones going back nine or ten years. During Plato's first visit to Dionysius's court, rumors about him were spread by Philistus (whom Plato here calls "Philistides"); Plato feels the weight of these earlier charges along with the new ones, and sets out to answer both. This two-layered approach, reminiscent of how he had structured Socrates' speech of defense, the *Apology*, allows him to go back over his dealings with Dionysius from the beginning. So he tells the whole tale of what brought him to the Younger's court in both 367 and 361, and what he did there, and how things went so awry.

The account emphasizes the contrast between Dionysius, a young, inexperienced ruler in 367, and Dion, a seasoned statesman. No doubt this was meant to elevate Dion, but its ostensible purpose is different. Plato wants to make clear that he took little part in public affairs and there-fore could not have impeded them as Dionysius has claimed. As soon as Dion was banished—only weeks after Plato's arrival—Plato saw no point any longer in helping the tyrant govern, since scheming courtiers were clearly in control. "Do you think," he asks Dionysius, in a tone of haughty contempt, "that there was at that time any partnership of political mat-ters between you and me, when I had lost my wise partner"—Dion—"and saw the foolish one left alone among many wicked people, not ruling (while thinking he did so) but being ruled by such men?"[41]

Plato says that he had no choice but to avoid politics after Dion's exile, "wary of slanders arising from jealousies"—the kind that had already brought Dion down. He put every effort instead toward getting Dion recalled and reconciling the brothers-in-law. With that as his sole moti-vation, he says, he went back to Syracuse in 361, well aware of what he would find there. "For I saw then, and I see now, that great and extrava-gant fortunes . . . nurture, the greater they are, a larger and more impres-sive cadre of slanderers and men who gather for pleasure that brings shame and harm."[42] Though couched in general terms, this presents a damning caricature of Dionysius's court with its lackeys surrounding the sovereign and indulging his appetites.

Plato then turns to the newer charges against him: the attempt to blame him for lack of progress in saving Greek Sicily. Here he addresses Dionysius, the source of the accusation, directly and personally. Plato reminds the tyrant of what was said at their parting, in the presence of two witnesses. In that exchange, the tyrant had sneered at Plato (see chapter 6) for wanting self-reform to precede other projects, including re-Hellenization. So the sneer indirectly confirmed that Plato *had* wanted Sicilian cities restored. Plato refutes the charge brought against him by quoting Dionysius himself.

Plato punctuates his record of this exchange with a cryptic remark. "On this account," Plato says, referring to the tyrant's contemptuous comments, "your *hubrisma* at that time has become a reality instead of a dream." It's hard to know what he means. *Hubrisma*, derived from the far more common word *hubris*, can denote an act of outrageous arrogance or, less often, the target of such bad treatment. Taking the word in the latter sense, it seems the *hubrisma* is the teaching that Dionysius had sneered at—the need to temper monarchic power with ethical principles.

If this reading is correct, then Plato allows himself a boast at his former student's expense. What you once mocked, he'd be saying to Dionysius, has now come to pass; Dion, a man who believes in my principles, is making a play to take your place. The triumphal tone seems out of tune with Plato's dialogues, where only the foolish, never the wise, say the equivalent of "gotcha;" but it coheres with the *Seventh Letter*, where Plato's prickliness is on full display, as we'll see.

The *Third Letter* leaves no doubt as to which side Plato was on in the struggle to come. It depicts Dion as a sage and Dionysius as a weak man manipulated by sycophants. But its principal goal is to revise the historical record. Plato insists he had not taken any hand in governing Syracuse; he had only gone there, on both recent occasions, for Dion's sake.

Plato wanted it to be known that *he* was not to blame for what had gone wrong in Syracuse. For clearly many things had, and worse was to come.

Dionysius's letter to Dion, read aloud to much of the demos, had planted seeds of doubt about Dion's intentions. Those doubts grew more insistent on account of a strange episode involving a fellow named Sosis. This ordinary Syracusan was known for his outspokenness in assemblies, a quality Plutarch castigates as tartness of tongue. He used that tongue to cast suspicion not only on Dion but on the hired army he led, a composite by this time of Greeks and non-Greeks.[43]

One day Sosis rose to speak his mind at a meeting of the assembly. His speech played on the theme of Dion's designs on power, and used more strident language than Syracuse had yet heard. "Don't you understand," Sosis asked the gathered citizens, "that you've simply exchanged a witless and drunken tyrant for one who's alert and sober?" Having thus made his opinions known, he walked out of the meeting.

The next day, shoppers in the market square were stunned when Sosis, naked and bleeding from cuts on his head, ran into their midst, saying he'd been wounded by Dion's soldiers. A crowd gathered around the wounded man. It seemed to many that Sosis had been attacked for his words against Dion. The apparent suppression of freedom of speech undermined the ideals for which Dion had claimed to be fighting. Murmurs began to spread that the revolution had indeed installed a new tyrant, just as Sosis had claimed.

Another assembly meeting was called and Dion strove to defend himself, claiming to be the victim of a conspiracy. "Dionysius has no hope of coming through safely," he pointed out, "except by stirring up your mistrusts and antagonisms." He pointed out that Sosis had a brother who served in Dionysius's army, implying the tyrant had engineered the whole scheme.

At this point, the story as told by Plutarch—our only source for it—takes a fantastical turn. A group of doctors examined Sosis's head and claimed they saw the marks of a razor, not the gash of a sword that a soldier would likely have used. What was more, they said, there were many small cuts, not one long one, as if someone had sought to draw blood without inflicting grave injury. Then, while this finding was being assessed, some prominent Syracusans arrived at the meeting, bearing a razor they'd found hidden under a rock. They explained that they'd discovered the blade where Sosis had first been spotted, bloody and screaming. The assembly then called in slaves belonging to Sosis, who testified that they'd seen their master leave his house in the hour before dawn carrying just such a razor.

The sequence of these revelations seems suspiciously well-timed and well suited to Dion's exoneration. It was just as easy, a skeptic might say, for Dion's supporters to plant false evidence and arrange false testimony as for Dionysius and Sosis to stage a false wounding. Nonetheless the assembly chose to believe that Sosis was guilty of fraud, as did Plutarch nearly five centuries later. Sosis was summarily sentenced to death.

Officially, Dion was vindicated, but the armed force on which he relied nonetheless created unease. His hardened soldiers owed their allegiance not to the city but to their paymaster. They looked all too much like the army maintained by the tyrant, now entrenched behind the walls of the Island.

Sosis had been convicted of lying, but many thought he'd told the truth when he talked of a sober tyrant replacing a drunken one. Meanwhile Dionysius was making other damaging claims and spreading them through the Greek world: that behind Dion's efforts stood Plato and the Academy, and that *they* were really the cause of the troubles of Syracuse.

*Dion enters Syracuse in triumph. An eighteenth-century tapestry designed by Victor Honoré Janssens.*

CHAPTER 11

# THE "NAVAL MOB"

## *(356–354 BC)*

The religious life of Syracusans had been curtailed since the start
of the revolution. The magnificent temples on the Island were
now off-limits to them, including the glorious shrine of Athena
with its doorway gleaming in ivory and gold. Average citizens, those
not part of the tyrant's cadre, had never had ready access to the Island,
though presumably they could go there on festival days. Now, if they even
approached the causeway, they encountered a zone of guard posts, walls,
and armed men, a Syracusan equivalent of the Berlin Wall.

One shrine however, not on the Island but on the mainland, remained a
vital focus of worship, because of the values it stood for. A colossal statue
of Zeus *Eleutherios*—Zeus who safeguards freedom—had been erected a
century before, after the fall of the tyranny founded by Gelon. A freedom
fest was held each year at the site, on the anniversary of that regime's
ouster. According to Diodorus, the annual rite included athletic games
and a sacrifice of over four hundred cattle on an enormous altar, their
roasted flesh feeding the demos as the smoke wafted upward toward
Zeus.[1] (The altar base seen at the site in Siracusa today, a platform over
six hundred feet long, is a later construction.)

With Dion's entry into the city, the statue of Zeus *Eleutherios* must have
become a symbol of the city's republican spirit, just as Michelangelo's

*David* would become for post-Medici Florence. The games and sacrifices at the fest of 356 BC must have had all the intensity of their first iteration. But unlike in that earlier case, the city's rejoicing was tinged with misgivings and fears. The new liberation was incomplete. A potent army lurked behind the gates of the Island, headed by a despot willing to use it.

Taking his cue from the cult statue, Dion issued coins that showed, on one face, the profile of a bearded Zeus surrounded by the engraved word *Eleutherios*. This was the first time that Zeus had appeared on Syracusan coins, which normally favored female figures, especially Arethusa. It was also the first time that any Greek coin had been stamped with such a clearly political slogan. The back of Dion's coins featured other symbols of Zeus, the thunderbolt or the eagle (or on one rarer issue, an unrelated image, an octopus). The message was one of moral right backed up by invincible might, in the service of Freedom, *Eleutheria*.

Perhaps, too, the coins had a subtler, almost subliminal message, promoting Dion himself. As we've seen, Dion's name was close in sound to oblique cases of Zeus's name, especially the genitive form, *Dios* ("of Zeus"). Plato, in his dialogue *Phaedrus*, seems (in some eyes) to have used this sound-alike word to refer obliquely to Dion, casting him as one of the Zeus-like souls who combine philosophy with political leadership. Dion may well have played on the same resonance when adopting the image of Zeus for his currency. The image shows the god in the prime of maturity, seemingly in his early fifties—the age that Dion had reached in 356.

The Greeks had barely begun, in Dion's time, to elevate living mortals

*The Zeus* Eleutherios *coin minted by Dion, with a stylized thunderbolt depicted on the reverse.*

to the level of gods (as they would do, with increasing ease, a few decades later). Interestingly, in an earlier case in which this had happened, it was a liberator of cities, the Spartan general Lysander, who got divine honors. This warrior had brought freedom (in his own view at least) to peoples who felt oppressed by imperial Athens, freeing them from a "tyrant city" (as Athens was known at the time). Dion had accomplished a similar feat of emancipation, at least in the view he put forward. So it made sense that those who believed in his cause regarded him as godlike, as Diodorus informs us.

Much of the coinage stamped by Dion went into the hands of his mercenaries, who were paid a drachma a day per man, perhaps more. Though initially hired by Dion out of his private wealth, these infantrymen were now on the city's payroll. The expenditure of public funds caused ill-will among Syracusans, in part because it recalled their lives under the Dionysii. Both father and son had squeezed them with taxes to pay for a huge foreign army. What good was a revolution, some started to ask, if poor folk ended up just as poor as before? And why were armed men, few of them Syracusan, many not even Greek, crowding their streets?

Amid these stirrings of discontent, a flotilla of warships arrived offshore, making its way toward Syracuse.[2] A wave of excitement went through the citizen body. Heraclides had come.

His ships had had a rough crossing as they made their way west from the Peloponnese but had gotten through safely. Heraclides, a former cavalryman, had learned a lot about seamanship in the preceding years, which he'd spent in Corinth, a seafaring town. He also understood the political clout that came with naval command. Syracusan warships were rowed by men who lacked the resources to maintain a horse; those wealthier citizens made up the cavalry corps. The throng of rowers was huge—perhaps twenty thousand—and because their ranks excluded the rich, their politics skewed democratic. They formed a powerful bloc in the assembly and rallied behind those who led them on expeditions, especially captains who brought them victories.

Plutarch portrays Heraclides as an amoral populist determined to exploit this "naval mob" (a disparaging phrase Plutarch borrowed from Aristotle). The caricature helps him explain why Heraclides, whom he dislikes, won wider support from Syracusans than Dion, whom he admires. Plutarch admits that Dion's aloof, haughty manner played poorly in the assembly, while Heraclides had the common touch; but he nonetheless holds the masses to blame for preferring the latter. "The license and boldness they'd taken on by gaining sovereignty made them want to be demagogued before becoming a demos [a unified people]," he writes.[3] Heraclides, in Plutarch's jaundiced view, pandered to that ignoble craving.

The Syracusan assembly welcomed Heraclides by voting him the title of "navarch" or admiral of the fleet. This posed a challenge to Dion's authority. Dion's title was *stratêgos autokratôr*, commander with executive power, and Dion argued that it implied command on *both* land and sea. At his behest the assembly canceled the admiralship—"unwillingly" says Plutarch—but then, in a private conclave, Heraclides bowed to Dion's senior position. At a second assembly meeting, the two men sought to project harmony. Dion himself reintroduced the navarch proposal and added a clause that Heraclides should have a bodyguard like his own. Heraclides, for his part, gave a speech paying tribute to Dion, and all between them seemed well—for the moment.

The people's navy had the task of stopping shipments of food from reaching the Island. The tyrant still had the larger fleet, much of it under command of Philistus, the tyranny's stalwart supporter. By now around eighty years old, the doughty hardliner had faced off twice against Plato and once against Dion, protecting the regime from what he perceived as threats. His third opponent, Heraclides, would prove his undoing.

In a battle at sea, Heraclides got the better of Philistus's naval squadron and surrounded its flagship. Philistus may then have killed himself, as Diodorus claims, but a witness quoted by Plutarch reports that he ran his ship aground and was captured alive as he tried to escape by land.[4] The "naval mob" then brought him back to a city hungry for vengeance.

The crowd on shore stripped Philistus bare and mocked his naked and aging physique. Then they cut off his head, and the rest of his body was dragged through the streets by gangs of boys. They towed Philistus's headless corpse by a rope they had tied to one leg—for everyone thought it was *he,* not Megacles, who had said that a tyrant should hold onto power until dragged off "by the leg." Then the remains were cast into the quarries, as if into prison.

The exultation over Philistus's corpse did not stop there. Decades later, Timaeus, the tyrant-hating Sicilian historian, described Philistus's death and disfigurement with such schadenfreude as to outrage a later writer, Plutarch. The great biographer pauses in his *Life of Dion* to remind his readers "not to mock at misfortunes with arrogance or jests, since nothing prevents the best of our kind from undergoing these things at the hands of chance." Conversely, Plutarch found the writings of Ephorus, another now-lost chronicler, too effusive in their support of Philistus, who was, after all, "the most tyrant-loving of any human being."[5]

In rejecting both these accounts of Philistus, one scathingly bitter, the other hagiographic, Plutarch reveals the moderate temper that wins over readers, century after century, to his *Parallel Lives.* "Whoever declines to praise the deeds of Philistus, and also does not rail at the man's misfortunes, is the most suitable writer," he comments, in what sounds like a self-description. But the case of Dion put his objectivity to the test. Under the influence of Plato he leaned hard into a positive view of Dion, despite ample evidence of a more complex picture.

Heraclides received a hero's reception after the death of Philistus, a worrisome development for Dion. Dion's mercenaries had nothing to show to compare to what the fleet had achieved; the Syracusans increasingly felt that these hired troops were useless, and far too expensive. The ships, they now said, were all that they needed; a naval blockade could starve out the men on the Island and bring victory. The navy inspired such confidence that when Dionysius offered, again, to surrender on terms—he asked for safe passage to Italy and the grant of a fertile province there—the demos turned him down. Nothing would satisfy them now except the tyrant's total capitulation.

Then, suddenly, Dionysius was gone. A small ship had rowed him out of the harbor by night and had slipped past the naval patrols. He made it safely to Italy and landed in Locri, together with a few of his family and much of his moveable wealth. This turn of events enraged Syracusans. In Locri, his mother's home city, the tyrant was safely beyond the reach of attack and able to gather resources from the Italian toe. What was worse, he had not abandoned his foothold in Syracuse. He'd left a contingent of troops hunkered down on the Island, under command of his teenage son, Apollocrates.

In a sudden about-face, the people cast scorn on Heraclides, who only a few days before had been their darling. Some must have wondered—as a modern historian does—whether he'd taken a bribe to let the tyrant escape. But soon, a new crisis made him a hero again, while thrusting Dion further into disfavor.

W ith the freedom to make its own laws for the first time in decades, the assembly took up a measure that the poor of Greece were always quick to adopt and the rich to suppress: land redistribution. Of the city's two leaders, Heraclides favored adoption, Dion, suppression. This financial wedge issue, as one would call it today, was about to split the revolution apart.

Like other cities in mid-fourth-century Greece, Syracuse had seen arable land become concentrated in fewer and fewer hands. Its two tyrants, especially Dionysius the Elder, had accelerated the trend by giving estates to those who had earned their favor. They'd also gathered the dispossessed from across Sicily, people made homeless or landless by war, and brought them to Syracuse, swelling its population and creating a large proletarian class. These urban poor felt that the deck that had been stacked against them ought now to be reshuffled.

A man named Hippon—a shill for Heraclides, according to Plutarch—introduced a land-reform act in a raucous assembly session. It easily passed, but Dion, drawing on his powers as *stratêgos autokratôr*, moved to block it. Urged on by Heraclides, the people passed it again and also went further, voting on measures designed to curb Dion's power. Swept up in a mood of defiance, they halted all payments to Dion's troops, the base on which his authority rested. They made clear they wanted new elections to choose a new slate of commanders.

With his brilliance at using metaphor, Plutarch, in various writings, often compares political passions to a disease and leaders to doctors who treat it. At this point in his *Life of Dion*, he turns the time-honored trope in a new direction. The Syracusans, he says, were like a patient who starts to feel well after shaking off a long illness. Exuberant at turning the corner, the patient leaps to his feet but stumbles and reels, discovering he has no strength. Dion, he says, was like a physician who urges caution and slowness. The advice is essential, but the patient, too eager to get out of bed, is bound to resent it.

The comparison configures Dion as a healer with only the interests of his patient at heart. That conception may have come from his reading of Plato, for Plato likewise thought in medical terms as he watched from afar the progress of Dion's invasion.

In a letter Plato sent to Dion from Athens—the *Fourth Letter* as we now know it—he gave his former student advice on "healing" the problems of Syracuse, including the conflict with Heraclides. He was worried by reports of that rivalry. "Everyone there [in Syracuse] says that, now that Dionysius is off the scene, there's much expectation that affairs will be wrecked by the ambitions of you, Heraclides, Theodotes, and the other notables," he writes to Dion. "May it turn out that no one behaves like that. But if someone *does*, then *you* must show yourself a doctor, and all will turn out for the best."[6]

Whereas Plato, by his own account, had at first disapproved of Dion's campaign, in the *Fourth Letter* he gives it a ringing endorsement. His very opening sentence declares his allegiance. "I think my enthusiasm for the events that have taken place has been clear to see throughout this whole time," he begins, "as has my eagerness to help them reach fulfillment, for no greater reason than ambitious pursuit of the good." His term for "the good," *tois kalois*, is the plural form of *to kalon*, philosophy's ultimate goal in *Republic*, the Form of the Good. Dion's revolution, Plato makes clear, deserves his support because it shares his loftiest aspirations.

Referring obliquely to the Academy and Dion's training there, Plato classes Dion among the people—"you know who I mean"—who need to live up to a higher standard than others, in the same way that adults are held to a higher standard than children. "We must reveal ourselves clearly to be the sort of people we claim we are," Plato urges, using "we" to group himself and Dion together as fellow philosophers.[7] Though he adds "this will be easy, with the help of god," his exhortations reveal a degree of concern. If ethical rule would be easy, what need of his letter?

Plato uses the adjective *phaneros* twice in the letter's first sentences, meaning "clear" in the sense of clearly apparent to others. (Our English "phenomena" started out as Greek *phainomena*, "things that are visible.") A verb derived from the same root occurs in Plato's injunction to Dion to "show yourself a doctor." The *phan-/phain-* cluster shows Plato thinking of how Syracusan events were *seen* across Greece. He makes this concern explicit as he continues impressing on Dion the need for the moral high ground. Other people, he writes, become famous only by traveling widely and winning esteem in the many places they visit; "but what's happened in *your* case is such as for people across the whole world (if I can speak with a bit too much heat) to look to *one* place, and to look at *you* most of all." He describes Dion as "seen by all" as he exhorts him to emulate Greece's greatest lawgivers. He might have used the phrase "seen by all" of himself, for he would be judged on how Dion managed his role.

In our own age, demonstrators are known to chant, in confrontations with authoritarian forces, "the whole world is watching." Thanks to smartphones with cameras, that sometimes is so. Plato, for his part, qualifies his statement about "the whole world" by conceding he's overheated (literally, "speaking too much like a teenage boy"). Nonetheless, his letter makes clear that *other* letters from Syracuse were going to cities in mainland Greece, carrying news of the revolution's progress. Heraclides and his uncle Theodotes, Plato reveals, had sent dispatches to Sparta and Aegina, giving *their* versions of what was taking place. We know from other sources that an Academy man, Timonides of Leucas, was writing from Syracuse to Speusippus at this same time.[8] The Greek world was staying informed, but getting different stories from different perspectives. Plato urges Dion to send a report of his own.

Aware of Dion's proud nature, Plato is careful not to preach or talk down to him. He casts himself not as a mentor but as a cheering spectator at an athletic event, helping Dion, the athlete, perform at his best. "Go ahead and vie for the prize," he writes, invoking the model of Olympic competition. But pride, in Dion's case, was a double-edged sword. Plato's final words in the letter carry a warning about Dion's haughty demeanor. "Keep in mind that you seem to some to be less solicitous than is fitting," he writes to Dion, slipping in his most urgent advice at the close. "Don't forget that it's through being pleasing to people that things get accomplished. Willfulness has solitude as its companion."⁹

Politics, as Plato had once told Dionysius, could not be conducted without reliable friends. But Dion's aloofness had often estranged him from those whose help he might need. In Athens, Plato had brought Dion together with his own nephew, Speusippus, a man known for warmth and a sense of humor. Dion had grown quite fond of Speusippus—had even passed on to him the house he had bought near the city—but had not learned much about levity.

There was little that Plato could do from afar to get Dion, essentially, to smile more. He sent the *Fourth Letter* to Syracuse and hoped for the best. "Good luck to you," he writes as a sign-off, a Greek way of saying goodbye. His former student was going to need more than luck.

According to Plutarch, Speusippus too was writing to Dion, with concerns very much like his uncle's. He warned Dion not to let the acclaim of women and children go to his head (implying perhaps that men, whose views mattered most, were not so impressed). "See to it that you adorn Sicily with reverence, justice, and laws of the best kind," he urged, then came to the main point: "and thereby put the Academy in good repute."¹⁰

If these were his words (we have only Plutarch's paraphrase), then Speusippus was keenly aware of how much was at stake for the school he was soon to inherit, as well as for his own image. He had done much—his polling of Syracusans—to link himself to Dion's campaign.

These two Academy leaders, Plato and his nephew Speusippus, were voicing the concerns of their institution. The Academy had trained Dion, and Dion, most likely, had helped fund the Academy. Whatever happened in Syracuse would be seen by many as an Academy venture, a real-world test of its theories. No one, perhaps, expected philosopher-kingship, but could *Republic* be proven right to a lesser degree—that a leader would be more effective, more just, if philosophically trained? Or would Plato become, as he feared, a mere *logos*, words without substance?


The salaries of Dion's troops had been stopped for weeks now, and Dion was unable or unwilling to make up their wages himself. The pay of the soldiers had fallen into arrears. The problems this might create had been shown all too clearly by Dionysius, who, a few years before this, had touched off a mutiny by reducing military pay. A crisis had been averted then, but now another was brewing.[11]

Syracuse had by this time divided along class lines, the wealthier folk supporting Dion and his land army, those less well-off, Heraclides and the fleet. Gradually the commoners got the upper hand. In an assembly meeting postponed by bad omens—a bull had gotten loose and rampaged through the city—the people elected a new board of leaders that included Heraclides but not Dion. In an instant Dion went from *stratêgos autokratôr*, commander-in-chief with plenipotentiary power, to ordinary citizen of free Syracuse.

With Dion demoted, his unpaid troops posed even more of a danger. Attempts were made to draw them away from their commander and absorb them into the demos; they were offered citizenship with full rights if they disavowed Dion. The troops, however, were still in mind of the pay they were owed, which neither Dion nor the city seemed inclined to provide. Flipping the situation on its head, they formed a plan to take over the state by force and invited Dion to join them. They told him that Syracuse had wronged him and so he had every right to ignore its laws.

What was Dion to do, with his city turning against him and his mercenaries proposing to make him dictator? Losing his hold on the revolution was unthinkable, but so was an army-backed putsch that would give the lie to his image as freedom fighter. With no good options within Syracuse, he hit on plan to go elsewhere. He'd continue on as the troops' commander but lead them to Leontini, a two-day march to the northwest. This city had joined the revolt against Dionysius when Dion had first arrived, then repelled an attempt by Philistus to force it back into line. It was populated by veterans who'd been given good land there, several decades before, by Dionysius the Elder.[12] Dion, who'd at that time been the Elder's chief aide, knew he could count on support from these men, or their sons. From Leontini he'd watch and wait for a chance to return.

A confrontation took place as Dion led his men out of Syracuse. As they marched toward the gates, the soldiers berated Syracusans they met for their treatment of Dion. Those provocations soon drew a crowd of angry citizens spoiling for a fight. Dion was keenly aware that the tense scene was being observed by the tyrant's forces, penned up on the Island but keeping close watch and hoping for discord of just this sort. He begged his countrymen not to create a rift by attacking the troops, but these entreaties, and the restraint of the soldiers, only emboldened the mob.

Dion finally ordered his men to advance with drawn weapons; the sight of those spears caused the crowd to scatter. It was ugly to present such a threat, but better than outright bloodshed. Soon though that threshold, too, would be crossed.

Dion's column marched off toward Leontini, while Syracusans regrouped and considered their options. Some now regarded the army of Dion, and Dion himself, as an enemy. A squad on horseback went in pursuit, hoping to chase Dion out of the region for good.

Dion had thus far held his men back, but when the Syracusan horsemen harassed and pelted them as they forded a river, he felt he had no choice. He ordered his troops to form up and attack, and they did so, inflicting casualties and putting the horsemen to flight. Plutarch, in his desire to downplay this episode, says that "not many" were killed, whereas Diodorus claims the fatalities were in fact "many."[13] A greater number were taken prisoner by Dion, but he generously released these without demanding a ransom. By keeping alive some thin shreds of trust, he hoped he might one day regain Syracuse.

Plato, in his *Fourth Letter,* had urged Dion to be a physician; now it turned out the role involved venesection, the opening of veins.

In Leontini, Dion was welcomed by families of soldiers he'd once settled there. His men were hired at full pay and offered citizen rights in the city. Leontini sent envoys to Syracuse to demand better treatment for Dion, a sentiment echoed by nearby cities, many also controlled by decommissioned soldiers. Dion seems to have forged a regional coalition, while Syracuse remained a determined opponent. Messages flew back and forth, one set accusing Dion of crimes and bad faith, the other defending his conduct. Neither argument did much to change the equation.

The struggle for Syracuse had gotten more complicated, with four contestants holding sway in four different places. Dion and his hired army held Leontini and the surrounding region; in mainland Syracuse, Heraclides was in full control, with support of the "naval mob;" on the Island, Apollocrates and his mercenaries were hunkered down with their stockpiles of weapons and food; while in Locri, on the Italian mainland, Dionysius presided over a government in exile and schemed at regaining his former seat.

For the moment, all four leaders were biding their time, awaiting the next turn of events. It was not long in coming.

On the Island, the troops in the tyrant's employ were at last beginning to starve. With their harbor blockaded, no transport ships had arrived to supply them with grain. Their commander, the tyrant's wine-soaked son, was doing his best to keep their spirits up, but even he had begun to despair.[14] At a conclave one night, the soldiers decided the end was at hand. In a process like that of a democratic assembly, they voted to send a spokesman at dawn to negotiate terms of surrender.

The following morning, this spokesman was on his way to the mainland when ships were seen approaching the Island. A relief convoy, sent from Locri by Dionysius, had gotten through the blockade, just in time. Its commander was a man named Nypsius, a soldier of fortune hired from what is now Naples. The ships tied up near the Island and began to unload.

Nypsius had brought not only grain and oil but fresh troops and chests of coin. Taking the men and money on shore, he convened a new conclave. The outcome of the earlier meeting was instantly canceled. Replenished by food and pay, those on the Island recommitted themselves to defending the tyrant's claim on Syracuse.

Meanwhile Heraclides' triremes rowed into the harbor to engage the tyrant's supply ships. Two fleets joined battle just off the shore of the Island. Once again, as in its fight with Philistus, the revolution's navy proved its mettle. It sank some of Nypsius's ships and seized others, finally overcoming resistance and stopping the resupply. Nypsius watched from the Island as his squadron went down to defeat. But he was not about to let things end there.

That day, and for much of the night, Syracusans went on a victory spree, celebrating with banquets and drinking bouts. With no stern "doctor" to reprimand them, they neglected their duties and rounds, as those on the Island could clearly observe from their towers. Even the guards on the isthmus wall drank deep and fell asleep on their watch. As the tower guards slumbered, Nypsius ordered a ladder set up; a small contingent ascended and killed all they found. Then, with the bolt-pin the guards had controlled, they opened the gate in the wall. The tyrant's armed forces poured into the city and fell on the Syracusans, many of whom were drunk.

Without a leader to rally them—Heraclides was somehow not on the scene—the Syracusans panicked and ran for safety instead of organizing resistance. The tyrant's troops seized control of the market, then invaded the houses nearby, seizing valuables, killing the men, taking women and children prisoner to sell as slaves. They sacked Achradina as though it were an enemy stronghold instead of a place their leader supposedly ruled. Small bands of Syracusans fought back in the dark in blind alleys; these narrow spaces quickly filled up with corpses.

As dawn arrived with the attack still in progress, Syracusans surveyed the ruin around them. They realized that one man could save them, a man who controlled a contingent of infantry: Dion. For a time no one dared speak of recalling Dion, but finally some of the cavalrymen—the wealthier class, among whom were Dion's supporters—proposed to go to Leontini and beg Dion to come back. Six horsemen set out at full gallop, arriving in Leontini at sunset. They threw themselves at Dion's feet and, their cheeks streaming with tears, described what was taking place in their city.

Plutarch, in his *Life of Dion*, sets this scene in the theater of Leontini— appropriately, for he stages it as a play. Dion, in Plutarch's telling, delivers a rousing speech straight out of a tragedy: "If I cannot save Syracuse, I will go to be buried there in the fire and the ruin." He asks his troops to join him and the entire company shouts agreement as one. The scene is crafted to glorify Dion as a man who put city before self, but of course in returning to help his city he was also helping himself. His second march on Syracuse, like the first, was part liberation crusade, part campaign of conquest, or, to some eyes, the second disguised to look like the first.

Dion and his troops set off at a rapid pace through the night. But in Syracuse, the tide of opinion was turning. Glutted with plunder and wary of counterattacks, the marauders unleashed by Nypsius had gone back to their barracks; in the calm that followed, the anti-Dion faction made its voice heard. The city had had good reason to kick Dion out, this faction insisted; it must not now let him in, but defend the gates against his return, just as though he were an invader. The Island could be sealed off once again, and its troops starved into submission, without his assistance.

A divided Syracuse sent opposite messages down the road toward Leontini, one set urging Dion to hurry, the other warning him to stay away. The anti-Dioneans manned the gates as instructed. Dion, unsure of the city's mood, kept slowing, then increasing his pace as he rode at the head of his column. In this way he marched through a night and a day; it was night again by the time he neared Syracuse.

On the Island, Nypsius learned, or guessed, that Dion was on his way. He launched a second assault, determined to wreak destruction while he still could. This time his troops knocked down the siege wall that blocked them off from the mainland and streamed into the undamaged parts of the city. They took no prisoners now but killed whomever they could and plundered at will. Then they set fires throughout the town with torches and flaming arrows.

As the blazes began to spread, those fleeing the flames were cut down in the streets or killed by collapsing houses. Rubble and burning timbers were strewn everywhere. "It was as though Dionysius wanted to bury his fallen tyranny within the city," Plutarch remarks, configuring Syracuse as an enormous funeral pyre.[15]

The nearer Dion drew to the walls, the more the messengers coming to meet him were of one mind: He must hurry. He'd been informed of the second attack and the spreading fires, and finally he heard that Heraclides, who'd at last entered the fray, had been wounded. To show his contrition, Heraclides sent his own uncle, Theodotes, to plead for Dion's help and assure him of his nephew's peaceful intentions. No doubt Heraclides had been among those who, only the day before, had urged that Dion be barred from passing the gates.

Several miles from those gates, Dion learned that the city's fate was nearly sealed. He urged his troops forward at speed, even though they'd been on the move for more than twenty-four hours. His best hope lay in surprise, for he'd traveled hard and would not be expected so soon. The refugees he met—thousands were fleeing—greeted him with tears and entreaties, and also informed him the slaughter was still underway. He increased his pace yet again; his approach had not yet been observed.

As he passed through the gates and saw the billowing smoke, he divided his men into columns to move on the tyrant's troops from several directions. Plutarch's tone becomes exultant as he depicts Dion in action: "When they saw him leading his men against the enemy, the Syracusans sent up a roar, cries of joy, and great shouting, together with prayers and appeals for help; they called Dion their savior and their god. . . . as he advanced at the forefront through blood and fire and the many corpses lying about in the streets."[16] It's an image fit for an epic poem, or a modern superhero film.

Dion's forces skirmished with those of the tyrant in narrow streets and along the destroyed isthmus wall. Gradually the tyrant's troops began to give ground. Over four thousand of their number lay dead; those who survived went back to the Island and barricaded its gates. Their devastating assault on the city was over.

Syracuse lay in ruins. Dion, who'd gone without sleep for three days now, supervised a night-long effort to put out the flames and preserve what little was left. The next day he set up a trophy, a monument made of captured weapons, to mark the point where the battle had turned, and led a sacrifice to the gods in thanks for his victory. An assembly convened amid the destruction voted once again to make Dion *stratêgos autokratôr*. He'd regained what he'd lost and had gotten a second chance.

All were expecting that Dion, once back in control, would take reprisals against those who'd forced him out or opposed his reentry. Most of these men fled the city but Heraclides stayed put and came before Dion, accompanied by Theodotes, in a spirit of contrition. Dion's advisors urged him to seize the moment and have the two killed, to eliminate what they called *dêmokopia*, "courtship of the masses." But Dion, according to Plutarch, invoked the lessons of Plato in rejecting their counsel. "Other commanders spend most of their training in weapons practice and war," Plutarch quotes him as saying, another speech the biographer may have invented. "But for me, my long stretch in the Academy was devoted to overcoming anger, envy, ambition. One doesn't display these restraints by dealing mildly with friends and *good* people, but rather, if one has been harmed, by being gentle with those who've done wrong and accepting appeasement."[17] He'd forgo revenge and allow Heraclides to stay in the city, unharmed.

Plutarch devised the phrase "philosopher-in-arms" to praise Alexander the Great, but it also sums up his conception of Dion. In the *Life of Dion* he's careful to keep Dion's soldierly prowess balanced with ethical virtues. Thus he provides Dion's calm meditation on mercy, allegedly the result of Academy training, as a counterweight to the blood-and-guts scenes of the previous night. It's an impressive portrait of a man for all seasons. But events to come were to make this balance impossible to maintain.

Dionysius had had good reason to choose Locri as his sanctuary; his mother, Doris, was Locrian by birth. The Locrians took him in willingly but soon discovered they'd lost their freedom when they opened their gates. With the armed force he'd brought, Dionysius seized their high ground and installed himself as their ruler. Locri was far smaller than Syracuse, but the confiscated estates of the rich kept his army well paid. As long as he could maintain his troops, he could stay in the game.

Living apart from his wife, who was still on the Island, and robbed of the Syracusan tables, Dionysius turned toward sexual predation. We're told that he exercised *droit du seigneur* with a vengeance, kidnapping brides before their weddings and sending them back deflowered to their bridegrooms. His troops arrested the wives of leading Locrians on specious charges and brought them to him to be raped.[18]

According to one report, these sexual crimes took place in a villa that Dionysius had commandeered. The floor of one room was strewn with sprigs of wild thyme and petals of roses. The tyrant used this fragrant matting to have his way with his victims, "omitting no outrage" in his treatment of them.[19] He was bearing out Plato's analysis in *Republic*, which links the will to power of tyrants with overactive or warped sex drives.

A second report that survives of the tyrant's Locrian crimes is so bizarre and unlikely that it seems, on the one hand, difficult to believe and, on the other, impossible for anyone to have invented. It comes from Strabo, a Greek geographic writer of the first century BC. According to Strabo, in Locri Dionysius had the most beautiful virgins brought to his rooms, stripped them bare, and forced them to run about chasing doves that he had released. Sometimes he made them wear shoes of unequal height, so that, as they chased the doves, their stride would be limping and awkward.[20] The story reveals a desire to humiliate women, a common theme in ancient accounts—whether true or invented—of despots.

While ravaging Locri, Dionysius kept his eye on Syracuse and the strife between factions there. Tyrants before him who'd been kicked out had sometimes gotten back in if their cities failed to stabilize in their absence. Omens had given him cause for hope: At the time he'd abandoned the Island, his seers had noted the swallows that lived there suddenly flying away. Since swallows were known to come back every year to their nests, the seers predicted that Dionysius, too, would soon return to his palace.[21]

The worse things got in his native city, the better were Dionysius's chances for restoration. It behooved him to wait and to watch in the hope that Dion would fail—and to try to make sure that he did so.

The power struggle in free Syracuse had become more straightforward, a classic *stasis* pitting the landed rich, who largely supported Dion, against the less wealthy, who backed Heraclides. The success of the revolution hinged on whether these factions could get along. A common enemy, the malevolent force on the Island, had brought them together, but now that the enemy seemed contained—Dion had sealed off the isthmus with a new wall—disputes erupted again.

At an assembly soon after the nights of the Nypsius terrors, Dion agreed, for the second time, to accept Heraclides as navarch. That pleased the demos, but then the divisive issue of land distribution again raised its head. Dion once more stood firm. The measure that had been passed was not yet in effect, and Dion continued to quash it, defending the interests of the propertied class. This move enraged Heraclides.

Plutarch reports that Heraclides from this point forward became committed to Dion's ouster. In speeches to the men in his fleet, he endorsed the idea put forward by Sosis, that Syracuse was only swapping one tyrant for another, and harped on the theme of Dion's kinship with Dionysius. Plutarch even asserts that Heraclides was *himself* in cahoots with Dionysius at this point, colluding with the enemy of his enemy. That arrangement would have made sense, but where Heraclides was concerned, Plutarch was inclined to believe ugly rumors.

The dissension that Plato had worried about, when he wrote the *Fourth Letter* to Dion, was now a reality. In that letter Plato urged Dion to bend his stiff neck in order to govern better, but this hadn't happened. A warmer or more adaptable person than Dion might have drawn Heraclides into a partnership, but Dion was not a warm man; all his life he'd kept to himself and hoarded authority. A charismatic orator who despised him, and whom the people adored, was a problem he was ill equipped to manage.

Heraclides nearly succeeded at one point in seizing the reins of power. Dion had left Syracuse to lead the army against a Spartan freebooter who'd arrived in Sicily. Heraclides, at sea with the fleet, turned the prows of his ships around and made straight for the city, intending to take control there and bar the gates against Dion. Someone brought word to Dion of the fleet's change of course. Dion took a flying column of horsemen and rode all night at top speed, arriving in Syracuse just before Heraclides. The fleet put back out to sea, having failed to carry out a second revolution. The power struggle became more fraught and intense.

A second Spartan arrived on the scene, a man named Gaesylus, otherwise unknown. He claimed to be an emissary from Sparta, but this would have been a convenient cover for a stateless soldier of fortune, which may have been his true identity. Heraclides made much of this man and tried to enlist his help against Dion, until Dion pointed out that *he* was a Spartan too, having been made a citizen during his exile.

Gaesylus dropped whatever game he'd been playing and turned peacemaker, arranging a truce between the two faction leaders. He vowed to Dion to use the soldiers he'd brought to keep Heraclides in line. A fragile accord took hold.

Then a new turn of events created more rifts between Heraclides and

Dion. As its food stocks ran low and its troops despaired of relief, the Island surrendered.

The assembly surely demanded heads on stakes, but Dion granted the tyrant's kin—his son Apollocrates, his two daughters, and his wife, Sôphrosynê—safe passage away from Sicily, along with five ships filled with soldiers and gear. The entire population of Syracuse—now greatly reduced—stood on the shore and watched these ships slip away, one by one through the harbor entrance, then turn northward toward Locri. Emotions ran high in the crowd: joy and elation, but anger as well, since men who'd butchered the city were going unpunished. All those who watched were aware that Dion, who'd allowed that to happen, was great-uncle to the tyrant's three children and uncle to Sôphrosynê.

When the ships had left, Dion made his way to the Island, a piece of land he'd called home for most of his life but had not glimpsed for eleven years. His son had been a toddler when he'd last lived there, and now that son, in his mid-teens, was coming to greet him, accompanied by Dion's sister, Aristomachê. Behind them came the boy's mother, Aretê, once Dion's wife, then married off by the tyrant to a regime loyalist. She wept as she came, overwhelmed by conflicting feelings. No one knew what to expect from the couple's reunion, least of all her.

Dion's emotions are hard to read in the two accounts of this moment. It's notable that, according to Plutarch, he hugged his sister and son at first meeting but didn't acknowledge his wife. Aristomachê, Plutarch reports, sensed his aloofness and forced him to make a choice: "Will she [Aretê] greet you as her husband or as her uncle?" She made clear that Aretê had remarried only under compulsion. At that point, says Plutarch, Dion's coldness gave way to tears and he finally embraced Aretê. Together with their son they went off to Dion's house to rebuild some version of family life.[22]

Unable to punish Dionysius, and now deprived of revenge on his kin, Syracusans tried to strike at his father, entombed on the Island beneath a magnificent monument. The assembly resolved to break up the tomb and cast out the corpse, a punishment no Greek city had seen enacted except on the tragic stage. Dion invoked his executive powers again, backed up by his troops, to block this proposal. In this, he played the stern "doctor," as Plutarch portrayed him, but also the loyal son-in-law, for he'd served the Elder for decades and married his daughter. His veto put him in greater disfavor among the popular party.

The fate of the acropolis—the tyrants' armory, fortress, and palace—was on everyone's mind. Dion had the good sense not to live there himself, preferring to stay in his modest home on the mainland. But he also did not destroy the place, as many believed that he should. The grim castle continued to stand, reminding Syracusans of the adamantine bonds in which they'd been held. We're told that Dion made the acropolis into a public space, though what this means is unclear.

The tensions of *stasis*, suppressed for a time by fear of those on the Island, began to mount once again now the fear was dispelled. The ranks of the poor had grown due to the wanton destruction, and the city no longer employed them as rowers; at Dion's behest, the navy had been disbanded. This was partly a cost-saving move but also a way to strip Heraclides of power by rendering him a navarch with no navy. Dion invited his rival to join his governing council, but Heraclides refused the subordinate role, saying he'd rather stay with the commons and cast his assembly vote just like all the rest.

Heraclides continued to channel the people's anger at Dion and stoke their mistrust. In assembly meetings, he mounted the speaker's platform to point out the ways that Dion had favored the few and thwarted the masses. He railed against a summons that Dion had sent to Corinth, Syracuse's mother city, requesting help in drafting a new constitution. Since Corinth was solidly oligarchic, any advisors arriving from there would no doubt favor the rich and prevent the tabled land measure from being revived.

Oligarchic advice was in fact just what Dion was seeking. His plan for Syracuse, related by Plutarch, involved a conservative power structure that "mixed the popular and the royal element"—a system of checks and balances. Just who Dion hoped would serve in the "royal" office, Plutarch doesn't say, but we can guess he reserved that spot for himself.

Dion and his inner circle feared that this constitution would fail if

Heraclides opposed it, as they felt sure that he would. And if the new laws failed, Dion would fail as a leader. Syracuse's future was on the line. Dion was told that something had to be done.

In the *Fourth Letter* Plato urged Dion to act as a doctor in dealing with Heraclides, but what did that mean? Doctors, after all, sometimes performed amputations. With grim resolve Dion gave the nod to what his council advised. His troops broke into his rival's home and stabbed Heraclides to death.

Three years after landing in Sicily, Dion at last took full control of his city.

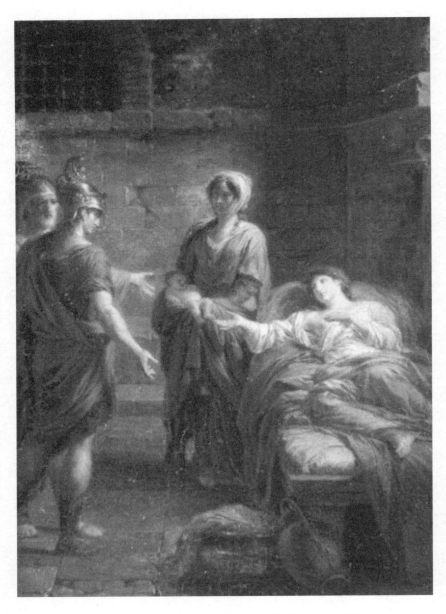

*Aretê, in prison, pleads with her guards not to take her baby son. Oil canvas by
Jean-Charles Nicaise Perrin (1754–1831).*

# CHAPTER 12

# THE FURY'S BROOM

## *(354 BC)*

In the passage of *Republic* that Platonist Paul Shorey calls "perhaps the most famous sentence in Plato," Socrates lays out two paths for bringing Callipolis, the perfectly just city-state, into being: A philosopher might become king, or a king might become a philosopher. Only in these two ways, *Republic* asserts, can the troubles of the human race be cured. Shorey notes the enormous influence that the sentence has had since Plato set it down: "A score of writers from Polybius to Bacon, Hobbes, More, Erasmus, and Bernard Shaw" have quoted or paraphrased it, most of them in support of what it conveys.[1]

The dream of a ruler who possesses absolute power, yet wields it with perfect justice, has burned brightly ever since Plato held it aloft, in both *Republic* and, as we've seen, in the *Seventh Letter*. Many political figures have been thought, either in their own times or afterward, to have made that dream a reality; a brief list compiled by Shorey stretches from Marcus Aurelius to Napoleon Bonaparte. Dion, though less illustrious than those later names, stands at the head of the list, in that he was the first western leader we know of to hoist philosophy's banners as he took control of a state. His career illustrates the potency of the dream but also the ease with which it can turn into nightmare.

Even Aristotle, in general an opponent of absolute rule, felt the allure of the dream. "If there is any man distinguished . . . in a surpassing degree of virtue," he writes in *Politics*, " . . . it's to be expected that such a man will be as a god among mortals. . . . Law does not exist in the case of such men, for they are themselves law."[2] As Plato had done in *Republic*, Aristotle tries to draw a bright line between good autocrats and bad ones, allowing the good ones license to do as they please. But his own former tutee, Alexander the Great, showed him it might not be easy to tell which was which.

The timeless appeal of the dream of philosopher-kingship is perhaps the best argument for keeping it at arm's length. Its power to move hearts and minds means that it inevitably gets misused, either by strongmen who want to be kings or by philosophers who want to be kingmakers. Whether Plato or Dion, or both, misused it in this way is a question that cannot be answered, but must nonetheless be asked. Over the centuries, misuse of the dream has been by far the more prevalent trend. Our skepticism has the endorsement of history.

News of Heraclides' murder must have hit hard when it reached Athens and the Academy. Plato, as he recounts in the *Seventh Letter*, had fought to save Heraclides' life when the tyrant had wanted him dead; he'd regarded Heraclides, along with his uncle Theodotes, as allies. Plato had urged Dion, in his *Fourth Letter*, to avoid a showdown with these men or a permanent rift. He'd stressed the need for Dion, as an Academy member, to meet a high moral standard, reminding him that the world was watching to see what he would do. What he'd then done was enough to dismay a good part of that world.

Among Plato's reasons to worry about Heraclides' death was the question of whether Academy members had been involved, or might appear to have been. According to Plutarch, it was Dion's "friends" who wanted Heraclides dead and to whom Dion entrusted the killing. Plutarch also makes clear that these friends did *not* include the soldiers Dion employed, so the logical alternative is his Academy allies.[3] Plutarch elsewhere mentions that Athenians were among Dion's "friends" and also makes clear that these "friends" had received bequests from Dion after the departure of Apollocrates.[4] Plutarch's vagueness about these people is striking, suggesting he was uncomfortable giving particulars.

Did Plato's students instigate the murder of Heraclides? Did they invoke Plato's doctrines to justify that deed? The question is complicated by a Platonic work, the dialogue *Statesman*, that advocates the use of assassination, provided the man who employs it is skilled in the arts of rule. The relationship between this text and Dion's career is controversial and hard to disentangle.

As we've seen, none of Plato's dialogues can be securely dated, but *Statesman* seems on stylistic grounds to belong to the late 360s or early 350s BC. That means it closely pre- or postdates Dion's takeover of Syracuse. Scholars have argued both ways; some see in *Statesman* a set of teachings that preceded Dion's coup and perhaps guided it, others, a subsequent text that may have been meant to justify Dion's actions. There's no way to be certain, but it's clear that anyone reading the work soon after 355 would connect its message with what had transpired in Syracuse.

The last third of *Statesman* seems especially apt, for here Plato defines statesmanship as an art that stands beyond law. Those who have mastered this art should not be constrained, *Statesman* claims, because they instinctively know what to do as rulers, even *whom to kill.*

The crucial passage is one in which Plato invokes the medical metaphor he also proposes to Dion in his *Fourth Letter.* A ruler is like the doctor of a city, the spokesman of *Statesman* avers. In this instance, though, Plato's focus is on the harsher methods a doctor, or ruler, might use. Just as doctors can still be healers even when causing pain—Plato mentions "cutting" and "burning," that is, amputation and cauterization—so statesmen are no less statesmen when taking harsh measures. "If they cleanse the state by killing some people or banishing them . . . so long as they do it by using understanding and justice, and take their city from worse to better so far as they can. . . . then *this* we must call the only upright form of government."[5]

The verb here translated "cleanse," *kathairein*, extends the medical metaphor into the realm of politics. In medical usage the word refers to purgation, elimination of noxious bile by vomiting or excretion. In the statesman's world it can only mean removal of those deemed harmful, exactly the argument Dion's "friends" made for getting rid of Heraclides. If those "friends" were Academy members, were they taking their cue from *Statesman*? Or was *Statesman* written to rationalize the "cleansing" they'd already done?

Or should we entertain a more disquieting thought? If *Statesman* was in circulation before the *Fourth Letter* was written, then Plato's mention of "doctoring" in the letter would have evoked his earlier use of the same metaphor in *Statesman*. Dion or his "friends," instructed by the letter to act as physicians, might have picked up the cross-reference and gotten a half-hidden message: If "cleansing" were deemed necessary, they ought to just go ahead and clean house. They might have understood Plato to be freeing their hands, in the letter to Dion, for extrajudicial killing.

Such speculations may seem overly dark, but it bears noting that Academy students *did* commit assassinations at about the time *Statesman* was written. Python of Aenus killed the king of Thrace, one Cotys, in 360 BC, with help from another follower of Plato; both escaped from Thrace and made it safely back to Athens, where they were honored as heroes. Then in 353 a third Academy member, Chion, slew the ruthless tyrant of Heraclea (on the Black Sea), Clearchus (whom we shall meet again at the end of this chapter). Chion's deed was seen as rooted in Platonist values to judge by the way it was later framed in *The Letters of Chion*, a Greek epistolary novel that still survives.

Python and Chion had slain autocrats, whereas Dion had slain a radical democrat, but all could claim to be acting on the principle Plato put forward in *Statesman*: Political wisdom gives one the right to kill.

Plutarch, our principal source for the killing of Heraclides, did his best to excuse the deed, wanting to see in Dion the good that Plato saw. He admits that Syracusans were "grieved" by Heraclides' death but claims that their grief was assuaged by Dion, who gave his victim a lavish funeral and delivered a ringing speech. That speech, as recounted by Plutarch, convinced Syracusans that "it was not possible for the city to cease from upheavals so long as Heraclides and Dion were both politically active."[6]

Plutarch appears to endorse the idea (or perhaps he supplied it himself) that a single death was a worthy trade to avoid political chaos. But elsewhere in his *Parallel Lives*, in biographies of Roman statesmen, Plutarch reviles the use of proscriptions, killings carried out in the name of preserving order. "Madness and rage drove them beyond the promptings of humanity," he writes of three Roman leaders who ordered the murder of Cicero for this reason. Whereas Plutarch compares those leaders to savage beasts, he portrays Dion as a rational man who'd shown restraint by waiting so long to take action. He repeats, in case we'd missed the point, his view that Heraclides was a rogue and a rabble-rouser, prone to stirring up *stasis*.

Cornelius Nepos, a Roman writer who preceded Plutarch by nearly a century, was also familiar with proscription, having witnessed it in his own lifetime. He saw in Dion's murder of Heraclides a pattern that all too closely resembled the Roman civil wars, still ongoing at the time he was writing. He says that, in the weeks leading up to the murder, Dion was heard reciting a line from Homer, to the effect that a state needs only *one* ruler. The killing of Heraclides, says Nepos, aroused "intense fear" among Syracusans and a sense that any of them might be next.

Nepos, relying on some now-lost writer who assessed Dion far more harshly than other sources, gives a damning account of how Dion changed in the wake of the killing. Sensing the uneasy mood in the city, Dion took to seizing estates and handing them out to his soldiers, says Nepos, desperately raising cash to secure their loyalty. In *Macbeth*-like fashion, crime begat crime and guilt begat paranoia. The Syracusans began to say openly that "a tyrant"—meaning Dion—"could not be endured."[7]

Nepos and Plutarch agree that Dion fell into depression after the death of Heraclides, but they see different causes behind this emotional downturn. According to Nepos, Dion was pained by the loss of his allies among the rich, for after he seized their estates, they turned against him. "He could not bear with an even temper being badly thought of by those whose praises, a little before, had lifted him up to the sky," Nepos says.[8]

Plutarch, by contrast, gives Dion the redeeming grace of a guilty conscience. "Troubled by the matter of Heraclides and that murder, regarding it as a stain on his life and his deeds, Dion was always weighed down and disturbed," Plutarch writes. "He said many times he was ready to die."[9] He even said he'd offer his throat to anyone who wanted to slit it.

It was not long before someone accepted that invitation.

Callippus had been at Dion's right hand for years, the principal "friend" and fellow Academy member who'd accompanied him from Athens. But proximity allowed Callippus to see all of Dion's shortcomings. Perceiving Dion's morose state of mind, and (according to some) suspecting him of tyrannic ambitions, Callippus laid plans in the spring of 354 to murder his chief and take Syracuse for himself. It's possible he had been recruited and bribed by Dionysius, as Plutarch implies and a second source, a papyrus recovered from Egypt, seems to confirm.[10]

The plans required the backing of Dion's troops, whose faith in Dion was by this time wavering. According to both Plutarch and Nepos, Callippus devised a means to enlist disaffected soldiers without revealing himself to Dion as a threat. He told Dion that discontent was on the rise in his ranks and offered himself as a spy; he even reported to Dion the mutinous things he had heard to retain Dion's trust. He began attending clandestine meetings of malcontent troops, ostensibly to take down names but really to recruit allies. When troops who were loyal to Dion reported that Callippus was taking part in these meetings, Dion assumed he was only doing his job and took no action.[11]

Dion, in his dejected mood, ignored what was plain to see for his wife and his sister. Aretê and Aristomachê became convinced that a plot was afoot but could not make Dion believe it. They distrusted Callippus when he protested his innocence, and made him swear "the great oath": In a temple of Demeter and Persephone—deities linked to the awesome powers of the underworld—he donned a ceremonial robe, held a torch in his hand, and, after solemn rites were performed, vowed before these great gods that he meant Dion no harm. That lie bought him time to put the plot into motion.

Sources differ as to whether Callippus led the coup on his own or in concert with his brother. Plato speaks in one place of two organizers, in another of one.[12] Plutarch mentions only Callippus, but Nepos—who calls Callippus "Callicrates"—assigns a prominent role to a brother named Philostratus. This brother was ordered to fill a warship with soldiers, on the day that had been selected for the attack on Dion, and have it rowed back and forth in the harbor as if for practice maneuvers. If the assassination miscarried, Callippus and Philostratus would make their escape in this vessel. Diodorus, a third source, does not mention the brother but gives short shrift to the whole affair, describing it in a single sentence.[13]

All sources agree that troops from Zacynthus, the island off the Peloponnese from which Dion had launched his invasion, were given the task of carrying out the killing. Dion was at home on a day in June when much of the city gathered elsewhere for a festival of Demeter, the very goddess before whom Callippus had sworn. With characteristic aloofness, Dion had declined to attend and was using the day to confer with his inner circle. These friends, as Plutarch calls them—again perhaps referring to Dion's Athenian cohort—were gathered with Dion in an upstairs room, stretched out on dining couches, when soldiers quietly took up positions surrounding the house.

The Zacynthian squad knew they could gain admission to Dion, having served under him for years. But they also feared they'd be searched, so they carried no weapons. When they'd all come into the upstairs room, the doors behind them slammed shut, barred from outside by their fellow conspirators. They fell upon Dion and started to choke him. This seemed like a sure way to kill him, but Dion's strength and determination kept them from closing his airways.

As Dion struggled for life, his assailants began to panic. They beat on the doors and called to their comrades outside to get them a sword, but the doors remained closed.

Throughout this attack Dion's friends and household staff, who could have come to his aid, stood aside and did nothing. With their divergent views of Dion, Plutarch and Nepos came to different conclusions about this failure to act. Plutarch focuses on the friends, presumably unarmed men, and claims that their fear for their own lives kept them out of the fray. Nepos looks instead at the soldiers whom Dion employed as his bodyguard, and who, though armed, ignored the sounds of a struggle. "From this anyone can easily understand," Nepos writes, "how hated a thing is sole rule, and how wretched the life of one who prefers to be feared rather than loved."[14]

Inside the sealed room, Dion gasped for life while his friends looked on in mute horror. In the women's quarters, Dion's wife, Aretê, and his sister, Aristomachê, were being seized and taken prisoner. Callippus did not want these women arousing the public's outrage, as they'd done when

Dion was sent into exile twelve years before. Perhaps, too, he already knew that Aretê was pregnant with Dion's child.

Dion's attackers grew desperate to finish their work. Through a window someone hailed a man passing by and urgently asked for a weapon. Maybe this man guessed what was happening or maybe he simply wanted to help those in need; in either case he entered his name in the annals of history: Lycon. He climbed up the stairs of a neighboring house and through its window passed his dagger, a short Spartan blade, to the hands that were reaching to grab it. That blade was used to slit Dion's throat. The messy, protracted assassination was over.

A crowd that included Dion's supporters collected outside the house. As rumors flew that Dion was dead, these pro-Dion Syracusans lashed out at soldiers they spotted nearby, killing several innocent men in their fury. Though many in Syracuse had judged Dion a would-be tyrant, the city, says Nepos, instantly shifted perspective and now saw him more as a martyr. Callippus bowed to this view and buried his victim with honors—exactly as Dion himself had honored Heraclides in death, after having him killed.[15]

In the grim prison cavern in which she was now confined, Aretê soon gave birth to a boy. The jailers let the child live, for this was not only Dion's son but Dionysius's nephew, a scion of both warring halves of the tyrant-house. No one could say at this point which half would prevail, if either, or what future heir the dynasty might need. So this offspring of Dion lived on into the post-Dion era—whatever chaotic shape that was going to take.

Though Dion's sister and wife had been thrown into prison, other members of Dion's family had not, nor had they been banished. Callippus did not yet have a strong enough grip on the city, never mind the larger empire, to eliminate enemies. Events were so much in flux, with splinter groups rising, combining, and disappearing, that the pro-Dion faction still had hope of regaining control. They reached out to Plato in Athens, in a letter that doesn't survive, asking his help "in word or in deed," as Plato recalls in his reply.[16] They seem to have felt that Plato owed them an intervention. Their request "might be expressed more bluntly thus: 'You got us into our present difficulties; it is your business to get us out again,'" in one scholar's view.[17]

Another Syracusan missive arrived at Athens around this same time. Callippus had sent an open letter, now lost, designed to put his deed in a positive light. We may guess that he sought to make Dion appear a tyrant and show himself as the true liberator. Perhaps he depicted himself as a philosopher-ruler, in contrast to Dion, who, as he might have claimed, only pretended to be one.

Plato composed the much-scrutinized *Seventh Letter* in response to the first of these dispatches, but in his reply he implicitly answers the second as well, and many other concerns. He addresses himself to the friends and supporters of Dion, but in fact writes at much greater length than their summons required and comments on matters of much wider interest. We've encountered parts of the *Seventh Letter* already, at points where the information it offers has filled in parts of our story; it's time now to deal with the letter head-on and in whole. First, however, we need to examine an issue that bears on the letter: the mysterious fate of Dion's eldest son.

The complexities start with a problem of nomenclature. Dion and Aretê named their first-born child Hipparinus, after Dion's father, but Dion's sister made the same choice and gave that name to *her* eldest son. Because of this overlap, Dion's son took on a nickname, Aretaeus, and I'll call him that here to keep the two cousins distinct. This Aretaeus was in his teens at the time of the revolution. When Dion took over the Island, as we've seen, he reclaimed his son after more than ten years, during which time the boy had been the ward of the tyrant and *his* son—that is, of his uncle and cousin.

According to Nepos, these two guardians, Dionysius and Apollo-crates, both heavy drinkers themselves, plied Aretaeus with alcohol and debauched him by giving him sexual partners when he was barely a teen. As a result, they'd corrupted his nature and made him a slave to the Syr-acusan tables. When Dion took his son back, he tried to undo the dam-age, assigning companions to monitor Aretaeus and curb his drinking. Whether because of the warped upbringing or the withdrawal of wine, the youth became emotionally unstable.[18]

Plutarch, by contrast, does not discuss Aretaeus's time as the ward of his uncle, but both he and Nepos agree that, during Dion's last days, the boy committed suicide by throwing himself off a roof. The tragedy, Plutarch says, fulfilled an omen that Dion had seen: One evening at twilight, a spectral figure resembling a Fury had made its way through his home, seeming to sweep it out with a giant broom. The supernatural overlay makes it apparent that, in Plutarch's eyes, Dion's loss of his son was a retribution sent by the gods for the killing of Heraclides.[19]

Plutarch reports that Callippus had tried to score political points from the death of Dion's son, by spreading a rumor that Dion, now childless, intended to adopt Apollocrates, Dionysius's son, as his own. Apollocrates was then in exile in Locri with his parents and siblings. Such an adoption, if Dion indeed entertained it, might have been a shrewd move, a splice with which to bind together the halves of the tyrant-house. As portrayed by Callippus, however, the alleged adoption plan meant only one thing: Dion's intention was not liberation but more generations of tyrannical rule.

All this is relevant to the *Seventh Letter* because Plato speaks there of a young man, Hipparinus, whom he considers a leading member of the Dionean faction. It's unclear whether he means the *son* of Dion, using his birth name rather than Aretaeus, or Dion's *nephew*, also called Hipparinus. According to Plutarch and Nepos, Aretaeus was dead by this time, so it seems at first glance Plato must mean Dion's nephew. But in a subsequent letter, the *Eighth*, Plato shows that he thinks Aretaeus is alive and well. So "Hipparinus" in the *Seventh Letter* could mean either person.

How is it Plato thought Aretaeus was living, at a point well after Plutarch and Nepos say he had died in a fall? Those who want to deny that Plato wrote the Syracuse letters have pointed to what they regard as a slip on the part of a forger. But by the strange logic of authorship questions, that "slip" does as much to support authenticity as to refute it. The author of the *Eighth Letter* is well informed on other counts; if he's a forger, he's clearly done his research. So how could he overlook such a crucial development as the death of Dion's son?

It seems more likely that Plutarch and Nepos got the chronology wrong. With their strong moralizing impulses, they wanted Dion's loss of his son to be seen as payback for the killing of Heraclides. Plutarch makes clear that a figure who seemed like a Fury appeared just before the boy's fall, and Nepos speaks of a fickle goddess, Fortuna, who brought Dion low by inflicting the loss of a child. Neither author's retributive scheme would work if Dion had died *before* his son, so they, or perhaps their common source, reversed the order of deaths.

If Aretaeus was indeed alive at the time the *Seventh Letter* was written, then it's likely that Plato means *him*, not his cousin, when he looks with hopeful eyes toward young "Hipparinus." It makes sense that he'd see Dion's *son* as the logical heir to his father's ideals and political program. Evidently that hope was misplaced, since we hear nothing more of Aretaeus beyond what's in Plato's letters. He played no further part in the story of Syracuse, unlike Hipparinus the nephew, who, as we shall see, played a large and unfortunate one.

So did Aretaeus really throw himself off of a roof? Was his mind destroyed by a childhood spent on the Island, with wine and sex pressed on him by his debauched relatives? Or was it his father's murder—an event he might well have witnessed—that caused him to take his own life? The sources do not permit us to answer these questions. All we can say is, he must have died young, barely past twenty, at a time when Plato seems to have been counting on him. That left only his infant brother, the babe born in prison, to give the Dionean faction the hope of a lineal heir.

The *Seventh Letter* is long—longer than some of Plato's dialogues, and more than five times as long as the next-longest letter. It owes its length to the number of things Plato tries to accomplish with it. Ostensibly his purpose is to advise the Dionean party, but he also grieves for Dion, dead perhaps only weeks, and reviles the assassins. He explains at length his reasons for going to Syracuse, especially on the last occasion in 361, and accounts for his failures there. At one point he drops these biographical themes and gives an exposition of philosophic doctrine, a segment that has greatly bewildered readers and kindled debate among scholars. Few ancient texts have so many different agendas.

The *Seventh Letter* is often described as an *apologia*, a tract of self-defense, and much of its tone is indeed defensive. Plato had clearly been nettled by questions about his motives in going to see Dionysius the Younger: "*This* was my intention in leaving home [for Syracuse], and not what some people suppose," as he says at one point.[20] He's especially eager to answer those who wondered why he'd gone *again* to the tyrant, in 361, after his 367 visit had ended badly. He describes his reply to this challenge as his *parerga*, his secondary task, as compared with his *erga*, his main task of helping the Dioneans.

The Dioneans wanted his help, but Plato had to be sure they would put his advice into practice. He compares himself to a doctor advising a patient, by now a familiar analogy. If the patient can't give up an unhealthy lifestyle and listen to counsel, then the doctor who counsels him wastes his breath, Plato says. He offers Dion and Dionysius as positive and negative examples: Dion had latched onto Plato's advice and become a good man; Dionysius had not, and had gone the opposite way. Dion's faction, he says, must be willing to take the positive path, the path that Plato had once laid out for the tyrant: forsaking the Syracusan tables and living a "Dorian" lifestyle, that is, one of spareness and rigor. In this way, he says, they'll gain true and faithful adherents.

Dion's devotion to justice is emphasized several times in the letter, as Plato seeks to burnish his friend's legacy. Dion's political goals are stated at the letter's outset—"He thought Syracusans ought to be free and live under the best laws"—and then expanded on later: "He would have adorned Syracusans with the best laws . . . he would have been eager to resettle all of Sicily and make it free from the barbarians," meaning the Carthaginians.[21] What "laws" Dion intended, or what form of government, Plato does not say. He strongly denies that Dion had any designs on a tyranny; that idea was a vicious slander, planted by the palace hardliners.[22]

To lionize Dion, of course, Plato had to obscure Dion's killing of Heraclides. He insists that Dion's path was one of nonviolence: Dion wanted "to bring about a life that was happy and true in the whole region, without the murders and deaths and evils that have now taken place."[23] The omission of Dion's one glaring murder is striking, especially given that, later on in the letter, Plato gives a detailed account of his own attempt to save Heraclides (an episode seen in chapter 8). That account helps achieve a separate goal of the letter, an explanation of how Plato's relations with Dionysius had broken down so completely; but it does so at a cost, since it makes Heraclides seem an innocent victim of oppression. Apparently that was a cost that Plato was willing to pay.

Plato turns often to mythic ideas to explain Dion's failure and fall, which was also in part his own failure. From his first arrival in Syracuse in 388, he writes, "it seems as though one of the greater powers was contriving to lay the foundation of the things that have now taken place regarding Dion and Syracuse."[24] He speaks of "some fortune greater than humankind," of a *daimôn* (a god or semidivine being), or, most intriguingly, of an *alitêrios*, a spirit of vengeance, that had wrecked his and Dion's plans. These references to supernatural forces cast a tragic glow over Dion while also downplaying Plato's agency. Plato does not admit to making mistakes in the course of his Syracuse journeys; he was merely a plaything of fortune. He does however concede, in an oddly phrased question, that he had unintentionally set in motion a dire chain of events: "How am I to say that my arrival in Sicily at that time"—meaning in 388, when he'd first met young Dion—"was the beginning of everything?"[25]

That Plato was conscious of error, or concerned that others might blame him, is clear from the space that he gives the *parerga*, his account of his final voyage. "It seemed to me that I had to explain the reasons I decided on a second voyage to Sicily," he writes, referring to the journey of 361, "because of the strange and irrational nature of subsequent events." That last word, "events," *genomenôn* in Greek, has been emended by one editor to *legomenôn*, "what's being said."[26] If that reading is the correct one, the defensive stance of the whole account becomes even clearer.

Among the likely things "being said" was a point that Plato takes pains to address in the letter. After what he had seen of Dionysius in 367, shouldn't he have known better than to return 361? He answers this implied challenge by adducing compelling reasons for the second voyage. He needed to plead Dion's case (as Dion himself had requested), and he'd been told, by reliable sources—the wise Archytas among them—that Dionysius was eager for education. It was those sources, not Plato himself, who'd been deceived, by the letter's logic.

Just as the letter accounts for Plato's apparent misjudgment of Dionysius, so too it excuses Dion's error in trusting Callippus. How had a talented statesman, Plato's protégé, been so easily ambushed? Plato admits that Dion had "stumbled," but draws on a seafaring metaphor to put the lapse in perspective. Even a "good" sea captain can see a storm coming but underestimate its intensity. "It's this that did Dion in," he concludes. "He didn't fail to perceive the evil of those who destroyed him, but he didn't realize what a depth of ignorance and other wickedness and greed they possessed. And on this account he was done in and lies fallen, casting Sicily into immeasurable grief."[27]

The letter vilifies Callippus and his brother, without naming either. Those who'd planned Dion's death are described as traitors and murderers, who, since they'd stood by "with weapons in hand" as the killing was carried out, were just as guilty as those who'd wielded the blade. The harm these two plotters have caused, Plato says, "not only to me but, practically speaking, to all other people," is equated with that done by Dionysius; both parties have helped extinguish the light of justice. Here, too, Plato seems to be answering skeptics and critics, for Callippus had been an Academy student and had no doubt maintained, in his own letters, that *he*, not Dion, was the true foe of tyranny.

In the letter's most revisionist passage, Plato maintains that Callippus's friendship with Dion had come about "not through philosophy," that is, not under the Academy's aegis (in fact the two had shared a home when both were Academy students). Instead, he asserts that a shallow bond had been formed when Callippus and his brother had helped initiate Dion into a religious order, far from Plato's own doorstep. This purely transactional friendship, Plato implies, had easily turned to betrayal. Plato contrasts this fickleness with his own devotion to Dion, born of "a sharing of liberal learning"; their bond had withstood the bribes of "money and many other honors" that Dionysius had offered and Plato had refused.[28]

Plato makes clear that Dion's "noble" death was a better outcome than the tyrant's "ignoble" life, at this point being spent (as Plato perhaps was aware) in violating the women of Locri. "None of us is immortal, and even if that could happen for someone, he wouldn't be happy, as people tend to believe," Plato writes.[29] He turns to mythic notions of life after death to exalt Dion's choices, claiming the soul of the virtuous man will reap immortal rewards while the vicious man's suffers. He drew on the same theme to end his *Republic*, as we shall see.

Plato offers a few concrete suggestions about the path forward for

Dion's party, his ostensible purpose in writing the letter. He's clearly afraid that *stasis* at Syracuse will spiral out of control. The pattern elsewhere in Greece suggested as much, for parties that came out on top in a *stasis* usually turned to punishing those they'd defeated. Plato advises the Dioneans against reprisals, should they take power. If they submit themselves to the laws and forgo retribution, their foes will do likewise and the cycle of violence will end. He urges them to convene a board of fifty lawgivers, men who have families and own property—a broad oligarchy. They should instruct these men to show no favor to either "the conquerors or the conquered" in drafting a constitution. (It's not clear whom he means by "the conquered," Callippus's forces or those of Dionysius; the Dioneans needed to overcome both to gain full control.)

Once the fifty-man board has drafted new laws, Plato says, the Dioneans must follow them unswervingly. If they do this, Plato predicts in dreamy tones, "everything will be filled with safety and prosperity, and all evils will take flight." Even so, he says, the state that results will be only the second-best kind, not as good as the one that he and Dion had tried for. "But some stroke of fortune, with greater than human power, tore that to pieces."[30]

These threads of the *Seventh Letter* already make an intricate weave, but there are still more. The letter answers implicit questions about Plato's role as teacher and ethical guide. By his own account he had gone to Syracuse, in both 367 and 361, to teach Dionysius, after others had said the tyrant was ripe for instruction. So why had the project failed? "I must tell the truth and endure it if someone, after hearing my account, scorns my philosophy and thinks that it's the tyrant who's wise," Plato writes, seemingly summarizing what his critics were saying.[31]

This challenge to Plato's reputation had been amplified by Dionysius himself, who, much to Plato's dismay, had by this time published his own philosophic treatise (since lost). The fact that the tyrant could write such a work suggested he *did* have potential for higher thought, which made Plato's failure to teach him more conspicuous. The treatise also offended Plato in another way: He hadn't read it (he says), but from what he had heard it pirated his teachings. Dionysius had claimed that the work was original, Plato reports, but nonetheless "he wrote about things he had heard back then," during Plato's two visits.[32]

Dionysius's treatise had raised the reputational stakes for Plato, and other events too must have made him more attuned to critique. At around the time that the *Seventh Letter* was written, Athenians attended a play put on by a comic playwright, Epicrates. It featured a mocking description of a pseudoscientific debate in which Academy students, guided by Plato, were trying, with parodic seriousness, to classify the gourd. One student said it belonged to the vegetable family, another to that of the grasses, a third, to the trees. A doctor passing by overheard the debate and found it so silly he farted at the discussants. Plato himself may have been present among the crowd that laughed at that crude joke.[33]

In several parts of the *Seventh Letter*, Plato seeks to explain the breakdown of his educational efforts on both his visits to Dionysius the Younger. The earlier instance, in 367, was a simpler matter: The tyrant had shrunk from engaging with Plato because the hardliners had scared him away, speaking of Plato's teachings as an attempt at a coup. The second round, in 361, required a more in-depth explanation. Plato had to account for his own breaking-off of the lessons after a single session, when the tyrant had failed his stamina test, and also for the fact that Dionysius somehow thought himself well-schooled enough to later write on Platonic themes. The paradox evokes some ingenious argumentation, a convincing sign of the letter's genuineness. Its strategies are more subtle than what an impostor could have produced, except perhaps an unparalleled genius.

Plato seeks to cast Dionysius as a poseur, a man who affects higher learning without being capable of it. He compares the tyrant to people whose skin gets a suntan—a brilliant adaptation of his own image, in *Republic*, that configured the highest truth, the Form of the Good, as the sun. He claims that Dionysius has published his book "out of a base pursuit of honor," whether the tyrant presented the ideas as his own or those of a teacher. The fact that some may believe the latter raises Plato's concern that *he* might be seen as the source of the treatise's doctrines, a thought he is quick to dismiss. "'God knows,' as the Theban says, how it happened," he writes, derisively quoting a well-known Boeotian expression, "that Dionysius acquired this learning from a single meeting; for as I have said, I explained it to him once only and never again after that."[34]

Plato comes back a second time to the termination of lessons, examining this breakdown in more depth. He proposes three explanations, each of which puts the onus onto the tyrant: Either Dionysius thought he already knew what Plato could teach; or, he thought the lessons worthless; or, he realized he was out of his depth and *couldn't* continue. Plato deals first with the middle, most damaging reason, rejecting it in a huff. "If it's 'worthless,' then he's at odds with many who attest to the opposite, and who would make very much more authoritative judges about these matters than Dionysius," he writes—an unusually petty instance of one-upmanship, though not the letter's pettiest move.[35]

In discussing the test he administered to Dionysius, Plato reports that the tyrant gave the first reason, prior knowledge, to explain why he wouldn't pursue further study. But Plato finds this implausible; the tyrant's unjust behavior toward Dion proves that he hadn't learned anything of real value. That leaves only the third alternative, inadequacy, to explain the tutorial's failure.

Plato's indignation can clearly be felt in his eagerness to blame Dionysius and assume the august role of "master" (*kurios*), the title he implicitly gives to himself.[36] Perhaps, as some have supposed, he was battling hedonist views that had once prevailed at Dionysius's court, espoused by Aristippus and others; the tyrant's treatise, perhaps, had endorsed such ideas or left the impression that Plato shared them. Whatever got under Plato's skin was irksome enough to prompt him to lay out his own philosophic doctrines in a section of the *Seventh Letter* that Plato calls a "wandering" from its main path. Depending on whom one asks, this excursus—about 15 percent of the letter's length—is either incoherent or one of the most important things Plato ever composed.

The impetus for the excursus comes not only from Dionysius's treatise but publications by other people, whom Plato does not name. "Who they are they do not know themselves," he says cryptically. These anonymous authors have, like Dionysius, addressed the themes on which Plato taught, themes Plato refers to as "the first and highest principles of nature."[37] What he means is unclear, especially since he asserts, in a sentence that has astonished many, that he's never once written about these matters and never will do so. "This can't at all be put into words like other kinds of learning," he writes, "but it is suddenly born in the soul and nurtures itself, from long association and mutual pursuit of it, like a torch-light ignited from a leaping flame." The striking image, of fire making a jump to a flammable object, recalls the sudden epiphany that Plato describes in *Republic* as the culmination of decades of mental training.

But Plato's goal here is not, as it was in *Republic*, to hold aloft a vision of philosophic transcendence. He's defending his turf and exposing poachers, among them the tyrant of Syracuse. In what amounts to an assertion of copyright, he makes this surprising statement: "This much I know, that if these things were written or spoken about, it had best be done by me; for I swear, if they're badly explained in writing then I suffer more than most." The idea that Plato "suffers" from bad expositions reveals the point of the coming excursus. He will show why not only writing, but language itself, fails at expressing the highest truths. Anyone trying to put those truths into words—Dionysius is called out by name—only "strews them about in an ill-befitting and unseemly manner."[38]

Plato demonstrates this failure of language in terms that echo *Republic*, so much so that, in the eyes of one scholar, he relies on his readers' acquaintance with that dialogue.[39] *Republic* explains the steps for the soul's ascent toward perception of truth, that is, of the Forms. The *Seventh Letter* plots these steps somewhat differently but concurs with *Republic*'s essential distinction, between reality, "that which is," and what we perceive with our senses. Yet unlike *Republic*, the letter stresses "the weakness of words" in getting past sense perceptions to ultimate truth. Plato uses geometry to make his point: "Nothing prevents the things now called circles from being called lines, and lines circles," he writes, yet the concept of circle is stable, whatever we call it.[40]

"For this reason," Plato concludes, "no one who has any sense will ever dare to commit to this weakness of words the things in his mind." A bit further on he repeats the same thought. "Every serious man who pursues serious things will in no way ever write them down. . . . If you see things in writing . . . you know that, if the author is truly serious, then he hasn't set down his most serious thoughts, but rather these are laid up in the finest place where he keeps his possessions."[41] The "finest place" seems to mean the philosopher's soul, the locus of apprehension of "that which is."

The *Seventh Letter*'s excursus agrees with *Republic* in separating the few who can progress toward the Forms—philosophers—from those who cannot. The latter group is described as "ill-framed with regard to learning and to what is called moral character." Intriguingly, Plato makes these non-philosophic souls, in metaphorical terms, half-blind: "Not even Lynceus"—a mythic hero famous for keen eyesight—"could make such men see," he writes disparagingly. The reference to weakened vision reminds us that Dionysius, who fits both types of "ill-framing," was known to be severely nearsighted.

Though referred to only obliquely in most of the excursus, Dionysius, attacked by name at both its beginning and end, lurks in the background throughout. To counter the tyrant's incursions into his territory, Plato has stretched and reframed the doctrines of *Republic*, emphasizing not just the steepness of ascent toward the Forms but the failure of language to help one climb upward. He's reserved for himself sole right to address his own themes but also denied that *anyone* could address them in writing with any success. He's thrust Dionysius out of the cadre to which he himself belonged, grouping him, implicitly, with those who get only a tan from their time in the sun.

With these ripostes to a former student who had somehow become a rival, Plato pursues yet another goal of the *Seventh Letter*: defense of his own pedagogy.

Ironically the philosophic excursus contained in the *Seventh Letter* has seemed to some scholars the work of a sun-tanner too, a man of superficial learning who could not have been Plato. "He might well be surprised," wrote Oxford professor of philosophy Myles Burnyeat in 2015, speaking of the author of the excursus, "at the number of readers, from antiquity to this day, who have taken him to be a philosopher, and even more surprised at those who have taken him to be Plato."[42] Burnyeat dismisses this man as a "philosophic incompetent," in a book with the polemical title *The Pseudo-Platonic Seventh Letter*, coauthored by another Oxford historian of philosophy, Michael Frede.

Burnyeat's dismissal of the excursus unwittingly raises its own rebuttal. A sizeable "number of readers" have indeed treated this passage as a serious exposition of Platonic philosophy, including some of the foremost Plato scholars of recent times. At least one specialist has even defended it, in print, *after* reading Burnyeat's takedown.[43] To claim that a "philosophic incompetent" produced the excursus implies that a large number of supposed experts not only cannot say, but cannot even tell, that the emperor has no clothes. Such widespread delusion seems inherently unlikely.

To be sure, the excursus, which deals with the problem of how to gain knowledge when language is so inadequate, varies somewhat from how the same theme is explored in Plato's dialogues (the details go beyond our current scope). But it also coheres with those dialogues to a substantial degree. What's more, the discontinuities can as easily point toward genuineness as to imposture. The letter's author, if someone other than Plato, was nonetheless a highly intelligent, literate person, as Burnyeat admits. He was capable of adhering unswervingly to doctrines from *Republic* and elsewhere if he wanted to seem to be Plato. "A forger would have stuck more closely to the letter of the Platonic doctrine," Glenn Morrow points out.[44]

"Why suppose that Plato was invariably consistent?" asked Hellenist Peter Brunt, in a probing 1991 inquiry into the authenticity of the *Seventh Letter*.[45] (He reserved judgment.) Over his six-decade career, Plato sometimes changed his views on even basic questions and experimented with alternatives. The dialogue *Parmenides*, today accepted as genuine, takes such a skeptical view of the Forms, those ideal entities central to other Platonic works, that, in the eighteenth century, many believed it could not be by Plato. The gap between the excursus of the *Seventh Letter* and Plato's other discussions of how we gain knowledge are small by comparison.

If the *Seventh Letter*'s excursus sometimes bewilders philosophy dons, that's because its goal is not so much philosophy as public relations. Plato deploys the doctrines he needs to put himself and Dionysius in separate intellectual classes and distance his own work and thought from that of the tyrant. The passage is thus very much of a piece with the *Seventh Letter* generally. From start to finish, that enormous missive is an ingenious, complex, and utterly plausible effort at spin control.

$P$lato was not alone in his need to manage the fallout of a failed intervention in politics. Isocrates, Plato's close contemporary and ideological rival, had to face an embarrassment of his own, the result of a tyrant who took inspiration from Dionysius the Elder but went much further in the direction of despotism. The resulting horrors unfolded in the Black Sea city of Heraclea, on the eastern fringe of the Greek world, at just the same time as the troubles of Syracuse.

Clearchus, a man who had once been Isocrates' student, established himself as tyrant of Heraclea in the 360s BC, in a manner that showed Syracusan autocracy starting to metastasize. Like Dionysius the Elder, Clearchus surrounded himself with armed might—hired soldiers—and built a fortified redoubt from which he could not be dislodged. With his assembly speeches he stoked the people's mistrust of the rich and got them to award him the title of *stratêgos autokratôr*, a license to do as he pleased. He freed Heraclean slaves to create more allies, then compelled the wives of their former masters to marry those he had freed, in a strategy learned from the Elder.[46] In tribute to his political model, he named one of his two sons Dionysius.

As they had done in Syracuse, the wealthy of Heraclea rose up and tried to oust this dangerous populist; but their rebellion was quashed, just as in Syracuse, by the tyrant's skilled mercenaries. Instead of exiling opponents as the Elder had done, Clearchus subjected those he had captured to public humiliation, torture, and execution. He fed the rage of the commons with cruel displays and stimulated their greed by divvying up ransom payments and seized estates. He raised brutality levels far beyond those the Elder had reached, thrilling the public with his transgressions of civilized norms.

Where his Syracusan model had sometimes behaved as though superhuman, Clearchus experimented with self-deification. He referred to himself as a son of Zeus and had a golden eagle, the symbol of Zeus, carried before him in the streets. He donned the footwear and robes of kings from the tragic stage, as Dionysius the Elder had done, then added a new theatrical touch by painting his face with a gleaming red dye. This was said to have created a terrifying effect.

All this was extremely bad news for Isocrates (and perhaps for Plato as well, who'd taught Clearchus more briefly). In the late 340s BC, a decade

after Clearchus had been assassinated—by the aforementioned Chion—
Isocrates addressed an open letter to the tyrant's elder son, Timotheus,
who'd by then taken power in Heraclea. In the letter he urges Timotheus
to use his power benevolently and earn the love of his subjects, his standard advice to monarchs. Then he raises the question that he imagines
will follow: Why had he offered no such counsel to Clearchus and tried
to curb his former student's abuses? The question implies Isocrates had
failed in his duty, standing by as Clearchus went down the wrong path—
the path that had led to his murder.

Isocrates tries to absolve himself. "During that time when Clearchus
was studying with me," he writes, "all who met him agreed he was the
most liberal-minded, gentlest, and most humane of those taking part in
my training. But later, when he got hold of rule, he seemed to depart so
far from these qualities that all who knew him before were amazed. For
these reasons," Isocrates adds, setting the record straight, "I separated
myself from him."[47]

The problems Isocrates faced from the Heraclea debacle were similar to those that confronted Plato in Syracuse. But Plato had less lee-
way to "separate himself" from that situation. He'd gotten more deeply
enmeshed than Isocrates had, not only with Dion but with Dionysius the
Younger, who was still very much on the scene. Plato had more at stake,
too, since Syracuse was a great and imperial power; tiny Heraclea was a
comparative backwater. The outcome of the struggle for Syracuse would
determine the fate of all Sicily, indeed the entire Greek West.

In the *Seventh Letter*, Plato shows he's still determined to influence
that outcome. By writing it he was visibly working to help the Dionean
party, which also meant, if things turned out well, repair of his own reputation. But things in Syracuse seemed to be getting worse, not better, and
that alarmed him. He'd make one more effort, and write one more letter,
before letting go as Isocrates had done.

# ACT V

## RESTORATION

*The death of Sôphrosynê, in an unfinished illustration from a fifteenth-century manuscript of Justin's* Epitome.

CHAPTER 13

# THE SECOND-BEST STATE

## (353–344 BC)

D ionysius the Elder had married two women on the same day and consummated the unions on the same night. In keeping with this symmetry, he had sired two sons by each wife. The Locrian sons, those by Doris, were older than those of Aristomachê and thus got first crack at ruling the empire. Dionysius the Younger had botched the task, and his younger full brother, Hermocritus, seems not to have tried (we have no record of him beyond his existence). With Doris's line having failed, the youths from the Syracuse branch—Hipparinus and Nysaeus, now in their early twenties—were ready to take their turn.

As boys, these two had been highly regarded by their uncle Dion, who touted them to Plato as eager philosophy students. "He said his young nephews . . . would be easily brought over to the life and the doctrine that I was always describing," Plato recalls Dion telling him in 367.[1] But instead of Plato, they'd had their older half-brother, Dionysius the Younger, as mentor, while Dion had been in exile. Their adolescence had been spent at the tyrant's court and at the Syracusan tables. It seems that, following family tradition, wine and high living had rotted their moral fiber.

As members of Dion's branch of the tyrant-house, these youths were allowed to remain in the city when the Locrian branch, Dionysius and kin, were cast out. Then, after Dion's death, they emerged as potential leaders of the Dionean faction. That group had been thrust out of power by Callippus and his mercenaries, then thrust out of Syracuse too, or else had left voluntarily, to take up position in Leontini. Hipparinus soon joined them, perhaps Nysaeus as well. By this point, even opponents of Dionysius wanted some member of the "royal" family to serve as their standard-bearer.

The Dioneans were mostly wealthier Syracusans who favored conservative governance, either Plato's ethical monarchy or Dion's mixed constitution. They hated the regime of Callippus, a military dictatorship with populist leanings. In Leontini they looked for a way to oust Callippus and set Syracuse back on the path that Dion and Plato had favored. Like Dion before them, they recruited the veteran troops who'd been settled in Leontini. These soldiers feared that Callippus would call for a redistribution of land, as populists often did, and take away their estates.

In July of 353, when Callippus brought his troops north to Catana, Hipparinus and the Dioneans made their move. They sent agents into Syracuse disguised as diplomats while Hipparinus and an armed squadron waited outside the walls. The infiltrators slew Callippus's guards and opened the gates to their comrades. In a single deft stroke, Hipparinus had taken control.

The recapture of Syracuse led to a liberation of Dion's imprisoned kin. Dion's sister, Aristomachê, was freed from the caverns, along with his widow, Aretê, and his posthumous son, by now a year old. Hipparinus entrusted these hardy survivors to the care of a family friend named Hicetas. This man arranged passage by ship for the three to the Peloponnese, presumably to get them out of harm's way. It seemed that these symbols of Dion's virtue—one of them even named "Virtue"—would survive the troubles of Syracuse, perhaps someday to return in a restoration.

But that hopeful future was not to be theirs. As their ship crossed the Ionian Sea, all three were thrown overboard and drowned. The turbid currents of Sicilian politics, which Plato had once compared to the lethal whirlpool Charybdis, had sucked down a new set of victims, the most innocent yet.

Hicetas was blamed for the deed, and later the Syracusans killed his wife and daughters to take revenge.[2] What his motive had been, if he was indeed guilty, is difficult to say. But one recent scholar, as we shall see, thought he'd been prompted, in part, by something Plato wrote in a letter.

Callippus, having lost Syracuse, set up a new base in Catana. He grimly joked that he'd traded a city for a cheese-grater, a humble object called *catanê* in regional slang. Still in command of skilled soldiers, among whom were the Zacynthian squad that he'd used to kill Dion, he looked for new places to seize and shake down, hoping to raise more money and hire more troops. He tried to take Messina but failed, losing some of his men in the effort. By now a pariah in Sicily, he crossed to Italy and took Rhegium, a city that had been recently reestablished.

Callippus had come a long way from Plato's Academy, where the Moriai, bearing Athena's sacred olives, once shaded geometry lessons. Now he found shade beneath the plane trees that Dionysius the Elder had had imported to grace his Rhegian game preserve.[3] His welfare depended on money, the only bond between him and his men, and money was running short. When he no longer had enough pay to keep them happy, two of their leaders stabbed him to death—using, says Plutarch, the very dagger with which he'd had Dion killed.[4]

The weapon was recognizable by the workmanship of its hilt. If Callippus saw that design as the blade sank in, his last thought must have been that Nemesis, goddess of vengeance, had come for him in the end.


In Athens, Plato had watched events in the West with ever increasing concern, and also a certain confusion. He seems not to have known of either the birth or the death of Dion's posthumous child, but believed Dion's older son, Aretaeus, was still alive (as he indeed may have been; see chapter 12). He thought Hipparinus was not yet in full control of Syracuse, but was threatened by a resurgent Dionysius. The tyrant may have been making incursions into Sicily or funding some kind of fifth column; either way, in Plato's eyes, he presented a danger.

Plato was now in his mid-seventies and his *Republic* was mostly, if not entirely, finished. He was writing a new political dialogue, *Laws*, an even longer work than *Republic*, in fact his longest work ever and, as far as is known, his last. In it, he turned away from his idealistic belief that knowledge of Justice could make people want to be just, even if the rewards of injustice were greater. He focused on making better laws rather than better souls. The course of events in Syracuse had helped put him on that more practical, realist path.

It had been fourteen years since Plato first disembarked on the Island and rode to the acropolis in the gleaming chariot driven by Dionysius the Younger. For nearly half that time Syracuse had been in a state of crisis. If the chaos continued or despotism returned, the Syracuse project would be judged a debacle. Events to come held grave implications for Plato, for his Academy, and for his *Republic*, the thesis of which—that philosophy was the best path to good governance—had already been badly damaged by Dion's missteps.

In the *Seventh Letter* Plato had burnished Dion's image, depicting him as an enduring icon of the Academy's values. He had insisted that Dion wanted "freedom" for Syracuse, meaning an end to domination by tyrants, and "the best laws," though Plato hadn't made clear what those were. He'd reviled Dion's assassins as embodiments of pure evil and erased the link between those killers and his Academy. He'd held up an idealized Dion as the lodestar by which Syracusans should steer. Since those who'd inherited Dion's mantle were now the best hope for the future, Plato continued his program of heroization.

In *Republic*, Plato lays out a plan for wise lawgivers to be revered, even worshiped as gods, after death. Socrates there advises the raising of statues before which the Callipolitans will offer sacrifice, treating departed statesmen as something greater than human. In *Laws* Plato proposes a more elaborate program: A board of elders will choose hymns, songs, and dances to be performed in public commemorations of the virtuous dead. Such pious tributes, Plato thought, would inspire the citizenry to follow the goals that the lawgivers had espoused. Religious awe, he implies in both works, should play an essential role in political life.[5]

Plato's funeral poem for Dion, likely written in 354, is a hymn of the kind that Plato prescribed in *Laws*. (The attribution of the poem to Plato is disputed, but on thin grounds, as discussed in chapter 4.) We've already looked at the poem's last line, which speaks of an *erôs* uniting Plato and Dion—perhaps a sexual bond, or perhaps a "Platonic" *erôs*, emotionally intense but physically chaste. The whole poem, written in the elegiac verse form used by the Greeks for farewells to the dead, runs as follows:

> *The Fates allotted tears to the Trojan women*
> *and Hecuba, at the time these women were born;*
> *but in your case, Dion—whose triumph lies in noble deeds—*
> *the gods poured out a stream of fair hopes.*
> *Honored by townsmen, you lie in your broad fatherland.*
> *Oh Dion! You drove my soul mad with the passion of love.*

As many Greek elegies do, this poem invokes mythic figures whose lives, or deaths, reflect on the honoree. Strangely, though, Dion is here compared not to a ruler or leader but to the conquered women of Troy, who'd perished or been enslaved when their city fell. The poem puts forward a contrast: The fates of those women, their "tears," had been predetermined at birth, and thus in a way were less painful than Dion's; Dion had had "fair hopes" poured out by the gods, an illusory promise of a successful life. His murder by Callippus, therefore, had cut those hopes unnaturally short, robbing the world of the grace it might have received.

Plato gives Dion full-throated support by asserting that Syracuse holds him in honor and that he himself had felt *erôs*. The last two lines are a cri de cœur by a grief-stricken man, but also, in the turbulent moment during which the poem was composed, a pledge of allegiance. Dion's nephew, Hipparinus, had either taken power or else was seeking to do so, in league with the other Dioneans. That faction had sought Plato's help, "in word or in deed," in the wake of Dion's death. To build a cult around Dion was one way, "in word," that Plato could give that help.

In 353 BC, soon after Hipparinus had ousted Callippus, Plato again looked to Dion, and the power of religious awe, in his last known intervention in Syracusan affairs. He wrote a second time to the Dioneans, the addressees of the *Seventh Letter*, in a shorter but still lengthy missive, the *Eighth Letter* as it is known. He tried once again to heal Syracuse's wounds and stop the cycle of violence. And once again, he sought to make Dion a greater than mortal being, in this case by resurrecting him from the dead.

Plato addresses the *Eighth Letter* to the Dionean party but, as with the other open letters, he has his sights on a wide readership. He includes among those who need his advice the entire city of Syracuse and, significantly, "the public and private enemies" of the Dioneans—the tyrant Dionysius, outside the city, and his supporters within it. Plato hopes that his counsel will benefit all these factions, not just his own allies. He excludes only "anyone who has done an unholy deed," that is, Callippus; Plato still does not utter that name, but it's clear whom he means when he speaks of "a stain that no one can ever wash clean."[6] Callippus, perhaps still alive at this point, was beyond redemption; not so, it seemed, the tyrant who lurked in Locri.

To explain how Syracuse came to this moment, Plato reviews the city's history going back fifty years, but presents a revisionist version. In his telling, Dionysius the Elder, at the time of his rise to power, was granted dictatorial powers by the Syracusan assembly, but so was the father of Dion, portrayed here as the Elder's partner in rule. Reliable sources make clear that this never happened; Plato is changing the record to suit his agenda.[7] If Dion's father could be portrayed as "co-tyrant" at the tyranny's founding, then Dion's battle for Syracuse became a just war, and the cause of his heirs also just.

Concerns over geopolitics dominate the *Eighth Letter*, even more than the *Seventh*. If Syracuse fails, Plato warns, all Sicily goes down with it. The Carthaginians would then be able to launch another invasion; non-Greek peoples, brought to the island as mercenaries, would form into armies and take over cities at will. Plato envisions Sicily turning into "a desert of the Greek language," populated and ruled by Phoenicians from Carthage and Oscans from Italy.[8] The western frontier of Hellenism, which Plato had fervently sought to expand, might radically shrink instead.

Rallying Hellenes against barbarian foes was good politics in this era, as seen in Isocrates' push for a Greek crusade against Persia. But Dion and Plato had not always seemed, in some eyes, sufficiently pro-Hellenic. Dion's connections to Carthage had gotten him exiled from Syracuse, and, upon his return, his collusion with Synalus, the Punic official who'd helped him transport his weapons, had not gone unnoticed. Plato, for his part, had been accused by Dionysius the Younger of blocking re-Hellenization rather than fostering it. The *Eighth Letter*'s exhortation to save Sicily for the Greeks has to be read with these charges in mind, as historian Lionel Sanders observed. Much of this letter, Sanders asserts, is intended as a response to "attacks upon Dion's dubious nationalistic credentials."[9]

As in his earlier *Seventh Letter*, Plato pleads in the *Eighth* for an end to the cycle of *stasis*, the pattern in which a victorious faction avenged itself on the defeated. He feels he must deter such reprisals, even if this "seems like a prayer—but let it be a prayer in any case, for all our talking and thinking should begin from the gods." He puts himself forward as mediator, comparing himself to the arbiter of a legal dispute.[10]

The parties Plato hopes to reconcile are "the tyrant and the tyrannized," a binary that lumps all those who opposed Dionysius into a single camp. Elsewhere in the letter Plato reinforces this view, claiming that "the party of the people" (*to dēmotikon genos*), also described as "those who seek freedom and flee the yoke of slavery," are fighting the supporters of tyranny.[11] The truth, as he knew, was more complicated, for those who had driven the tyrant out were split along class lines, as seen in the days when Dion had vied against Heraclides. It was best, from Plato's perspective, that those divides be forgotten, and the struggle for Syracuse be simplified, as in the *Seventh Letter*, into a struggle for liberation.

But liberation can go too far if the demos gets too much power, as Plato makes clear in the *Eighth Letter*. It was excess freedom, he there asserts, that initially brought the Dionysii to power. He cites an episode six decades old, from the time just before the tyranny's rise, in which, as he claims, the demos illegally stoned to death a board of ten men they mistrusted. "It was from *this* that tyrannies came about for the citizenry," he asserts.[12] Once again he has revised history in a way that suits his agenda; the stoning, in fact, had taken place elsewhere than Syracuse.[13] It's unclear whether Plato's memory failed him or he tarred the radical democrats with the biggest brush he could find.

Successful states, Plato says, are a blend of democracy and autocracy, a mean between two extremes. "Both slavery and freedom in excess are entirely evil, but in due measure, entirely good," he asserts. Then he extends the idea of "due measure" into the sphere of religious piety. "Due measure is an enslavement to god," he writes, "whereas lack of measure is enslavement to human beings. The god of the wise is Law; of the foolish, Pleasure."[14]

These were ideas that Plato was working out, at much the same time, in his *Laws*, where he also equates "enslavement to laws" with "enslavement to the gods."[15] The opposition between Law and Pleasure, however, is found nowhere else in Plato's writings. It seems he designed it to fit the problem of Syracuse and its luxurious tables.

At its midpoint, the *Eighth Letter* makes a sudden swerve into necromancy. Plato declares he will act as mouthpiece for Dion, "the sharer of my counsels," as if that man were alive and able to speak. "What then would he say?" Plato asks, in a well-worn rhetorical ploy. What follows are Dion's words, spoken as if from the underworld—presumably from the happy Elysian Fields, where the souls of wise lawgivers go, according to *Republic*. This summoning of a voice from the grave—a device Plato borrowed from tragic drama—gives the sense that what we will hear has the authority of the divine.

The ventriloquized Dion opens his speech by condemning the corrosive effect of wealth. Syracuse must have new laws that will combat desire for money, he says, and instead "enslave" that desire to the needs of the soul and the body. The prescription applies in particular to the Syracusan poor, whom Dion, in life, had denied their promised land grants. Plato makes clear, by implication, that Dion was right to do so. Revolutions should be about values, not riches; "the reasoning that labels rich men happy is itself wretched, and makes wretched those who believe it," he has Dion say.[16]

Speaking as the revivified Dion, Plato proposes a unity government for Syracuse, with opposing parties holding joint power. The antityrannical faction would thus get "freedom with kingly rule," a formula similar to Plato's "due measure" between liberty and control. The opposing faction is to be given "kingly power that's subject to oversight, with the laws acting as sovereigns over the kings themselves."[17] Plato had long ago urged Dionysius to place himself under law; the *Eighth Letter* underscores the point, even though *Statesman*, by now almost certainly in circulation, asserted that truly gifted rulers were laws unto themselves.

But who was to hold "kingly power"? The answer the *Eighth Letter* gives is surprising. "Set up as your king," the ghost of Dion tells Syracuse, "first of all, my son"—presumably, Aretaeus (see previous chapter)—"and second, the one who has the same name as my father, the son of Dionysius [the Elder]"—Dion's nephew, Hipparinus. Two kindred kings ruling jointly had long been the custom in Sparta, a widely admired model. But Plato, speaking through Dion, goes one step further, onto entirely new constitutional turf. "And third, you must summon to take his place as king of the Syracusans, by his own accord and that of the city, the man who's now in command of an enemy army, Dionysius, the son of Dionysius." The Younger is to be restored—provided, of course, he submits to law—and given equal power in the royal troika.[18]

After all that had transpired in Syracuse, could Plato really want Dionysius back in the city, or allow Dion's ghost to extend the invitation? The *Eighth Letter* proposes a remarkable amnesty, in the name of knitting the tyrant-house back together. The unity of that house, Plato felt, held out the best hope for the future of Syracuse, and his own best chances of absolution. His presence at court, in all three of his Sicilian sojourns, had done much to split the family apart at the seam of its maternal lines.

Dion's ghost goes on to plan out the state over which this trio will preside. "Ambassadors" are to be chosen, from both Syracuse and elsewhere, to draw up a new constitution. The kings, in spite of their royal title, will have mainly religious duties; they'll basically be figureheads. Policy matters will fall to a board of *nomophulakes*, "guardians of the laws." An assembly and its governing board, representing the demos, are to have an advisory role and perhaps the right to elect the *nomophulakes* (Plato leaves vague the process by which they are chosen). A high court will be made up of the *nomophulakes* plus the magistrates who've proven themselves most just. The three kings will have no part in judging capital cases or imposing banishments.

This moderate, mixed constitution, Dion's ghost says, had been his objective in life, but Erinyes, "Furies," had blocked him from achieving his goal.[19] Similarly, in the *Seventh Letter*, Plato had mentioned an *alitêrios*, a spirit of vengeance, among the supernatural forces to blame for Dion's failure. Furies, too, are avenging deities, charged in particular with punishing those who've committed murder. By alluding to divine vengeance in both of these letters, Plato hints at the problem of Dion's killing of Heraclides, a deed he never discusses in explicit terms. Plutarch would later raise the same problem with his tale of a spectral woman, "resembling in features and clothing a Fury [Erinys] from tragedy," that swept out Dion's house with a giant broom.

Dion's speech closes with prayers that the plan it lays out, described as "like the heaven-sent dreams that people have while awake," can come to fruition. The *Eighth Letter* is indeed dreamlike, since its proposals come forth from the mouth of a ghost. With Syracuse in disarray, with his own reputation at stake, Plato reached for the power of religious awe in his quest for a resolution. Whether any Syracusans were listening is not known.

The *Eighth Letter*'s mention of "Dion's son" as one of three titular kings returns us to the problem of Aretaeus's death. We have seen that Plutarch and Nepos both place that event before Dion's own demise, most likely wrongly. Plato seems to have thought Aretaeus was still alive when he wrote the *Eighth Letter*, though he never calls him by name. He has Dion refer to him only as "my son," which could be taken to mean "my younger son," the boy born to Aretê in prison (his name is unknown).

But Dion's ghost goes on to declare that the soul of his "son" is in concord with that of Hipparinus regarding governance. It seems that the son in question must be already grown—that is, Aretaeus—since toddlers don't normally hold political views. But L. A. Post, a Haverford College classics professor, tried in the 1920s to claim that the "son" was in fact the younger of Dion's offspring. "Plato had great faith in heredity," writes Post, and might well have thought that a baby shared its father's nature from birth. He thus could have written that Dion's son, even when just learning to talk, was in harmony with his much older cousin.

Post's view has found no defenders and won't be defended here, but it's worth our noting a grim line of thinking that follows from it. Post observed, as part of his argument, that Hicetas (as we have seen) ordered the infant thrown overboard en route to the Peloponnese. In Post's view, the prospect that Plato put forward—the idea that the child might be enthroned as part of the royal troika—provided the motive for that otherwise motiveless crime. "Plato's *Eighth Letter* evidently had its effect," Post writes. Faced with a rival who had the backing of Plato, Hicetas, who wanted Syracuse for himself (and later tried to seize it), snuffed the boy out.[20]

Even to entertain Post's theory adds a horrific final twist to the tale of Plato's Syracuse interventions. In Post's reconstruction, Plato, like a cursed figure from myth, had destroyed Dion's son by trying to help him—as he had done, in a way, to Dion himself.

The long years of strife and disorder were eating away at once-mighty Syracuse. Its population had dwindled, reduced by killings, banishments, and emigration. We're told that, at this point, horses were grazing in what had been a bustling market square, as their grooms stretched out on the grass.[21] The neighborhoods that had burned in the rampage unleashed by Nypsius likely had not been restored. Only the Island remained intact, its walls and fortified palace still seeming to promise safety, pleasure, and power for any who held it.

The Greeks were learning how destabilizing such strongholds could be, since they tempted adventurous warlords to occupy them. At Thebes in 382 BC, the fortified hill called the Cadmeia had been seized in a Spartan aggression, then used as a base to control the city below. In Piraeus, the harbor town serving Athens, a hill called Munychia offered such strength that Athenians, so it was said, would have gladly torn it apart with their teeth. A towering rise above Corinth, the Acrocorinth, was soon to be known (if it wasn't already) as one of the "shackles of Greece," the means by which the entire region might be enslaved.

Dionysius the Elder had used a similar shackling metaphor for the Island, dubbing it one of the "adamantine bonds" by which he held onto his power. His son, Dionysius the Younger, had proven how well the place could hold out against the rest of the city. With its stockpiles of food, infantry gear, and state-of-the-art artillery weapons,[22] it had made first him, then his son Apollocrates, largely invulnerable, while its magical spring, Arethusa, supplied them and their troops with plentiful drinking water.

Then Dion had taken over the Island. As self-proclaimed liberator, he might have destroyed its defensive works, thus putting an end to the era of tyranny. He'd have gained huge acclaim by so doing, but he must have decided the stronghold the Island offered was a more valuable asset. In the era of Hipparinus, the barracks and dockyards still stood, as did the fortified palace where the Dionysioflatterers, now scattered to less troubled tables, had once feigned blindness and helplessly groped for their plates.

Hipparinus, too, must have fallen under the spell of the Island, the sense of impunity it conveyed. He took to drinking and reveling once installed there, and dallying as well with a beautiful boy named Achaeus. We're told that Hipparinus took on a certain superior air, which also made him mean and abusive when drunk, as he frequently was.[23] This didn't advance his image as an enlightened leader. Only two years into his reign he fell to a dagger, though not an assassin's blade like the one that had slain his uncle. His death was a manslaughter, not a murder, brought on by a heady mixture of wine and lust.

Parthenius, a collector of salacious stories, relates the tale—impossible to confirm but too good not to tell. It seems Hipparinus had brought Achaeus to live with him in the palace, but feared that the young man's beauty would make him a target for rape. When he had to leave Achaeus alone and lead the defense of the city, he gave him a dagger and told him to use it on any would-be assailant. After a victory in the field, Hipparinus drank deep at a banquet, then hastened to visit Achaeus for celebratory sex. Outside the boy's door, on a drunken whim, he put on a foreign accent and pretended to be a Thessalian soldier who'd killed Hipparinus in battle. Achaeus flew into a rage, threw open the door and stabbed at the figure he failed to recognize in the dark. Grievously wounded, Hipparinus lingered three days before dying—during which time he absolved Achaeus of guilt.[24]

Nysaeus, Hipparinus's brother, took over as ruler of Syracuse. He too behaved badly, indulging himself at the Syracusan tables and preying on women and boys who caught his fancy. Among the signs of his nature our sources list a gaudy four-horse chariot and an embroidered robe, evidently part of the kit handed down from his father and half-brother.[25] These regal trappings made clear to Syracusans, if it hadn't been clear already, that their run of tyrants had never really ended. Before, in the days of Dion, they'd been warned of exchanging a drunken tyrant for a sober one; it now seemed they were swapping out drunks for more drunks, without gaining any measure of freedom.

In Locri, on Italy's toe, another wine-soaked despot, Dionysius the Younger, still lurked, watching the slow decay of Syracuse and the failures of his half-brothers. He'd continued building his power, largely by building his wealth. His mercenaries required pay, and if he had more pay to offer, more could be hired. The West was by now teeming with stateless, landless soldiers eager for work. And so Dionysius embarked on a devious fundraising venture, as Justin describes.

More than a century before this time, the city of Locri had made a religious vow that had gone unfulfilled. When engaged in a war against neighboring Rhegium, Locrians vowed that, if they won, they would make a precious offering to Aphrodite: the virginities of their young women. The maidens would, in accord with Near Eastern customs, sit in the city's temple of Aphrodite and consent to have sex with any man who came by. The Locrians did indeed win the war, but then reneged on their vow. They simply ignored their promise to Aphrodite.

Turn the clock forward again to the late 350s BC, the time of Dionysius's reign over Locri. A new war erupted then, pitting the Locrians against nearby Lucanians. Dionysius stirred up the Locrians' fears that they'd lose because of the goddess's unappeased anger. Then he proposed an ingenious plan: A hundred young women from leading families, wives and daughters of the nobility, could sit in the temple, dressed in fine clothing and jewels—but the men of the city would be forbidden to touch them. In this way, the long-ago vow would be fulfilled, in letter if not in spirit. To guarantee that these women incurred no shame, Dionysius suggested a rule that *they* must all be matched with husbands before any other weddings took place. They could not be penalized in the marriage market.

The Locrians approved this plan, bizarre though it was, and the women, richly adorned, took their places in Aphrodite's temple. No one, it seems, raised the point that a man who'd preyed on their virgins might have ulterior motives.

Dionysius had taken a lesson from his tyrannical father about using piety as a means of extortion. He sent his soldiers to Aphrodite's temple to strip the women of all their gold and fine clothes, then held them hostage until their families surrendered the rest of their wealth. If the families did not comply, Dionysius ordered the women tortured until they revealed where their valuables had been hidden. The temple of Aphrodite became, not a shrine to sexual love, but a monument to cruelty, greed, and cunning.

The Locrians learned once again the high cost of giving a tyrant sanctuary. But out of their suffering was to come a new order. The humiliation of the Locrian women, and the loss of the city's wealth, were soon to provoke a counterreaction. A Fury was coming for Dionysius too.

As he neared the age of eighty, Plato turned once again to the question that had occupied him since youth: how to arrest, or reverse, the downward momentum of Greek politics and build an entirely new kind of state. In his last years he produced his longest, but also saddest and driest, work, *Laws*—his only dialogue that does not include Socrates. Plato's mask in this work is an old and nameless Athenian, addressed as "Stranger" by his two interlocutors, a Cretan and a Spartan. Some have theorized that this Stranger *is* Socrates, but he has none of that character's lively, ironic wit. More likely he's Plato himself, appearing incognito and, unusually, at his true age; his other dialogues are set much earlier than the time in which they were written.

Not only is this stranger an elderly man, but elderly, too, are the Cretan, Cleinias, and the Spartan, Megillus. The three old men converse as they make their way to a famous cave in the mountains of Crete, and the uphill walk tires them. The absence of younger participants, and the backdrop of physical strain, mirrors not only the stage of life that Plato had reached but the moral exhaustion of mid-fourth-century Greece. Gone are the vibrant energies that youthful Glaucon and Adeimantus— not to mention the ever-vivacious Socrates—had brought to *Republic*. We are left with the generation of Cephalus, the aged father of Lysias and Polemarchus, who exited early from *Republic* after admitting he no longer had any sex drive.

Unlike in *Republic* and other dialogues, none of the speakers in *Laws* are based on known figures; they have no past that might convey a personality or an outlook. They function instead as tokens of the places they dwell and the systems under which they've been governed. Sparta and Crete both belonged, ethnically, to the Dorian branch of the Greek family, known for its moral rigor. Both places were thought to preserve ancient virtues thanks to their stable constitutions. Cleinias and Megillus thus represent a backward-looking conservativism, in contrast to the innovative Stranger. The collaboration of these different "types" produces a plan for a new political order.

The state constructed in *Laws* is defined as "second-best," and it's clear that what it's "second" to is the one described in *Republic*. The best state, as the Stranger maintains, would be a commune, in which all property, wives, and children are shared—exactly as in *Republic*'s Callipolis. "No one will ever lay down a more upright or better definition than these precepts, as regards the furthest extension of virtue," the Stranger says. But that ideal state seems largely beyond human reach; it's said to be inhabited by "gods or the children of gods."[26] In its place, the Stranger constructs a compromise constitution; private property will be permitted but not allowed to exceed certain moderate limits.

Along with the disappearance of Socrates, of youth, and of utopian communism, the Forms have also vanished from *Laws*. No longer does Plato speak of a blazing sun, the Form of the Good, that guides the making of policy, or of any eternal, perfect objects of knowledge. The philosopher-king of *Republic* has disappeared, replaced by a set of legal and constitutional precepts. "The importance of law overshadows all," writes Platonist Trevor Saunders, "and the ideal ruler with his expert knowledge of moral values is barely mentioned."[27] If the best legal code is simply supplied—as it is in *Laws*—then the only knowledge that rulers need is how to enforce it.

Though many things divide them, one point remains consistent between *Republic* and *Laws*: the idea that a monarch with unconstrained power offers the world its best chance for change. That idea, of course, was central to the Syracuse project and to Plato's defense of it in the *Seventh Letter*. Its recurrence in *Laws*, in language that seems to point toward Syracuse, reveals that Plato still felt the need to mount that defense as he neared the end of his life.

In *Republic* Plato expressed the hope that a ruler, or ruler's son, might be converted to philosophic ideas. He referred there to "kings," "dynasts," and "sons of kings" as the potential converts. In *Laws*, he alters his terms and dares to suggest that a *tyrant* would be the best candidate. "Give me a city ruled by a tyrant," says the Stranger (a quote we have looked at before), describing the best way to institute change. "And let the tyrant be young, with a good memory, ready to learn, brave, and great-hearted." No one would fit that glowing description to Dionysius the Younger, but the use of "tyrant," in place of *Republic*'s "king," marks a significant shift. "There is not, nor could there ever be, a quicker or better way of establishing a constitution," says the Stranger.[28]

But even a virtuous tyrant cannot succeed by himself; he needs an advisor. He must be "lucky, in that, in his time, a lawgiver worthy of praise was born," says the Stranger, "and luck brought them together; and if this should happen, then god would have done nearly everything that he does when he wants a city to fare especially well." That sounds like an idealized description of Plato's Syracuse project, a vision of what might have been. Had Dionysius been able to master his desire for pleasure, or had Dion lived and ruled longer, then Plato, a "lawgiver worthy of praise," might have completed the magical formula.

*Laws* is thought to have been the last treatise Plato composed. It seems distinctly the work of a tired man, perhaps a lonely one, too, for the Stranger who represents Plato has no connection to Cleinias and Megillus, beyond their shared walk to the cave. The Cretan and Spartan never learn, or ask, the Athenian's name. In the last lines of the work they speak of him in the third person, making clear that, without saying farewell, he has departed their company. They resolve to beg him to stay, but the dialogue intimates that he's already gone.

Plato died in 347 BC, at the age of eighty-one. We have several accounts of the cause of death, but our oldest source, Philodemus, reports that he suffered from fever for several days. In his will, a document quoted in full by Diogenes Laertius, he left his land and property—a very modest estate—to "Adeimantus," presumably not his older brother but that man's grandson. His body was buried in the Academy, and his nephew Speusippus took over as head of his school.

Two years after Plato's death, the tyrant Dionysius, driven out of Locri by an outraged populace, sailed back to the Island and wrested control from Nysaeus, his half-brother. He'd heeded the lesson once taught to his father, to cling to the tyranny like a rider clings to a horse, refusing to leave it unless dragged off by the leg. In fact, he'd taken that maxim further, resolutely climbing back on the horse after being dragged off.

Dionysius imprisoned Nysaeus for months, delaying his death for some unknown reason. While awaiting execution, Nysaeus passed his time in gluttonous eating and drinking.[29] He remained a devotee of the Syracusan tables, the center of life in the tyrant-house, right up to the end.

The fifth change of ruler in thirteen years had brought back to power a man whom many reviled but some no doubt saw as a welcome end to the chaos. The family civil war now appeared to be over, since all of the kin on the junior side—those connected to Aristomachê—were dead. Dionysius, by contrast, had as yet lost no one from *his* branch, except his mother and father, who'd died long before. He had brought his eldest son, Apollocrates, now in his twenties, with him from Locri to Syracuse; his wife, Sôphrosynê, and two daughters, along with his younger son, had stayed behind in Locri, under the watchful eyes of a bodyguard corps.

Dionysius surely intended to send for his kin in due time, but before he could do so, events took a course of their own. Preyed upon for too long, the Locrians were bent on revenge. They overpowered the guards and took the tyrant's wife and three children prisoner. Dionysius offered limitless ransom and got his Tarentine allies to intercede on his behalf, but the Locrians refused to negotiate. Dionysius brought his army against them, laid siege to their city and ravaged the outlying fields, but even then they didn't give in. Finally the tyrant withdrew.

The Locrians vented their rage on their captives, a fury built up over years of the tyrant's predations. The daughters were forced to prostitute themselves along public roads, while Sôphrosynê, in the lurid language of Plutarch, "was violated by her enemies with the most licentious pleasures inflicted on her body."[30] Then the entire family was tortured by means of needles thrust under their fingernails. In the end, all the prisoners were strangled to death, their bodies dismembered, and their bones ground to powder in mortars.

All that was still not enough. According to sources, the Locrians took the flesh of the bodies and milled it in with the flour that went to making the town's bread supply.[31] Thus the whole population enjoyed the horrific thrill of grinding their tormentor's kin between their teeth. Whatever they did not cannibalize they cast into the sea.

Dionysius went back to the Island, the glittering gem he still possessed, though everything around it had turned to ash. He'd paid a terrible price for his strange predilections and his determination to stay in power. His life seemed to bear out Plato's view in *Republic*, that the lot of the tyrant is the most unhappy of human conditions. But fate had a strange resolution in store for him yet.

When the soul of Plato departed the earthly plane, it was launched on an astral journey that would, after a thousand years, lead to reincarnation. Thanks to Plato's pursuit of knowledge, his soul, at that journey's end, had hopes of avoiding the error that other souls would be all too eager to make: to come back as a tyrant.

Our souls' experience after death is described in the final segment of *Republic*, in some of Plato's most inspired prose. Here Plato employs a spokesman brought from beyond the grave, a device he had also deployed in his *Eighth Letter*. The revenant in *Republic* is not Dion but someone named Er, a barbarian soldier who'd been seemingly killed in a battle but then had revived twelve days later—sent back to the world as a messenger from the divine. The Myth of Er, as this final stretch of *Republic* is called, is described by Socrates, who relates it as a thing that might "save" us if we attend to its lessons.[32] It puts *Republic*'s teachings into a larger framework, indeed the largest possible, the entire universe.

If Plato's soul followed the journey described by Er, it came first to a place of judgment, not unlike the Christian seat of St. Peter. Two paths diverged; Plato was sent on the right-hand path, along with the souls of the just, on a journey into the sky, a place of "visions of indescribable beauty." *Republic* is vague on what these visions contained, but it's a fair guess that the "indescribable beauty" came from Beauty itself, that is, from the Forms. Meanwhile, the souls of the wicked, especially tyrants, were sent to the left and down into the earth, condemned to centuries of hideous torment.

At the end of his thousand-year journey (at about the time of the death of the prophet Muhammad), Plato's soul descended out of the sky and entered a peaceful meadow. There it congregated with other souls in a festival setting. When a week had gone by, Plato was granted further beatific visions and heard ineffable music. The cosmos was laid out before him, with planets, stars, and the moon and sun whirling around an axis that looked like a giant spindle. Accompanying these rotating orbs were a chorus of Sirens, each singing a single note; together these notes produced the harmony of the spheres. The spindle was propped on the knees of the goddess Anankê, "Necessity."

Turning the spindle with their hands were three Fates, one singing of the past, another of the present, a third of the future. Plato and the other just souls were summoned to stand before the Fate called Lachesis, she who assigns human lots. In the lap of this goddess Plato saw many tokens for casting lots, and also "patterns of lives"—the futures that lay ahead for the reincarnated. An attending priest cast both the lots and the lives on the ground, and bid the souls to make ready to choose. Their next life, he told them, was up to them: "The blame belongs to the chooser; god is blameless."

The lots determined the order in which the souls selected their lives from the "patterns" laid out on the ground. This moment of choosing is described by *Republic* as "the entire danger for humankind"—the point at which we can make the greatest mistake. All that we've learned in earthly life comes to bear on this moment. If we've gained enough knowledge to tell a good life from a bad one, we'll choose well. The highest such knowledge, of course, is that gained from philosophic inquiry.

In the choosing witnessed by Er and described in *Republic*, the soul who had gotten the very first choice dashed forward with glee and selected the greatest tyranny he could find. In his previous life, *Republic*

explains, this soul had not belonged to an evil man, only an unphilosophic one. Having never reflected on the essence of virtue, this soul had
no way to know what horrors awaited it in the life of a tyrant—ghastly
crimes, including the worst yet mentioned, child-cannibalism (see chapter 3). As the soul inspected the life it had chosen, it wailed in agony, but
the choice was irrevocable.

Plato knew what life he must choose, but he also needed some luck. If
the lottery put him last or near last, the best lives might have been taken,
and he'd have to settle. In the choosing witnessed by Er, the final choice
fell to the hero Odysseus, who took the life of a private and unremarkable
man—the very one, as he said, that he would have chosen if he'd gone
first. Perhaps that's a good life, *Republic* implies, but not a path to true
happiness. In Plato's terms, it's the best one can do if one never escapes
from the cave.

After all the choices were made, Plato marched with the other souls
across the plain of Lethe, "Forgetfulness," a hot, dry place without any
shade-giving trees. Even though disembodied, they still experienced
thirst in these arid conditions. When they camped at a river called
Amelês, "Heedless," they were told they could drink but only in moderation. Some of the souls, "not rescued by reason," gulped down the river's
waters greedily. Those guzzlers got an overdose of oblivion. Their memories of what they had seen in the heavens were completely erased.

Refreshed, the souls slept, then woke to a rumble of thunder. In an
instant all were sent to their chosen lives, streaming toward birth like
comets or shooting stars. Those who had drunk only moderately had not
quite lost an impression of the "visions of indescribable beauty" they'd
seen in the astral realm. In time, with hard work, they might recover
those visions—the task of philosophy.

With the Myth of Er, Plato gives *Republic* a transcendent and totaliz-
ing finale. Up to this point the work has examined justice in the soul and
in the city, reading the soul's smaller "letters" by using bigger ones as a
guide. In the work's last segment, Plato leaps to yet a larger level, a leap of
quantum dimensions. He finds justice not only in souls and cities, but in
the fabric of the cosmos, written into the motions of stars and planets. To
practice philosophy, he suggests, is to strive to join those heavenly bodies.

The Myth of Er also shows us, again, how Plato's sojourns in Syracuse, and his tortured relations with that city's ruling family, informed his *Republic*. The last trial that the souls undergo is precisely the one that the Dionysii consistently failed. At the river of Amelês, it is restraint of a very specific kind that distinguishes souls that are educable from those condemned to lose their visions of beauty. The latter are barred from philosophy in their next life because, like those ill-fated tyrants, they could not stop drinking.

*Timoleon departs for Syracuse with the blessing of heaven. From an early twentieth-century edition of* Plutarch's Lives.

# CHAPTER 14

# THE MUSIC TEACHER

*(343 BC and after)*

Plutarch compared the reign of Dionysius the Elder to a tragic play, but as we've seen, that reign was only the first act of a very long drama. In the second act, Dionysius the Younger had taken the helm and split the tyrant-house by exiling Dion, while also making a clumsy and demanding attempt to bring Plato into his court. The third act had returned Plato to Syracuse for a second, in this case very brief, attempt at making a tyrant into a king. His efforts on behalf of Dion and Dion's allies had offended Dionysius and brought real danger upon himself, until Archytas swept in to save the day. In the fourth act Dion had taken center stage and had been revealed as a complex figure, to some a liberator, to others an autocrat like his two brothers-in-law. He'd alienated many by murdering his chief rival before being murdered himself.

The fifth act began with a series of debauched despots holding sway in rapid succession. Plutarch describes the state of mind that the demos had reached by this point: "They were overflowing with ills and enraged against all who led armies," he writes; they had come to regard the former tyranny, ousted by Dion, as "a golden age." But when that tyranny resumed, the tyrant, Dionysius, was likewise "enraged," says Plutarch, and treated his fellow citizens as his slaves.[1]

No one could have foreseen that the drama's resolution would feature a *deus ex machina*, with a savior dropped in from afar as though by a crane (the "machine" of the famous phrase). Nor could anyone have anticipated the denouement of Dionysius's story, a peripety that astonished all Greece. To make that surprise ending possible, Dionysius, as he claimed, had drawn on his lessons with Plato—a course of instruction at last bearing fruit well after the teacher was dead.

The *deus* that came to Syracuse *ex machina* was not in fact a god but a mortal, and an unremarkable one at that. Timoleon was a private Corinthian citizen, already in his mid-fifties in 343 BC. In his youth he'd shown promise as a military commander but opted out of public life after a traumatic episode: When his brother had tried to seize power and rule Corinth as a tyrant, he'd taken part in the plot that got the man killed (see chapter 8). For twenty years thereafter, stained by the sin of fratricide, he'd withdrawn into a self-imposed isolation.

In 343 the people of Syracuse, desperate to end their string of tyrants and restore their homeland, reached out to Corinth—their mother city—for help. No Corinthian leader wanted the job, which seemed sure to result in failure. The collapse of Greek Sicily appeared all but certain; the Carthaginians, sensing the end was at hand, had begun sending ships once again into Syracusan waters. But Corinth could not abandon a former colony without making a token effort. They sent Timoleon, a highly expendable person, in command of a small squad of mercenaries. Their expectations for what might happen were low.

Before the battalion even set sail, word arrived that most of Syracuse had fallen to a Greek warlord, Hicetas—the man suspected of having Dion's kin drowned—who'd made common cause with Carthage. Dionysius had been driven back behind the walls of the Island and had dug in there with his troops, in a pattern by this time distressingly familiar. Another grim siege was about to take place, with Syracusans again caught between besieged and besieger. But Timoleon's arrival was about to change everything.

Drawing on tactical skills that had lain dormant for two decades,

Timoleon used a surprise attack to deal a defeat to Hicetas. Then, a messenger from the Island arrived in the Corinthian camp. Against all odds, Dionysius, perceiving Timoleon as an ally, was offering to surrender his troops and his forts in exchange for safe passage to Corinth. Nothing in the tyrant's past suggested he'd give up power so easily, yet somehow the fight had gone out of him. Rejecting the maxim that tyranny makes a fine shroud, he was handing the Island over, with its soldiers, cavalry horses, artillery weapons, siege engines, food stocks, and seventy thousand sets of infantry gear.[2]

In a stealth operation, Dionysius was rowed past a naval blockade and brought in disguise to Timoleon's camp. Timoleon held up his end of the joint agreement. A single skiff took away the man who had once possessed a fleet hundreds strong and brought him to exile in Corinth. The last, most unlikely chapter of Dionysius's life was set to begin.


No Greek city had hosted a tyrant before who had fallen from such a great height. Dionysius's arrival aroused high emotions in Corinth, in some cases pity, in others schadenfreude. Mostly there was astonishment at the banality of his new lifestyle. "That era revealed no work of nature or art to rival this work of Fortune," writes Plutarch. "The one who had a little before been tyrant of Sicily, now in Corinth, passing his time in a fishmonger's shop, or sitting in a perfumer's, or drinking watered-down wine in the taverns, or squabbling in public with 'ladies of the night,' or giving the music-girls instruction in singing odes."[3]

Corinthians could not understand why a former monarch would let himself be seen in such tawdry pursuits. Some thought he was merely indulging innate hedonism. Others thought he was bored and seeking the thrill of the demimonde. Still others developed a theory that his behavior was an elaborate ploy: Sensing that Corinth feared his will to power, the former tyrant was acting a part, debasing himself so as to seem harmless. If this was indeed Dionysius's plan, it was working, for, according to one source, he was three times acquitted at trial on charges of seeking some sort of restoration.[4]

Among those who marveled at Dionysius's lowness was another recent arrival at Corinth, the acid-tongued Cynic, Diogenes of Sinopê. Plutarch records the first meeting between the two men, both formerly wealthy but no longer so.

"How unworthy you are of this life, Dionysius," the Cynic declared. Dionysius thanked him for what he took to be fellow feeling, but Diogenes corrected the misunderstanding. "Did you think I was sympathizing?" he said. "I was peeved that a slave like you, who ought to have grown old and died in a tyrant's estate like your father, should be here, enjoying our jokes and high living." To the Cynic, with his disdain of wealth and power, a fall from the heights was a *better* fate than Dionysius deserved.[5]

After only a few months in Corinth, Dionysius was joined by his cousin Leptines, son of his uncle of the same name, who had tried his hand at the family trade of tyrannical rule. Leptines had been ousted from power by Timoleon but, like Dionysius, had received a grant of safe passage to the Peloponnese. Apparently this transfer was part of a plan to teach a political lesson to all of Hellas. "Timoleon thought it a fine thing," writes Plutarch, "to have the Greeks see the tyrants of Sicily living the miserable life of an exile."[6] Leptines and Dionysius could provide real-world cases in point of Plato's *Republic* doctrines.

By this time Dionysius had no surviving kinsman besides Leptines. He had seen his wife and two other half-siblings, four children, and two nephews disappear into the maelstrom, all because he could not get along with his brother-in-law. One ancient writer notes, with evident satisfaction, that none of the tyrant's family members died in such a way that their corpses could be recovered for burial.[7]

As he spent his time in taverns and shops, Dionysius left himself open to the snipes and gibes of the public. Observers saw a streak of masochism in his willingness to be taunted and in his new choice of career: a humble music instructor who gave lessons to children in public squares. Centuries later, Cicero came to a different conclusion about that late-life occupation. Teaching the young, Cicero writes, was merely, for Dionysius, an exercise of tyrannical power on a smaller scale.[8]

Sometimes the former tyrant gave as good as he got when Corinthians mocked his fallen condition. Once, a visitor to his house pretended to shake out his clothes as he entered, in the way that, in former days, Syracusan courtiers had proved that they carried no weapons. After the meeting ended and the man was leaving, Dionysius insisted he shake out his clothes again—to prove he had not stolen anything while he had been there.

Two fascinating exchanges between Dionysius and those he met in Corinth, both reported by Plutarch, centered on his former relations with Plato. During his lifetime, Plato, in Athens, had had to face scrutiny over that bond and explain its rather abrupt dissolution. Now, in Corinth, Dionysius took his turn at answering similar questions.

One of the tyrant's interrogators was Aristoxenus, a musical theorist who, as a native of Tarentum, had once lived close to the borders of Dionysius's empire. Perhaps he remembered, from childhood, that Tarentines had rescued Plato from the tyrant's machinations. Now, in the streets of Corinth, he asked Dionysius what fault he had found in Plato that caused the breakdown of his partnership with the sage. Dionysius blamed his courtiers for leading him astray. "Of the many ills of which tyranny is replete, there's none so great," he declared, "as the inability of one's so-called friends to speak their minds. Because of these people I was robbed of Plato's good will."[9] If that was indeed his answer, Dionysius had at last learned his lesson about the hollow fellowship of the Syracusan tables.

In another exchange, a stranger needled Dionysius over his vaunted philosophic ambitions during the days when he'd ruled Syracuse. "What help are you getting now from Plato's wisdom?" the man scoffed. Dionysius kept his cool and gave a reply that Plato, had he heard it, might have found gratifying. "Do you think," he said, "that I've gotten no benefit from Plato, when I endure, as you see, my reversal of fortune?"[10]

After he'd been in Corinth for several years, Dionysius got into a testy exchange with Speusippus, now head of Plato's school and keeper of his legacy. Two sources have left us a record of a bitter verbal duel, conducted by letter. It included a petty attempt by Dionysius to pull himself up by pulling a moral philosopher down, and to show that, whatever his own flaws, he would not be preached to by the Academy.

Speusippus had been writing, or perhaps talking, disparagingly about

Dionysius's greed. The tyrant shot back, in a letter quoted or paraphrased by both sources, that Speusippus was a worse money-grubber. "Plato made those who came to study with him exempt from fees, but *you* assess fees and collect them, from both those willing to pay and those not willing," Dionysius writes. He accuses Speusippus of borrowing money—with the intent of not paying it back, he must mean—and of raising funds to reimburse himself after he'd paid off the debts of a former Academy student named Hermeias.[11]

Dionysius didn't stop there. He threw in Speusippus's face his relations with Lastheneia, a female Academy student who'd come to Athens from Arcadia. She and another woman, Axiothea of Phlius, had broken through Greek philosophy's gender barrier by joining the group around Plato (though one account says they put on male clothes in order to do so). Lastheneia remained "on campus" after Plato's death and, according to Dionysius, Speusippus was sleeping with her.

In the course of the previous decade Dionysius, by all reports, had committed outrageous sex crimes, and, throughout adult life, had indulged in drunken debauches. He had made hedonism a way of life and entertained Aristippus, chief priest of that school, at his court. How it must have gratified him to charge an Academy head, the standard-bearer of sobriety and self-restraint, with shameless pursuit of pleasure. "One can learn the scope of your 'wisdom,'" he wrote to Speusippus in scornful tones, "from your female student, the Arcadian woman."[12] His remark was more cutting for his omission of Lastheneia's name.

The last words we have from Dionysius date to 338 BC, some six years after his abdication. Philip of Macedon, fresh from his triumph over Athens and Thebes at the battle of Chaeronea, arrived in Corinth that year to supervise the Greek League, his newly established treaty organization. He reportedly sought out Dionysius for a consultation, a rising monarch hoping to learn from a fallen one's mistakes.

Philip boldly asked Dionysius how he had managed to lose a position so stoutly fortified by his father. "My father left me his tyranny, but not his luck," was the tyrant's reply.[13] In a different version of this exchange, Dionysius explained that his father's era had held democracy in contempt, whereas *his* era felt an equal disdain for tyrannical rule.[14]

Dionysius is said to have lived to advanced age at Corinth; no information survives as to how he died. In the strangest report of all, preserved in two sources, we're told that he ended his days as a priest of the goddess Cybele, traveling about the countryside in female garb, dancing wildly while beating a tambourine.[15]

Dionysius's reversal of fortune became proverbial in the Greek world, apparently even during his lifetime. When Philip, at the height of his power, was threatening Sparta with invasion, the Spartans sent him a message, typically terse: "Dionysius is in Corinth."[16] The moral to be drawn was that even the highest may end up the lowest, so Philip should not take for granted that he would succeed. The pithy expression was still in use several centuries later.[17]

Ethicists treated the fall of Dionysius as a warning against ambition for wealth and power. It provided "an illustration for humankind," as one author wrote, "to instill the lessons of moderation and an orderly lifestyle."[18] The word denoting "moderation," *sôphrosynê*, was the name of Dionysius's wife but a lesson the tyrant had never managed to learn. In Corinth he could at least teach it to others.

Even as Greeks made a parable out of Dionysius's fall, they continued to puzzle over his association with Plato. The shadow cast by that partnership darkened Plato's name well after both men had passed from the scene. Decades after Plato's death, Epicurus—founder of the philosophic school that bears his name—went so far as to call the Academy members "Dionysioflatterers," and to snarkily label Plato "golden," referring both to his elegant prose style and to rumors he'd gotten rich by paying court to a despot.

The problems presented by Plato's Syracuse project were still unresolved in the first century BC. At that time a Greek rhetorician named Molon, a teacher of Cicero, wrought his own twist on the apophthegm coined by the Spartans.

"The amazing thing was not 'Dionysius in Corinth,'" he wrote, "but rather 'Plato in Sicily.'"[19]

To return to the fifth act of the drama of Syracuse: Timoleon managed to get firm control of the ruined city and rally eastern Sicily to his cause. He embarked on a reclamation campaign, uprooting Sicilian warlords and despots and pushing the Carthaginians back to the western third of the island. As conflicts eased, the region began to recover. In mainland Greece, at festival sites like Olympia, criers announced that Syracusans who'd fled their homes could now reclaim them and new colonists could acquire land on the cheap. Tens of thousands streamed across the Ionian Sea to resume their old lives or build new ones.[20]

Sicily was being re-Hellenized, exactly as Plato had urged in his letters and in his counsel to Dionysius. Indeed, the way Timoleon dealt with the region followed Plato's plans so closely that some scholars suppose he had read the *Eighth Letter* and used it as a blueprint.[21] There's no evidence to support these theories but nothing rules them out either. It's appealing to think that Plato's efforts to save the Greek West *did* bear some fruit in the end.

Though he could have made himself ruler of Syracuse, Timoleon gave up his office—most likely that of *stratêgos autokratôr*—and left the city to govern itself, under a new constitution. Before returning to private life, he took the step that none of the previous "liberators" had had the courage to take. He leveled the Island, stone by stone, making it useless to anyone grasping at power.[22]

All Syracusans who wished were allowed to bring iron tools to the site and take part in the demolition. One imagines that nearly the whole population did so. Down came the monument at the Royal Gates where Dionysius the Elder was buried; down came the grim acropolis, the palace in which, one by one, five members of a drunken, dysfunctional family had once held dominion.

On the spot where that palace had stood, Timoleon built a complex of law courts, a move that would have meant much to Plato had he lived to see it.[23] The symbolism was surely intentional. At the heart of the Island, the seat of the old tyranny, the city would henceforth seek for justice, and perhaps, "with the help of god," find it.

# ACKNOWLEDGMENTS

Many people have helped make this book possible or, in its formative phase, *seem* possible. I wish to thank above all my agents, Nate Muscato and David Kuhn of Aevitas Creative Management, and my editor at Norton, Dan Gerstle, for faith in this project and for wise guidance throughout the three years it occupied. Nearly every page of this book has been improved by Dan Gerstle's sharp eyes, as well as by the keen ear of Steve Coates, reader and friend extraordinaire, whose suggestions helped knit together many a broken train of thought or heal a wounded sentence. Norton's Zeba Arora has heroically managed the production process despite all the entropy I created, and copy editors Bob Byrne and Rebecca Rider have dealt patiently with my slovenly citations and orthography.

This book has benefited from a Public Scholars Fellowship awarded by the National Endowment for the Humanities (NEH). I am grateful to the NEH for this generous support and to the anonymous readers of my grant proposal, who offered salutary criticisms. The Public Scholars program's goal, of bringing well-researched, serious humanistic inquiries before the eyes of general readers, is hugely important in an era of increasing academic specialization, and the NEH deserves all our thanks for instituting it.

Among the colleagues in Classics and Philosophy who have generously

lent an ear, shared an unpublished manuscript, or answered an impor-
tunate question, I can list the following, in alphabetical order: Carol
Atack, Eva Atanassow, Paul Cartledge, Rob Cioffi, Carolyn Dewald,
Jay Elliott, Richard Evans, Killian Fleischer, Filippo Forcignanò, Dan-
iel Mendelsohn, Pamela Mensch, Debra Nails, Josh Ober, Vasilis Politis,
Jamie Redfield, David Rosenbloom, and Robin Waterfield. Jay Elliott,
Richard Evans, and Pam Mensch did me the enormous favor of reading and commenting on early drafts. Sam Dresser of *Aeon* and essayist
Adam Kirsch both commented on an article discussing the authorship
debate surrounding Plato's *Epistles*, and Harvey Yunis sponsored a lecture and discussion at Rice University that produced many helpful criticisms and comments on the same topic. Conversations with Rob Tempio,
Stefan Vranka, and Jim Ottaway Jr. have, as always, been encouraging
and enlightening.

Invaluable help with illustrations came from Markley Boyer, Killian
Fleischer, Brad Nelson, and the digital imaging departments of Oxford's
Bodleian Library and the Harvard Art Museum. Kelly Sandefer of Beehive Mapping prepared the superb maps and genealogical chart. Rights
and permissions have been secured with the help of the tireless Sarah
Palmer. For the beautiful design of the book and the expert handling of
its illustrations, I have Joe Lops and Chris Welch to thank, and for the
marvelous cover design, art director Ingsu Liu.

My loving and lovely wife, artist Tanya Marcuse, and our three children, Jacob, Abby, and Jonah, have helped me stay sane as I took on the
most difficult book I have yet written or ever hope to write. Tanya has
given me courage to tread on the hallowed ground of Plato scholarship,
where I often felt like a trespasser, and her response to the manuscript
made all my labors seem worthwhile. My dad, to whom the book is dedicated, often said while I was writing that he looked forward to reading
it but likely knew at the time he wouldn't be able to. I hope it would have
pleased him.

# NOTES

Source citations take the name Plato to be implicit in the case of references to *Republic*, *Laws*, or the *Third*, *Fourth*, *Seventh*, *Eighth*, and *Thirteenth Epistle*. Other ancient works are cited by author and title. All translations from Greek and Latin are my own.

## Introduction

1. Abby Jackson, "The Most Popular Required Reading at America's Top 10 Colleges," *Business Insider*, February 5, 2016.
2. Thomas Jefferson to John Adams, July 5, 1814, in *The Papers of Thomas Jefferson, Retirement Series, vol. 7, 28 November 1813 to 30 September 1814*, ed. J. Jefferson Looney (Princeton: Princeton University Press, 2010), 453.
3. Popper, *The Open Society and Its Enemies*, xxxix; this 2020 edition is a one-volume edition. The first volume of the two-volume work is *The Spell of Plato*. This work was originally published in 1945.
4. Diodorus Siculus, *Library of History* 2.5 and 14.42; Aelian, *Varia Historia* 6.12.
5. Waterfield, *Plato of Athens*, ix.
6. Machines were proficient enough, even decades ago, to compare the styles of works within the same genre—to establish, say, that a certain dialogue thought to be Plato's is not by the person who wrote *Republic*. But comparing works that cross genre boundaries—as do letters and dialogues—is a much harder task. In a 1989 computer-based study, statistician Gerald Ledger employed an analytic method designed to overcome the gap between genres, and found the *Third*, *Seventh*, and *Eighth Letters* to be genuine Plato and leaned toward the same conclusion for the *Thirteenth* (the other epistles he deemed too short for analysis). But reviewers have disputed the validity of his study (see Nails, *Agora, Academy, and Conduct*, 1995).
7. Misch, *History of Autobiography*, 111.
8. Politis, "Plato's Seventh Letter"; Forcignanò, *Platone: Settima Lettera*; and Waterfield, *Plato of Athens*, have argued for the authenticity of the *Seventh Letter*, along with the *Third* and

*Eighth* in the case of Waterfield. The book-length study by Helfer, *Plato's Letters,* defends Platonic authorship of *all* of the letters. James Redfield has shared with me portions of his forthcoming book on the *Seventh Letter,* which will make an eloquent case for the authenticity of that epistle.

9. Burnyeat and Frede, *Pseudo-Platonic Seventh Letter.*

10. A letter apparently sent by Speusippus, Plato's nephew, to Philip II of Macedon, was declared authentic in a recent book-length study (Natoli, *Letter of Speusippus*). Natoli's work was ignored by Michael Frede in his attempt to dismiss the letter (Burnyeat and Frede, *Pseudo-Platonic Seventh Letter*). Six letters attributed to Demosthenes, dating to 323 BC, were examined from every angle by classicist Jonathan Goldstein (Goldstein, *Letters of Demosthenes*); his conclusion, accepted by his reviewers, was that four of the six were almost certainly genuine.

11. Gallazzi, "Plato, *Epistulae* VIII 356a."

12. L. A. Post (*Thirteen Epistles of Plato,* 15) notes this divide with regard to the *Thirteenth Letter.*

13. Morrow, *Plato's Epistles,* 16.

14. I developed this argument further in Romm, "The Sage and His Foibles."

15. Prefatory note to *Epistle XIII* in the Loeb Classical Library edition of Plato's works, vol. 9 610–11.

16. "Plato's Letters," *Classical Quarterly* 38 (1924): 29. Other defenders of the *Thirteenth* are listed by Thesleff, *Studies in Platonic Chronology,* 235n99.

## Chapter 1: Tyrants and Kings

1. The assessment of his contemporary, Isocrates (*Philip* 65).

2. The term "archon" is used of Dionysius in Athenian inscriptions, but there is dispute over whether it originated from Dionysius himself; see Oost, "Tyrant Kings of Syracuse," 234–5, notes 45 and 48.

3. Lysias, *Olympic Oration* 5.

4. Dionysius of Halicarnassus, *Lysias* 29. Diodorus Siculus, *Library of History* 14.109. Diodorus says that the crowd rioted over the recitation of Dionysius's verses, but this seems less likely. See also Plutarch, *Moralia* 836d.

5. Diodorus Siculus, *Library of History* 14.109.

6. Diodorus Siculus, *Library of History* 11.26.

7. See Kraay, *Greek Coins and History,* chapter 2, and Kraay, "The Demareteion Reconsidered." Kraay thought in the earlier piece that the Damareteion was a small gold coin; in the later essay he accepted its usual identification as a silver decadrachm.

8. Diodorus Siculus, *Library of History* 5.3.5–6. The myth that connected the spring to Arethusa's attempt to escape being raped by Alpheus, a river god, seems to postdate the classical era.

9. Diodorus Siculus, *Library of History* 11.87. The procedure was terminated after a few years under pressure from the nobility.

10. Diodorus Siculus, *Library of History* 13.75.

11. Cicero, *On Divination* 1.73.

12. Diodorus Siculus, *Library of History* 13.111–12.

13. Aelian, *Varia Historia* 4.8 (placing the episode during a Carthaginian attack, and giving the name Ellopides rather than Heloris); Isocrates, *Archidamus* 44 (in the same context as Aelian); Diodorus Siculus, *Library of History* 14.8.

14. Diodorus Siculus, *Library of History* 20.78. At 14.8 Diodorus tells the same story but attributes the saying to Philistus.

15. Plutarch, *Dion* 7; Diodorus Siculus, *Library of History* 16.5.3.

16. Diodorus Siculus, *Library of History* 14.18; see Evans, "Misleading Representation of Dion," 113; and Karlsson, *Fortification Towers and Masonry Techniques,* 14. When the Epipolae wall

was later completed, perhaps in 385, it was the largest circuit wall of any Greek city, according to Diodorus Siculus (*Library of History* 15.35).

17. Diodorus Siculus, *Library of History* 14.112.
18. Diodorus Siculus, *Library of History* 15.13.
19. I. F. Stone, *Trial of Socrates* 66–67.
20. Plato's birth date is disputed. I have adopted the consensus view, and that of the ancient sources, that he was born in 428 or 427 BC. Some scholars prefer a date of 424 on the grounds that we hear nothing of military service by Plato during the Peloponnesian War, which ended in 404; had he reached the age of twenty before the war's end, we'd expect that he would have served. But Plato was certainly old enough to serve in the Corinthian War (395–387 BC), yet there's no evidence in his works that he did. Could he have had some kind of exemption? The silence about his military service is puzzling, but not, in my view, a sound basis for dating his birth.
21. *Seventh Letter* 324d.
22. *Seventh Letter* 324e.
23. *Seventh Letter* 325b.
24. *Seventh Letter* 326a.
25. Diodorus Siculus, *Library of History* 10.7; Plutarch, *Moralia* 551a; Cicero, *Tusculan Disputations* 4.36.78.
26. Huffman, *Archytas of Tarentum*, 41. See also Johnson, "Sources for Philosophy of Archytas," 182–3.
27. Huffman, *Archytas of Tarentum*, 36n16, 609.
28. Harward, *The Platonic Epistles*, 229.
29. Strabo, *Geography* 6.1.10; see Caven, *Dionysius I*, 146, and Stroheker, *Dionysios I*, 223n60.
30. Pindar, *Olympian* 1, lines 12 and 23; discussion in Morgan, *Pindar and Construction of Monarchy*.
31. Sanders, "Dionysius I of Syracuse," 281.
32. Xenophon, *Memorabilia* 4.6.12.
33. Plato, *Statesman* 291e.
34. Xenophon, *Memorabilia* 2.1.17, e.g.; Plato, *Statesman* 276b.
35. *Republic* 571c–d.
36. *Republic* 572a.
37. *Republic* 586a.
38. *Republic* 587e.
39. There is an ancient tradition, almost certainly apocryphal, that Plato also visited Egypt on his way to Sicily (rejected by Thesleff, *Studies in Platonic Chronology*, 28).

## Chapter 2: Syracusan Tables

1. *Seventh Letter* 326b.
2. Athenaeus, *Deipnosophistae* 1.11.
3. Athenaeus, *Deipnosophistae* 1.5.
4. Sometimes attributed to a different Philoxenus, but probably wrongly (see John Wilkins, *The Boastful Chef* [Oxford: Oxford University Press, 2001] 344–6).
5. Diodorus Siculus, *Library of History* 15.6.
6. Aelian, *Varia Historia* 12.44.
7. Diodorus Siculus, *Library of History* 15.6.
8. Plutarch, *Moralia* 334c.
9. Diodorus Siculus, *Library of History* 14.44; Caven, *Dionysius I*, 99.
10. Aelian, *Varia Historia* 13.10.
11. Aelian, *Varia Historia* 13.45.
12. Nails, *People of Plato*, 131.

13. Cornelius Nepos, *Dion* 2. See Riginos, *Platonica: The Anecdotes*, 74–76.
14. *Seventh Letter* 327a–b.
15. Paul Shorey in his note on the passage (Shorey, *Plato: The Republic*, 2.473).
16. *Republic* 5.473d, *Seventh Letter* 326a–b.
17. Athenaeus, *Deipnosophistae* 507c.
18. Jo Marchant, "First Passages of Rolled-Up Herculaneum Scroll Revealed," *Nature* news, February 5, 2024.
19. Recent and current methods discussed in Fleischer, *Philodem: Geschichte der Akademie*. Fleischer's text is the basis of the passages translated in this chapter.
20. Philodemus, *Index Academicorum* Column 10, lines 5–18.
21. Plutarch, *Dion* 5.
22. Diogenes Laertius, *Lives of the Philosophers* 3.18.
23. Diodorus Siculus, *Library of History* 15.7.
24. Discussion by Fleischer in *Philodem: Geschichte der Akademie*.
25. Thesleff has speculated, seemingly with this same thought in mind, that Dion brought Plato to Syracuse at a time when Dionysius was out of the city, pursuing his war against Rhegium (Thesleff, "Platonic Chronology," 5).
26. Isaeus, *Orations* 5.29. Property values may have been higher at "downtown" addresses (those inside the city walls).
27. It was Plato who started the Greek word down the path toward its modern meaning. In his last dialogue, the *Laws*, he discussed the need for young men to be educated in philosophical abstractions and to strive for excellence "in the *scholais* of these things" (820c)—"leisures" here understood to mean "free time spent in discussion of ideas."
28. Dillon, "What Happened to Plato's Garden?," 58.
29. Aristotle (*Metaphysics* 987b) credits Plato with the invention of dialectic.
30. Ostwald and Lynch, "The Growth of Schools and the Advance of Knowledge," 605, 610.
31. See Cameron, "Last Days of the Academy," 11, 21.
32. Sources cited by Riginos, *Platonica: The Anecdotes*, 139.
33. *Republic* 537d–540a.
34. *Republic* 514a–517b.
35. Stobaeus, *Anthology* 4.22.33.
36. Diogenes Laertius, *Lives of the Philosophers* 3.28. I follow the line assignments of the Goulet-Cazé translation.
37. Diogenes Laertius, *Lives of the Philosophers* 3.28.
38. The anecdote is related by Aristoxenus in his treatise *Harmonics* (2.1), but attributed, reliably, to Aristotle, who was no doubt present on the occasion. Riginos (*Platonica: The Anecdotes*, 125) says the report "may be accepted as true."
39. *Republic* 479e.
40. *Republic* 7.539e.
41. *Republic* 5.473c.
42. I rely here on the solution of Sedley ("Philosophy, the Forms and the Art of Ruling," 2007) to the notorious problem of why the philosopher reenters the cave once he's left it.
43. It's said he declined the job when he found he could not institute one of the crucial doctrines espoused in *Republic*, communal ownership of property. Diogenes Laertius, *Lives of the Philosophers* 3.23; Plutarch, *Moralia* 1126c.
44. Saunders, "The RAND Corporation of Antiquity," 1986.

## Chapter 3: "Adamantine Bonds"

1. Plutarch, *Moralia* 338c.
2. Diodorus Siculus, *Library of History* 13.96.
3. Isocrates, *Panegyricus* 169.

4. *Inscriptiones Graecae* II².18, housed in the Epigraphic Museum of Athens.
5. "Plato has borrowed several features from the career of . . . Dionysius I of Syracuse" (Adam, *Republic of Plato*, 2.250; "The references to Syracuse are unmistakable" (Caven, *Dionysius I*, 167). For a different view see Meulder, "Est-il possible d'identifier le tyran. . . ."
6. *Republic* 577a–b.
7. Adam, *Republic of Plato*, 2.333.
8. *Seventh Letter* 326d.
9. *Republic* 565e–566a.
10. *Republic* 619c.
11. *Republic* 567d.
12. Bridgman ( "The 'Gallic Disaster' ") has made the intriguing suggestion that the Gallic sack of Rome in 386 BC may have been ordered by Dionysius.
13. Justin, *Epitome* 20.5.1–6.
14. Diodorus Siculus, *Library of History* 14.100–102.
15. Diodorus Siculus, *Library of History* 13.62.5.
16. Diodorus Siculus, *Library of History* 14.75.
17. *Republic* 567d–568a.
18. *Republic* 569b.
19. Diodorus Siculus, *Library of History* 14.58, 14.96; Cicero, *Tusculan Disputations* 5.58.
20. Aeneas Tacticus, *Life under Siege* 40.2–3; see also Polyaenus, *Strategems* 5.2.20.
21. A leader who took Dionysius as a model, Clearchus of Heraclea, is said to have used the same tactic (Justin, *Epitome* 16.5); see chapter 12. Polybius (*Histories* 16.13.1) attributes the same device to a Spartan tyrant named Nabis.
22. *Republic* 568c–569b.
23. Cicero, *On the Nature of the Gods* 3.83–4.
24. Aristotle, *Politics* 1313b27–30. Presumably Aristotle refers to Dionysius the Elder, since we know the Younger tried to reduce tax burdens.
25. Pseudo-Aristotle, *Economics* 1349a.
26. Bullock, "Dionysius of Syracuse, Financier," 266.
27. *Republic* 567b–c.
28. Lucian, *The Ignorant Book-Seller* 15.
29. Anonymous, *Life of Euripides* 83–4.
30. Suda, *Lexicon* 4.729s.
31. Plutarch, *Moralia* 833b.
32. Aristotle, *Politics* 1313b.
33. Polyaenus, *Strategems* 5.2.13.
34. Aristotle, *Politics* 1259a29–31.
35. Athenaeus, *Deipnosophistae* 261b.
36. Plutarch, *Moralia* 176b.
37. Cicero, *Tusculan Disputations* 5.57. Plutarch (*Dion* 9) has a similar story but omits the daughters and speaks only of coals, not walnut shells.
38. Duncan, "Theseus Outside Athens," 140.
39. Plutarch, *Dion* 9.
40. Cicero, *Tusculan Disputations* 5.59; Ammianus Marcellinus, *History* 16.8.10.
41. Aelian, *Varia Historia* 13.34; Cicero, *Tusculan Disputations* 5.60 (where the youth is anonymous).
42. Scholiast to Aeschines, *On the False Embassy* 10, quoted by Baron, *Timaeus of Tauromenium*, 126. A different version of the story is related by Valerius Maximus (see Pownall, "Dionysius I and the Woman of Himera"). A rival story, told by Philistus, concerned a more positive dream omen (Cicero, *On Divination* 1.39).
43. Polyaenus, *Strategems* 5.2.3; Plutarch, *Moralia* 176.
44. Polyaenus, *Strategems* 5.2.4.

45. Polyaenus, *Strategems* 5.2.12.
46. Plutarch, *Dion* 9–10. The story has been doubted on grounds that Dionysius the Younger did not later seem to be emotionally damaged. But his insecurity and lack of confidence make Plutarch's picture of his childhood isolation a credible one.
47. Plutarch, *Moralia* 175e.
48. Diodorus Siculus, *Library of History* 15.7.
49. Aeneas Tacticus, *Life under Siege* 10.21–2.
50. Plutarch, *Moralia* 338c.
51. Cicero, *Tusculan Disputations* 5.61. A variation of the story is given by Ammianus Marcellinus, *History* 29.10.
52. *Republic* 566e.
53. Diodorus Siculus, *Library of History* 15.74.
54. Diodorus Siculus, *Library of History* 14.65–69. On the attribution of the speech to Timaeus, see the sources cited by Sanders, "Diodorus Siculus and Dionysius I," 397n10. Sanders himself reaches a different conclusion but only by tendentious reasoning.
55. Diodorus Siculus, *Library of History* 15.74.
56. Diodorus Siculus, *Library of History* 15.74.
57. Diodorus Siculus, *Library of History* 15.74.
58. Pearson (*The Greek Historians of the West*) traces the speech's content to Timaeus and regards it as pure invention, for "the tyrant's guards would have suppressed him [Theodorus] before he made much progress" (p. 180). But this ignores the fact that the Spartan troops were wavering in their loyalties until they got direction from Pharacidas. The speech may well have at least a kernel of historical truth.
59. Diodorus Siculus, *Library of History* 14.42.
60. Diodorus Siculus, *Library of History* 15.24.
61. Justin, *Epitome* 20.5.
62. Isocrates, *Letters* 1.7.
63. Isocrates, *Letters* 1.4.
64. Tod, *Selection of Greek Historical Inscriptions*, II.133, housed in the Epigraphic Museum at Athens.
65. Tod, *Selection of Greek Historical Inscriptions*, II.136, also in the Athens Epigraphic Museum.
66. Diodorus Siculus, *Library of History* 15.73.
67. Diodorus Siculus, *Library of History* 15.74.
68. Nepos (*Dion* 2.4–5), Plutarch (*Dion* 6), and Justin (*Epitome* 20.5) all describe the death as a murder. Cicero (*On the Nature of the Gods* 3.84) believes the death was a peaceful and natural one.
69. Diodorus Siculus, *Library of History* 15.74.
70. Plutarch, *Pelopidas* 34.

## Chapter 4: "Wolf-Love"

1. *Republic* 6.502a–b.
2. *Seventh Letter* 328a.
3. Justin, *Epitome* 21.2.
4. Alcoholism: Aelian, *Varia Historia* 2.41 and 6.12; Athenaeus, *Deipnosophistae* 435d–e. Near-sightedness: Justin, *Epitome* 21.2. Palimpsest: Plutarch, *Moralia* 779c.
5. Plutarch, *Dion* 8.
6. Nepos, *Dion* 2, and Plutarch, *Dion* 6. It has been argued (see Porter, *Plutarch: Life of Dion*, 55) that Dionysius the Younger could not have suspected Dion of any such interference in the succession since he retained him as chief counselor; but a new ruler, with such limited preparation, could not have afforded to lose an experienced statesman.
7. Beloch is quoted by Porter, *Plutarch: Life of Dion*, 63; Westlake, "Dion: A Study in Liberation," 252.

8. *Seventh Letter* 327a–b.
9. *Seventh Letter* 328b–c.
10. *Seventh Letter* 328e–329a.
11. *Seventh Letter* 329a–b.
12. Plutarch, *Dion* 7.
13. Plutarch, *Dion* 6.
14. Plutarch, *Dion* 10.
15. *Thirteenth Letter* 360a–b.
16. Plutarch, *Dion* 13.
17. Plutarch, *Dion* 13.
18. Plutarch, *Dion* 14.
19. *Seventh Letter* 329b–c.
20. The poem is preserved by Diogenes Laertius (*Lives of the Philosophers* 3.30), who also records the report that it was inscribed on Dion's tomb. The poem is also found in the collection of Greek poems known as the Palatine Anthology (*Anthologia Palatina* 7.99).
21. See, e.g., Pisani, "Su un Epigramma attribuito a Platone."
22. Page, *Further Greek Epigrams*, 169; Brunt, "Plato's Academy and Politics," 329n94.
23. The online *Oxford Dictionary of National Biography* reports of Brunt: "He never contemplated marriage thereafter, her photograph remaining on his bookcase to the end."
24. Taylor, *Plato, the Man and His Work*, 554.
25. Bowra, "Plato's Epigram on Dion's Death," 403–4.
26. Plato, *Phaedrus* 252e.
27. Nussbaum, *Fragility of Goodness*, 228–30. Yunis (*Plato: Phaedrus*), in his comments on the passage in question, rejects Nussbaum's reading but largely because he considers the funeral epigram spurious.
28. Plutarch, *Dion* 16.
29. Plutarch, *Antony* 67.
30. *Third Letter* 318e.
31. *Laws* 906d.
32. *Laws* 709e–710d.
33. *Seventh Letter* 338d.
34. Plutarch, *Dion* 9.
35. *Seventh Letter* 332d.
36. *Seventh Letter* 332c.
37. *Seventh Letter* 332e–333a.
38. *Third Letter* 319c.
39. Plato also seems to have offered Dionysius practical, policy-based advice. He says in his *Third Letter* that he worked with the tyrant on "political matters" including the drafting of what he calls "preambles to the laws." It's hard to know what he means, but in his dialogue *Laws*, he speaks of "preambles" as explanations designed to prepare and persuade the public. He compares them to preludes in music that prepare the ear for what follows. Perhaps his Syracusan "preambles" were works of this type, an overture, as it were, to a new constitution.
40. Plutarch, *Dion* 14.
41. *Seventh Letter* 329c.
42. *Seventh Letter* 329d.
43. *Seventh Letter* 329d–e.
44. *Seventh Letter* 330b.
45. *Seventh Letter* 333d. The time frame of this passage is vague and it could be taken to refer to the visit of 361 rather than 367 BC.
46. Plutarch, *Dion* 16.

## Chapter 5: One Night in Piraeus

1. Gray's opinion is quoted approvingly by Adam, *Republic of Plato*, 2.38.
2. The German works that pursued these methods are summarized by Keyser, "Stylometric Method and Chronology," 61–4. The Keyser article is a review of Brandwood's *Chronology of Plato's Dialogues*.
3. Keyser, "Stylometric Method and Chronology," 65, 67.
4. Thesleff, *Studies in Platonic Chronology*, 8–17.
5. Thesleff, *Studies in Platonic Chronology*, 101.
6. Dionysius of Halicarnassus, *On the Composition of Words* 25.209; Quintilian, *Institutio Oratoria* 8.6.64; Diogenes Laertius, *Lives of the Philosophers* 3.37. See Riginos, *Platonica: The Anecdotes*, 185–6.
7. The playwright Aeschylus uses the phrase in his play *Eumenides*, written 458 BC, but this use only reaffirms the phrase's Sicilian provenance, since Aeschylus had been to Sicily before that time. Xenophon, who never went west, does not use the phrase in any of his Socratic dialogues, a large body of work containing numerous places it might have been used.
8. Keyser, "Stylometric Method and Chronology," 60–61.
9. In his *Timaeus*, a late dialogue, Plato imagines that Socrates had been addressing four friends, three of whom are there named, when he gave the report that makes up *Republic*. But those four friends are nowhere referred to in *Republic* itself; it's likely they were only invented later.
10. At places throughout *Republic*, Plato reminds us of our place in this frame by having Socrates "pause" his narration and address an aside to *us*, his implied auditors.
11. Glaucon appears in one other work, *Parmenides*, but only in the opening frame, as one of the people listening to an account of a conversation. I agree with the many scholars who take the Glaucon mentioned in the frame of *Symposium* to be a different person than Plato's brother.
12. Nails, "The Dramatic Date of Plato's *Republic*."
13. *Republic* 327c.
14. The account that follows is taken from Lysias, *Against Eratosthenes* 6–20.
15. Lysias, *Against Eratosthenes* 25 and 28.
16. Plutarch, *Moralia* 835c.
17. Found in Sextus Empiricus, *Against the Physicists* 1.54.
18. *Republic* 336d–e.
19. *Republic* 344a–c.
20. *Republic* 404d.

## Chapter 6: The Dionysioflatterers

1. Plutarch, *Moralia* 176c.
2. Athenaeus, *Deipnosophistae* 6.56.
3. Xenophon, *Memorabilia* 2.1.
4. Aristotle, *Rhetoric* 2.23.12.
5. Aristotle, *Metaphysics* 996a.
6. Plato, *Phaedo* 59c.
7. Diogenes Laertius, *Lives of the Philosophers* 2.72.
8. Diogenes Laertius, *Lives of the Philosophers* 2.80.
9. Diogenes Laertius, *Lives of the Philosophers* 2.66.
10. Diogenes Laertius, *Lives of the Philosophers* 2.67.
11. Diogenes Laertius, *Lives of the Philosophers* 2.66.
12. Athenaeus, *Deipnosophistae* 8.30.
13. Lucian, *Parasite* 34.

14. Diogenes Laertius, *Lives of the Philosophers* 2.79.
15. Diogenes Laertius, *Lives of the Philosophers* 2.67.
16. Diogenes Laertius, *Lives of the Philosophers* 2.75; Cicero, *Letters to Friends* 9.26.
17. Plutarch, *Moralia* 750d–e.
18. Diogenes Laertius, *Lives of the Philosophers* 2.82.
19. Lucian, *Parasite* 32–3.
20. Plutarch, *Moralia* 67d–e; Diogenes Laertius, *Lives of the Philosophers* 2.61–2.
21. Athenaeus, *Deipnosophistae* 12.64–65.
22. Cicero, *De Senectute* 12.39–41; see Huffman, *Archytas of Tarentum*, 323 ff.
23. Plutarch, *Moralia* 718e–f and 14. See Riginos, *Platonica: The Anecdotes*, 145–6.
24. Mueller, "Greek arithmetic, geometry and harmonics," 312n23.
25. Aristotle, *Politics* 8.1340b.
26. For discussion of the mechanics see Johnson, "Sources for the Philosophy of Archytas," 187–8 and sources cited there.
27. Aulus Gellius, *Attic Nights* 10.12.8–10; discussed by Huffman, *Archytas of Tarentum*, 572–9.
28. *Seventh Letter* 338d and 339d.
29. *Seventh Letter* 339d.
30. *Thirteenth Letter* 360b.
31. *Thirteenth Letter* 360e.
32. *Thirteenth Letter* 361a–b.
33. Morrow, *Plato's Epistles*, 161.
34. Morrow, *Plato's Epistles*, 104.
35. Plutarch, *Aristides* 1.4 and *Dion* 17.5.
36. *Thirteenth Letter* 362a. Morrow, *Plato's Epistles*, 266, translates according to his own interpretation: "who would *advance* the money" (my emphasis).
37. Harward, *The Platonic Epistles*, 159.
38. The phrase is translated from the German of the great Ulrich von Wilamowitz-Moellendorff; Harward, *The Platonic Epistles*, 232, with a number of judgments of this kind.
39. Morrow, *Plato's Epistles*, 104.
40. *Thirteenth Letter* 362d.
41. *Thirteenth Letter* 362e.
42. Plutarch, *Dion* 21.
43. Harward, *The Platonic Epistles*, 161.
44. Hackforth, *Authorship of the Platonic Epistles*, 168.
45. Romm, "The Sage and His Foibles."
46. Morrow, *Plato's Epistles*, 105–6.
47. Gilbert Ryle, who in his book *Plato's Progress* devotes great ingenuity to explaining the motives of forgers who (in his view) created the Platonic letters, admits to difficulties explaining the *Thirteenth*. "The purposes of the forger of the *Thirteenth Letter* are obscure," he concedes (Ryle, *Plato's Progress*, 84). Ryle is also so impressed by the "natural ring" of the letter that he speculates that it's a doctored version of a letter actually written by Plato, before dismissing that notion as "unpalatably intricate."
48. Diogenes Laertius, *Lives of the Philosophers* 3.9.
49. Stobaeus, *Anthology* 3.13.68.
50. Diogenes Laertius, *Lives of the Philosophers* 6.26.
51. Diogenes Laertius, *Lives of the Philosophers* 6.67.
52. See Steiner, "Diogenes' Mouse and the Royal Dog," 37: "In most ancient contexts . . . Diogenes and Aristippus are remembered and used rather like figures from myth, not for what they ever actually were, but for what they can represent."
53. Diogenes Laertius, *Lives of the Philosophers* 6.58.
54. Diogenes Laertius, *Lives of the Philosophers* 6.25.
55. Diogenes Laertius, *Lives of the Philosophers* 6.29–31, 6.74–5.

56. Diogenes Laertius, *Lives of the Philosophers* 8.85; see Chroust, "Plato's Detractors in Antiquity," 110.
57. Diogenes Laertius, *Lives of the Philosophers* 3.9–16.
58. Diogenes Laertius, *Lives of the Philosophers* 3.9.

## Chapter 7: The Education of Glaucon

1. *Republic* 358b.
2. Xenophon, *Memorabilia* 3.6.
3. Gyges, as Herodotus thought, had seized the Lydian throne by exploiting an erotic liaison with the Lydian queen, just as Plato's nameless shepherd does. The two usurpation legends related by the two authors overlap so closely that, in one passage of *Republic* (612b), Plato refers to "the ring of Gyges" as though it were Gyges, not his ancestor, who'd found it.
4. *Republic* 360b–c.
5. *Republic* 474d–e.
6. *Republic* 468b–c.
7. Paul Shorey, trans., *Plato: Republic*, Books 1–5 (Loeb Classic Library, 1930), 489.
8. Nails, *People of Plato*, 108.
9. Xenophon, *Memorabilia* 1.2.
10. *Republic* 417a–b.
11. *Republic* 420e–421a.
12. *Republic* 420a–421c.
13. *Republic* 424a.
14. Munn, *The School of History*, 239.
15. Howland, *Glaucon's Fate*, 6.
16. Howland, *Glaucon's Fate*, 40–41.

## Chapter 8: Return to Charybdis

1. *Seventh Letter* 338c.
2. Plutarch, *Dion* 17.
3. *Seventh Letter* 339b–c.
4. *Seventh Letter* 339e.
5. *Third Letter* 317c.
6. *Seventh Letter* 340a.
7. *Seventh Letter* 345c–e, quoting Homer, *Odyssey* 12.428.
8. Justin, *Epitome* 21.1.
9. Riginos, *Platonica*, 184–5.
10. *Seventh Letter* 341a.
11. Plutarch, *Dion* 19.
12. *Seventh Letter* 345d.
13. *Seventh Letter* 347a.
14. *Seventh Letter* 346b.
15. Plutarch, *Dion* 17.
16. Plutarch, *Dion* 22.
17. *Seventh Letter* 331a.
18. Preserved in Andocides, *On the Mysteries* 97.
19. *Seventh Letter* 347e.
20. The account that follows is based on *Seventh Letter* 348c–350a and *Third Letter* 318c.
21. Generally the dialogue is dated to around 360 BC. See Aalders, "Date and Intention of Xenophon's *Hiero*," 208–14.
22. Aalders, "Date and Intention of Xenophon's *Hiero*," 213 and 213n4.

23. Isocrates, *Antidosis* 266.
24. Isocrates, *Antidosis* 40.
25. Isocrates, *Evagoras* 78.
26. Georges Mathieu and Richard Jebb, as noted by LaRue Van Hook in the introduction to
    *Evagoras* in the Loeb edition (*Isocrates III*, Cambridge, MA, 1945). Benoit, "Isocrates and
    Plato on Rhetoric," does not include the speech in his tentative chronology, but dates the
    earlier *To Nicocles* to 368 BC.
27. The account that follows is taken from the *Seventh Letter* 349d–350b.
28. Diogenes Laertius, *Lives of the Philosophers* 3.21–2.
29. Huffman, *Archytas of Tarentum*, 608.
30. *Seventh Letter* 350b.
31. *Third Letter* 319a–c.
32. Brunt, "Plato's Academy and Politics," 330.

## Chapter 9: The Evils of Change

1. Demosthenes, *Against Timocrates* 139; Diodorus Siculus, *Library of History* 12.17.
2. Thucydides, *Peloponnesian War* 1.18.
3. Plutarch, *Lycurgus* 29.
4. Athenaeus, *Deipnosophistae* 11.66.
5. *Republic* 415a–c.
6. Crossman, *Plato Today*, chapter 9; Popper, *The Open Society and Its Enemies*, 132.
7. *Republic* 415d.
8. *Republic* 459d–e.
9. *Republic* 546c–d.
10. *Republic* 547a.
11. Cicero, *Letters to Atticus* 7.13.
12. *Republic* 546c.
13. Popper, *The Open Society and Its Enemies*, 557–60n39; 144.
14. Popper, *The Open Society and Its Enemies*, 597.
15. Popper, *The Open Society and Its Enemies*, 143–4.
16. Popper, *The Open Society and Its Enemies*, 146.
17. Popper, *The Open Society and Its Enemies*, 146.
18. Popper, *The Open Society and Its Enemies*, 87.
19. The point is disputed (see Lampert and Planeaux, "Who's Who in Plato's *Timaeus-Critias*,"
    90n10). It matters little for my purposes whether the previous night's discussion was *Republic* itself or another conversation just like it.
20. Plato, *Critias* 108c.
21. Critias is not mentioned among those attending the discussion that is *Republic*, though here
    he speaks as though he had been there. He may have been among the unnamed "others" who
    accost Socrates in the street, along with Polemarchus and Adeimantus (see Nails, *People of
    Plato*, 326). The same issue has been raised regarding Timaeus and Hermocrates.
22. Hale, *Himmler's Crusade*, 26, 119–120.
23. *Laws* 713e.
24. Plato, *Statesman* 271d–273e.
25. Gill, "Plato's Unfinished Trilogy," 43.

## Chapter 10: "Drunken and Sober Tyrants"

1. *Seventh Letter* 350d.
2. *Seventh Letter* 350b–e.
3. *Seventh Letter* 350c.

4. *Seventh Letter* 350b–e.
5. *Seventh Letter* 351c.
6. Sanders, *Legend of Dion*, 219–20 and 220n503.
7. Plutarch, *Comparison of Dion and Brutus* 3–5.
8. Plutarch, *Dion* 22.
9. Plutarch counts two thousand sets of infantry gear, while Diodorus Siculus says five thousand. Either way, Dion's resources were minuscule compared to those of Dionysius, whose armories on the Island could outfit 140,000 fighting men.
10. Plutarch, *Dion* 32.
11. The account of Dion's voyage to Sicily and ouster of Dionysius derives from Plutarch, *Dion* 22–31; Diodorus Siculus, *Library of History* 16.9–12; Nepos, *Dion* 5; and Polyaenus, *Stratagems* 5.2.7–8. We're told by Plutarch that Dion had only two vessels, but this must be wrong, since two merchant vessels could hardly have carried eight hundred men, accompanied by thousands of sets of armor. I'm grateful to Richard Evans for this observation.
12. Aristotle, *Politics* 1312a39.
13. Plutarch, *Dion* 24.
14. Diogenes Laertius, *Lives of the Philosophers* 2.78.
15. Athenaeus, *Deipnosophistae* 6.56.
16. Plutarch, *Moralia* 330f.
17. Plutarch, *Moralia* 41e and 333f–334a.
18. Plutarch, *Moralia* 176d.
19. Pseudo-Aristotle, *Problems* 949a.
20. Plutarch, *Dion* 7.7; attributed to Aristotle by Athenaeus, *Deipnosophistae* 435e.
21. Aristotle, *Politics* 1312a5.
22. Plutarch, *Moralia* 338b.
23. Athenaeus, *Deipnosophistae* 436a–b.
24. The story is found in Diodorus Siculus (*Library of History* 10.4), in Cicero's *De Officiis* (3.45) and *Tusculan Disputations* (5.22), and in Iamblichus's *Life of Pythagoras* 233. A similar tale is told by Polyaenus, *Stratagems* 5.22.
25. Plutarch, *Moralia* 175e.
26. The account that follows is based on Plutarch's *Dion* 25–30 and Diodorus Siculus, *Library of History* 16.9–13.
27. The coded message is found in the military handbook of Aeneas Tacticus, sometimes titled *Life under Siege*, 31.30–31. R. Schöne gave the message coherent meaning in his Teubner edition of the work (Leipzig, 1911).
28. Thucydides, *Peloponnesian War* 3.81.
29. Diodorus Siculus, *Library of History* 15.58.
30. Austin, "Society and Economy," 533.
31. Aeneas Tacticus, *Life under Siege* 11.13–15.
32. Aeneas Tacticus, *Life under Siege* 14.2.
33. Strabo, *Geography* 6.1.4.
34. Diodorus Siculus, *Library of History* 16.12; Plutarch, *Dion* 30.
35. Diodorus Siculus, *Library of History* 16.13.
36. Plutarch, *Dion* 31; Polyaenus, *Stratagems* 5.2.7.
37. *Third Letter* 315d–e.
38. *Third Letter* 315b–c. As Glenn Morrow points out (*Plato's Epistles*, 199–200), the wish expressed in the line is ambiguously phrased, such that "the tyrant" could be either Dionysius or Apollo.
39. *Third Letter* 315c.
40. *Third Letter* 315c.
41. *Third Letter* 316d.
42. *Third Letter* 317c–d.

43. The account that follows is taken from Plutarch, *Dion* 34–5.

## Chapter 11: The "Naval Mob"

1. Diodorus Siculus, *Library of History* 11.72.
2. Heraclides had twenty ships, according to Diodorus Siculus (*Library of History* 16.16); Plutarch says seven (*Dion* 32).
3. Plutarch, *Dion* 32.
4. Diodorus Siculus, *Library of History* 16.16; Plutarch, *Dion* 35.
5. Plutarch, *Dion* 36.
6. *Fourth Letter* 320e.
7. *Fourth Letter* 320c.
8. Plutarch, *Dion* 35.
9. *Fourth Letter* 321b.
10. Plutarch, *Moralia* 70a.
11. The account that follows is based on Plutarch, *Dion* 38–45.
12. Diodorus Siculus, *Library of History* 14.78.
13. Plutarch, *Dion* 39; Diodorus Siculus, *Library of History* 16.17.
14. On Apollocrates' drunkenness, see Athenaeus, *Deipnosophistae* 435b, with testimony from Theopompus; Aelian, *Historical Miscellany* 2.41. Aristotle (*Rhetoric* 2.15) described the descendants of Dionysius the Elder as afflicted by "insane habits," likely referring to alcoholism (see Cromey, "Aristotle on Destruction of Dionysios I's Family").
15. Plutarch, *Dion* 44.
16. Plutarch, *Dion* 46.
17. Plutarch, *Dion* 47.
18. Justin, *Epitome* 21.2.
19. Athenaeus, *Deipnosophistae* 12.58.
20. Strabo, *Geography* 6.1.8.
21. Aelian, *On Animals* 10.34.
22. The account is found not only in Plutarch (*Dion* 51) but in Aelian's *Varia Historia* (12.47).

## Chapter 12: The Fury's Broom

1. Shorey, *Plato: The Republic* 2.473–4, note a.
2. Aristotle, *Politics* 1284a.
3. This is assumed by Porter, *Plutarch: Life of Dion*, 90–92; see also Westlake, "Friends and Successors of Dion," 162n5.
4. Plutarch, *Dion* 52, where the phrase *en astei*, "in the city," refers to Athens.
5. Plato, *Statesman* 293a–e.
6. Plutarch, *Dion* 53.
7. Cornelius Nepos, *Dion* 7.
8. Cornelius Nepos, *Dion* 7.
9. Plutarch, *Dion* 56.
10. Plutarch, *Dion* 54, where "Dion's enemies" (unspecified) are said to have given Callippus 20 talents; P. Oxy. 12 lines 1–7, with the name "Dion" supplied where the papyrus is broken.
11. Plutarch, *Dion* 54.
12. *Seventh Letter* 335c and e.
13. Plutarch, *Dion* 54–8; Cornelius Nepos, *Dion* 9; Diodorus Siculus, *Library of History* 16.31.
14. Cornelius Nepos, *Dion* 9.
15. Cornelius Nepos, *Dion* 10.
16. *Seventh Letter* 323e.
17. Hackforth, *Authorship of Platonic Epistles*, 97, quoted approvingly by Bluck, *Plato's Seventh and Eighth Letters*, 20n1.

18. Cornelius Nepos, *Dion* 4.
19. Plutarch, *Dion* 55; Cornelius Nepos, *Dion* 4. See also Plutarch, *Moralia* 119b, where it's unclear (as it may have been at the time) whether Aretaeus's fall had been accidental or intentional.
20. *Seventh Letter* 328c.
21. *Seventh Letter* 336a–b.
22. *Seventh Letter* 333c–d.
23. *Seventh Letter* 327d.
24. *Seventh Letter* 326e.
25. *Seventh Letter* 326e.
26. Emendation proposed by Karsten in "Commentatio Critica."
27. *Seventh Letter* 351d–e.
28. *Seventh Letter* 333d.
29. *Seventh Letter* 334e.
30. *Seventh Letter* 337d.
31. *Seventh Letter* 339a.
32. *Seventh Letter* 341b.
33. Epicrates, *Plays* fr. 6; see Olson, *Broken Laughter*, 228–9 and 446.
34. *Seventh Letter* 345a.
35. *Seventh Letter* 345b.
36. *Seventh Letter* 345c.
37. *Seventh Letter* 344d.
38. *Seventh Letter* 344d.
39. Politis, "Plato's Seventh Letter," 66–69.
40. *Seventh Letter* 342b–c.
41. *Seventh Letter* 344c.
42. Burnyeat and Frede, *The Pseudo-Platonic Seventh Letter*, 133.
43. Politis, "Plato's Seventh Letter," with a pointed reply to Burnyeat at 72–74.
44. Morrow, *Plato's Epistles*, 73.
45. Brunt, "Plato's Academy and Politics," 328n88.
46. Justin, *Epitome* 16.5.
47. Isocrates, *Letters* 7.12–13.

## Chapter 13: The Second-Best State

1. *Seventh Letter* 328a.
2. Plutarch, *Timoleon* 33.
3. Theophrastus, *Inquiry into Plants* 4.6.
4. Plutarch, *Dion* 58.
5. *Laws* 801e–802c.
6. *Eighth Letter* 352c.
7. A version of events in which Dion's father had merely been a supporter of Dionysius is given by both Diodorus (*Library of History* 12.94) and Aristotle (*Politics* 5.5.6).
8. *Eighth Letter* 353e.
9. Sanders, "Nationalistic Recommendations and Policies," 82.
10. *Eighth Letter* 353a.
11. *Eighth Letter* 353e.
12. *Eighth Letter* 354e.
13. The stoning is set in Acragas by Diodorus (*Library of History* 13.87).
14. *Eighth Letter* 354e.
15. *Laws* 762e.
16. *Eighth Letter* 355b–c.

17. *Eighth Letter* 355d.
18. *Eighth Letter* 356a–b.
19. *Eighth Letter* 357a.
20. Post, "A Supposed Historical Discrepancy," 324.
21. Plutarch, *Timoleon* 22.
22. Aelian, *Varia Historia* 6.12.
23. Athenaeus, *Deipnosophistae* 11.47.
24. Parthenius, *Love Romances* 7.
25. Athenaeus, *Deipnosophistae* 436a–b.
26. *Laws* 739d.
27. Saunders, *Plato: The Laws*, 26.
28. *Laws* 709e–710d.
29. Athenaeus, *Deipnosophistae* 435f.
30. Plutarch, *Timoleon* 13.
31. Athenaeus, *Deipnosophistae* 12.58; Strabo, *Geography* 6.1.8.
32. What follows, up to the end of the chapter, is taken from *Republic* 614b–621d.

## Chapter 14: The Music Teacher

1. Plutarch, *Timoleon* 11.
2. Aelian, *Varia Historia* 6.12.
3. Plutarch, *Timoleon* 14.
4. Justin, *Epitome* 21.5.
5. Plutarch, *Moralia* 783d.
6. Plutarch, *Timoleon* 24.
7. Aelian, *Varia Historia* 6.12.
8. Cicero, *Tusculan Disputations* 3.12.
9. Plutarch, *Timoleon* 15.
10. Plutarch, *Timoleon* 15.
11. Diogenes Laertius, *Lives of the Philosophers* 4.2; Athenaeus, *Deipnosophistae* 279e, 546d.
12. Diogenes Laertius, *Lives of the Philosophers* 4.2.
13. Aelian, *Varia Historia* 12.60; Plutarch, *Moralia* 176e.
14. Plutarch, *Moralia* 176d.
15. Athenaeus, *Deipnosophistae* 541d; Aelian, *Varia Historia* 9.8.
16. Plutarch, *Moralia* 511e; Demetrius, *On Style* 6, 102, 241.
17. Found in the handbook *Peri Tropôn* attributed to Tryphon (2.9), a work of the late first century BC.
18. Aelian, *Varia Historia* 6.12.
19. Diogenes Laertius, *Lives of the Philosophers* 3.34.
20. Plutarch, *Timoleon* 23.
21. Opinions discussed by Talbert, *Timoleon and the Revival of Greek Sicily*, 116–22. Talbert himself rejects these views.
22. Diodorus Siculus, *Library of History* 16.70.
23. Plutarch, *Timoleon* 22.

# BIBLIOGRAPHY

## Primary Sources

Primary sources are discussed in the introduction. With very few exceptions the ancient authors I have cited can be accessed through the Perseus online database or can be found in the Loeb Classical Library, available either in print or (with a subscription) online. The letters of Plato can be accessed, in English and in their entirety, in those two places, as well as in John M. Cooper's 1997 edition of *Plato: Complete Works* (Hackett Publishing), and in the monograph by Helfer cited below. A forthcoming volume of philosophic epistles, edited by Christopher Moore, will contain translations of all the letters done by myself and Pamela Mensch (expected 2026 from Oxford University Press).

## Secondary Sources

Aalders, G. J. D. "Date and Intention of Xenophon's *Hiero*." *Mnemosyne* 6, no. 3 (1953): 208–15.

———. "Political Thought and Political Programs in the Platonic Epistles." In *Pseudepigrapha*, Vol. I, edited by Kurt von Fritz, 147–87. Vandœuvres, Switzerland: Fondation Hardt, 1972.

Adam, James. *The Republic of Plato.* 2 vols. Cambridge: Cambridge University Press, 1902.

Arruzza, Cinzia. *A Wolf in the City: Tyranny and the Tyrant in Plato's Republic.* Oxford, UK: Oxford University Press.

Atack, Carol. *The Discourse of Kingship in Classical Greece.* London: Routledge, 2019.

Austin, M. M. "Society and Economy." In *The Cambridge Ancient History: Vol. VI, The Fourth Century BC*, edited by D. M. Lewis, John Boardman, Simon Hornblower, and M. Ostwald, 528–64. New York: Cambridge University Press, 1994.

Balot, Ryan K. *Greed and Injustice in Classical Athens.* Princeton, NJ: Princeton University Press, 2002.

Baltes, Matthais. "Plato's School, the Academy." *Hermathena* 155 (Winter 1993): 5–26.

Baron, Christopher A. *Timaeus of Tauromenium and Hellenistic Historiography.* Cambridge: Cambridge University Press, 2013.

Benoit, William L. "Isocrates and Plato on Rhetoric and Rhetorical Education." *Rhetoric Society Quarterly* 21, no. 1 (Winter 1991): 60–71.

Bluck, R. S. *Plato's Life and Thought*. London: Routledge and Paul, 1949.

———. *Plato's Seventh and Eighth Letters*. Cambridge: Cambridge University Press, 1947.

Boas, George. "Fact and Legend in the Biography of Plato." *Philosophical Review* 57, no. 5 (September 1948): 439–57.

Bonacasa, Nicola, Lorenzo Braccesi, and Ernesto De Miro, eds. *La Sicilia dei Due Dionisî*. Rome: L'Erma di Bretschneider, 2002.

Bosher, Kathryn, ed. *Theater Outside Athens: Drama in Greek Sicily and South Italy*. Cambridge: Cambridge University Press, 2012.

Bosman, Philip R. *Intellectual and Empire in Greco-Roman Antiquity*. London: Routledge, 2019.

Bowra, C. M. "Plato's Epigram on Dion's Death." *American Journal of Philology* 59, no. 4 (1938): 394–404.

Brandwood, Leonard. *The Chronology of Plato's Dialogues*. Cambridge: Cambridge University Press, 1990.

Bridgman, Timothy P. "The 'Gallic Disaster': Did Dionysius I of Syracuse Order It?" *Proceedings of the Harvard Celtic Colloquium* 23 (2003): 40–51.

Brumbaugh, Robert S. "Digression and Dialogue: The Seventh Letter and Plato's Literary Form." In *Platonic Writings/Platonic Readings*, edited by Charles L. Griswold, 84–92. University Park: Penn State University Press, 1988.

Brunt, P. A. "Plato's Academy and Politics." In *Studies in Greek History and Thought*, 282–342. Oxford: Oxford University Press, 1993.

Bullock, C. J. "Dionysius of Syracuse, Financier." *Classical Journal* 25, no. 4 (1930): 260–76.

Burnyeat, Myles, and Michael Frede. *The Pseudo-Platonic Seventh Letter*. Oxford: Oxford University Press, 2015.

Cameron, Alan. "The Last Days of the Academy at Athens." *Proceedings of the Cambridge Philological Society* 15, no. 195 (1969): 7–29.

Canfora, Luciani. "Platone e i tiranni." In *La Sicilia dei Due Dionisî*, edited by Nicola Bonacasa, Lorenzo Braccesi, and Ernesto De Miro, 11–18. Rome: L'Erma di Bretschneider, 2002.

Carter, B. E. "The Function of the Myth of the Earthborn in the *Republic*." *Classical Journal* 48, no. 8 (1953): 297–302.

Caven, Brian. *Dionysius I: Warlord of Sicily*. New Haven, CT: Yale University Press, 1990.

Chapoutot, Johann. *Greeks, Romans, Germans: How the Nazis Usurped Europe's Classical Past*. Berkeley: University of California Press, 2016.

Chroust, Anton-Herman. "Plato's Detractors in Antiquity." *Review of Metaphysics* 16 (1962): 98–118.

Coppola, Alessandra. "Mito e propaganda alla corte Dionisiana." In *La Sicilia dei Due Dionisî*, edited by Nicola Bonacasa, Lorenzo Braccesi, and Ernesto De Miro, 373–88. Rome: L'Erma di Bretschneider, 2002.

Crick, Nathan. "Isocrates's *Nicocles* and the Hymn to Hegemony." In *Rhetoric and Power: The Drama of Classical Greece*, 171–97. Columbia: University of South Carolina Press, 2015.

Cromey, Robert D. "Aristotle on the Destruction of Dionysios I's Family." *Revue Belge de philologie et d'histoire* 57, no. 1 (1979): 5–17.

Crossman, R. H. L. *Plato Today*, 2nd ed. London: Routledge, 1959.

de Blois, Lukas. "Dionysius II, Dion and Timoleon." *Mededelingen van het Nederlandisch historisch Instituut te Rome* 40 (1978): 113–49.

———. "Political Concepts in Plutarch's *Dion* and *Timoleon*." *Ancient Society* 28 (1997): 209–24.

Dillon, John. *The Heirs of Plato: A Study of the Old Academy (347–274 BC)*. Oxford: Clarendon Press, 2003.

———. "What Happened to Plato's Garden?" *Hermathena* 134 (Summer 1983): 51–59.

Duncan, Anne. "A Theseus Outside Athens: Dionysius I of Syracuse and Tragic Self-Presentation." In *Theater Outside Athens: Drama in Greek Sicily and South Italy*, edited by Kathryn Bosher, 137–55. Cambridge: Cambridge University Press, 2015.

Edelstein, Ludwig. *Plato's Seventh Letter*. Leiden, Netherlands: Brill, 1966.

Evans, Richard. *Ancient Syracuse: From Foundation to Fourth Century Collapse*. London: Routledge, 2016.

——. "The Misleading Representation of Dion as Philosopher-General in Plutarch's *Life*." In *Intellectual and Empire in Greco-Roman Antiquity*, edited by Phillip R. Bosman, 102–15. London: Routledge, 2018.

Ferrari, G. R. F. *The Cambridge Companion to Plato's Republic*. Cambridge: Cambridge University Press, 2007.

Finley, Moses I. *Ancient Sicily to the Arab Conquest*, vol. 1 of *A History of Sicily*. New York: Viking, 1968.

Fite, Warner. *The Platonic Legend*. New York: Charles Scribner's Sons, 1934.

Fleischer, Killian. *Philodem: Geschichte der Akademie*. Leiden, Netherlands: Brill, 2023.

Forcignanò, Filippo. *Platone: Settima Lettera*. Rome: Carocci, 2020.

Freeman, Edward A. *The History of Sicily from the Earliest Times*, vol. 4. Oxford: Oxford University Press, 1894.

Friedlander, Paul. *Plato: An Introduction*. Translated by Hans Meyerhoff. Princeton: Princeton University Press, 1970.

Fuks, Alexander. "Redistribution of Lands and Houses in Syracuse in 356 BC and Its Ideological Aspects." *Classical Quarterly* 18, no. 2 (1968): 207–23.

Gallazzi, Claudio. "Plato, *Epistulae* VIII 356a, 6–8." In *Sixty-Five Papyrological Texts Presented to Klaas A. Worp on the Occasion of his 65th Birthday*, edited by F. A. J. Hoogendijk and B. P. Muhs, 6–8. Leiden, Netherlands: Brill, 2008.

Gaiser, Konrad. "Platone come 'Kolax' in una lettera apocrifa (13a Epist.)." *Sandalion* 4 (1981): 71–94.

Gill, Mary Louise. "Plato's Unfinished Trilogy: *Timaeus—Critias—Hermocrates*." In *Plato's Styles and Characters: Between Literature and Philosophy*, edited by Gabriele Cornelli, 33–46. Berlin: Walter De Gruyter, 2015.

Glucker, John. "Plato in the Academy: Some Cautious Reflections." In *Plato's Academy: Its Workings and Its History*, edited by Paul Kalligas, Chloe Balla, Effie Baziotopoulou-Valavani and Vassilis Karasmanis, 89–107. Cambridge: Cambridge University Press, 2020.

Goldstein, Jonathan A. *The Letters of Demosthenes*. New York: Columbia University Press, 1968.

Gray, Vivienne J. *Xenophon on Government*. Cambridge: Cambridge University Press, 2007.

Griswold Jr., Charles L., ed., *Platonic Writings/Platonic Readings*. University Park: Penn State University Press, 1988.

Gulley, Norman. "The Authenticity of the Platonic Epistles." In *Pseudepigrapha*, Vol. I, edited by Kurt von Fritz, 105–143. Vandœuvres, Switzerland: Fondation Hardt, 1972.

Haake, Matthias. "The Academy in Athenian Politics and Society—Between Disintegration and Integration: The First Eighty Years (387/6–306/5)." In *Plato's Academy: Its Workings and Its History*, edited by Paul Kalligas, Chloe Balla, Effie Baziotopoulou-Valavani, and Vassilis Karasmanis, 65–88. Cambridge: Cambridge University Press, 2020.

Hackforth, Reginald. *The Authorship of the Platonic Epistles*. Manchester, UK: Manchester University Press, 1913.

Hale, Christopher. *Himmler's Crusade: The Nazi Expedition to Find the Origins of the Aryan Race*. Hoboken, NJ: John Wiley and Sons, 2003.

Halliwell, Stephen. "The Life-and-Death Journey of the Soul: Interpreting the Myth of Er." In *The Cambridge Companion to Plato's Republic*, edited by G.R.F. Ferrari, 445–72. Cambridge: Cambridge University Press, 2007.

Hankins, James. *Plato in the Italian Renaissance*. 2 vols. Leiden, Netherlands: Brill, 1990.

Harward, J. *The Platonic Epistles*. Cambridge: Cambridge University Press, 1932.

Head, Barclay V. "On the Chronological Sequence of the Coins of Syracuse." *The Numismatic Chronicle and Journal of the Numismatic Society* 14 (1874): 1–80.

Helfer, Ariel. *Plato's Letters: The Political Challenges of the Philosophic Life*. Ithaca, NY: Cornell University Press, 2023.

Herter, Hans. "Platons Dionepigramm." *Rheinisches Museum für Philologie* 92, no. 4 (January 1944): 289–302.

Holloway, R. Ross. *The Archaeology of Ancient Sicily*. London: Routledge, 2000.

Howland, Jacob. *Glaucon's Fate: History, Myth and Character in Plato's Republic*. Philadelphia: Paul Dry Books, 2018.

Hoyos, Dexter. *Carthage's Other Wars: Carthaginian Warfare Outside the "Punic Wars" against Rome*. Yorkshire, UK: Pen and Sword, 2019.

Huffman, Carl A. *Archytas of Tarentum: Pythagorean, Philosopher and Mathematician King*. Cambridge: Cambridge University Press, 2005.

Innocenti, Piero. *Platone: Lettere*. Milan: Biblioteca Universale Rizzoli, 1986.

Irwin, Terry. "The Inside Story of the Seventh Platonic Letter: A Sceptical Introduction." *Rhizai* 2 (2009): 127–60.

Isnardi Parente, Margherita. *L'Accademia e le lettere Platoniche*. Napoli, Italy: G. Macchiaroli, 1955.

———. "Sulle *Epistolae Platonis* di Leonardo Bruni." *Rivista di Storia della Filosofia* 61, no. 2 (2006): 245–61.

Isnardi Parente, Margherita, and Maria Grazia Ciani. *Platone: Lettere*. 2nd ed. Milan, Italy: Arnoldo Mondadori, 2014.

Johnson, Monte Ransome. "Sources for the Philosophy of Archytas." *Ancient Philosophy* 28, no. 1 (Spring 2008): 173–99.

Jonasch, Melanie, ed. *The Fight for Greek Sicily: Society, Politics, and Landscape*. Oxford: Oxbow Books, 2020.

Kahn, Charles H. "On Platonic Chronology." In *New Perspectives on Plato, Modern and Ancient*, edited by Julia Annas and Christopher Rowe, 93–127. Washington, DC: Center for Hellenic Studies, 2002.

Kalligas, Paul, Chloe Balla, Effie Baziotopoulou-Valavani, and Vassilis Karasmanis, eds. *Plato's Academy: Its Workings and Its History*. Cambridge: Cambridge University Press, 2020.

Karasmanis, Vassilis. "Plato and the Mathematics of the Academy." In *Plato's Academy: Its Workings and Its History*, edited by Paul Kalligas, Chloe Balla, Effie Baziotopoulou-Valavani, and Vassilis Karasmanis, 108–40. Cambridge: Cambridge University Press, 2020.

Karlsson, Lars. *Fortification Towers and Masonry Techniques in the Hegemony of Syracuse, 405–211 B.C.* Stockholm: Paul Aströms Förlag, 1992.

Karsten, H. T. "Commentatio Critica de Platonis Quae Feruntur Epistolis: Praecipue Tertia, Septima, et Octava." PhD diss., University of Chicago, 1864. Microfilm.

Keyser, Paul T. "Orreries, the Date of [Plato] *Letter* ii, and Eudoros of Alexandria." *Archiv für Geschichte der Philosophie* 80, no 3 (January 1998): 241–67.

———. "Stylometric Method and the Chronology of Plato's Works," a review of Leonard Brandwood, *The Chronology of Plato's Dialogues*. *Bryn Mawr Classical Review* 3.1 (January 12, 1992): 58–74.

Kraay, Colin M. "The Demareteion Reconsidered: A Reply." *Numismatic Chronicle* 12 (1972): 13–24.

———. *Greek Coins and History: Some Current Problems*. London: Methuen and Co., 1969.

Laistner, M. L. W. "The Influence of Isocrates's Political Doctrines on Some Fourth Century Men of Affairs." *Classical Weekly* 23, no. 17 (March 10, 1930): 129–31.

Lampe, Kurt. *The Birth of Hedonism: The Cyrenaic Philosophers and Pleasure as a Way of Life*. Princeton: Princeton University Press, 2015.

Lampert, Lawrence, and Christopher Planeaux. "Who's Who in Plato's *Timaeus-Critias* and Why." *Review of Metaphysics* 52, no. 1 (September 1998): 87–125.

Lehmann, G. A. "Dion und Herakleides." *Historia* 19 (November 1970): 401–6.

Levinson, Ronald B. *In Defense of Plato*. Cambridge: Harvard University Press, 1953.

Lewis, Sian, ed. *Ancient Tyranny*. Edinburgh: Edinburgh University Press, 2006.

Lewis, V. Bradley. "The Rhetoric of Philosophical Politics in Plato's 'Seventh Letter.'" *Philosophy and Rhetoric* 33, no.1 (2000): 23–34.

Lintott, Andrew. *Violence, Civil Strife and Revolution in the Classical City*. Baltimore: Johns Hopkins University Press, 1982.

Lloyd, G. E. R. "Plato and Archytas in the Seventh Letter." *Phronesis* 35, no. 2 (1990): 159–74.

Lomas, Kathryn. "Tyrants and the Polis: Migration, Identity and Urban Development in Sicily." In *Ancient Tyranny*, edited by Sian Lewis, 95–118. Edinburgh: Edinburgh University Press, 2006.

Ludwig, Paul. "Eros in the *Republic*." In *The Cambridge Companion to Plato's Republic*, edited by G. R. F. Ferrari, 202–31. Cambridge: Cambridge University Press, 2007.

Lygouri-Tolia, Eutychia. "The Gymnasium of the Academy and the School of Plato." In *Plato's Academy: Its Workings and Its History*, edited by Paul Kalligas, Chloe Balla, Effie Baziotopoulou-Valavani, and Vassilis Karasmanis, 46–64. Cambridge: Cambridge University Press, 2020.

Mathieu, Bernard. "Archytas de Tarente, pythagoricien et ami de Platon." *Parola del Passato* 10 (1955): 239–55.

McBrayer, Gregory A., ed. *Xenophon: The Shorter Writings*. Ithaca: Cornell University Press, 2018.

Merrill, Jacqueline Pfeffer. "The Organization of Plato's *Statesman* and the Statesman's Rule as a Herdsman." *Phoenix* 57, no. 1/2 (Spring–Summer 2004): 35–56.

Meulder, Marcel. "Est-il possible d'identifier le tyran dêcrit par Platon dans la *République*?" *Revue belge de Philologie et d'Histoire* 67, no. 1 (1989): 30–52.

Miller, James. *Examined Lives: From Socrates to Nietzsche*. New York: Picador, 2011.

Miller, Mitchell H., Jr. *The Philosopher in Plato's* Statesman. The Hague: Martinus Nijhoff, 1980.

Misch, Georg. *A History of Autobiography in Antiquity*, vol. 1. London: Routledge and Kegan Paul, 1950.

Monoson, S. Sara. *Plato's Democratic Entanglements: Athenian Politics and the Practice of Philosophy*. Princeton: Princeton University Press, 2000.

Morgan, Kathryn A. *Pindar and the Construction of Syracusan Monarchy in the Fifth Century B.C.* Oxford: Oxford University Press, 2015.

Morrison, Donald, L.-A. Dorion, and G. Mosquera. "Tyrannie et royauté selon le Socrate de Xenophon." *Les Études Philosophiques* 2, no. 69 (2004): 177–92.

Morrison, Donald R. "The Utopian Character of Plato's Ideal City." In *The Cambridge Companion to Plato's Republic*, edited by G. R. F. Ferrari, 232–55. Cambridge: Cambridge University Press, 2007.

Morrow, Glenn. *Plato: Epistles*. New York: Bobbs Merrill, 1962.

——. *Plato's Cretan City: A Historical Interpretation of the Laws*. Princeton: Princeton University Press, 1960.

Mossé, Claude. *La tyrannie dans la Grèce antique*. Paris: Presses Universitaires, 1969.

——. "Plutarch and the Sicilian Tyrants." In *Ancient Tyranny*, edited by Sian Lewis, 188–96. Edinburgh: Edinburgh University Press, 2006.

Mueller, Ian. "Greek Arithmetic, Geometry and Harmonics: Thales to Plato." In *Routledge History of Philosophy. Volume I: From the Beginning to Plato*, edited by C. C. W. Taylor, 271–322. London: Routledge, 1997.

Munn, Mark. *The School of History: Athens in the Age of Socrates*. Berkeley: University of California Press, 2000.

Nails, Debra. *Agora, Academy, and the Conduct of Philosophy*. Boston: Kluwer Academic Publishers, 1995.

——. "The Dramatic Date of Plato's *Republic*." *Classical Journal* 93, no. 4 (1998): 383–96.

——. *The People of Plato: A Prosopography of Plato and Other Socratics*. Indianapolis: Hackett, 2002.

——. "Plato's *Republic* in Its Athenian Context." *History of Political Thought* 33, no. 1 (Spring 2012): 1–23.

Natoli, Anthony Francis. *The Letter of Speusippus to Philip II: Introduction, Text, Translation and Commentary. Historia Einzelschriften 176*. Stuttgart: Franz Steiner Verlag, 2004.

Nerdahl, Michael. "Flattery and Platonic Philosophy: The Limits of Education in Plutarch's *Life of Dion*." *Classical World* 104, no. 3 (2011): 295–309.

Nussbaum, Martha. *The Fragility of Goodness: Luck and Ethics in Greek Tragedy and Philosophy*. Cambridge: Cambridge University Press, 1986.

Ober, Josiah. *Political Dissent in Democratic Athens: Intellectual Critics of Popular Rule*. Princeton: Princeton University Press, 1998.

Olson, S. Douglas. *Broken Laughter: Select Fragments of Greek Comedy*. Oxford: Oxford University Press, 2007.

Oost, Stewart Irvin. "The Tyrant Kings of Syracuse." *Classical Philology* 71, no. 3 (July 1976): 224–36.

Orth, Wolfgang. "Der Syrakusaner Herakleides als Politiker." *Historia* 28, no. 1 (1979): 51–64.

Ostwald, Martin and David Lynch. "The Growth of Schools and the Advance of Knowledge." In *The Cambridge Ancient History: Vol. VI, The Fourth Century BC*, edited by D. M. Lewis, John Boardman, Simon Hornblower, and M. Ostwald, 592–633. New York: Cambridge University Press, 1994.

Page, Denys L., ed. *Further Greek Epigrams: Epigrams before AD 50 from the Greek Anthology and Other Sources, Not Included in "Hellenistic Epigrams" or "The Garland of Philip."* Cambridge: Cambridge University Press, 2008.

Parry, Richard D. "The Unhappy Tyrant and the Craft of Inner Rule." *The Cambridge Companion to Plato's Republic*, edited by G. R. F. Ferrari, 386–414. Cambridge: Cambridge University Press, 2007.

Pasquali, Giorgio. *Le lettere di Platone*. Florence: G. Sansoni, 1967.

Pearson, Lionel. *The Greek Historians of the West: Timaeus and His Predecessors*. Atlanta: Scholars Press, 1988.

Pisani, V. "Su un Epigramma attribuito a Platone." *Paideia* 6 (1951): 297–300.

Politis, Vasilis. "Plato's Seventh Letter." *Classics Ireland* 27 (2020): 56–77.

Popper, Karl. *The Open Society and Its Enemies*. Princeton: Princeton University Press, 2020.

Porter, W. H. *Plutarch: Life of Dion with Introduction and Notes*. Dublin: Hodges, Figgis and Co., 1952.

Post, Levi Arnold. "An Attempt to Reconstruct the First Edition of Plato's *Republic*." *Classical Weekly* 21, no. 6 (November 14, 1927): 41–44.

———. "The Preludes to Plato's *Laws*." *Transactions of the American Philological Association* 60 (1929): 5–24.

———. "The Seventh and Eighth Platonic Epistles." *Classical Quarterly* 24, no. 2 (1930): 113–15.

———. "A Supposed Historical Discrepancy in the Platonic Epistles." *The American Journal of Philology* 45, no. 4 (1924): 371–76.

———. *Thirteen Epistles of Plato: Introduction, Translation, and Notes*. Oxford: Clarendon Press, 1925.

Pownall, Frances. "Dionysius I and the Woman of Himera: A Case Study in the Perils of Political Religion." In *Political Religions in the Greco-Roman World*, edited by Elias Koulakiotis and Charlotte Dunn, 16–33. Newcastle upon Tyne: Cambridge Scholars, 2019.

Riginos, Alice Swift. *Platonica: The Anecdotes Concerning the Life and Writings of Plato*. Leiden, Netherlands: Brill, 1976.

Robinson, Eric W. "Democracy in Syracuse, 466–412 B.C." *Harvard Studies in Classical Philology* 100 (2000): 189–205.

Romm, James. "The Sage and His Foibles." *Aeon Magazine* (online), March 30, 2023.

Rowe, Christopher. "The Place of the *Republic* in Plato's Political Thought." In *The Cambridge Companion to Plato's Republic*, edited by G. R. F. Ferrari, 27–54. Cambridge: Cambridge University Press, 2007.

Rowe, Christopher, and Malcolm Schofield, eds. *The Cambridge History of Greek and Roman Political Thought*. Cambridge: Cambridge University Press, 2008.

Ryle, Gilbert. *Plato's Progress*. Cambridge: Cambridge University Press, 1966.

Sanders, L. J. "Diodorus Siculus and Dionysius I of Syracuse." *Historia* 30, no. 4 (Fourth Quarter 1981): 394–411.

———. *Dionysius I of Syracuse and Greek Tyranny*. London: Croom Helm, 1987.

———. "Dionysius I of Syracuse and the Origins of the Ruler Cult in the Greek World." *Historia* 40 (1991): 275–87.

———. "Dionysius I of Syracuse and the Validity of the Hostile Tradition." *Scripta Classica Israelica* 5 (1979): 64–84.

———. *The Legend of Dion*. Toronto: Edgar Kent, 2008.

———. "Nationalistic Recommendations and Policies in the Seventh and Eighth Platonic Epistles." *Ancient History Bulletin* 8 (1994): 76–85.

———. "The Relations of Syracuse and Magna Graecia in the Era of the Dionysii." In *La Sicilia dei Due Dionisî*, edited by Nicola Bonacasa, Lorenzo Braccesi, and Ernesto De Miro, 473–92. Rome: L'Erma di Bretschneider, 2002.

———. "What Did Timaeus Think of Dion?" *Hermes* 120, no. 2 (1992): 205–15.

Saunders, Trevor J. *Plato: The Laws*. New York: Penguin Classics, 1970.

———. "The RAND Corporation of Antiquity: Plato's Academy and Greek Politics," In *Studies in Honor of T.B.L. Webster*, vol.1, edited by J. H. Betts, J. T. Hooker, and J. R. Green, 200–10. London: Bristol Classical Press, 1986.

Sayre, Kenneth M. "Plato's Dialogues in Light of the Seventh Letter." In *Platonic Writings/Platonic Readings*, edited by Charles Griswold Jr., 93–109. University Park: Penn State University Press, 1988.

Schofield, Malcolm. "Approaching the *Republic*." In *The Cambridge History of Greek and Roman Political Thought*, edited by Christopher Rowe and Malcolm Schofield, 190–232. Cambridge: Cambridge University Press, 2008.

———. "Plato and Practical Politics." In *The Cambridge History of Greek and Roman Political Thought*, edited by Christopher Rowe and Malcolm Schofield, 293–302. Cambridge: Cambridge University Press, 2008.

Sedley, David. "Philosophy, the Forms and the Art of Ruling." In *The Cambridge Companion to Plato's Republic*, edited by G. R. F. Ferrari, 256–83. Cambridge: Cambridge University Press, 2007.

Shorey, Paul. *Plato: The Republic*. 2 vols. London: William Heinemann, 1969.

Skemp, J.B. *Plato's Statesman*. London: Routledge and Kegan Paul, 1952.

Solmsen, Friedrich. Review of Ludwig Edelstein, *Plato's Seventh Letter*. *Gnomon* 41, no. 1 (February 1969): 29–34.

Sourvinou-Inwood, C. "The Votum of 477/6 B.C. and the Foundation Legend of Locri Epizephyrii." *Classical Quarterly* 24 (December 1974): 186–98.

Steiner, G. "Diogenes' Mouse and the Royal Dog: Conformity in Nonconformity." *Classical Journal* 72 (1976): 36–46.

Stone, I. F. *The Trial of Socrates*. New York: Knopf, 1989.

Stroheker, Karl Friedrich. *Dionysios I: Gestalt und Geschichte des Tyrannen von Syrakus*. Wiesbaden: Franz Steiner, 1958.

———. "Platon und Dionysios I von Syrakus." *Historische Zeitschrift* 173 (1952): 225–59.

Stylianou, P. J. *A Historical Commentary on Diodorus Siculus, Book 15*. Oxford: Clarendon Press, 1999.

Syme, Ronald. "Fraud and Imposture." In *Pseudepigrapha I*, edited by Kurt von Fritz, 3–21. Geneva: Fondation Hardt, 1972.

Talbert, R. J. A. *Timoleon and the Revival of Greek Sicily 344–317 B.C.* Cambridge: Cambridge University Press, 1974.

Tarán, Leonardo. *Speusippus of Athens: A Critical Study with a Collection of the Related Texts and Commentary*. Leiden, Netherlands: Brill, 1981.

Taylor, A. E. "The Analysis of ἐπιστήμη in Plato's Seventh Epistle." *Mind* 21 (1912): 347–70.

———. *Plato, the Man and His Work*. London: Methuen, 1926.

Tenca, Ada. *Dione e Platone*. Florence: E. Ariani, 1932.

Thatcher, Mark. "Syracusan Identity Between Tyranny and Democracy." *Bulletin of the Institute for Classical Studies* 55, no. 2 (December 2012): 73–90.

Thesleff, Holger. "Platonic Chronology." *Phronesis* 34, no. 1 (1989): 1–26.

———. *Platonic Patterns: A Collection of Studies*. Las Vegas: Parmenides Publishing, 2009.

———. *Studies in Platonic Chronology*. Helsinki: Societas Scientiarum Fennica,1982.

Tod, M. N. *A Selection of Greek Historical Inscriptions to the End of the Fifth Century B.C.*, 2nd edition. Oxford: Clarendon Press, 1946.

Trampedach, Kai. *Platon, die Akademie und die zeitgenössische Politik*. Stuttgart: Franz Steiner Verlag, 1994.

Vatai, Frank Leslie. *Intellectuals in Politics in the Greek World: from Earliest Times to the Hellenistic Age*. London: Croom Helm, 1984.

von Fritz, Kurt. "Conservative Reaction and One Man Rule in Ancient Greece." *Political Science Quarterly* 56, no. 1 (March 1941): 51–83.

———. *Platon in Sizilien und das Problem der Philosophenherrschaft*. Berlin: De Gruyter, 1968.

———, ed. *Pseudepigrapha I*. Geneva: Fondation Hardt, 1972.

Walbank, F. W. "The Historians of Greek Sicily." *Kokalos* 14–15 (1968): 476–97.

Wareh, Tarik. *The Theory and Practice of Life: Isocrates and the Philosophers*. Washington, DC: Center for Hellenic Studies, 2012.

Waterfield, Robin. *Plato of Athens: A Life in Philosophy*. New York: Oxford University Press, 2023.

Westlake, Henry D. "Dion: A Study in Liberation." *Durham University Journal* 38 (1946): 37–44. Reprinted in *Essays on the Greek Historians and Greek History*. Manchester: Manchester University Press 1969.

———. "Friends and Successors of Dion." *Historia* 32, no. 2 (1983): 161–72.

———. *Timoleon and His Relations with Tyrants*. Manchester: Manchester University Press,1952.

———. "Timoleon and the Reconstruction of Syracuse." *Cambridge Historical Journal* (1942): vii. Reprinted in *Essays on the Greek Historians and Greek History*. Manchester: Manchester University Press, 1969.

Wohl, Victoria. "Plato Avant la Lettre: Authenticity in Plato's Epistles." *Ramus* 27, no. 1 (1998): 60–93.

Youtie, Herbert C. "Σημεῖον in the Papyri and its Significance for Plato, Epistle 13 (360a-b)." *Zeitschrift für Papyrologie und Epigraphik* 6 (1970): 105–16.

Yunis, Harvey, ed. *Plato: Phaedrus*. Cambridge: Cambridge University Press, 2011.

# ILLUSTRATION CREDITS

190 Drawing of Dionysius sentencing Phintias to death, by Giovanni Francesco Barbieri: Penta Springs Limited/Alamy.

216 Eighteenth-century tapestry of Dion entering Syracuse, by Victor Honoré Janssens: Interfoto/Alamy.

218 Zeus *Eleutherios* coin minted by Dion: CNG LLC.

238 Oil painting of Aretê pleading with her prison guards, by Jean-Charles Nicaise Perrin: The Picture Art Collection/Alamy.

262 The death of Sôphrosynê, in an unfinished illustration from a fifteenth-century manuscript of Justin's *Epitome*: The Bodleian Libraries, University of Oxford, MS Auct. F 2.29, fol. 067r.

284 Illustration of Timoleon departing for Syracuse, from an early-twentieth-century edition of *Plutarch's Lives*: Ivy Close Images/Alamy.

# INDEX